DUST
ON THE
THRONE

THE SEARCH
FOR BUDDHISM IN
MODERN INDIA

DUST
ON THE
THRONE

Douglas Ober

Stanford University Press
Stanford, California

Stanford University Press
Stanford, California

Printed in the United States of America on acid-free, archival-quality paper

Library of Congress Cataloging-in-Publication Data

Names: Ober, Douglas, author.
Title: Dust on the throne : the search for Buddhism
    in modern India / Douglas Ober.
Other titles: South Asia in motion.
Description: Stanford, California : Stanford University Press, 2023. | Series:
    South Asia in motion | Includes bibliographical references and index.
Identifiers: LCCN 2022041144 (print) | LCCN 2022041145
    (ebook) | ISBN 9781503635029 (cloth) | ISBN 9781503635036
    (paperback) | ISBN 9781503635777 (ebook)
Subjects: LCSH: Buddhism—India—History—19th century.
    | Buddhism—India—History—20th century.
Classification: LCC BQ345 .O34 2023 (print) | LCC BQ345
    (ebook) | DDC 294.30954—dc23/eng/20220912
LC record available at https://lccn.loc.gov/2022041144
LC ebook record available at https://lccn.loc.gov/2022041145

Cover design: Lindy Kasler
Photograph: Indian laborers repairing the Great Stupa at Sanchi in the early 1880s, one of the oldest and most revered Buddhist complexes in India. The site was a thriving center of Buddhist activity from the third century BCE up to the 12th century CE. After its rediscovery in the early 1800s, the site underwent extensive repairs by British and Indian officials and is often considered one of the best preserved Buddhist monuments in India today. British Library, London, UK © British Library Board. All Rights Reserved / Bridgeman Images."

MAPPING BUDDHISM IN SOUTH ASIA

BAMIYAN

SHAHJI-KI-DHERI

PESHAWAR

GUJARAT

GIRNAR

BARODA

DANDI

NASHIK

SOPARA

BOMBAY

PUNE

ARABIAN SEA

MODERN NATIONS

RUSSIA

MONGOLIA

AFGHANISTAN

PAKISTAN

NEPAL TIBET

JAPAN

INDIA BANGLADESH CHINA

MYANMAR
(BURMA)

SRI LANKA
(CEYLON)

THAILAND
(SIAM)

VIETNAM
(COCHINCHINA)

CAMBODIA

INDONESIA

TRAVAN

LADAKH

LEH

RINAGAR

TIBET

LHASA

HARIDWAR

HIMALAYAS

DELHI

LUMBINI
(TILAURAKOT)

SIKKIM

YATUNG

MATHURA

KATHMANDU GANGTOK

SHRAVASTI KUSHINAGAR

DARJEELING

LUCKNOW

ASSAM

UTTAR
PRADESH

KANPUR

BENARAS DARBHANGA

ALLAHABAD

ARRAH

PATNA
(PATALIPUTRA)

BHARHUT SARNATH

BODH
GAYA

BENGAL

SANCHI-
SATDHARA

BHOPAL

BIHAR

RAJGIR
(NALANDA)

BURDWAN

AGARTALA

MAYURBHANJ

CALCUTTA CHITTAGONG

NAGPUR

KHANDAGIRI

CUTTACK

MANDALAY

PAUNI

DHAULI

JANTA KARLI

PURI

ARAKAN
& BURMA

MAHARASHTRA

HUBLI

AMARAVATI

BAY OF
BENGAL

PEGU

RANGOON

TAMIL NADU

MADRAS

BANGALORE

RE

OOTACAMUND

CALICUT NAGAPATTINAM

TRICHUR

MAVELIKKARA

TUTICORIN KANDY

COLOMBO

● CITIES
◆ VILLAGES
⛰ MOUNTAINS & RANGES
Ⓐ STATES & REGIONS
⌂ CAVES

Contents

Abbreviations

Cited Texts

ABP	*Amrita Bazar Patrika*. Calcutta.
BAWS	*Dr. Babasaheb Ambedkar Writings and Speeches*, Vols 1–20, edited by Vasant Moon. Mumbai: Education Department, Government of Maharashtra.
BBA	*Annual Report for the Bengal Buddhist Association: Bauddha Dharmankur Sabha*. Calcutta.
BI	*Buddhist India: Journal of the All-India Buddhist Conference*. Calcutta and Rangoon.
BC	*Bombay Chronicle*. Bombay.
BP	*Buddha-prabha*. Bombay.
BYB	*Brahmo Year Book*. London.
CAD	*Constituent Assembly Debates: Official Reports*. Government of India.
Chogyal	Private papers of Chogyal Sidkeong Tulku, the 10th Chogyal of Sikkim, Institute of Tibetology, Gangtok.
CWMG	*Collected Works of Mahatma Gandhi*, Volumes 1–98. New Delhi: Publications Division, Government of India.
Darbar	Darbar, Sikkim State Archives, Gangtok, India.
DD	*Dharmadoot*. Sarnath.
DEEB	Government of India, Department of Education: Education Branch. National Archives of India, New Delhi.
DpD	Anagarika Dharmapala Diaries (#497–502). National Archives of Sri Lanka. Colombo.
DpNb	Anagarika Dharmapala Notebooks. Dharmapala Museum of the Maha Bodhi Society of India. Sarnath.
EADEBS	Government of India, External Affairs Department: External Branch

	(Secret). National Archives of India, New Delhi.
FDE	Government of India, Foreign Department External. National Archives of India, New Delhi.
FDSE	Government of India, Foreign Department: Secret External. National Archives of India, New Delhi.
FPDGB	Government of India, Foreign and Political Department: General Branch. National Archives of India, New Delhi.
HDBPB	Government of India, Home Department: Books and Publications Branch. National Archives of India, New Delhi.
HDP	Government of India, Home Department: Political Branch. National Archives of India, New Delhi.
HDPB	Government of India, Home Department: Public Branch. National Archives of India, New Delhi.
HO	*Hindu Outlook*. Organ of the Hindu Maha Sabha. New Delhi.
HT	*Hindustan Times*. New Delhi.
IM	*Indian Mirror*. Calcutta.
ISR	*Indian Social Reformer*. Bombay.
JBTSI	*Journal of the Buddhist Text Society*. Calcutta.
MBJ	*Journal of the Maha Bodhi Society / Maha Bodhi and the United Buddhist World*. Calcutta.
MEABB	Government of India, Ministry of External Affairs: Burma Branch. National Archives of India, New Delhi.
MEAEB	Government of India, Ministry of External Affairs: External Branch. National Archives of India, New Delhi.
MEAFEA	Government of India, Ministry of External Affairs: FEA Branch. National Archives of India, New Delhi.
MEAIANZ	Government of India, Ministry of External Affairs: IANZ Branch. National Archives of India, New Delhi.
MEANEF	Government of India, Ministry of External Affairs: NEF Branch. National Archives of India, New Delhi.
MEANEFS	Government of India, Ministry of External Affairs: NEF Branch (Secret). National Archives of India, New Delhi.
MEARIB	Government of India, Ministry of External Affairs: R&I Branch. National Archives of India, New Delhi.
MEASEA	Government of India, Ministry of External Affairs: SEA Branch. National Archives of India, New Delhi.
MMPP	M.M. Malaviya Private Papers, Nehru Memorial Museum and Library, New Delhi.
MSKB	Government of India, Ministry of States: Kashmir Branch. National Archives of India, New Delhi.
RPCSD	*Dr. Rajendra Prasad: Correspondence and Select Documents*, Vols. 3–10. Edited by Valmiki Choudhary. New Delhi and Ahmedabad: Allied Publishers.
RPENWP	*Report on the Progress of Education in the Northwestern Provinces.*

	Allahabad: Government Press.
RPPP	Dr. (President) Rajendra Prasad Private Papers, National Archives of India, New Delhi.
SPM	Syama Prasad Mookerjee Private Papers, Nehru Memorial Museum and Library, New Delhi.
SupTheo	*Supplement of The Theosophist*. Adyar.
SWJN	*Selected works of Jawaharlal Nehru*. Vols. 1–9. Edited by S. Gopal. New Delhi: Jawaharlal Nehru Memorial Fund.
Theo	*The Theosophist*. Adyar.
TheoIn	*Theosophy in India*. Benares.
TOI	*Times of India*. New Delhi.

Others

AAS	Association for Asian Studies
AIBS	All-India Buddhist Society
ASI	Archaeological Survey of India
BBA	Bengal Buddhist Association
BHU	Banaras Hindu University
BJP	Bharatiya Janata Party
BJS	Bharatiya Jana Sangh
BSP	Bahujan Samaj Party
BSRS	Buddhist Shrines Restoration Society
BTS	Buddhist Theosophical Society
CPI	Communist Party of India
CPI-M	Communist Party of India-Marxist
CSP	Congress Socialist Party
EIC	East India Company
NAM	Non-Aligned Movement
NEH	National Endowment for the Humanities
OBC	Other Backward Class
RSS	Rashtriya Swayamsevak Sangh
SC	Scheduled Caste
SIBS	South Indian Buddhist Society
SNDP	Sri Narayana Dharma Paripalana Yogam
ST	Scheduled Tribe
TBMSG	Trailokya Bauddha Mahasangha Sahayaka Gana
TS	Theosophical Society
UBC	University of British Columbia
USIEF	United States–India Education Foundation

Language Matters

South Asia truly is a babel of tongues. While this poses less of a problem for its numerous polyglots, it proves challenging for scholars and writers trying to convey its lingual diversity to an English readership. Most of the South Asian primary source material in this book is derived from Hindi and English, but it also draws upon sources originally composed in such diverse languages as Bengali, Burmese, French, Japanese, Malayalam, Marathi, Nepali, Pali, Persian, Russian, Sanskrit, Tamil, Telugu, Tibetan, and Urdu. In order to accurately convey the original spelling (but not necessarily the pronunciation) of these disparate linguistic registers, one is required to use a number of different transliteration systems, characterized by specific diacritical marks. While this provides much-needed clarity and accuracy for specialists, it comes at the cost of readability. Since all writers do not follow the same transliteration system, the exercise becomes a fool's errand.

For these reasons, this work dispenses with all diacritical marks. To provide three examples, I write "Krishna" rather than the Hindi "*Kṛṣn*," "lama" rather than the Tibetan "*bla ma*," and "sangha" rather than the Sanskrit "*saṃgha*". The first time Sanskrit, Pali, Hindi, etc., terms are used, they appear in italicized form. All uses thereafter appear without italics. The transliteration of personal names and places follows the most frequently encountered English spelling in use at the time.

When using common Buddhist terms, I generally follow the Sanskrit usages better known in anglophone publics (for instance, *dharma* as opposed to the Pali *dhamma*). However, because the figures studied in this book used Pali or other Prakrits as much as Sanskrit, I often move between both sets of terminology. To some readers, this may be jarring, but language matters, and the use of certain linguistic registers, particularly Pali, was—and still is—of important cultural and political significance. To miss this component would be short-sighted.

Other than learning all of Babel's languages, there is no single solution to presenting their differences in a format pleasing to everyone. While I realize some will be disappointed by the lack of diacritics, I hope this opens the book up to a wider audience.

Accurately conveying linguistic differences is not the only challenge this book faces. Much of *Dust on the Throne* touches on questions of social identity, nation building, and geography. Writing about caste identities is particularly fraught.

Writing about caste formations and social identities in historical South Asia (like elsewhere) is no less contested. If part of a historian's responsibility is to be faithful to the way language is used in the past, they also have an obligation to do so in a manner that is not insensitive to those populaces who bore the heavy burden of that language which was deeply harmful. When I use terms like untouchable, low caste, upper caste, and the names of both specific South Asian castes (jati) and generic ones (varna), it is the context of their use at that historical time. It is not intended to validate their meaning or perpetuate their usage. In South Asia today, former untouchables often prefer the term dalit. These terms are often used interchangeably throughout the book but none are capitalized.

A Dependent Arising

Around the time of Indian independence in August 1947, a curious set of events transpired in the highest echelons of state power. The first occurred on 14 August, the day before the formal transfer of power, when a group of seventy-two women entered New Delhi's Constituent Assembly and unfurled the newly chosen national flag. In a sudden change decided only three weeks before, the Gandhian charkha, spinning wheel, had been replaced by the Ashokan *dhammachakra*, dharma wheel, as the flag's central symbol. The second event occurred a few months later, when the Central cabinet publicly disclosed the official state emblem of the new nation. This time the image chosen was that of the Ashokan Lion Seal from Sarnath, a site known both for the 1904–05 discovery of its half-broken lion pillar and as the sacred ground where the Buddha delivered his first teaching. The third, and arguably most definitive moment, occurred in January 1950 at the Government House in New Delhi, where a cadre of ministers, military officers, royalty, political elites, and journalists gathered beneath a massive, 1,800-year-old sandstone image of the Buddha to witness Rajendra Prasad take oath as the first president of the Republic of India.

Such connections to Buddhism may seem perplexing to many today. India is widely considered a secular state, albeit with a Hindu majority that has expressed increasing scorn for the republic's non-religious foundation. Even further, at the time of Independence, Buddhism was considered "extinct" in India for nearly eight hundred years, and less than 1 per cent of the population explicitly identified as Buddhist.[1] But demography and entrenched theories are not always reliable indicators of cultural conscience.

Beginning in the nineteenth century, Buddhism captured the imagination of an eclectic range of people around the world—from African-American writers and British nobles to devout clergymen, socialist freethinkers, radical pacifists, and imperial adventurers. Within colonial India, a new generation of equally diverse figures forged their own Buddhist publics. These included migrant laborers, anti-caste activists, self-styled Hindu reformers, Indian Orientalists, Marxists, and Gandhian nationalists. Forming club associations, temples, and publishing houses, they discovered modern messages in ancient suttas (Sanskrit, sutra) and debated Buddhist histories in scholarly journals and popular magazines. By the 1950s, Buddhism was a source of immense national pride and critical to new understandings of the subcontinent's past. It became integral to the techne of the postcolonial Indian state, part of diplomatic initiatives abroad and cultural celebrations at home. Buddhism also brought about what is arguably the largest conversion movement in world history, when the Indian jurist and civil rights leader, B.R. Ambedkar, led some half a million dalits (formerly known as "untouchables") to the religion in 1956. Despite these monumental interventions, modern Indian Buddhism is often disparaged as having little relevance outside Ambedkar's followers, or among Himalayan Buddhists and exiled Tibetans. Even when these communities are acknowledged, most scholars treat them as anomalies, choosing instead to characterize India as little more than a museum of tattered Buddhist manuscripts and ancient ruins for scholarly study and curious traveler–pilgrims.

From the late-nineteenth century onwards, those who spoke of this new Buddhist resurgence invariably called it a "revival". Their use of the term was based on a series of assumptions concerning Buddhism's historical rise, decline—and now rebirth—in the Indian subcontinent over the past two-and-a-half millenia. According to these histories, roughly 2,500 years ago, a prince named Siddhattha Gotama (Sanskrit, Siddhartha Gautama), was born in Lumbini, a small hamlet not far from Kapilavatthu the capital of the Sakya kingdom, in what is today southern Nepal. Early Buddhist tradition records that this was the last of his countless rebirths: the culmination of a practice founded on moral conduct (*sila*), mental discipline (samadhi), and wisdom (*panna*), perfected over many lifetimes. At the age of twenty-nine, Gotama renounced the luxuries of royal life, and traveled on foot across the Gangetic Plains in search of liberation from human suffering (*dukkha*). After six torturous years mastering yogic techniques and attaining the highest states of meditative consciousness (dhyana /*jhana*), he came to the conclusion that neither self-denial nor hedonism were meaningful paths.

While sitting under a bo tree in Bodh Gaya (in modern-day India's Bihar), he "awakened" to the true nature of suffering and the path that leads to its cessation (nirvana). During the next forty-five years, he organized a community (sangha) of disciples, all the while teaching the dhamma to kings and queens, merchants and mendicants, farmers and criminals, all and sundry. At the age of eighty, he laid his head between two *sala* trees at Kushinagar (modern-day Uttar Pradesh), attaining *mahaparinirvana* or ultimate release from the cycle of life and death. In the centuries after his death, South Asian political and mercantile elites continued to support the community of monastics gathered in his name. There were many great patrons, none more luminous than the enigmatic Mauryan emperor, Ashoka (r. 269–232 BCE). Inspired by Buddhism's message of universal equality and loving kindness, Ashoka renounced war and evangelized the Buddha's Word (*buddhavacana*) across his empire and beyond. For centuries after, nearly all South Asians gave praise to the Fully Awakened One (*samyak sambuddha*). Even as respect for the great teacher of gods (*shasta deva*) gathered momentum across the rest of Asia, it gradually lost support in its homeland. While the precise reasons behind Buddhism's decline in India remain debated, the scholarly community is fairly unified in its belief that by the thirteenth to fourteenth centuries, it had "all but disappeared".[2]

Scholarship on Indian Buddhism, between its purported disappearance and modern revival, has grown significantly in recent years. Yet, it constitutes only a fraction of the literature focused elsewhere in Asia or on other periods of Indian history. The consensus is threefold. First, most Buddhists in contemporary India are dalits, who began converting to Buddhism en masse under the leadership of Dr B.R. Ambedkar (1891–1956). Second, just a century prior to this momentous turn, most of India's ancient Buddhist spaces were decrepit, more likely to be visited by British antiquarians than Buddhist monks. Third, only after the founding of Anagarika Dharmapala's

Maha Bodhi Society in Calcutta in 1891, did Buddhists from across the globe begin traveling to India in large numbers, thereby reinvigorating and reshaping ancient networks of pilgrimage and cultural exchange. This three-pronged narrative, however, belies a much more complex history.

In rewriting this narrative, *Dust on the Throne* makes four specific interventions. First, it contends that the theory of Buddhism's "disappearance" from the subcontinent is little more than a useful fiction, deployed to wash over a more complicated historical terrain involving periodic Buddhist resurgences and trans-regional pilgrimage networks. Second, to the extent that Buddhist institutions declined in the subcontinent—and there is no doubt that they were decimated—it argues that their colonial revival was led as much by Indians and other Asians as it was by Europeans, who are still regularly credited with Buddhism's rediscovery and revival (Almond 1988; Allen 2002, 2010, 2012). Third, the book shows that India's modern Buddhist revival began nearly a century before 1956, when the Indian government celebrated "2,500 years of Buddhism" and when Ambedkar led half a million converts to the dhamma in an unprecedented public event. Fourth, it argues that the revival of Buddhism in colonial and early postcolonial India gave significant shape to modern Indian history, from the making of Hindu nationalism and Hindu reform movements, to dalit and anti-caste activism, Indian leftism, and Nehruvian secular democracy. By recovering the history of Buddhism in India *by Indians* of all stripes, the book offers a corrective to the pervasive Eurocentrism of so much anglophone scholarship on the subject. *Dust on the Throne* primarily studies the period from the early decades of the nineteenth century up through the middle of the twentieth, looking at the disparate colonial-era Indian figures and institutions whose efforts to revive—or suppress—Buddhism have largely gone unnoticed.[3]

Un-archived Histories and Useful Fictions

In retelling the history of modern Buddhism in India, we must first acknowledge what can and cannot be done. All histories are selective. Its writing comprises selection and criticism, framing and simplification. The very work of writing history involves erasure, just as remembering involves forgetting (Davis and Zhong 2017). As histories develop, so do theories that structure narratives and create the conditions through which reasonable inquiries can be made. When confronted with data that does not fit into existing paradigms, historians have been known to disregard the evidence, uneasy with narratives that challenge the ones they invest in and create.

Reconstructions of the past, then, are full of what the historian, Gyanendra Pandey (2012, 2013), calls "un-archived histories". An un-archived history is not a history that does not have an archive, but rather that which has been "un-archived"—marginalized, ignored, disenfranchised, and pushed out of reference or recall. "The very process of archiving," Pandey (2012: 38) writes, "is accompanied by a process of 'un-archiving': rendering many aspects of social, cultural, political relations in the past and the present as *incidental, chaotic, trivial, inconsequential, and therefore unhistorical.*"[4] All cultures suffer from it, whether in the marginalization of working-class and peasant histories, the silencing of racialized and indigenous peoples in the Americas, or the erasure of dalit voices in South Asian historiography. The figures, institutions, and ideas explored in this book were at times, and to varying degrees, also prone to this kind of un-archiving. But their histories, long absent in the academy, have much bearing on the study of India, and of Buddhism more widely.

Contemporary historians tend to have a nuanced understanding of the rise and fall of Indian Buddhism thanks to an abundance of specialist literature on art, literature, sociology, philosophy, ethics, economics, among the many other sub-topics which are often further divided along regional and linguistic lines. Despite this, since the very founding of Buddhist studies and Indology in the early- to mid-nineteenth century, scholars have remained almost unanimous in dating Indian Buddhism's disappearance to sometime between the twelfth and fourteenth centuries. This "end" is precisely what enables the idea of a modern revival, thus marking a convenient starting point of the revival movement. With rare exception, the twelfth-to-fourteenth-century "end" of Buddhism is often denoted by terms like death, disappearance, or annihilation, rather than something more appropriate like collapse or downfall.[5] By then, one learns, Indian Buddhism "was an endangered species" (Sarao 2002: 101), had "pretty much died out" (Strong 2015: 10), "virtually disappeared" (Gethin 1998: 2), or in the most common of phrases, it had "all but disappeared".[6] The timidity of all the above statements ("pretty much," "virtually," "all but") is not a coincidence, since even the most eminent scholars propagate these narratives despite knowing that they are mere fictions.[7] Two centuries of archaeological excavation and textual scholarship now point to a long, enduring, and "unarchived" Indian Buddhist afterlife that extends to the modern day.

A brief survey of just some of these Buddhist "afterlives" demonstrates the wider point. Sometime around 1776, a roughly two-foot-tall ruby- and turquoise-encrusted image of the Bodhisattva Tara was installed inside a temple complex on the banks of the Ganges in Howrah, near Calcutta. The "two-storied house of worship" with a central "gateway facing the river" (Bysack 1890: 50) was adorned with carpets and cloth banners shipped by Tibet's Sixth Panchen Lama (1738–80) to the East India Company with the assistance of the Panchen's Indian agent, the Shaiva yogi, Puran Giri (1745–95).[8] The temple was never exclusively Buddhist. Hindu images and associated relics filled a separate chamber: it contained multiple Shivalingams and shaligramas. And yet, for a brief period, at least until the early 1800s, the crowned Tara image along with other similar ones, including Avalokiteshvara (Padmapani) and Cakrasamvara, were worshipped according to Buddhist rites by travelers from across the Himalayas and the Tibetan Plateau.

Although the construction of a Tibetan Buddhist temple in eighteenth-century-Bengal was a remarkable intervention in the religious landscape, a Buddhist presence in India was hardly uncommon. Toni Huber (2008) has traced the more than millennia-long history of Tibetan pilgrimage to Buddhist sites across India, including a detailed account of the Himalayan yogin, Garshapa Sonam Rabgye's, visit to Bodh Gaya and Nalanda as late as 1752. Newar Buddhists from the Kathmandu Valley were no less active in their pilgrimages to Bodh Gaya. Nepalese Buddhist chronicles describe the visit of a Newar vajracharya (tantric Buddhist priest) to Bodh Gaya in the early to mid 1600s (Slusser 1988: 126). Such a tradition appears to have continued unabated. In the early 1800s, the famed Newar Buddhist scholar Amritananda Bandya (d. 1835), spoke of his childhood visit to the Maha Bodhi temple complex, the famed site in Bodh Gaya built over many centuries to mark and honor the Buddha's enlightenment under the Bodhi tree (Hodgson 1827: 221–22). Buddhists from across the Himalayas and western Tibetan Plateau were not the only pilgrims either. As late as 1412 CE, a Ming dynasty envoy named Hou Xian (fl. 1403–27) traveled to Bodh Gaya (Ray 1993: 78).[9] Architectural evidence from recreations of the Maha Bodhi temple in present-day Myanmar and Thailand suggests that Southeast Asian Buddhists may have continued making transcontinental journeys to Bodh Gaya as late as the fifteenth century (Brown 1988: 106–11).[10] Eyewitness accounts confirm the continued presence of Burmese Buddhist pilgrims in north India throughout the late eighteenth and early nineteenth century (Geary 2017: 48–50).

It is difficult to surmise why such developments have failed to impact the wider historiography. It is possible they were marginalized because the events themselves are seen as inconsequential to the "big" histories of the subcontinent. After all, when the Lahauli Buddhist mendicant, Garshapa Sonam Rabgye, visited Nalanda in 1752, he was unable to restore the ancient monument as a seat of Buddhist learning. He came, he saw, and returned home (and to history's good fortune, accounts of his journey were preserved). All these visits do signify something of value. They are evidence of a steady stream of Buddhists from across Asia who sought out sacred spaces in the ancient heartland of Buddhism long after the thirteenth and fourteenth centuries.

Then there were the Indian Buddhists who dotted the Gangetic Plains in the centuries after their religion's so-called disappearance. Amidst a dwindling sangha and volatile political conditions, the Bengali monk, Shariputra (1335–1426), was installed as the "last abbot of Bodh Gaya" around the year 1400 (McKeown 2019). Documentary evidence in the form of Sanskrit manuscripts composed some fifty years later attest that scribes "with faith in [the Bodhisattva of Wisdom] Manjushri" continued to copy Buddhist scriptures in parts of rural Bihar (Shin'ichirō 2015, 2017).[11] Such compositions were increasingly rare but not unknown. Indian teachers— monastics and non-monastics—who typically came from south and east India, like Shariputra, Vanaratna (1384–1468), Buddhagupta (1514–1610), and Krishnacarya (d. ~1640) traveled through India, Nepal, Tibet, and China as living votaries of Buddhist Sanskrit learning, Mahayana practices, and Vajrayana lineages.

Read collectively, these accounts reveal a bustle of ritual activity and pilgrimage at the *axis mundi* of the Buddhist world, which continued well into the colonial period. So, when the most seminal scholars repeat like a mantra that Buddhism had "all but disappeared" by the thirteenth to fourteenth century, their assertions cement into facts, diminishing our historical imagination and marginalizing what was a minor, but living, part of Indic religious life during the next several centuries. In a recent and important intervention on Buddhism's "end days," Arthur McKeown (2019: 19) argues, on the basis of little-studied Chinese, Tibetan, and Sanskrit sources, that the period between the sixteenth and the eighteenth centuries is a more accurate estimate of Indian Buddhism's "demise" and that its decline was "neither drastic, dramatic nor catacalysmic but a more even downward slope with periodic resurgences." McKeown's work should encourage historians to rethink Buddhism's putative death in the Gangetic Plains. His research, however, has a narrow geographical and temporal scope, and therefore discounts other areas in the subcontinent where these kinds of activities were equally evident and lasted just as long. That is, it has long been clear that Buddhism continued to be the center of a thriving public culture up through the present day in places like the Kathmandu Valley, Chittagong, the high Himalayas, and parts of north-east India.

Newar Buddhists from the Kathmandu Valley in Nepal, for instance, have, from the Gupta era onwards, followed Sanskrit Mahayana practices and deities alongside Vajrayana initiations while surviving in a wider Hindu world (Gellner 1992).[12] As the anthropologist Todd Lewis (2000: 13) writes, this "small but vibrant oasis of tradition ... disproves the often-repeated assertion that Indic Buddhism ever completely died". Yet, almost all histories of South Asian Buddhism consciously and knowingly exclude post-fourteenth-century Newar Buddhism from their narratives. Certainly, one of the driving forces behind this is a nation-state paradigm in which present-day national boundaries are projected anachronistically into the past. Nepal is not a part of India, and therefore Newar Buddhism is "Nepal's Buddhism," not India's. The nationalist appropriation cuts both ways. While many Indians today are content to claim Ladakh as part of the Indian nation, and along with it, Ladakhi Buddhism as Indian Buddhism, this is largely a matter of political convenience. Few scholars would contend that Buddhist practices in Ladakh are closer to an imagined "Indian" Buddhism than those of Newar Buddhists. This kind of nationalist and territorial argumentation has seeped into other arenas of Buddhist history as well. In response to the idea that the Buddha was an Indian, the Nepali public has expressed outrage, demanding that it is Lord Buddha's birthright to be recognized as Nepali![13] Nepal is not the only blind spot in the wider historiography.

Buddhism also survived as a living practice up through the present day in Chittagong, the coastal and hilly region in what is today south-eastern Bangladesh. Before Arakanese monks "converted" Chittagong Buddhists to an Irawaddy Valley–inspired mode of Pali aesthetics in the nineteenth century, the region was a fulcrum for Buddhist tantra and a significant conduit for the dissemination of Buddhist poetry in Persian, Bengali, and Arabic (Charney 2002: 218–21; Leider 2010: 145–62; D'Hubert 2019). Even as late as 1798, some fifty years before the region's Chakma queen (rani), Kalindi (r. 1844–73), invited Theravadin Buddhist monks into the royal court, the East India Company surveyor, Francis Buchanan (1762–1829), was able to clearly identify the Bengali-speaking community's practices and customs as tied to the Buddha (Buchanan [1798] 1992: 57–58, 98). These were the same communities whose Bengali-language translations of Pali scriptures one century later would fire the imagination of intellectuals like Rabindranath Tagore. However, nationalist histories of India have no place for the Buddhism of Chittagong. The horrendous events of 1947 involved as much a Partition of the past as it did of borders and identities. A similar appropriation of history has occurred in Bangladesh, only this time with religious overtones, where a million-plus Bengali-speaking Buddhists in Chittagong find no place in nationalist narratives which privilege Muslim identities (D.M. Barua n.d.).[14]

The marginalization of Nepal and Chittagong, like that of Sikkim, Kinnaur, Spiti, Ladakh, and other "borderlands" could be attributed to their geographical positioning at the periphery.[15] However, there is ample evidence in the form of inscriptions and literary texts that document the persistence of Buddhism even in more "centrally located" and less-disputed Indian locales long after the fifteenth century. In peninsular India, there are signs of a self-conscious Buddhist presence that lasted well into the late sixteenth century and possibly even beyond. According to the Kalyani inscription erected in

Pegu by the Burmese king, Dhammaceti, in 1479, a group of Burmese monks (*theras*) returning from Lanka were shipwrecked and ended up in the South Indian town of Nagapattinam.[16] There, they visited a pagoda-shaped vihara taller than "Kanaka Giri" (Mount Meru) and worshipped an image of the Buddha in a cave constructed by the "Maharaja of *Cinadesa* (China)". After the town's "Chinese Pagoda" was demolished by the British in 1867 to make way for what is today St Joseph's College, more than three hundred bronze images of the Buddha, Avalokiteshvara, Maitreya, Lokeshvara, Vasudhara, and Tara were uncovered. According to the art historian Vidya Dehejia (1988: 73), the discoveries evidenced "a generous patronage of Buddhism as late as 1700 A.D."[17] While little is known about the use and production of these images, it is clear from other sources that socially distinct Buddhist communities still populated the region through the late 1500s.[18]

Similar evidence for the survival of Buddhism well into the sixteenth century is found throughout the Prachi Valley southeast of Bhubaneswar in Odisha. This region, abounding in massive Buddhist monuments and structures dating from the tenth to twelfth centuries, appears to have been the scene of a rather violent conflict in the early 1500s. According to both the Odia-language chronicle, *Madalapanji*, and Ishvara Das's Bengali-language *Chaitanya Bhagavat* (c. 1580s), the Gajapati king, Prataparudra Deva (r. 1497–1540), perpetrated large-scale persecution of several hundred Buddhists around the year 1530. The leader of these "crypto-Buddhists," as the scholar Nagendranath Vasu (1911: clxxvi) called them, was a *nath* siddha adept named Veersingh, who, under the threat of death, adopted external Vaishnava doctrines and adornments while privately adhering to Buddhist teachings. Despite Vasu's concerns about whether these communities were "pure" and "authentic" Buddhists—hence the "crypto" moniker—what is less debated is Prataparudra's persecution of a community understood locally as Buddhist in the early sixteenth century (Verardi 2011: 372–76; Mukherjee 1940: 53–54).

When one considers these developments and the near continuous flows of Buddhist pilgrims to Bodh Gaya up through the colonial period, the narrative around Buddhism's disappearance begins to look quite different. And yet, most scholars write these histories off as anomalies. They appear to be incidental, erratic, trivial, and therefore "inconsequential," as Gyanendra Pandey (2012: 38) would put it. These "anomalies" in the historical archive also help explain the very jarring differences in the dating of Indian Buddhism's decline. To a minority of dissenting scholars like Vidya Dehejia (1988), Stephen Berkwitz (2010), Giovanni Verardi (2011), and Arthur McKeown (2019), all of this documentary evidence is proof that Indian Buddhism, despite its fragmented state, existed well into the sixteenth and seventeenth centuries. This radical discrepancy in the dating of Buddhism's "disappearance" should raise alarm. After all, their difference of opinion with other leading scholars on this matter is not based on years or even decades, but on centuries.

One major source of disagreement among these scholars is less in the set of data being examined than in its interpretation. That is, this is as much a matter of how one defines what is Indian (or Indic) as it is a matter of how one defines Buddhism.[19] A useful litmus test for gauging this vexed issue is the case of the sixteenth-century yogi, Buddhagupta-natha (1514–1610). Buddhagupta was neither an ordained monk (bhikkhu) nor the product of a major monastic institute (mahavihara), but a yogi who had studied with a number of other non-monastics (Waddel 1893; Tucci 1931; Templeman 1997). The accounts of Buddhagupta's studies with Buddhist teachers in India, described in a colorful seventeenth-century Tibetan biography (namthar), are often dismissed on the grounds that his instructors belonged to wandering groups of ascetics (naths), which comprised both Buddhist and non-Buddhist (primarily Shaiva) communities (siddha sampradaya). Uncomfortable with these religiously plural arrangements, some scholars (cf. Huber 2008: 171–72, 205–07) have argued that Buddhagupta's teachings were essentially tainted, having been mistaken as Buddhist by his all too gullible student, the Jonangpa Buddhist master and historian, Taranatha (1575–1635). That is, Buddhagupta's Buddhist credentials, despite being (mostly) acceptable to Taranatha, fell somewhat short of the normative standards of what many colonial and postcolonial scholars considered "authentic Buddhism".

The fact that Buddhagupta was shaped as much by Shaiva customs as by Vajrayana Buddhist norms is not to be dismissed. It speaks to Indian Buddhism's precarious position in the early seventeenth-century world. Equally, none of this should make us blind to the fact that in that historical moment, there still existed a few Indians who were seen as fully capable of teaching the words of the Buddha (Mallinson 2019). Now, the fact that most accounts of other Buddhagupta-like figures emerge from the pens of Tibetan rather than Indian writers may say more about Tibetan notions of Buddhism than about existing Indian attitudes. But the underlying point remains the same: simply because it does not look Buddhist to us today does not mean it was not seen as Buddhist then.[20]

Numerous scholars (cf. Lopez 1995; Almond 1988) have shown that the colonial figures who defined Buddhism in the nineteenth and twentieth centuries associated it with a rational, textual tradition typically codified through Pali (and, to a lesser degree, Sanskrit) scriptures. Whether they were themselves Protestant Christians or not, these scholars tended to understand Buddhism in terms of Christian history. It was, in their eyes, a religion that not only fought against a caste-obsessed brahmanical priesthood (the equivalent to the Pharisees) but had also deviated from its "original" teaching, which had become (like the Catholic Church) bound by superstitious practices and "absurd" theological complexities. As they constructed the grand narrative of India's Buddhist past, there was a palpable scholarly deference towards the "true" geographical landscape that Buddha Shakyamuni was believed to have traversed (Allen 2002, 2012). It is these factors that appear to be so closely linked to the enduring theory of Buddhism's "disappearance" between the twelfth and thirteenth centuries, for this was precisely the period when the kinds of Buddhism so privileged by colonial scholars—institutionalized, monastic, nikaya forms—disappeared. What remained were traditions of wandering yogis, outcastes, tribal practitioners of tantra and magic—forms of practice deemed "un-Buddhist" by the religion's modern curators. When they encountered evidence that contradicted theories of Buddhism's disappearance, they cleverly redefined their terms, thereby ignoring the relationships of patronage, lay praxis, and intra-religious discussion that continued well into later centuries (Davidson 2002). Despite Gregory Schopen's (1991) important argument that studies of Buddhism in India have been driven by Protestant suppositions that locate "authentic Buddhism" within elite texts and monastic walls, there is a stubborn reluctance to extend the lens through which we understand Buddhism's late Indic formations. In other words, simply because Indic Buddhism after the fourteenth century did not meet the normative definition of what scholars and practitioners (European, Asian, or otherwise) felt a Buddhist was or should look like, does not mean that it died. The only way to substantiate such a claim is to view India as a hermetically sealed container, bounded by national walls that had yet to be built and religious divisions that had yet to crystallize with such concrete force.

The Architecture of the Argument

Buddhist revival in India was often discussed in the colonial period as if it was a singular monolithic movement. In reality, it produced a wide spectrum of interpretations and therefore requires a number of different lenses. Like the history of modern Buddhism more widely, Indian Buddhism's modern formation was deeply shaped by global networks. Scholars who study these networks have demonstrated that changes wrought by the expansion of imperial power, international commercial interests, and the "death of long distance"—the communications and transportation revolutions wrought by steamships, railways, telegraphs, etc.—laid the foundation for an unprecedented era of global religious activity.[21] In the nineteenth and twentieth centuries, it was the expansion of British rule over the Indian subcontinent and the formation of empires and colonies across Asia that conditioned the nature and flow of these networks (C. Bayly 1998, 2004).[22]

The main body of this book is loosely chronological with each chapter exploring different facets of modern Indian Buddhism. Chapter 1 surveys the long history of Buddhism in India, as conceived of and remembered by Indians during the early colonial encounter. By looking at a variety of primary sources, including Sanskrit, Odia, Tamil, and Bengali texts (hagiographies, temple chronicles, Puranas, and scholastic manuals) as well as early nineteenth-century surveyors' reports, memoirs, correspondence, and scholarly articles, the chapter provides concrete evidence of a robust memory of and conversation regarding Buddhism among indigenous scholars, literati, and ascetics up through the early decades of the colonial encounter.

The second chapter highlights how popular Indian memories of Buddhists and the Buddha were re-evaluated in light of new epistemological interpretations provided by philologists and archaeologists in the second half of the nineteenth century. The stage for this discussion was provided by the dramatic shifts in Britain's colonial education policies during the 1850s and the institutionalization of "scientific" methodologies. These gave rise to a new generation of English-educated Indians with critical "academic" interests in Buddhist material culture and ideas. How was the new interpretation of Buddhism received in the public sphere? The following chapter turns away from the specialized world of critical Indian scholarship and examines the public culture and religious networks and associations that propelled Buddhism's popularity in the late nineteenth and early twentieth century. Buddhist images and ideas had by then become familiar and commonplace to many Indians through popular literature, military service in Buddhist lands, and new religious movements. Knowledge of Buddhism, however, was not a mass phenomenon, being more likely to be held by literate upper-caste males in the urban strongholds of provincial capitals; although, Buddhist borderlands and hubs like Bodh Gaya or Darjeeling always proved important exceptions as did the movement among casteless Tamils in southern India. The pan-Indian popularity of works like Sir Edwin Arnold's *The Light of Asia* (1879) speaks precisely to this phenomenon (Ober 2021; Ramesh 2021). The chapter follows these trends by turning to the interlinked but often competing views of Buddhism espoused by diverse groups like the regional monastic networks in Arakan, the Theosophical Society, the new Buddhist organizations led by dalits in southern India, the Chittagong Buddhists in Bengal, and the South Asian Hindu–Buddhist elites in the Maha Bodhi Society.

Chapter 4 shifts attention to the dominant Indian and, in particular, brahmanical–Hindu response to these developments. The modern Hindu appropriation of Buddhism—captured succinctly by the popular phrase, "The Buddha was born, lived, and died a Hindu"—was molded by socio-political circumstance. Driven by political pragmatism, a growing sense of pan-Asianism, and the rise of Hindutva ideologies, a number of Hindu groups and intellectuals immersed themselves in Buddhist teachings and practices. It was, however, the right-wing Hindu organization, the All-India

Hindu Maha Sabha, and its industrialist sponsors, the Birlas, that became the foremost patrons of Buddhist construction and publishing projects. This had wide-ranging and contradictory effects. The Maha Sabha and other Hindu associations' support helped transform brahmanical Hindu attitudes towards Buddhism from stigma and exclusion to lukewarm adoration and unease. At the same time, they appropriated it for their own ends, characterizing it as little more than modern Hindu values, thereby erasing distinctive Buddhist qualities and, in effect, invalidating Buddhism's very existence as a separate tradition (for an apt illustration of this, see Sarvepalli Radhakrishnan's (1950) introduction to his translation of the *Dhammapada*). This process of Buddhist engagement via total amalgamation remains the dominant lens through which most Hindus understand the religion today.

However, not all Indians subscribed to the above view. Dissent was strongest among an influential group of Indian leftists and dalit intellectuals who felt that the rhetoric of a Hindu Buddha washed over a long history of distinctive identities and religious tensions. Set against a backdrop of emergent socialist paradigms and national debates on caste reform, the fifth and sixth chapters show how these two groups forged a revolutionary Buddhist ethos based on the ideals of socio-economic equality and anti-caste politics. Although the groups shared similar concerns for the suffering of India's impoverished populations and drew from common pools of Buddhist thought, the political strategies they employed and ideological conventions on which they depended led them down different paths. From the subaltern publics of Lucknow, Madras, and Calicut arose an anti-caste Buddhist activism that later found voice in the mass conversions of Ambedkarite dalits from 1956 onwards. Concurrent political shifts in Congress politics and the Soviet Union led a number of Indian leftists to understand "pure" Buddhism as a kind of socialist humanism that could engender a world of radical equality and enlightened social beings. In the former anti-caste movement, being Buddhist was at the forefront of one's non-Hindu caste-free identity, whereas in the latter leftist movement, attachments to religious identities, including Buddhism, were seen as revisionist and counter-revolutionary. And still, both movements considered Buddhism to be at the forefront of a modern movement for inclusion, equality, and a life well lived.

Among those influenced by the colonial search for Buddhism was India's first prime minister, Jawaharlal Nehru. The final chapter argues that visions of a Buddhist past, particularly under the Mauryan emperor Ashoka, had a powerful impact on Nehru and the members of his cabinet. The chapter delves into "Nehruvian Buddhism," or the state's promotion of Buddhism in both domestic and foreign affairs. By integrating ancient rituals of devotion to Buddhist relics in diplomatic and state projects, Nehruvian Buddhism attempted to forge a new consciousness and identity, not just for India but all of Asia. While Nehru's use of Buddhism as a form of soft power was effectively dismantled by the mass conversions of Ambedkarite Buddhists in 1956, followed by the exile of the Dalai Lama to India in 1959, and finally, the Chinese invasion of India in 1962, it continues to play a role in India's external affairs to this day.

The beginning and end of the book are both marked by two symbolic moments. The first moment took place in 1839. That year, the ghost of India's Buddhist past returned to the subcontinent through the translation and publication of a newly "discovered" Sanskrit Buddhist manuscript, the *Vajrasuchi,* whose sustained criticism of entrenched brahmanical Hindu norms did not go unnoticed. Over the next century, the *Vajrasuchi,* in all its many translations, became a staple of modern Indian Buddhist ideology. At the opposite end of the spectrum, the book ends around 1956, a year that for scholars of South Asia holds a much more obvious bearing. Not only did some half a million dalits convert to Buddhism in October that year, in a striking demonstration of unity and defiance, the event also coincided with a very differently imagined year-long celebration honoring "2,500 Years of Buddhism," orchestrated by Prime Minister Nehru. These prominent events in the 1950s mark the end of this survey. After which, India's encounters and conversations with Buddhism were gradually pulled in other directions.

Place-Making and Social Publics

Reconstructing the past is far from simple, even in places and times with detailed written records (Rahman 2010; Finney 2014). According to the British philosopher and historian, R.G. Collingwood ([1933] 2013: 82), the only solid things history possess are the "traces of itself," the concrete relics in the form of texts, art, objects, and so on. There may be visual, oral, and literary accounts to help guide our reading of these materials—the how, what, when, and where of history—but our ability to truly grasp the world in which they dwelled is to a large degree guided by human imagination. The more that imagination is informed, the more sophisticated our understanding can be.

Ordinarily, non-specialists do not engage in the sort of formalized historical reconstructions that Collingwood describes. Instead, history is typically conceived through what the anthropologist Keith Basso (1996: 7) called "place-making," or bringing the past into the present. According to Basso, thinking about the past and our relationship to it, is probably the most consequential tool in the study of history. The past is always there, and even the most trivial of things can instigate the journey:

> The restrictions on local travel are virtually nonexistent (memory and imagination, the most intimate and inventive of traveling companions, always see to that) … [and] getting there is quick and efficient (a quiet moment or two is usually sufficient to make the transition) (3).

In day-to-day place-making, deep histories may not be recognized at all, with most time spent dwelling on the familiar, mundane, and trivial. Yet, our surroundings, Basso tells us, carry the marks of time, and occasionally something does unsettle our habitual patterns of thought and move us to contemplate other place-worlds. The catalyst may be instantaneous, time changes and "ordinary perceptions begin to loosen their hold … [awareness] has shifted its footing, and the character of the place, now transfigured by thoughts of an earlier day, swiftly takes on a new and foreign look" (4).

This revitalization of places where memories are stored, that carry the mark of time, reveals the underlying conceptual shifts in the making of modern Indian Buddhism. In his memoir, written in the mid-1940s, Jawaharlal Nehru engaged in his own place-making:

> In my own city of Allahabad or in Hardwar I would go to the great bathing festivals, the *Kumbh Mela*, and see hundreds of thousands of people come, as their forebears had come for thousands of years from all over India, to bathe in the Ganges. I would remember descriptions of these festivals written thirteen hundred years ago by Chinese pilgrims and others, and even these *melas* were ancient and lost in an

unknown antiquity .... To a somewhat bare intellectual understanding was added an emotional appreciation, and gradually a sense of reality began to creep into my mental picture of India, and the land of my forefathers became peopled with living beings, who laughed and wept, loved and suffered (Nehru [1946] 1985a: 131–32).

As Nehru traveled across India for thousands of miles, campaigning as a leading Congress politician, shaking the hands of strangers, and visiting India's storied sites, memories of a long-gone past intensified his understanding of the land. When he traveled to Sarnath to visit the famous Deer Park (*Mrigadava*), Nehru invented a place-world swept by the ethical guidelines inscribed on the Ashokan pillar and where the Buddha spoke words of wisdom under the shade of a banyan tree. "Tell all the people," the Buddha says in Nehru's voice, "the poor and the lowly, the rich and the high, are all one, and that all castes unite in this religion as do rivers in the sea" (129). Within this familiar, yet distant realm, Nehru lingered, until, as Basso (1996: 6) explains, "it started to fade, as every place-world must."

According to Basso, the places-worlds we visit are shaped by the "congenial places of experiential terrain: the terrain of one's youth, perhaps, or of where one's forebears lived, or of decisive events that altered the course of history" (3). Yet, building place-worlds is not only about reviving times gone by and reliving the past but also about *revising* them and shaping them in new ways. Place-worlds, in other words, may be constitutive of past historical moments, but their significance and meaning will forever be constructed, interrogated, and fashioned for someone actively imagining them. This process of creating place-worlds, of comparing contents, evaluating strengths and weaknesses, and pondering their significance is a regular, collective, social process, "as common and straightforward as it is sometimes highly inventive" (7).

This book tells the stories of individuals and communities who wished to make "the stuff" (7) of Buddhist place-worlds alive again. As the following chapters describe, this task could not be so easily accomplished. For if the place-maker's main objective is to speak the past into being, to summon it with words and objects, and give it dramatic, living form, to *produce* an experience of place-worlds and not just speak of them, there was an even greater number of individuals who sought to produce the experiences of place-worlds either wholly separate from Buddhist ones or impressioned with a different lens. That is, the process through which one place-world becomes more widely accepted than another may depend on how credible and convincing they seem, the charisma and authority of those who describe them, or even the political conditions under which certain accounts may be authorized, archived, and un-archived. This work aims to recover the complexity of this pivotal moment in modern Indian and modern Buddhist history.

1

The Agony of Memory

It all began with a conversation. In the spring of 1835, a British diplomat named Lancelot Wilkinson (1805–41) and his Sanskrit tutor, Pandit Subaji Bapu (dates unknown), began talking about an old Buddhist Sanskrit manuscript, the *Vajrasuchi*, that Wilkinson had recently acquired from a Hindu sannyasi on a trip to Nashik in western India.[1] In thirteen printed pages the *Vajrasuchi* or Diamond Cutter, lays out a scathing critique of the brahmanical view of caste (varna). The purported author of the text, Ashvaghosha, a first century CE Buddhist scholar, begins by asking the reader simple questions: "What is Brahmanhood? Is it life (*jiva*)? Is it caste (*varna*)? Is it wisdom (*jnana*)" (Hodgson 1831: 161)?[2] Then, quoting from different Hindu scriptures (smriti), his cutting logic turns the sources on their head and systematically demolishes the notion of a brahmin's superior status. In Ashvaghosha's view, all humans belong to one caste. Only those who are filled with compassion for all beings and have gained control over their bodily and psychological senses can be called "true Brahmins". "Brahminhood," Ashvaghosha concludes, is not a quality of birth but "merely a quality of good men" (164).[3]

Subaji was resistant when Wilkinson told him of his wish to publish a bilingual English–Sanskrit edition of the manuscript and distribute it widely. By all accounts, this appears to have been the first major hiccup in what had otherwise been a long and relatively fruitful relationship. Throughout his nearly decade-long service for Wilkinson, Subaji had proven himself to be "anything but an orthodox Hindoo" (Letter from Wilkinson to Brian Hodgson, 11 May 1835, quoted in Young 2003: 208). He had become a proponent of Copernican science and even produced Marathi-language tracts arguing against Vyasa's conception of the universe (which governed brahmanical–Hindu metaphysics). A Telugu-speaking brahmin of "wonderful acuteness, intelligence and sound judgment" (Wilkinson 1837: 401), Subaji had followed Wilkinson from one princely state to another before ending up in Bhopal. Here, the latter became the British resident and Subaji the star attraction of Sehore Pathshala, the local Sanskrit school. Wilkinson, for his part, was considered a colonial oddity, "a subaltern of Orientalism" (Kopf 1969: 278) whose unwavering support for Sanskrit and regional lingua francas had earned him the support of local leaders.[4]

But their conversation about the *Vajrasuchi* went poorly. In a private letter written to a colleague, Wilkinson reported that Subaji's eyes "glistened with anger when he heard the arguments expounded" (Wilkinson 1834, quoted in Young 2003: 208). Eventually, Subaji agreed to help edit the text, but only if it was published along with his own rebuttal. Wilkinson consented, and in a forty-seven page critique—more than three times the length of the *Vajrasuchi* itself—Subaji attacked the tract's core reasoning by arguing that caste (varna) is prior to all behavior and a universal inherent in the nature of reality.[5] In 1839, the manuscript, which included Subaji's commentary, officially went to print as *The Wujra Soochi, or Refutation of the Arguments upon which the Brahmanical Institution of Caste is Founded, by the Learned Boodhist Ashwa Ghoshu (with a Translation by B.H. Hodgson and a Preface by L. Wilkinson), Also the Tunku, by Soobajee Bapoo, Being a Reply to the Wujra Soochi.*[6]

For decades after its publication, the Wilkinson–Hodgson–Subaji edition of the *Vajrasuchi* remained a big hit. It was widely known across India and Europe, being circulated among Christian missionaries, Hindu social reformers, and later Buddhist missionaries. Museum libraries, state archives, and research centers acquired it; popular magazines, literary reviews, and scholarly journals debated its merits. By the end of the century, the text was a favorite among anti-caste activists like Tukaram Tatya Padwal (1838–98), Dadoba Pandurang (1814–82), and Jotirao Phule (1827–90), who published their own Marathi editions of the text (O'Hanlon 1985: 225–27).

The Hindu nationalist, V.D. Savarkar (1883–1966), praised it, as did the Nepali Buddhist organizer, D.A. Dharmacharya (1902–63), and the Sinhalese Buddhist activist, Anagarika Dharmapala (1864–1933). In the decades that followed, the text was translated into Bengali, Tamil, Hindi, and Nepali alongside numerous reprints of the English editions.[7] Nineteenth- and twentieth-century Indian publics were clearly convinced that the words of an ancient Buddhist monk were still relevant in the modern day.

At the time that the Wilkinson–Hodgson–Subaji edition of the *Vajrasuchi* was published, the professional enterprise that later became Buddhist Studies and Indology was still embryonic. Eugène Burnouf's *Introduction à l'histoire du Buddhisme Indien* (1844) and Alexander Cunningham's *Bhilsa Topes* (1854), two of the most significant early nineteenth-century studies to firmly place the Buddha and Buddhist traditions in India's history, were still years away. Anagarika Dharmapala, the figure often credited with launching India's Buddhist revival, was not born until a quarter century later. It may seem strange to begin a history of modern Indian Buddhism with the raw criticism of one of its brahmanical opponents. But the story of the Wilkinson–Hodgson–Subaji edition of the *Vajrasuchi* speaks well to the wider social and intellectual attitude towards Buddhists and the Buddha among many late eighteenth- and early nineteenth-century Indians.

Memories of the Buddha and Buddhists

Scholars have dedicated much of their time in recent years to further their understanding of how the "West discovered Buddhism" (see, App 2012; Lopez 2013) or more tangibly, how late eighteenth- and early nineteenth-century European intellectuals came to the conclusion that the Buddha had been an Indian and that the variegated traditions across Asia that developed in his wake had first blossomed in the rich soil of the Gangetic Plains. By contrast, almost nothing has been said about how Indians actually understood him at that time and what roles they played in the development of European knowledge of Buddhism. Instead, most scholars have proceeded on the false assumption that by the time the surveyors of the East India Company began unearthing Buddhist monuments across the subcontinent, Indians had lost all knowledge of who the Buddha was. In a paradigmatic example of contemporary scholarship, the French philosopher Roger-Pol Droit ([1997] 2003: 7) asserts that by the eighteenth century, "Brahmans appear to have almost completely lost any recollection of their argument with Buddhism". The brilliant Indian linguist S.K. Chatterji was equally emphatic: "Till the beginning of the nineteenth century, Buddhism was a *forgotten* creed in the land of its origin" (quoted in Barua 2007: 54, italics mine). The obvious counterpart to this argument is that Indian memory must have been a veritable *tabula rasa,* a blank slate upon which European Orientalist visions of Buddhism were constructed.

Even if India's so-called "lack of historical consciousness" continues to be the subject of much spilled ink (Pollock 1989; Sharma 2003; Trautmann 2012), it should not lead one to assume that Indians did not possess living depictions of the Buddhist past. Sustained engagement with Buddhist texts and practices may have been pushed to Himalayan enclaves and remote frontier regions when the first Europeans established colonies on the subcontinent, but many Indians still encountered an imagined Buddhism in popular literary works, performances, and oral traditions. These "storehouses of memory" included Puranic scriptures, hagiographies, technical philosophical works, ballads, popular plays, poems, art, and iconography. It is in these materials that visions of Buddhism remained a living force among Indian populaces before European colonialism. As Sheldon Pollock (2011: 1) once remarked in a simple but profound way: "we cannot know how colonialism changed South Asia if we do not know what was there to be changed."

Due to the contingent nature of these materials, in terms of both their dynamic and shifting interpretations as well as their sheer availability in different geographical regions, several limitations must be recognized. Surveying them in a limited manner involves a risk of homogenizing the diversity of views involved, as if there were a uniform early colonial attitude towards Buddhists across South Asia. The reconstruction and transmission of memory and knowledge has always varied immensely across the subcontinent, with contradictions across regions being the norm rather than the exception (Guha 2019). Further challenges are posed by the epistemological problems inherent in South Asian history and its diverse, often opposing, sets of evidence. There are also important questions of chronology. While coins and inscriptions often provide concrete dates, the dating of manuscripts is notoriously contested. Most manuscripts were traditionally composed on palm leaves and birch bark, both of which perish quickly in the tropical Indian climate.[8] Even after paper was introduced around the thirteenth century, manuscripts had to be recopied (a laborious task) and passages were often consciously or unconsciously altered, omitted or added. Thus, almost all manuscripts should be seen as composite texts, the products of multiple authors and editors at different stages in time. And in most regions, such work was often the prerogative of brahmins.

Nonetheless, when viewed in conjunction with one another, these materials provide clear evidence that, as late as the nineteenth century, Buddhists (*bauddha, saugata*) continued to be the subject of much conversation in India. For roughly two thousand years India transmitted its knowledge through what scholars call "manuscript cultures" (Houben and Rath 2012). In the first few centuries of the Common Era, Sanskrit emerged as the premier "cosmopolitan" language, transmitting systems of scientific, literary, and religious thought across southern Asia (Pollock 2006).[9] The circulation of Sanskrit manuscripts among the brahmin literati, wealthy patrons, and royal courts and, after the fourteenth century, the subcontinent's extensive network of Hindu monasteries (*matha*), always depended on a variety of cultural, economic, and political conditions. Focusing on those manuscript cultures whose cultural production is noted for its regional or even "pan-Indian" popularity is especially valuable for understanding the attitude towards Buddhism in the pre-colonial world.

Early brahmanical literature in Sanskrit expressed less scorn towards Buddhists than it did to those who did not follow the the householder traditions of *varna-ashram-dharma*, (a brahmanical ideological model that divided society into four castes [varna] and four ashrams, or stages in life) as a whole. In the *Manusmriti* (second to third centuries CE) and the shastric redactions of Kautilya's *Arthashastra* (third to fifth centuries CE), Buddhists are generally grouped together with the non-Vedic groups that "produce no reward after death" (*Manu's Code of Law* 2005: 349, verse 12.95). Like Jains, Carvakas, and other non-Vedic groups, Buddhists were classified as *pashandika*s (impostors) and *nastika*s (literally, deniers), terms that derogatorily but rightly labeled them as ones who denied the Vedas, the notion of a Supreme God (*Ishvara*), and the authority of the brahmin priestly castes.[10] These classifications were largely maintained in other genres of Sanskrit writing, the most important of which, for our purposes, is the Puranic–*Itihas* literature. The Puranas were a body of eighteen central texts, *Mahapurana*s, besides a much larger number of lesser texts (*upapurana*). Puranic literature was the dominant form of Sanskrit historical writing. It recalls the past (itihasa) in the language of the gods (deva), the languages of sages (rishi) and their descendants. While temporal considerations are not irrelevant, they are generally accorded secondary importance to what their brahmin authors considered more weighty matters—the nature of the universe and tales of war between deities and demons.

As the principal scriptures of theistic Hinduism, the puranas also provide the central motifs and stories for many popular Hindu practices. Although, as a whole, the genre does not contain extensive discussion of Buddhist systems, Buddhists appear as frequent interlocutors. It is thus an important source for understanding the wider brahmanical Hindu view of Buddhist traditions. The most notable feature of several major puranas is their acceptance of the Buddha as the (typically) ninth avatar or incarnation of Vishnu.[11] Many colonial Indians even argued that the "crowning" of the Buddha as an avatar of Vishnu was evidence of the general spirit of Hindu tolerance and inclusiveness. This line of reasoning continues to have wide radiance today. But a closer reading of the Buddha avatar mythology suggests that the real motivation in incorporating him into the pantheon of Vishnu avatars stemmed more from religio-political pragmatism than from any genuine respect or adoration.

In the *Vishnu Purana* (fourth to fifth centuries CE), where the Buddha avatar is discussed in greatest detail, the Buddha is introduced as one of many forms of the *mayamoha* (delusive power) of Vishnu.[12] The story begins by describing how demonic rule and unrighteousness (*adharma*) have gained ascendancy in the world. As is customary in Vaishnava scriptures, it then explains why and how Vishnu, the Supreme Being, must descend to the earth from his heavenly abode to restore social order. The narrator describes Vishnu taking the form of the Buddha, dressed in a red garment, speaking gently, sweetly, and calmly. The nature of his character is overt. Unlike his earlier incarnations where Vishnu wields weapons and uses physical force to defeat the unrighteous, the Buddha avatar's tactics are noticeably different. Since the demons (*daityas*) are too powerful to be defeated using force, he must demoralize them from within, a process described by the Indologist, Klaus Klostermaier (1979: 65), as a kind of "psychological warfare". The demons listen carefully to the Buddha's seductive and gentle words, which are broadly consistent with early Buddhist teachings: the slaughter of animals for sacrifices should be stopped; the universe is a product of the mind; the world is without support from the gods; humanity's veneration of the Vedas is based on ignorance. All of these teachings are in direct opposition to the most centrally held Vaishnava beliefs. Yet, the Buddha's charisma and "trickery" are seemingly impossible to resist. The demons cease their worship of the Vedas, abandoning brahmanical rituals and the smritis. As they do so, they also begin coaxing other "misguided ones" to take refuge in the Buddha until veneration for him swells across the land. Those who accept him as their master, however, become noticeably weak. The Purana describes them as "naked" (*nagna*) of "the armor of dharma [Vedic righteousness]" that protects the righteous and orthodox from malicious forces (*Vishnu Purana*, Book III, Chapter 18, Verse 33). The message is clear: those who follow the Buddha's teachings and abandon the Vedas will meet destruction.

Not all Puranas discuss Buddhists, but those that do are explicit in describing how Buddhists and other dissenters should be (mis)treated.[13] All social contact with them must be broken. Those who dine with Buddhists go to hell. Even the sight of a Buddhist is ritually polluting and can lead to one's demise. To illustrate this, the *Vishnu Purana* (Verses 53–104) tells the story of King Shatadhanu and his pious wife, Shaivya. When a Buddhist (or possibly a Jain)[14] renunciate approaches the king after bathing in the Bhagirathi River, they engage in conversation while his wife wisely turns away. The text explains that while the wife's decision maintained her purity, the king had to suffer many low rebirths as a dog, a jackal, a wolf, a vulture, a crow, and finally a peacock before assuming a human body again. The story closes by explaining that one should avoid all contact with wicked apostates, and that all merit earned that day will be lost if you even speak to the "naked"—those who "shave their heads," "disregard the rules of purity," "eat food prepared by members of the lower orders," or "oppose Vedic teachings" (Verses 97–102).

Perhaps the only thing worse than socializing with a Buddhist is being or becoming one.[15]

Contemporary scholarship believes most of the major Puranas to have been composed between the fifth and tenth centuries, a period which in parts of India also marked growing tensions between Buddhist and non-Buddhist communities. However, in many later Sanskrit works composed between the eighth and tenth centuries—when Buddhist institutions may have been seen as a reduced threat to brahmanical norms—the Buddha avatar is characterized in less explicitly hostile terms (Doniger 1976: 187–211). In the *Bhagavata Purana* (c. tenth century), for instance, Vishnu takes form as the Buddha to protect humanity from ignorance. Similarly, in Jayadeva's *Gita Govinda* (tenth century), the Buddha avatar is born out of Vishnu's compassion for animals and to end bloody sacrifices. As texts of tremendous cultural and supra-regional importance (particularly for theistic Hindus), these manuscripts were composed, copied, and edited by scribes and scholars, then read and recited at royal courts and in the homes of wealthy merchants up through the colonial period. The frequent recourse to and study of these manuscripts conditioned a familiar yet dismissive attitude towards Buddhists among an influential section of the subcontinent's populace.

It is worth asking whether this hostile, and later, ambivalent, feeling towards Buddhists was simply the product of a north Indian brahmanical priestly conservatism. After all, it is widely known that there was a robust cross-fertilization of ideas and practices among Jains, Shaivas, Vaishnavas, Lingayats, and various Buddhist sects throughout the first millennium. The period between the seventh to fifteenth centuries, in particular, is often seen as the high point of Indic scholasticism, a time when philosophers of every persuasion honed their logic at pluralistic courts. One outcome of these urbane and closely knit lineages of learning was that Buddhist doctrines became deeply enmeshed in Indic intellectual culture. Even as late as the seventeenth century—when Buddhist scholars had long lost the support of South Asian rulers in the plains—scholastic manuals and commentaries produced by the Vedanta and Nyaya traditions continued to show surprisingly faithful understandings of basic Buddhist doctrines (Nicholson 2010: 192; Freschi 2016: 65–99). In manuals like Shankara's

Brahmasutrabhasha (eighth century), Jayanta Bhatta's *Nyaymanjari* (ninth century), and Madhava's *Sarvadarshanasamgraha* (fourteenth century), Buddhists served as the propagators of what Andrew Nicholson (2010: 192) calls "the prototypical *nastika* school".[16] For students of these influential works, understanding and defeating the arguments of the nastika system was a necessary step on the way to self-realization and prestige. Buddhists were the "scholastic other," the fundamental foil, against whom Hindu *astika*s (affirmers) redefined and reimagined themselves. Long after Buddhists had left the stage and were no longer providing live responses to Mimamsaka, Vedantic, and other astika interlocutors, Hindu philosophers still felt compelled to converse with the ghosts of the Buddhist past.

Many of these manuals were widely circulated among philosophic and religious authorities up through the early colonial period. In the many hagiographies and commentaries of the influential seventh-century Mimamsaka scholar, Kumarila Bhatta, memories of a Buddhist past are in vivid display.[17] Described as a brilliant logician with a profound wit and an equally sharp tongue, Kumarila Bhatta is remembered not only as a votary of Indic intellectualism but for his stunning and often violent attacks on Buddhists. By nearly all accounts, Kumarila Bhatta appears to have studied under an unnamed Buddhist guru at a young age before becoming convinced that Buddhist views were mistaken. Leaving his former guru, he became a zealous proponent of the Mimamsakas, castigating other mistaken "Hindu" sects like the Samkhya, Pancharatra, and Pashupatas, but always reserving particular scorn for his former Buddhist teachers. He ridicules the argument that the Buddha was omniscient, asking how someone who is not omniscient himself could know that someone else is. Such a teaching, he contends, is only fit for and practised by the symbolically polluted: outcastes, foreigners (*mleccha*), and other "animal-like" tribals (Klostermaier 1979: 67–68). Although he never withdrew his attacks on Buddhists, he later burned himself to death on a funeral pyre, or in some recensions, tossed himself off a building after realizing what a terrible thing he had done by defaming his former Buddhist master (betraying one's teacher being the *maxima mea culpa* in Indic learning circles).[18]

Despite being more "exclusivist" than many of his contemporaries, Kumarila Bhatta is a fair representation of the general sentiment held against

Buddhists by scholastics at this time. As Nicholson (2010: 188) argues in his study of twelfth- to seventeenth-century South Asian philosophy, those thinkers with "marked inclusivist tendencies" still drew a clear line between "insiders and outsiders, *astikas* and *nastikas*" (ibid). Even the decidedly inclusivist philosopher, Vijnanabhikshu (sixteenth to seventeeth centuries), who was willing to make room for "difference and non-difference" with regard to multiple insider, or astika, positions, argued that "non-difference" does not come into play when discussing Buddhism. In fact, while Vijnanabhikshu rarely descends into polemics against astika thinkers, he is relentless in his attacks on Buddhists. Only the Advaita Vedantins—his true antagonists—are treated more harshly. The term he uses to deride them, however, is telling: he calls them "hidden Buddhists" (*pracchannabauddha*), a common term of oral and literary slander which throughout the centuries has been used to exploit "the strong popular sentiment against Buddhism" (Klostermaier 1979: 71).[19]

The eighth-century Vedantic philosopher, Shankara, was similarly hostile towards Buddhist institutions. Indeed, his post–fourteenth century reputation as the "destroyer" of Buddhism—the truth of which is greatly contested by scholars—is perhaps only superseded by his reputation as the foremost interpreter of Vedanta. After the fourteenth century, when a series of hagiographies describing Shankara's "conquest of the four quarters" of India gained wide circulation, he attained a prized place in popular Hindu consciousness (Bader 1991). His own scholastic commentaries, which were required reading for post–fourteenth century Advaita Vedantins, showcase a clear and lucid awareness of three different Buddhist philosophical schools (*nikaya*). Shankara's advice to his audience is to avoid the Buddhists if they have any "regard for their own happiness" (Klostermaier 1979: 69–70; see also, Bader 1991: 137).

While there is only scattered evidence for the persistence of Buddhism in the ancient Buddhist heartland (Pali, *Majjhima Desa*) after the fifteenth century, it is clear that even if most Indians did not meet living Buddhists or access physical Buddhist texts, they continued to be well aware of their historical existence and their continued presence on the borders. In Madhava's *Shankaradigvijaya,* a seventeenth- to eighteenth-century Sanskrit hagiography of Shankara that quickly eclipsed all earlier Shankara legends and was essential reading for devotees, Buddhists are given ample space. Admittedly, the subtle nuances of anti-Buddhist argumentation appear to have been lost, and recensions from the eighteenth century no longer detail the sharp analytical swipes at Buddhist logic typical of the past. Instead, they turn to metaphors of gruesome violence and destruction to showcase Buddhist failings. For instance, in an influential eighteenth-century version of the *Shankaradigvijaya*, studied in detail by Bader (1991), Buddhists and Jains are crushed by the famed Mimamsaka master, Kumarila Bhatta, with weapons and not just words.

Buddhists, it is clear, were no longer the primary scholastic adversaries at this point in time. They were simply the defeated "other," driven to the margins and no longer deserving of sustained targeting and debate. Nonetheless, memories of Buddhists continued to be hashed out through live performances of popular Sanskrit dramas, like the late ninth-century *Agamadambara* (Bhatta Jayanta 2005) and the eleventh-century *Prabodhacandrodaya* (Krishna Mishra 2009), where the saffron-robe-clad monastics are the subject of much satire and comedy, appearing as little more than progenitors of faulty views and hedonistic lifestyles.[20] There were undoubtedly some exceptions to this trend: Hindu intellectuals who recognized Buddhists as formidable sparring partners in their centuries-long conversations about self and non-self, existence and non-existence, realization, beauty, logic, death, knowledge, and the numerous other categories that consumed the Sanskrit cosmopolis. But their stories appear to be the exception that proves the rule.[21]

Geographies of Exclusion

For the often polyglot populaces of the subcontinent, Sanskrit literature only serves as one domain where intimations of a Buddhist past are stored. Indeed, between the tenth and sixteenth centuries, there was a marked turn towards "vernacular" literature across India (although this process developed much earlier in the south, where linguistic choices in literary traditions were more varied and complex, on which see Pollock 2006). Literary sources from sixth- to thirteenth-century south India, popularized in later centuries through devotional hymns, temple artworks, and the networks of charismatic saints, provide equally rich—but disturbing—insights into conventional brahmanical views on Buddhists. Many of the most popular devotional works from this period rigorously condemn Buddhists, turning what Anne Monius (2001: 84) called a "geography of inclusion" into "a rabidly sectarian vision of the Tamil landscape." Buddhists (and Jains) are ridiculed for everything from their style of dress and manner of eating to their lack of respect for Vedic rites and the use of the Prakrit rather than refined "classical" tongues.[22]

Nowhere is this enmity more evident than in the poems and narratives surrounding the seventh-century child prodigy, Sambandar (or Campantar). Popularly remembered for his heartfelt prayers to Shiva, and worshipped with offerings across Tamil-speaking south India to this day, Sambandar's life—like other Shaiva Nayanar poet–saints—was characterized by itinerancy and use of lyrical devotional melodies. His bhakti or devotion was also concerned with converting courtly elites away from Jain and Buddhist institutions. In most of his hymns, Sambandar reserved the tenth verse for the denunciation of the two creeds. Buddhists—clearly identified by their shaved heads and ochre robes—are described as "wicked scoundrels," "worthless, wily rogues," and "fat, degenerate men" (Peterson 1989: 10). In other hymns, they are considered stupid, deluded, overfed, overdressed, linguistically challenged, and the teachers of a dharma that leads to misfortune and ruin (1–23, 270–83).

These signs of stigmatism were sometimes accompanied by violence, as the still popular twelfth-century Tamil epic, *Periya Puranam* (Great Purana), makes clear. In one of the more memorable stories from this text, Sambandar accepts an invitation to debate with the logician Buddha Nandi, the head (thera) of a local Buddhist vihara (*St. Sekkizhaar's Periya Puranam* 1995: 176–81, Ch. 33, Verses 904–26). Praying to Shiva for victory, Sambandar recites a single mantra, and the monk's head is severed from his spine. Aghast, the monk's disciples challenge him again, insisting this time on a debate conducted not through "flawless mantric disputation" but with "words" (178, Ch. 33, Verse 911). Unfortunately for the Buddhists, they are forced to submit to Shiva's strength after Sambandar proves that "the omniscience of the Buddha was hollow like his *moksa* [salvation]" (181, Ch. 33, Verse 924). Whether such violence should be read literally or figuratively is often contested, but the underlying message is the same: Buddhists encourage forms of socially unacceptable behavior. As Wendy Doniger (2009: 483) rightly observes, brahmanical criticism of Buddhists was often stated in terms of both orthopraxy and orthodoxy: Buddhists teach people the wrong belief—to stop venerating the Vedas and brahmin castes. With the wrong belief, people will begin doing the wrong things. The justification of these tales may be morally ambiguous by contemporary liberal standards, but in the historical context, these kinds of pedagogies were fundamental in reminding people to "live right".

Although these sources—temple chronicles, devotional poetry, and songs—were widely read and recited in public spaces and religious sites (giving them a popularity not always evident in their small readership), art and iconography were other media through which narratives concerning Buddhists were transmitted across generations. Brahmin literati, land owning castes, and Vishnu-oriented devotees living in early colonial south India, for example, would have been well aware of the Buddhist exploits of Thirumangai Alvar (eighth-to-ninth century), one of the twelve great Tamil poet–saints who espoused bhakti to Vishnu. In a popular story that recalls the early history of the massive Sri Ranganathaswamy Vishnu temple complex at Srirangam—one of the largest Hindu complexes in the world today—Thirumangai, in effect, sanctions theft against Buddhists when he funds his construction of the temple walls by stealing and melting a golden image of the Buddha housed in the seaside enclave of Nagapattinam (Dehejia 1988: 58). Likewise, at the Lakshmi temple of the Jagannath complex in Puri, a fresco depicts a Vaishnava priest threatening a Buddhist monk at the point of a dagger (Tripathy 1988: 188).[23] Regional accounts recall these incidents in vivid detail. In the twelfth century Odia-language chronicle *Madalapanji* (2009), the Ganga king, Rajaraja II (c. 1171–94), calls for a debate between brahmins and Buddhists to see "who were omniscient and whose words were true" (34).[24] Philosophical proofs are laid out, and despite the Buddhists winning, the king executes them (34–35).[25] Another story from both a later edition of the *Madalapanji* and the Bengali-language *Chaitanya Bhagavat* (c. 1540s) describes the King Madana Mahadeva's persecution of large groups of Buddhists and the burning of nearly all their manuscripts (Kulke 1993: 187; Mukherjee 1940: 52–53).

Sixteenth- and seventeenth-century hagiographies circulated in Bengal among Gaudiya Vaishnavas, one of the most successful Vaishnava movements of the past five centuries, provide similarly lively (and antagonistic) depictions of Buddhists. Centered on the Bengali brahmin priest, Chaitanya (c. 1468–1533)—believed by his devotees to be the *Mahaprabhu* (Great God)—this movement may have only gained popularity in the nineteenth century, but its sixteenth and seventeenth century luminaries produced a number of influential manuscripts detailing Chaitanya's interactions with Buddhists. In the *Chaitanya Charitamrita* (c. 1540s), the author Krishnadasa Kaviraja describes Chaitanya's visit to a village led by a young Buddhist acharya (master) near Vriddha-Kasi in present-day Tamil Nadu (*Chaitanya Charitamrita* 1999: 464–65, Ch. 9, Verses 40–57). Despite admitting that Buddhists are unfit to be conversed with or even seen, Chaitanya agrees to debate with the acharya in order to shatter his pride. Expectedly, the acharya is humiliated by Chaitanya's wit and logic. However, rather than surrendering and "converting" to the opponent's position, as is often the custom in these stories, the acharya and his disciples try to poison Chaitanya by offering him a plate of impure food (*apavitra anna*) disguised as a religious offering (prasad). At the very moment the food is being offered, a large bird swoops down, grasps the plate, sweeps back into the sky and drops the plate on the acharya's head, striking him dead. Terrified, the acharya's disciples beg Chaitanya to revive their guru. In his great compassion, Chaitanya does so but only after ordering all of the Buddhists to join in singing praise to Krishna (Krishna *sankirtan*). At that moment, the defeated acharya wakes with the word of God (*Krishnabali*) bursting from his mouth.[26]

In the many religious debates that took place at the Mughal emperor Akbar's (r. 1556–1605), imperial court, Jain theologians and brahmin intellectuals argued about the connection of Buddhist doctrines to Shaiva and Islamic conceptions of a monotheistic God (*paramishvara*) (Truschke 2015: 1327, 1332). In fact, Akbar's *vizir* and court historian, Abu al'Fazl (1551–1602), wrote at length about the "tribe of Boodh [Buddha]".[27] Buddhists appear in all three volumes of his Persian-language *Ain-e-Akbari*, including a comprehensive report in Volume III (*Ain-e-Akbari* 1873–1907: 211–17) where he describes four different schools of Buddhist philosophy, the nature of Buddhist praxis, brahmanical antagonism towards Buddhists, and the widespread influence that Buddhists once held over the land. Long after Akbar's reign, Mughal rulers continued to engage in political negotiation with Buddhist monastic governments at both ends of the Himalayas, showing significant familiarity with their customs and doctrines. Even in seventeenth-century Rajasthan, where Buddhism had been supplanted nearly a millennium before, Buddhists continued to be spoken about in the songs and hymns of the Dadupanthis. This devotional sect of monastic and lay communities, founded by the *sant*, Dadu (1554–1603), taught that Buddhists were one of the six schools (*saddarshana*) who "wear false religious costumes" (*sabai kapata ke bhekha*) (quoted in Hortsman 2015: 36). Some six hundred miles south of the Dadupanthis' *karmabhoomi,* a host of Maharashtrian saints and their devotees extolled the name of the Buddha in art, sculpture, and poetry. Except now, his Vishnu-inspired identity as the incarnation (avatar) of deception had been transfigured into the holy persona of Vitthal (Vithoba), the most popular god in the western state (Dhere 2011: 173–88). The phenomenon led Ramachandra Chintaman Dhere, the great scholar of Maharashtrian culture, to declare: "in Indian traditions nothing ever gets destroyed: it only gets transformed, taking on different names and forms" (187).

The violence and othering contained in so many of these texts are striking. While some scholars argue that these features are clear manifestations of social tensions (Verardi 2011), others argue that the hostilities evidenced in literary sources are not visible in archaeological records. They point to what appears as a long history of religious pluralism at sites like Bodh Gaya, Amaravati, Nagarjunakonda, Ellora, and elsewhere (Singh and Lahiri 2010; Ray 2007). In everyday practice, religious identity in South Asia has largely been malleable and dependent on context, yet it is also clear that caste and ethnic-group practices are tied to familial and communal traditions that police peoples' behaviors and thoughts. Religious communalism is not inevitable, and a broad examination of Indic history reveals as much intra-religious sectarianism as it does extra-religious animosity. Buddhists argued amongst one another as vociferously as they did with non-Buddhists. They were also vicious in their denunciations of brahmins and no less invested in polemics (Black 2009).

Scholars are not exactly amiss when they contend that brahmanical culture absorbed much of the ethical and philosophical basis of Buddhism (and vice versa). Despite this, Buddhists were still stigmatized as objects of derision and this was largely how they came to be remembered in India after the fifteenth century. Difference does not always lead to understanding or empathy. Shared spaces can also be sources of conflict. While there is no doubting the long history of communion at the multilayered altar of Indic religious life, religious elites also understand that they follow disparate religious paths that present substantially different world views and ethics. In the realpolitik of competition for patronage and political support, these differences often come to the fore. It is here, as a means of gaining resources, tangible and intangible, that the severe Buddhist critiques leveled against brahmanical authority (and vice versa) took on forms of social and political tension and which were remembered for generations to come.

What is inarguable is the depth and breadth of materials in conversation with Buddhists in the era before British colonization. Of course, significant obstacles arise in our reading of these materials, the most crucial of which is our (in)ability to gauge how well known they were in the wider "public sphere". As a whole, social and religious interactions at the popular level in pre-modern India still remain little understood. Despite roughly thirty million manuscripts still extant—clear proof of a rich and vibrant "popular" pre-modern culture—there are very few studies of manuscript cultures in terms of understanding their actual production and use (Pollock 2006). Simply put, we still don't know enough about how deeply the knowledge systems and stories crafted and created by these manuscript cultures permeated beyond the elite communities that formed them. However, it is evident that in pre-colonial India, knowledge of these texts was geographically widespread, for not just individual thinkers, but a larger Indic intellectual culture deeply conversant with Buddhist peoples, philosophy, and praxis.

Jan Kampani and the Agony of Memory

In the eighteenth century, the British-owned East India Company (EIC) consolidated power across South Asia. By 1773, the Company had established a capital in Calcutta and appointed its first governor general, Warren

Hastings. The administration of the regions it annexed required a sizable number of officials from Europe. For many who served in the upper ranks of the Company, India was envisioned as a land of opportunity where, as the popular historian, Charles Allen (2002: 12), put it, "a young gentleman blessed with patronage and a stout constitution could give the pagoda tree a good hard shake and return home with a modest fortune before acquiring so much as one grey hair upon his head."[28] Although few Company officers had university degrees, they were largely products of a social class where sons acquired a solid grounding in Greek, Latin, mathematics, and philosophy. It was among this genteel class of administrators, officers, surveyors, and lawyers, living in colonial entrepôts like Calcutta, Madras, Bombay, and Benares, that a new conversation with Indians commenced.

Amidst the wider Orientalist discussions about the nature of India's past, its social and religious customs, and the relationship between Sanskrit and Greek, were a series of unanswered questions about the figure called the Buddha.[29] While the concept "Buddhism" had yet to be coined, the meaning of the term "Buddha" was hotly debated by European intellectuals. Modern European encounters with Buddhist traditions had begun several centuries before, but despite growing interactions with the rich tapestry of localized traditions across Asia—worshipping *fo* ("Buddha" in Chinese), *hotoke* (Japanese), *sangay* (Tibetan), *samana Gotam* (Thai), and many more—there was no universal consensus regarding his singular Indian origin (Lach 1965–93; App 2012). By the late eighteenth and early nineteenth centuries, a flood of new literary and archaeological evidence gathered from European colonies across Asia began disclosing the early Indian origins of the Buddhist traditions of Asia (Lopez 2013: 134–54). While much of Europe's growing understanding of India's Buddhist past stemmed from the critical editing of Buddhist manuscripts by armchair scholars in faraway European universities, a number of the most influential interpreters were employees of the Company.

As the Company expanded its mercantile interests across the Indian subcontinent, surveyors and soldiers increasingly encountered artifacts of Buddhist material culture buried in the soil, hidden in dense jungles, or being reused and recycled for other construction projects. During this early phase of exploration, Buddhist discoveries were rare but often opened radical new perspectives into the subcontinent's past. In 1785, for example, one Mr Wilmot copied a Sanskrit inscription from a stone found at Bodh Gaya—the town in modern Bihar now recognized as the site of the Buddha's enlightenment. Three years later, the Sanskritist and veteran Company writer, Charles Wilkins, published a translation of the inscription in the *Asiatick Researches*, proclaiming it as the "house of Bood-dha" (Wilkins 1788: 287).[30] Just a few years later, two twelfth-century urns honoring the Buddha were discovered near Sarnath, the small town in modern Uttar Pradesh believed to be the site of the Buddha's first teaching. It would be decades before the full significance of these kinds of findings were realized. But as the skeletal outline of the Buddha's life and India's Buddhist past began to take shape, there was a re-evaluation of the conventional narratives driving European and Indian understandings of the subcontinent's history.[31]

A fine illustration of the way that some of the most astute of Company officials pieced together these historical traces is evident in the career of the Scottish surgeon and botanist, Francis Buchanan (1762–1829). Between 1794 and 1816, Buchanan traveled large swathes of the subcontinent by horse, foot, and boat as a surveyor for the Company. Within two years of his arrival, he accompanied the British mission to the royal court of Ava (Burma) where he met the Buddhist monarch, Bodawpaya (r. 1782–1819), and visited the venerated *Mahamuni* image that had been recently taken by the Burmese as war booty from the neighboring kingdom of Arakan. While traveling through Chittagong, Buchanan recognized quite a few similarities between the Bengali-speaking populace there and the Buddhists in Arakan, including the worship of "Godama [Gotama Buddha]" (Buchanan [1798] 1992: 98). Buchanan's observations also included notes on caste distinctions, "Brahmanical superstitions," and the "bloody sacrifices to the Devtas" that he witnessed among the Chittagong Buddhists and that he felt had "corrupted" their "pure" Buddhist identity (98). Buchanan's discomfort with cultural mixing and application of botanical concepts of taxonomy to his ethnological studies was typical of the scientific men of his Scottish homeland. Yet, it would be a mistake to see such attitudes as uniquely European. At the same time that Buchanan traveled the Chittagong–Arakan borderlands, a growing network of Arakanese Buddhist monastics were visiting the villages and temple towns of the region in order to "reform"

Chittagong Buddhist customs and "cleanse" them of brahmanical and Islamic influence (Charney 2002: 218–21). To these monastics, such "mixing," particularly animal sacrifice, was to be harshly condemned.

Buchanan's biases against brahmins are notable, and his reports therefore demand additional scrutiny. And yet his penchant for reading against the grain led him to be one of the first European scholars to consistently highlight non-brahmanical and non-Islamic histories of the subcontinent. This was an unusual effort in the early decades of the Asiatic Society. In his 1801 publication, "On the Religion and Literature of the Burmas", he pointed Orientalists to the existence of an until then largely unacknowledged Buddhist past and its heterogeneous co-mingling with tribal, Hindu and Islamic practices. His conclusion that the Buddha of Burma was the same as the Buddha of India, and that of Siam, Cambodia, China, Cochinchina, Japan, and Tonkin, was a significant breakthrough in Orientalist knowledge (Buchanan 1801: 163). Not long after, while returning from an official mission to Nepal (1802–03), he published reports of his trip in *Asiatick Researches*, noting the clear doctrinal affinities between the Burmese and Newars, and their shared reverence for the Shakyamuni, Siddhatta Gotama. In 1807, Buchanan began a seven-year geographical survey of the Bengal Presidency, a region that included many of the oldest Buddhist pilgrimage and ritual sites in the world. While traveling through this region in the winter of 1811–12, he learned from the Shaiva mahant (the temple head), who managed the Maha Bodhi complex where the Buddha had been enlightened, that a group of Burmese Buddhists had only recently passed through the area. One of the mahant's disciples, a rajput ascetic, Buchanan learned, had even "converted to the doctrines of the Buddhs [sic]" (Buchanan 1925: 6). Buchanan met with the rajput Buddhist, who in turn gave him a tour of the temple complex, explaining the sacred significance of each ritual corridor as described by his Burmese masters. These reports of a Buddhist past—and living Buddhist present—came at a time when many Europeans were still debating the Buddha's identity and origins. Some contended he was of African or Siamese origin; others suggested he was actually a planet or a Norse god (Lopez 2013).

Through their many decades of work with or alongside *"Jan Kampani"*

(John Company), as the EIC was often known in Indian circles (after one of its founder–inverstors, John Watts), these surveyors, diplomats, officers, and administrators gained a more grounded, ethnographic knowledge of living Buddhist traditions along the frontier regions and of Buddhist material culture in the form of manuscripts, artifacts, and ruins. The most stunning example of the collections acquired by Company officials is the cache of Sanskrit Buddhist manuscripts collected by Brian Hodgson, the British resident in Kathmandu between 1820 and 1843 (Waterhouse 2004; Allen 2015). Between 1827 and 1845, Hodgson shipped some 430 Buddhist palm-leaf manuscripts to educational institutions and scholars in Calcutta, London, Oxford, and Paris. While the translation and study of these works formed the nucleus of the Orientalist understanding of Buddhism, the copious amounts of reports and studies penned by "amateur" scholars like Hodgson and Buchanan on the ground left an enduring imprint on the nascent field of Buddhist studies and Indology. It is not surprising, then, that many of the influential early nineteenth-century Buddhological journals were produced at institutes based in India.[32]

What is less often discussed in the histories of these scholars and explorers are the vast networks of South Asians who worked alongside them, both voluntarily and involuntarily. Senior Company officials in India were regularly accompanied by native scholars (pandit), teachers, interpreters (munshi / *dubashi*), and other luminaries connected with tombs, temples, mosques, and landed estates. These figures are often invisible in the colonial record, which makes them all the more difficult to track, but their influence should not be underestimated. In the context of colonial Ceylon, for instance, Charles Hallisey (1995) has written persuasively about the influence of the venerable bhikkhus, Waskaduve Subhuti (1835–1917) and Yataramulle Unnanse (dates unknown), on T.W. Rhys Davids (1843–1922), the founder of the Pali Text Society and arguably the most influential Western scholar of Pali in the early twentieth century.

Rhys Davids wasn't alone in his reliance on local expertise. Brian Hodgson's Newar Buddhist informant, Amritananda Bandya (d. 1835), was an accomplished scholar who guided Hodgson's understanding of South Asian literatures and history. The Ceylon-based British civil servant, George Turnour (1799–1843), whose translation of the Pali-language

Mahavamsa in 1837 significantly altered the understandings of India's early Buddhist history, was frequently assisted by his Buddhist tutor named "Galle" (Turnour 1837: ii). James Prinsep (1799–1840), the assayist best remembered for deciphering the Kharoshthi and Brahmi scripts that led to the rediscovery of the Mauryan emperor, Ashoka, frequently relied upon a Sinhalese Christian named Ratna Paula.[33] Although figures like Sir William Jones warned other Europeans that "it was found highly dangerous to employ natives as interpreters, upon whose fidelity they could not depend" (quoted in Lopez 1995: 5), few appear to have heeded his advice.

Europeans in India had long relied on learned Indians for the interpretation of texts composed in Persian, Sanskrit, Tamil, and other local languages. But, when it came to deciphering the Buddhist past, the British castigated Indians of all social circles as being especially unreliable. Much of this distrust stemmed from deep-seated colonial arrogance, bigotry, and racial prejudice. However, in many cases, this was also a response to India's long history of transforming Buddhist sites through the age-old process of place-making. When Alexander Cunningham traveled to Sankissa, the storied site in contemporary Uttar Pradesh, where ancient Buddhists built magnificent structures to honor the Buddha's descent from "the Heaven of the Thirty-three Gods," his informants explained to him that the ancient Buddhist stupa was in fact the "kitchen" of the great Hindu heroine, Sita (Cunningham 1843: 245). In the early 1880s, when the brilliant epigraphist, Bhagavanlal Indraji, began studying the ancient Buddhist ruins in Sopara, a village in western India, he was told that the Ashokan pillar and the adjoining stupa were remnants of the "Fort of the Basket King" (Indraji 1882). In response, colonial scholars advanced the idea that not only had Buddhism vanished from the subcontinent but that Indians themselves had no conception of the Buddha or even Buddhists. They had simply forgotten who the Buddha was. Then again, where there was silencing and transformation, there was also remembrance.

Close readings of colonial records display lively and often agonizing discussions about Buddhism emanating from Indian elites. In the German Lutheran missionary Bartholomäus Ziegenbalg's invaluable compendium of early eighteenth-century Tamil writings, Buddhists are condemned by his informants for their dangerous teachings, "evil sects," and criticisms of Vishnu (Ziegenbalg [1713] 2005: 93). More than seven decades later and some thousand miles to the north, Sir William Jones reported that his own Sanskrit teachers "universally spoke of the *Bauddhas* [Buddhists] with all the malignity of an intolerant spirit" (Jones 1790: 123).[34] While traveling through Nepal in the spring of 1803, Buchanan's Bengali brahmin interpreter found the doctrines of the Buddhists of Kathmandu "so shockingly impious" that Buchanan "could not induce him to converse on the subject with their learned men" (Buchanan 1819: 32). Less than a decade later, while camping amidst the ruins that would later be identified as Nalanda, Buchanan met a Jain ascetic who explained that "all the images and ruins" belonged to a time when the bulk of the "infidels ... worshipped the Buddhas" (Martin 1838: 95).[35] When in 1808, the Bengali scholar and "colossus of literature," Mrityunjay Vidyalankar (c. 1762–1819), composed the first Bengali-language history of India (*Rajabali*) for British students at Calcutta's Fort William College, he described the "fifteen kings of the Nastika [heretical] faith ... all of the Gautama [Buddha] lineage." For the four hundred years under their rule, the textbook proclaims, "the *nastika* views enjoyed such currency that the *Vaidika* [Hindu] religion was almost eradicated" (quoted in Chatterjee 2010: 63).[36]

A decade later, a young administrator named Andrew Stirling visited a rocky hill (Khandagiri) just five miles west of Bhubaneswar in Odisha. According to Stirling's report (Cumberland 1865), the ascetics living amongst the rock-cut caves said that, "the place had its origin in the time of Buddha, and that it was last inhabited by the Rani of the famous Raja Lalat Indra Kesari, a favourer of the Buddhist religion" (116–17). When Stirling approached the so-called *Hathigumpha* or "Elephant's Cave", he found an inscription the ascetics claimed was from "the *Budh Ka Amel*, or time when the Buddhist doctrines prevailed". The brahmins, he reported, look at the cave with "shuddering and disgust ... and are reluctant even to speak on the subject" (117). Nearly two decades later, this would be identified as one of the major Buddhist sites associated with Emperor Ashoka's edicts at Dhauli, roughly six miles away. During a visit to Gaya in the spring of 1821, Colonel Colin Mackenzie's Jain assistant informed him of the once violent relations between Buddhists and Shaivas in the city (Burgess 1902). When Brian Hodgson began compiling oral traditions in the Kathmandu Valley, his own pandits described similar animosity (Hodgson [1827–28] 1874: 135–36). While traveling through the Krishna district of modern Andhra Pradesh in 1870, J.A.C. Boswell learned that nearly all of the hundred-plus Buddhist remains scattered through the district were universally known in Telugu by the demeaning phrase *lanja dib-balu* or "prostitute hill" (Boswell 1872: 152–53).[37]

Despite significant transformations of material landscapes, the Buddhist past had been immortalized as part of the vocabulary through which brahminized intellectuals, elites, and other serious students of Vedic dharma redefined and imagined themselves. Records like these make clear that Indians were far from being empty vessels that white colonizers filled with the knowledge of Buddhist history. Instead, for many eighteenth- and nineteenth-century Indian intellectuals, the Buddha and Buddhists symbolized the ruptures of the past. Such processes are not unusual. Some histories so profoundly penetrate society's deepest mores that even hundreds and thousands of years later, their scars are visible. Like Christians pondering on the meaning of the Old Testament, Jews reckoning with the trauma of the destruction of the Second Temple, British imperialists invoking an imagined relationship to the Roman Empire: dwelling on the past is a universal condition. The past is never dead and even what is seemingly buried is never truly gone. It can always be resurrected.

While Buddhism was not the only dissident voice in the pre-modern Indic world, it left an enduring mark. Giovanni Verardi (2011) is right when he asserts that over the millennia, "even where Buddhism structured itself in such a way as to be compatible with Brahmanical principles, it remained a symbol for all anti-Brahmanical identities" (201). The conversation about the Buddha and the "fifteen kings of the Nastik faith" invoked memories of a haunted past when brahmanical doctrines were in decay and the lifeblood of a varna-ashram-dharma society was under threat. For those who subscribed to brahmanical views, these were traumatic moments in time. One solution to these ruptures was to erase the past and to redescribe it, to try to create new meaning in the world. Here we understand the esteemed literary scholar, Velcheru Narayan Rao, when he writes that for orthodox Telugu-speaking brahmins in the late nineteenth century, the term "Buddhist" had simply become "the harshest term fathers could hurl against their sons when young boys deviated from Brahminic practices" (Rao 2008: 96).

The conversations between Jan Kampani and its attendant army of pandits reveals not forgetting but a memory of struggle and conquest. What emerged from the mouths of these pandits was not positive adoration but, rather, a largely critical assessment of an *upadharma,* a lesser teaching and way of living, that had been rightfully defeated and driven from their holy land (Bharatvarsha). This attitude alongside the long history of Indian place-making led European scholars to argue that Indian notions of Buddhism were biased, unreliable, and ultimately unimportant. As the nineteenth century wore on, many Orientalists increasingly praised Buddhism over brahmanism, and when their primarily brahmin pandits did not, they retorted that it was because India had forgotten what a great man the Buddha truly was.

When the Past Becomes the Present

When the British officer Lancelot Wilkinson's desire to publish the *Vajrasuchi* or Diamond Cutter in 1839 was met with resistance from the brahmin pandit Subaji Bapu, the former had to agree to publish the latter's sub-commentary alongside the text. The cultural impact of the *Vajrasuchi*—that is, its popularity, persuasiveness, distribution, and circulation—was so great that by the end of the century, it was reproduced at least a dozen more times in more than seven different languages. Wilkinson, it should be remembered, was a member of the diplomatic corps and the British resident in the princely state of Bhopal. As the primary patron of a Sanskrit school, he was a major figure behind the spread of Copernican science through Sanskrit and other "native" languages (as opposed to English). In addition to his pedagogic efforts, he also had a keen interest in social reform and encouraged the pandits at the Sehore school to search for and publicize indigenous literature that supported British views on widow remarriage, infanticide, and sati. Many teachers in the school applauded his support for indigenous rather than Christian critiques. Wilkinson, in other words, appeared to have as good a relationship as one might expect an alien ruler to have with the local community.

Subaji Bapu was the most respected teacher at the school. From

Wilkinson's perspective, and by extension the Raj's, Subaji was something of the crème de la crème of pandits. Just a few years before, Subaji had composed a series of Sanskrit tracts arguing that Copernicus's understanding of the solar system disproved Vyasa's conception of the universe (which was the dominant Hindu model). This brought him a fair bit of accolades and awards from Governor General Lord William Bentinck, including *sanad*s (affidavits) in Sanskrit and English that guaranteed him safe passage through British territories, in recognition of his contribution to disseminating "useful knowledge". In other words, Subaji was a "model native scholar," someone whom the Raj considered, what Richard Fox Young (2003: 200) calls, an "affirmer of modernity." However, his support of Copernican science made him deeply unpopular with some Indian colleagues. Threats were made, and a learned ascetic (*gosain*) in Mathura even implemented a "bann [sic] of excommunication" on anyone studying Western science in the school (Wilkinson 1834). Jan Kampani, as the rebellions of 1857 revealed with ruthless force, was disliked by many.

It was in this context that Wilkinson told Subaji of his recent acquisition of an old Sanskrit manuscript that challenged the brahmanical argument for caste. The text, attributed to the first-century Buddhist scholar—and brahmin apostate—Ashvaghosha, turns brahmanical arguments on their head, asking how there can be four castes (varna) when all people have proceeded from one god (Brahma)?

> If I have four sons by one wife, the four sons, having one father and mother, must be essentially alike ... the foot of the elephant is very different from that of the horse; that of the tiger unlike that of the deer; and so of the rest .... But I have never heard that the foot of a Kshatriya ["warrior caste"] was different from that of a Brahman, or that of a Sudra ["servant caste"]. All men are formed alike ... is a Brahman's sense of pleasure and pain different from that of a Kshatriya (Hodgson 1831: 166–67).[38]

Continuing this kind of question-and-answer methodology, Ashvaghosha applies "a withering, analytical logic to the concept of Brahmanhood, reducing it to an absurdity" (Young 2003: 208). When Wilkinson told Subaji that he intended to circulate a bilingual Sanskrit–

English edition of the text, he found himself, for the first time, in conflict with the scholar. As Wilkinson recounted in a letter written to the British resident in Nepal, Brian Hodgson, Subaji was visibly upset:

> My shastree [Subaji], who was with me when I got your letter [containing an English translation of the text], listened to my version of it into Maratha with the utmost uneasiness .... He was obliged to acknowledge the truth of all it contained. Indeed, he is anything but an orthodox Hindoo now. But still his eye glistened with anger when he heard the arguments expounded and all the long-buried animosities of the Brahman for the [Buddhist] were evident in him ... (letter from Wilkinson, 11 May 1835, quoted in Young 2003: 208).

Despite Subaji's disapproval of the argument, Wilkinson insisted that it be published, but agreed in the "spirit of free inquiry" to print it along with Subaji's own commentary. In a forty-seven-page counter-attack entitled the *Laghutanka* or Little Chisel, Subaji cites sources from legal treatises, epic literature, and the Puranas to refute the *Vajrasuchi*'s arguments. "A donkey, even a good one, can never become a horse," Subaji declares. "A mongrel that thinks itself a lion won't be able to roar, no matter how hard it tries" (quoted in Young 2003: 209).

The question that remains unanswered is why Subaji felt it so important to write a nearly fifty-page rebuttal—more than three times the length of the *Vajrasuchi*—to a text authored by a religious community that lacked any tangible presence in day-to-day Indian life? Young argues that Subaji's long attack on Ashvaghosha was an indication that there were "limits to his modernity" and that the longer he associated with Wilkinson, "the more insecure his identity as a Hindu became" (209).[39] Yet not all at the school responded so unfavorably. According to a letter Wilkinson wrote four months later, there were:

> ... two or three learned men about me, so far enlightened, or perhaps so much annoyed by the reflections of their ignorant friends upon their new doctrines, that they are quite delighted with this attack on their own Brahmanism. They have not only taken copies for themselves but have also been lending copies of it to their learned orthodox friends who have been provoking them by attacks on their abandonment of

Vyas' system of the world (Wilkinson, quoted in Young 2003: 208fn51).

Thus, Subaji's counter-attack wasn't just symptomatic of an "insecure" Hindu.[40] While Subaji's ability to counter Ashvaghosha's argumentation was due to his own erudition and familiarity with brahmanical–Buddhist philosophical debates, his long diatribe also spoke to the new political context: for the first time in several hundred years, that great heretic, the outstanding dissenter, and foremost ancient challenger to brahmanical orthodoxy, was returning to the public sphere. As one of the most distinguished pandits living in India at the time, Subaji would have certainly been familiar with the discoveries of Buddhism taking place across the subcontinent and the new conversation about the Buddha that Jan Kampani was initiating. Some Indians, as will be seen in later chapters, were greatly inspired by the new developments, but others, like Subaji, may have remembered more keenly the danger of the Diamond Cutter. It was one thing to have a critique against the revealed knowledge of the Vedas leveled by a Buddhist, but to have it spread by a colonial government, whose sympathies for the Buddha were increasingly public, was simply too much to bear.

Dispelling Darkness

In the decades after the *Vajrasuchi* controversy, the public conversation about Buddhism gained a new sense of urgency among the small but influential class of English-educated Indian elites. The way these "new elites" discussed Buddhism, both amongst themselves and with European colonizers, provides insights into the changing nature of Indian society and the role Buddhism played in it.[1] Many among them worked in new public enterprises such as government education departments, the Archaeological Survey of India (ASI), and the Census Commission as well as in innumerable research societies. In close proximity to the higher echelons of a society in flux, this constituency powered popular Buddhist campaigns and activities, producing a robust discourse about Buddhism in the decades before the Maha Bodhi Society established its headquarters in Calcutta in 1891.

Before the British Crown took over the East India Company's charter in 1858, only a small number of colonial educational institutions had been established across Indian territories. Missionaries set up their own schools, and some civil administrators collaborated with local elites to open Hindu and Islamic colleges. However, enrollment at these was often segregated by religion, gender, and caste.[2] Likewise, while scholarly societies emerged in major cities and urban and provincial centers, they did not attempt to impart any systematic education to non-European communities. After an inquiry led by the British Parliament concluded that the Company was failing to fulfill the Anglicist vision of disseminating Western education, a formal educational scheme was implemented under Wood's Despatch of 1854.

In the following decades, each presidency—Calcutta, Madras, and Bombay—came to be overseen by a department of public instruction which built provincial universities, expanded the secondary education sector, and increased the number of vernacular and technical schools. Under the new initiative, most government institutions taught a standard curriculum that included literature, philosophy, history, geography, and mathematics. Although it was not until the early 1900s that Buddhism became a discrete subject in any higher educational institution, the Victorian tendency to understand religion as the foundation of "Oriental cultures" led to an environment in which the study of Buddhism formed an integral part of curriculum, particularly in history and geography classes.

Imagining Buddhism in Colonial India's Education System

In 1864, the department of public instruction in Allahabad published the first of a three-volume Hindi textbook, *Itihas Timir Nashak* or History as the Dispeller of Darkness. Composed by the Indian educator, Raja Sivaprasad (1823–95), the *Itihas* was one of the most popular school textbooks in nineteenth-century India, remaining part of the standard curriculum for history and geography classes from the fourth to the tenth grade in the North-western Provinces, from 1864 up until the turn of the century. While Sivaprasad was not a scholar of Buddhism, he was, as Ulrike Stark (2012) has argued, a "hybrid intellectual" who mastered both Indian and British systems of learning and then used those skills to engage the colonizers "as interlocutor and cultural broker [rather] than merely as 'native informant'" (71). This makes his vision of Buddhism of particular interest since he approached it not from the position of a specialist but from that of an intellectual whose background and training lay within the wider north Indian current.

Born into a family of wealthy Jain merchants, Sivaprasad received a private education in Persian and Sanskrit before enrolling in Benares Sanskrit College, an institution first established by the Company administrator, John Duncan, in 1791. Like most Indian elites, he was multilingual, but his linguistic and intellectual gifts were exceptional. By the age of sixteen, his in-depth knowledge of Jain, Hindu, and Islamic works, alongside his growing mastery of English, Bengali, and Arabic, gained him a position as the ambassador (vakeel) to the maharaja of Bharatpur at the British Rajputana Agency. Not long after, he joined the foreign department as a munshi, later rising to *meer munshi* (chief clerk) of the Simla Agency and becoming private secretary to H.M. Elliot, the well-known British historian and civil servant.[3] The manner in which he carried himself and rose to the top of the colonial hierarchy was as much a matter of contempt to some as it was inspiration to others, a sentiment well captured by this contemporary's assessment:

> [Sivaprasad was] throughout life a supple courtier, who curried favor with every European official, played the sycophant and got titles, estates, and honors of sorts, earned the contempt of his compatriots and, at the same time, that of the whites to whom he "bent the pregnant hinges of the knee that"—well, that he might get what he coveted (Olcott 1900: 270).

As the description indicates, Sivaprasad's accomplishments were many, and in 1856, he became the first non-European inspector of schools in the North-western Provinces—a position he held until his retirement in 1878. Here, he began transforming the way the wider populace conceived of the subcontinent's history, and Buddhism in tow.

In the opening pages of the *Itihas,* Sivaprasad outlines his reasons for composing the textbook. First, he found the existing histories of India, written by Lord Elphinstone and other British writers, to be full of errors and historical fallacies. Second, he wished "to prove to my countrymen that, notwithstanding their very strong antipathy to 'change', they *have* changed, and *will* change" (Sivaprasad [1864] 1883: ii).[4] In Sivaprasad's view, the study of the past was necessary for improvement and to understand contemporary predicaments. "Our readers must learn what history means," he writes, "and with this knowledge they will not take offense at what we write ... no sober man is expected to go through these pages and again believe in the mythology of the Puranas" (Sivaprasad [1874] 1880: 12, ii).[5] A firm believer in the model of "scientific history" invoked by his former teachers Elliot and

James Prinsep, Sivaprasad drove a harsh wedge between myth and history. The stories of Rama and Krishna, of Jesus as the Messiah, and Muhammad as Prophet—these may all be believed, but "we ought never to mix it with the authentic [*pramanika*] events of history" (10).[6] To determine that which is authentic, students were instructed to base their arguments on objectivity (*yatharth*) and strong evidence (*prabal praman*), being forever warned about those individuals that claim that the contents of their books (*pothi*) could not possibly be false (10–11).

Having outlined his historical method, Sivaprasad explains that the first step in determining the *true* (*sachcha*) Indian past is to realize that Indians could no longer afford to ignore the era of the "Buddha which begins from Shakyamuni" (5).[7] Then, over the course of roughly fifty pages, or one half of volume three, the *Itihas* proceeds to outline details of the Buddhist tradition that had been largely unexpressed in this part of India for the past several centuries.[8] Admittedly, many aspects of his outline diverge from what today might be considered standard accounts of Indic Buddhism. While this is due largely to the inadequacy of the scholarship at the time, his was the first modern Hindi text to recount the Buddha's life in terms (semi-) faithful to normative Buddhist accounts.

Narrating the story of the Buddha's life, Sivaprasad recalls plots familiar to Buddhist cultures worldwide: the young prince abandons his life of luxury, practices various austerities before realizing the error of asceticism and gains enlightenment under the Bodhi tree, where he remains in a meditative state for forty-nine days. Although he does not always specify his sources, much of the content appears to have been drawn from Pali-language suttas, the English translations of which he likely took from George Turnour's "Pali Buddhistical Annals," published in 1837–38.[9] Perhaps the most striking divergence from normative biographies of the Buddha is Sivaprasad's argument—contained in a long footnote—that the Buddha (Shakyamuni) and Mahavira, the historical founder of Jainism, were actually the same person. Of Jain background himself, Sivaprasad anticipated criticism from Jain scholars but he was adamant in his view that ancient Jains and Buddhists were originally followers of a single figure named "Buddh Mahavir" and only later, just "as a river flowing to some distance branches off into two streams named separately," did the two form separate paths (Sivaprasad [1874] 1880: 13fn1).[10] The argument that Mahavira and the Buddha were identical may seem odd today, but according to John Cort (2012: 158fn34), it was only after the towering German Indologist and scholar of Jain texts, Hermann Jacobi, published the *Kalpasutras* in 1879, that Orientalist scholars became convinced of their differences.[11] Despite this (mis)interpretation, the descriptive narrative that Sivaprasad provides is surprisingly faithful to Pali Buddhist sources and contains none of the demonizing of Puranic scriptures better known at the time. In alignment with his own humanistic lens, Sivaprasad also firmly placed the Buddha in temporal history, providing the reader with precise dates and times at which certain events occurred in his life. Moreover, while the cosmological element of the Buddha's enlightenment is not ignored, the accent on his humanity is obvious.

As for Buddhism itself, he declares it to be a "progressive and modern creed" (*unnati ka naya dhang*) that "prevailed throughout the whole of Bharatvarsha [India]" for more than a thousand years (Sivaprasad [1874] 1880: 50, 13fn1). The school textbook explains how when Buddhism was at its apex, people from across the globe (*sari duniya*) visited India to study at its universities (*vidyalaya*). Rulers outlawed capital punishment (*qatal ki saza*) and built large hospitals where the poor and sick could be relieved of their suffering. He tells the reader how the bones of two of the Buddha's most renowned disciples were recently discovered near Bhopal, the princely state whose Muslim begums would decades later go to great lengths to protect the famed Sanchi stupa.[12] He also reports that large Buddhist ruins had been found near the Hindu holy city of Benares. Narrating the accounts of the medieval Chinese pilgrims, Xuanzang and Fa-Hsien, Sivaprasad explains how in the provincial city of Patna (ancient Pataliputra), the Buddha's birthday was celebrated with great pomp: there were gripping plays and performances (*natak aur lila ka hangama*), night-time illuminations (*rat ko roshni ka tamasha*), and four-wheeled chariots carrying statues of Buddhas and Bodhisattvas (76–77).

By Sivaprasad's reckoning, the Buddha's message of equality and non-violence was a direct challenge to the brahmanical elites (*vedon ki mahima langhan*). In a remarkable passage, he even frames early Buddhism as a popular protest movement against the tyranny of society, comparing its fight against brahmanical caste supremacy and Vedic sacrifice to US president Abraham Lincoln's, struggle "for the emancipation of slaves" (*ghulami se nikalne*) in the American Civil War (1861–65) and the Russian tsar (*badshah*) Alexander II's freeing of the serfs in 1861 (49).[13] Before the Buddha arrived on the scene, the shudras or lower castes were treated as no better than cattle, he argues. "But how long," Sivaprasad asks rhetorically, "can a wooden vessel be heated without setting it aflame? ... [I]t is a general rule that an institution based on the deprivation (*nuqsan*) of the many for the profit (*phaida*) of a few has not long to last" (49–50).[14] Thus, when Shakyamuni spoke against the "evil of violence" (*himsa ki burai*) and proclaimed that "Aryan and non-Aryans, men as well as women, were all alike able to choose their own religion (*dharma*)," the number of Indians who took to the Buddha's message soared (49–50).[15] "It was autumn for the Sanskrit and spring for the Prakrit. The brahmins had become [pale like] morning stars while the shudras ... bloomed like lotus flowers before the sun" (49–50).

Despite these progressive qualities, Sivaprasad explains that there was a fundamental flaw in the Buddha's teaching. It is "beyond the sphere of ordinary reasoning," he contends, "attainable only by intuition and deep and patient meditation"—unrealistic skills for the majority populace (79). Thus, by the time of Ashoka, the teachings of the Buddha had weakened the people, allowing sacrilege (*dharmaghata*), ostentatiousness (*ayyashi*), and idol worship (*murti puja*) to take root (72). In fact, the real danger was not its idealism, but its pacifism. In a statement that anticipates the later writings of twentieth-century Hindu nationalists like V.D. Savarkar and R.S. Moonje, he writes that Buddhist non-violence so "softened the heart to the detriment of the land" that "the tame spirit of petty traffickers, banias, fell upon the kshatriyas [ruling classes] ... [and] the cruelty, hardheartedness, rapacity and debauchery of the Muhammadans demoralized both [the merchants and ruling classes]" (118).[16] By the thirteenth century, Buddhism vanished.

From the moment it was printed, Sivaprasad's *Itihas* ruffled the feathers of a wide swathe of Indian society. Many protested against its anti-Muslim bias. Others were uneasy with his image of an ever-fragmented Hinduism. Educators complained about its excessive footnoting and pedantic prose (Stark 2012: 76–85). But despite calls for the book to be removed from state curricula, it only grew in popularity. In its first three years of use

(1864–67), the department of education in the North-western Provinces published more than twenty thousand copies of the text. When the government issued translations into Urdu (1867) and in "a rare reversal of colonial textual hierarchy" (Stark 2012: 82), even English (1874), the number of copies circulating in classrooms across the subcontinent nearly tripled each year.[17] By 1870, more than eighteen thousand copies were being printed annually. This number nearly doubled by 1883.[18] Buddhism may not have found its place among north India's largest private publishing houses, like Naval Kishore's "Empire of Books" (Stark 2007), but it had found a grand new patron in the state's educational campaigns to "civilize the natives".[19]

The widespread use of the *Itihas* in government schools is of great significance considering the radically different views of the past being imparted in customary centers of learning.[20] Popular Hindu works like the *Vishnu Purana* demonized Buddhists. Temple art and chronicles depicted Buddhists as dangerous to society and degenerate. One catches glimpses of these attitudes in contemporaneous memoirs. For instance, in Rahul Sankrityayan's autobiographical portrait of his childhood education in the village schools (pathshala) of late 1890s Azamgarh (in modern-day Uttar Pradesh), he recalls a fascinating moment when his grandfather tells him that the carved Buddha images at Ajanta were of "demons" (*rakshasas*) frozen into stone by Hindu heroes (Sankrityayan [1944–63] 2014). Colonial schools not only challenged these views but attacked their very epistemological foundations. This was a pivotal change. In the textbooks, the Buddha became a modern icon: a veritable Abraham Lincoln *and* Jesus Christ, the latter of which comparison Sivaprasad ([1874] 1880: 50fn4) could not resist employing (in an ode to Max Müller). Sivaprasad's interpretations strengthened the tendency to understand the history of Buddhists and the Buddha as part of the existing discourse on world religion, an intellectual object on par with Christianity. Like all "world religions," Buddhism was ancient, geographically widespread, had its own historical founder, and a fixed "canon" of "classical" scriptures (typically associated with Sanskrit or Pali).[21]

Although Sivaprasad was deeply conversant with Orientalist thought, one needs to be careful in over-interpreting its influence. The historian Avril Powell (1999) has shown how many of Sivaprasad's inferences were drawn from his readings of Persian texts and much vaster knowledge of that literature. Furthermore, Sivaprasad composed the *Itihas* because he found existing British histories of India inadequate (and he was courageous enough to say so). While Sivaprasad's reading of primary Buddhist sources in Pali seems to have relied upon English translations, many of the conclusions he drew must be situated within a larger Jain and brahmanical Hindu framework. His assertion that Buddhist non-violence and laxity of morals led to India's downfall was, for instance, the modern extension of an entrenched Puranic argument about Buddhism leading to social disorder and decay. The idea that Buddhist monastics were hypocrites and hedonists dwelling in luxury was also a common trope in satirical Sanskrit literature (Bhatta Jayanta 2005; Krishna Mishra 2009), in which Sivaprasad was likely well read.

The argument that the Buddha was a kind of socio-religious reformer, a Lincoln and Luther combined into one, was certainly a novel proclamation that can be traced to his intimate knowledge of Euro-American history and current events. While the notion that the Buddha was a reformer may be a historical anachronism, it has maintained its steam to the present day because Sivaprasad's critique of Vedic norms has deep and discursive underpinnings in the literary traditions of both Buddhists and brahmins (Black 2009; Eltschinger 2012). Lastly, his argument that Buddhists once formed the majority of the Indian population, particularly among oppressed castes, has had an equally long shelf life, with real-life repercussions among colonial and post-colonial dalit–bahujan[22] populations. Ultimately, many of his claims regarding Buddhist history are derived from both pre-modern sources and colonial scholarship. The *Itihas* is best seen in this vein, as a hybrid intellectual's synthesis of the available materials (Stark 2012).

Apart from the important issues regarding the nature of Sivaprasad's interpretation, the *Itihas* is a significant text for the simple fact that it was so widely known. While the number of students attending colonial schools was proportionally small—and thus those who would have acquired the basic framework that the *Itihas* provided would have been even smaller— this should not mask the influence these school graduates came to wield in future generations (Vishwanathan [1989] 2014). In his landmark study of the rise of the Sikh Singh Sabha in the nineteenth- and early twentieth-century Punjab, Harjot Oberoi (1994: 262) highlights how "bilingual skills and western education became a form of capital in a colonial society that could be effectively used to acquire power, privilege and the ability to strike bargains". Put in more concrete terms, British schools taught the kinds of skills that allowed graduates to negotiate the bureaucratic apparatuses and run the voluntary associations and publishing houses that were becoming increasingly central to modern civic life. With these tools, graduates were able, as Oberoi remarks, to "appropriate both the channels of communication and, more importantly, the signifiers they generated. This control gave them an unprecedented sway over the production of symbols, texts and stories, the elements out of which any culture is created" (277). As for the Singh Sabha with Sikhism, the new Indian elites would become key stakeholders in the making of modern Buddhism.

Admittedly, it is difficult to gauge the *Itihas*'s actual classroom reception. Was it eagerly palmed page by page by an overachiever or simply drilled rote-fashion into the ears of bored adolescents? Despite these ambiguities, evidence outside the classroom indicates that it was consulted widely as a standard historical resource by mature Indian thinkers.[23] It is easy to surmise that Sivaprasad's sound knowledge of existing scholarship on Indian Buddhism and the translation of that knowledge into local languages gave students the conceptual vocabulary and historical framework to understand discussions of Buddhism taking place in the public sphere. By the time Sivaprasad retired from the department of public instruction in 1878, the specialized study of Buddhism's past via material and literary remains had ceased being an enterprise whose public face was monopolized by European Orientalists. A new generation of Indians, typically trained at colonial schools where they mastered the tools of the Orientalist trade, was using its own linguistic skill and know-how to shape the colonial consensus on Buddhism.

Like the Nalanda of "Bygone Times"

The colonial state saw itself as engaged in a civilizing mission (Mann 2004). But the spread of education and morality across the provinces only served to alleviate part of the "white man's burden," to use Rudyard Kipling's famous expression. An aspect of that "burden" also entailed the retrieval of the lost history of Her Majesty's conquered territories, a landscape of ancient sites waiting to be identified, described, classified, and conserved. Cast in the role of "ignorant natives," Indians were widely perceived by European authorities and colonizers as being incapable of using their critical faculties and making sound, historical assessments (Singh 2004: 290–354; Guha-Thakurta 2004: 185–239). Yet, as the process of cataloguing and documenting the ancient past gained speed, the need for educated critical thinkers—which the government felt only it could produce—became increasingly evident.

By the early 1860s, programs in Oriental studies and Sanskrit studies at the universities of Bombay, Calcutta, and Madras had emerged as important venues where students could study Buddhist history and comprehend the poems (*gatha*) of the ancient theras (monks) and *theris* (nuns). Although formal programs in Pali, or in Buddhist studies, let alone history, did not take form until the turn of the century, there was an enduring sense among the leaders of these institutes that the study of Buddhism was at the avant-garde of human inquiry. As the *Bombay Journal of the Asiatic Society* described it in 1847: "There is scarcely any subject ... which has excited more interest, or is better deserving of investigation than the origins and progress of Buddhism" (Bird 1847: iii).

Academic programs often reflected the sentiment. In Bombay University's Elphinstone College (est. 1856), Sanskrit studies was headed by the German Indologist, Georg Bühler (1837–98). As one of the foremost authorities on Buddhist caves and manuscripts, Bühler's passion for exploring and piecing together Buddhism's past rubbed off on many of his students and field assistants. Among the latter were men like Bhagavanlal Indraji (1839–88), the Gujarati epigraphist and autodidact who, before joining Bühler at Buddhist sites in Nepal and Bodh Gaya, had trained as a draftsman, drawing Buddhist caves and stupas at Ajanta and Karli in the 1860s. Despite being inhibited by his only "tolerable" English, a shortcoming which forced him to rely on others to disseminate his findings among the wider scholarly community, he became a well-known genealogist and explorer of ancient mounds. The most notable of his achievements was the discovery of the Ashokan edict and Buddha relics at Sopara in 1882, a feat that helped him earn an honorary doctorate from Leiden University two years later (Yajnik 1889).[24]

Among the most well known of Bühler's classroom pupils to take an interest in Buddhism was the Sanskritist, R.G. Bhandarkar (1837–1925), who in 1868 took over as head of Sanskrit studies at Elphinstone. One of the most prolific historians of his generation, Bhandarkar published on an incredible array of subjects, edited the prominent journal, *Indian Antiquary*, and was one of the first Indians to complete a doctorate from a European university (University of Göttingen, 1885). During his long and distinguished career, most of it spent at Deccan College in Pune, where he formed the Bhandarkar Oriental Research Institute in 1917, Bhandarkar made a name for himself as one of the foremost authorities on Buddhist kingship in Mauryan India. Although he personally found Buddhist metaphysics lacking and was critical of his colleagues who wished to see the seed of Buddha dhamma sprout in India again, he was adamant that any historian of ancient India worth their salt needed to carefully consider the Buddhist past.[25]

At Calcutta University, the first batches of Sanskrit graduates were equally adept at applying the methodologies and theories the British taught them to the study of Buddhist remains. As early as 1870, Babu Chandrasekhara Banerji began using his free time as the deputy magistrate in Jajapur, Odisha, to publish essays on the Buddhist antiquities scattered across the Cuttack hills (Banerji 1870). Conducting research while holding coveted government jobs was not unusual, a popular hobby (*shauq*) for many nineteenth-century Indian bureaucrats.[26] Others, like Haraprasad Shastri (1853–1931) would transform the antiquarian pursuit into a full-fledged profession, using his BA (1876) and MA (1877) in Sanskrit from Calcutta University to help catapult his status from "native pandit" to "perhaps the most important scholar" of "[Sanskrit] Buddhist literature" in his lifetime (Sylvain Lévi, quoted in Nariman 1920: 1). In fact, almost all of the great nineteenth-century Indian scholars of Buddhism began their careers at government colleges, local libraries, museums, or as assistants on archaeological expeditions.

Throughout the entire colonial period, the premier Indian hub for Buddhist scholarship was Calcutta, the heart of the Bengal Presidency and then capital of the British Empire in Asia. Home to the Asiatic Society headquarters, Indian Museum (est. 1814), the Imperial Library, and the

University of Calcutta and its numerous affiliated colleges, the city attracted and produced the country's most influential scholars. Much of its draw derived from its outstanding collections of material artifacts and manuscripts acquired from across the Empire. Indian visitors to the city with an interest in Buddhism could view everything from the mundane to the monumental. At the Indian Museum, known more popularly as the *Jadu Ghar* or "House of Magic", visitors in 1876 would have beheld copper land-grant plates, Kushana coins and small Buddhist icons next to entire rooms overflowing with reassembled monastic walls and pillars from Bharhut.[27]

Many of the city's most impressive collections were literary, a consequence of Lord Lawrence's 1868 order to the government to search for historical manuscripts. Although the vast majority of manuscripts were in Sanskrit and dealt with non-Buddhist topics, a significant portion of the Asiatic Society, Imperial Library, and Calcutta University collections, to name just three of the largest archives in the city, opened vast windows into the history, philosophy, and practice of Buddhism. Most represented "Northern Buddhism," the colonial categorization that included what are better known today as Mahayana and Vajrayana sects. Take the catalogue of the Asiatic Society for the year 1882, which listed complete sets of the Tibetan "canon" of Kagyur (*bka'-'gyur*) and Tengyur (*bstan-'gyur*), 256 Tibetan xylographs, more than 150 Sanskrit Buddhist manuscripts, and 350 Chinese xylographs of mixed genres (Mitra, Hoernle, and Bose 1885: 27–28).[28] While large numbers of these had been deposited by European officials between the 1830s and 1860s, one cannot discount the contributions of the many dynamic Indian manuscript hunters. This included the Bengali scholar–explorer–spy, Sarat Chandra Das (1849–1917), who returned from his state-sponsored journeys to Central Tibet in 1879 and 1881–82 with over two hundred Tibetan volumes. The towering Bengali savants Rajendralal Mitra and Haraprasad Shastri added over a hundred more Sanskrit, Prakrit, Bengali, and Newari (Nepal Bhasha) Buddhist texts to the state coffers, following their own research excursions in Bengal and Nepal.[29]

Sources for the study of "Southern Buddhism," or Pali-language-mediated traditions of southern Asia were no less extensive. Once again, many of the collections were derived from the city's imperial connections, this time with royal and religious elites in Siam, Burma, and Ceylon. A survey of the Asiatic Society library in 1882, for instance, revealed not only significant portions of the Pali "canon" or *Tipitaka*, but "about 125 bundles" of uncatalogued Burmese, Siamese, Javanese, and Sinhalese palm-leaf manuscripts (Mitra, Hoernle, and Bose 1885: 27–28). In other words, by the late 1880s, the city housed one of the most linguistically diverse, albeit fragmented, collections of Buddhist manuscripts in the world. These were significant resources for a scholarly enterprise that only decades before had doubted the very existence of Buddhism in India.

Of equal importance to the sources themselves was the fact that the city hosted a growing body of native scholars who could read and interpret them. To understand the city's late nineteenth-century academic Buddhist scene, the short-lived Buddhist Text Society (est. 1892) is key. When Sarat Chandra Das and Rajendralal Mitra proposed the formation of the society in early 1891, they did so in the hope that by establishing a site in Calcutta, Japanese and Sinhalese Buddhists would come to study Sanskrit at the local colleges.[30] In its early days, the Buddhist Text Society consisted of nine university-educated Indian scholars, a handful of Sanskrit pandits, several Buddhist Theosophists, Indian elites, and a few British civil servants.[31] According to its frontispiece, the objects of the society were twofold: first, to edit and publish Sanskrit or Tibetan texts relating to Indian Buddhism, geography, and Indo–Aryan thought, and second, "to discuss in the Journal of the Society topics of various kinds connected with that interesting subject".[32] By 1895, the society had more than four hundred members, nearly three quarters of whom resided in India (*JBTSI* 1895: viii). The increase speaks clearly to the new enthusiasm for studying Buddhism and the growing sentiment that the Buddha represented one of India's greatest cultural assets. Under government pressure, in 1897 the Society added anthropology—"the science of mankind, which comprised an inquiry into the habits, customs, manners of the human race"—to its scope, electing Herbert Hope Risley as its president, and was renamed the Buddhist Text and Anthropological Society. Although it remained Das's pet project until 1907, as he acquired numerous state grants to collect and publish rare Buddhist texts, Risley's two-year term as president took the organization in more social-scientific and pseudoscientific directions (HDBPB October 1905, nos. 42–43).[33] The added emphasis diluted aspects of its Buddhist focus, and the promise of a wider circulation never blossomed, leaving the group to drop the anthropological title in 1904. By 1907, the renamed "Buddhist Text and Research Society" disappeared in a merger with the Indian Research Society, ending the fifteen-year life of colonial India's first academic organization dedicated solely to the study of Buddhist literature.

Archaeology and the "Natives"

Most of the major Buddhist sites rediscovered in nineteenth-century India sat far outside the new colonial centers of power. Although increasingly connected by an ever-expanding network of railways and *pakka* roads, most of India's abandoned Buddhist sites were at least a full day's journey from the nearest urban hub. Inevitably, geography and economics played a critical role in how one could encounter Buddhist ruins in situ. Traveling to these sites, as several colonial-era accounts attest to, could be a grueling affair.[34] Unsanitary conditions, little to no available lodging, and the threat of disease, robbery, or animal attacks were commonly reported. Yet, for thousands of nineteenth-century Indians, who were in some way connected with the government's conservation efforts, visits to and encounters with Buddhist place-worlds became a reality.

The initiative to protect and study India's ancient sites began in the early 1840s when field-engineers-turned-archaeologists, like Alexander Cunningham (1814–93), argued that the government had a moral obligation to implement a thorough and regimented investigation of all existing ancient Indian monuments. For Cunningham, whose role in nineteenth-century archaeology is difficult to overestimate (Imam 1966), almost nothing was more important than the recovery of the Buddhist past. Within just months of his arrival in India as a nineteen-year-old army cadet in 1833, he drove a 110-foot shaft down through the center of the even taller Dhamek stupa in Sarnath, revealing the ancient Buddhist words, *ye dharma hetu prabhava* (all phenomena arise from causes) inscribed on a stone slab inside. "The act opened up not just the *stupa*," art historian Tapati Guha-Thakurta (2004: 28) rightly asserts, "but a whole area of investigative technique that became his special forte".[35] During the nearly five decades that Cunningham lived in India, much of them in "the field," from Burma and Afghanistan to Ladakh

Sir Alexander Cunningham, the first director general of the Archaeological Survey of India

and Bhopal, he used similar methods of guerilla archaeology to open at least another twenty-seven stupas and excavate many more. In 1854, at the so-called *chaitya giri*, or "hill of shrines", near Sanchi in central India, he recovered two relic boxes with inscriptions describing the remains inside as the bones of Mogallana and Sariputta, two of the Buddha's disciples whose names were by then well known to Orientalist scholars from their readings of Pali texts acquired in Ceylon and Burma. Despite causing extensive and often irreversible damage to millennia-old structures, Cunningham's numerous finds inside mostly alabaster and brick monuments were groundbreaking, widely reported in the news, and tragically inspired others to excavate and loot ruins in search of ancient treasures.

By 1861, archaeology finally caught the ear of Viceroy Lord Canning, and he formally approved the formation of the Archaeological Survey of India. From here, the field of study took on an increasingly Buddhist flare with Cunningham its most zealous advocate. The French translation of two Chinese pilgrim accounts, one by the fifth-century Fa-Hsien and the other of the seventh-century Xuanzang, both of which detailed the location and expanse of Buddhist sites in India at that time, had changed the way Cunningham and other archaeologists conducted their research. With the pilgrims' handbooks as his guide, Cunningham and his draftsman, Babu Jamna Shankar Bhatt (dates unknown), traversed the subcontinent, attempting to match Chinese place names with local toponyms and Sanskrit–Prakrit inscriptions.[36] The results were astonishing: during the first four winter surveys conducted during 1861–65, they identified more than 160 Buddhist sites in north India *alone* (Cunningham 1871).[37] By the turn of the century, archaeologists and art historians were churning out books and articles, describing the "wonderful works" of art and architecture the Buddhists of ancient India had produced. From the 180-foot Buddha statues carved into rock at Bamiyan (Afghanistan), caches of Indo-Greek coins with Buddhist images near Peshawar (Pakistan), three-story monastic universities at Nalanda (Bihar), colorful cave paintings of Bodhisattvas at Ajanta (Maharashtra), and towering *mahachaitya*s at Amaravati (Andhra Pradesh), Buddhism was firmly placed on the Indian map.

Archaeology, and the related fields of art history, numismatics, and epigraphy, allowed for the temporal charting of literary traditions, providing not just illustrative materials for the texts but lending a tangible basis to historical events, locales, and memories (Trautmann and Sinopoli 2002; Singh 2004; Lahiri 2012). Such immediate relevance lent archaeology a prestige—without it, myth and history were difficult to separate. Votive inscriptions at Sanchi, for instance, revealed the names of a great many female donors, allowing archaeologists to realize the important role women played in early Buddhist traditions, a relationship that can otherwise be difficult to determine from the literary tradition. Equally important was the manner in which archaeology and its underlining positivism brought the materiality of Buddhism to the fore. Where Puranic and epic accounts of Hindu kings and avatars often fell flat, leaving no physical traces of the magnificent kingdoms and realms they described, the textual past of

Buddhism could be located in the monumental architecture and rock-cut viharas and chaityas found across the subcontinent.

As local authorities and government branches received circulars instructing officials to make lists and collect photographs of these grand remains, one of the problems the colonial government faced was the high number of monuments located inside princely states where the ASI had no legal authority.[38] At its height, the British Empire in India covered approximately three-fifths of the subcontinent, with native rulers possessing (nominal) authority over the rest. With a number of smaller monasteries dotting these kingdoms, from Mayurabhanj to Sanchi in the Bhopal state, Bharhut in Nagod to Ajanta in Hyderabad, princely states possessed legal jurisdiction over many Buddhist remains. Archaeological officials were often convinced that such rulers were unfit to manage their own archaeological resources and frequently decried the way that Buddhist sites were "vandalized" inside native jurisdictions. But, as Upinder Singh's (2004) masterful study of nineteenth-century archaeology demonstrates, there was no single paradigm that shaped princely attitudes towards conservation. The nizam of Hyderabad, for example, was "quite willing" to cooperate with conservation authorities and spent "considerable amounts of money from the state exchequer" (299) to help safeguard the Buddhist frescoes at Ajanta. Likewise, the nineteenth- and twentieth-century Muslim begums of Bhopal generously supported conservation efforts at Sanchi, both acts directly contradicting British refrains that a Muslim ruler could not possibly have sincere interests in protecting non-Islamic heritage (Lahiri 2012).

Elite officials in princely states, however, were not the only Indians to come in contact with the archaeology of Buddhism. Although the ASI only began to resemble the expansive machine it is today when John Marshall took over the Survey of India from 1902 to 1928, the colonial government had long employed large bodies of workers to assist in documenting the Empire's antiquities. As early as 1854, the British had established the School of Industrial Arts (present-day Government College of Arts and Crafts) in Calcutta, where students were trained in new sets of vocational and technical skills. From drawing and plastering casts to using the camera lucida, the School churned out "a skilled battery of drawing masters, draftsmen, surveyors, engravers, and lithographers" (Guha-Thakurta 2004: 143). Epigraphy was another area where colonial officials, recognizing the multilingual talents of the local population, made special efforts to increase expenditures. By the 1880s, special funds were allocated and prizes offered by government schools to train and encourage students in archaeological sciences. For privileged and motivated Indians, conservation and archaeology became an avenue through which to climb the ladder of rank and file as a "native" in colonial society.

Precise figures for the number of skilled workers supported by the colonial government's various quasi-archaeological units are difficult to estimate, but towards the end of the nineteenth century, tens of thousands of individuals constituted this body. ASI was not alone in its requirement for skilled (and many more unskilled) workers to assist in interpreting Buddhist sites. The public works department, education department, foreign department, and so on, also frequently called upon their services. In the late 1890s, during the excavations at Lumbini (Tilaurakot,) where the Buddha was purported to have spent his youth, surveyors described, "about 200 coolies, mostly *Tharus* [a large ethnic group found across the Terai], being employed for a week at a time, who returned to their villages; and then a fresh relay of labourers took their place" (Mukherji 1899: 1). Alongside this sizeable body of laborers, there were individuals like Lala Deen Dayal (1844– 1905), from Sardhana, who in 1866 took a job as a draftsman in the princely kingdom of Indore. A skilled photographer, his family firm, Lala Deen Dayal & Sons (est. 1868), became one of the most sought-after photography companies in India, commissioned by Lepel Henry Griffin in 1882–83 to lead an extensive photographic survey of Buddhist ruins in central India.[39] While the growing interest in colonial portraits allowed Dayal to expand his business into different markets, other portrait photographers like D.N. Bali, of Bali & Sons in Rawalpindi (modern-day Pakistan), became so enthralled by the "noble Doctrine of Buddha" that he used his own profits to support an Urdu biography of the Buddha based on "authentic sources" (*MBJ* Vol. 8/11, 1899–1900: 110).[40]

Other trained draftsmen like Ghulam Rasool Beg and P.C. Mukherji appear to have been less struck by the Buddha's doctrines than they were by his remains. The former spent several seasons working at Kushinagar, the site of the Buddha's mahaparinirvana. In 1901, he even enjoyed a brief stint in charge of all operations, a position which would have certainly led him to encounter the Hindu wrestler-turned-bhikkhu, Mahavir, and his cohort of wealthy Arakanese patrons, building the town's first modern rest house and temple (*dharamshala-vihara*).[41] Mukherji, on the other hand, began his career as a draftsman in 1884 and spent much of the next two decades working on early Buddhist sites in the North-western Provinces. In addition to his own stunning finds of the Kumraharbagh Ashoka pillar and bell fragment near Patna in 1896–97, Mukherji is best remembered for uncovering the rather inconvenient truth that his superior, Dr Anton Führer, was fabricating evidence and supplying Buddhist priests with forged Buddha relics in order to justify claims about having discovered the Buddha's birthplace.[42]

Despite an awareness of many such figures whose lives were spent in the study of Buddhism, our understanding of their precise thoughts and actions remains cloudy. Firstly, because there was a deep and enduring prejudice against indigenous scholars and workers: they were considered little more than informants and assistants whose contributions were not worth recalling in published reports. One outcome of this is that many Indians who participated in the study of Buddhism are either ignored in colonial records or simply (un)marked through anonymizing and paternalistic labels such as "*my* babu," "*my* assistant," "*my* pandit," and so on. Second, the anglophone and Eurocentric nature of British archaeology prevented many otherwise capable and accomplished Indian scholars from disseminating their findings in scholarly journals. A close scrutiny of colonial records reveals the names of many Indians whose contributions went unacknowledged (Singh 2004: 290–354; Guha-Thakurta 2004: 185–239). For instance, P.C. Ghosh, the librarian at the Asiatic Society, regularly assisted scholars in their searches for manuscripts and materials, and Babu Deva Shastri, the professor of mathematics at Benares College, helped scholars in matters of chronology. Others, like the outstanding epigraphist, Bhagavanlal Indraji—whose only scholarly crime was his rudimentary English—were made popular by colleagues and friends who translated all of their works into English (Dharamsey 2012: 14). Similarly, when Buddhist relics were discovered in the Swat Valley in 1896 and credited to Major F.C. Maisey—a veteran surveyor—the latter wrote an open letter, reprinted in a number of newspapers, stating that the relic casket was actually discovered by two "energetic" field assistants, Ghulam Ali and Fazldud Khan. Both men, he applauded, had "of their own accord" been busy "digging up Buddhist images" and "getting volunteers from among their men to dig .... I hope, in time, these working parties will receive some remuneration from Government" (*MBJ* Vol. 4/6, 1895–96: 50).

While the true underbelly of colonial archaeology—comprising *lascars* (servants) and *bhishtis* (water-carriers), *mehtars* (sweepers) and *dhobis* (washermen), coolies (porters), *chaukidars* (watchmen), and other caste subalterns—remains largely outside our historical understanding, with only fleeting glimpses provided in contemporary accounts, one has to wonder about the degree to which the discussion about the Buddhist sites permeated their social worlds. Certainly, there were the caste-oppressed intellectuals like Jotirao Phule and Iyothee Thass, who, although not involved directly in the archaeological enterprise, drew on its findings to reinterpret the past as one not just dominated by landowning castes and brahmanical elites. But, as always, one wonders about the common laborers' reading of the government signposts and surveying crews that transformed the divine realms of the epics and Puranas into a historical materiality linked not to folk deities, Hindu heroes, and saintly pirs, but Buddhist kings and monks. How did they react and contend with the babus' and sahibs' story that the massive Ashokan pillars strewn across the subcontinent were not in fact Bhim's giant walking sticks (*Bhim ka lath*) from the Mahabharata, as many oral histories recalled, but the political symbol of an ancient Buddhist emperor? What did they say when the Indian Orientalist, Nagendranath Vasu (1912: xlvii), told the "ignorant villagers" in Midnapur district that their city of Dantan (city of the tooth) was not named after the Hindu saint Chaitanya's toothbrush, as local custom proclaimed, but instead, as Vasu argued, after the area's ancient connections to the Buddha's tooth relic, described in the *Dathavamsa*? When the art curator and outspoken critic, Henry Cole, griped that the Buddhist stupa inside the Karli caves was not *really* a Shivalingam, as the priests had painted and shaped it to be, what did locals think (Singh 2004: 295)? Did the sahibs' empiricism trump customary

views, or did the culturally embedded meanings of a sacred landscape make their science (*vidya*) appear empty and hollow?

If the memoirs of the Buddhist pilgrims are any indicator, the responses were often of dissent and resistance. Consider, for instance, the story told by the Indian scholar–monk, Dharmanand Kosambi ([1924] 2010), when he joined Anagarika Dharmapala in 1904–05 to preach to a group of locals at Sarnath that the stupa there had actually been built by King Ashoka and was not an "oil-presser"s mill", as local tradition held. The message fell flat, and Kosambi admitted that, "I think it did not have the effect that was hoped for" (161–62).[43] Kosambi may have failed that day, but his later writings would inspire generations, proving that every time the Tathagata Buddha's story was told, a new storyteller was potentially born. And with each rendition, Buddhist history was reimagined in ways subject to the values and conditions of the audience and storyteller.

From Pandit to Scholar: Some Case Studies

According to Tapati Guha-Thakurta (2004), there was always a fine line in colonial India between the pandits on the one hand and the epigraphists and draftsmen on the other. While the former "embodied the traditional fund of learning that British Orientalists had drawn on since the eighteenth century, the other embodied a small slice of the new training and employment that the colonial government generated" (89). Both were necessary, she argues, for the surveying work the government pursued, but between them, there was the need "for a group of *modernized pandits* suited to the new requirements of the time" (89, emphasis added). The metaphysical transition from pandit to scholar, she argues, was based on a variety of idealized traits: of rationality and accuracy, of critical judgement and objectivity. To be more than just a "native informant," the Indian pandit had to make "the crucial passage from prejudice to reason, from tradition to modernity" (96). Those that successfully made that transition were awarded with grand titles like "Raja," "Commander of the Indian Empire (CIE)," "Shastri" (Learned One), "Mahamahopadhyaya" (Greatest of Teachers), and while most had no real political power, their influence on sociocultural norms and government projects was significant.

Rajendralal Mitra and The Relics of the Past

In 1877, the Bengali savant and permanent fixture in Calcutta's Asiatic Society, Rajendralal Mitra (1824–91), finished editing the *Lalitavistara Sutra*, an ornate Sanskrit biography of the Buddha, originally composed around the third century CE.[44] In the introduction to the text, Mitra highlighted the general historical outline of Buddhism as it was then known among the Orientalists. After describing its diffusion from the north of India to the far corners of Asia, he lamented that as great as this tradition once was, the history of the Buddha's life had been obscured "in mysteries which the light of modern research has yet scarcely dispelled" (Mitra 1877: 2). "India never had her Xenophon or Thucydides," he decried. Instead, "her heroes and reformers, like her other great men, have to look for immortality in the ballads of her bards, or the legends of romancers .... [Yet,] Sakya Sinha [Buddha] had not even that advantage. He was known only through the misrepresentations of his enemies, the Brahmans" (2). These tragic circumstances, however, were now slowly being reversed:

> The orientalist ... has now no longer to complain of paucity of information regarding him [the Buddha]. The discoveries of [Brian] Hodgson in Nepal, of [Edward] Upham and [George] Turnour in Ceylon, of [Sándor] Csoma de Korosi in [Kinnaur] Tibet, and of [Julius] Kalporth [sic], [Jean-Pierre Abel-] Rémusat, [Samuel] Beal and others in China, have placed at his disposal a large mass of legends in Sanskrit, Pali, Tibetan and Chinese, which record with more than Boswellian zeal and assiduity ... even the most trivial circumstances of the life and preachings of the great reformer (2–3).

Mitra's life story has been rightly described as being "a story of firsts" (Guha-Thakurta 2004: 86): the first Indian to edit and publish Sanskrit texts in the highly regarded *Bibliotheca Indica* series; the first Indian appointed by the government to direct an archaeological survey; the first Indian director of Calcutta's Wards Institution; a founding member of the British Indian Association; and a founding editor of two Bengali monthlies. Born in 1824 in a distinguished high-caste family of scribes (*kayasthas*) previously employed by the Mughals, Mitra was groomed at an early age to become a doctor or a lawyer. After failing to complete his medical and law courses, he began an intensive study of language in 1842. A gifted linguist, Mitra's mastery over more than ten South Asian and European languages led to his first appointment at the Asiatic Society four years later.[45] When, in 1885, he was elected president of the Asiatic Society, he became the first non-European to hold the office. His election was a milestone and a cause célèbre, for although he continued to be the object of incessant racist diatribes masquerading as scholarly critiques, his position meant that a colonial subject, a "brown babu," now headed one of the most illustrious scholarly organizations in the Empire, one whose members were predominantly white and male.

Mitra's reputation hinged on his staunch empiricism, mastery of critical Western methodologies, and nearly unsurpassed knowledge of Sanskrit Buddhist literature. In publications like *Antiquities of Orissa* (2 vols., 1875–80), *Buddha Gaya: the Hermitage of Shákya Muni* (1878) and the multi-volume *Sanskrit Buddhist Literature of Nepal* (1882), Mitra demonstrated a profound ability to connect material remains with the literary record. More than just a scholar of Buddhism, Mitra was an educator who felt that it was his duty to recover and popularize the Buddhist past whose elusive meanings had been defiled by woeful negligence and slander. To prevent Buddhism's further disappearance, he amassed a huge collection—at private and government expense—of rare Buddhist manuscripts and antiquities, adamant that these "relics of the past, weeping over a lost civilization and an extinguished grandeur" required urgent protection and public visibility (Mitra 1875: i).[46] It was here, as a collector and historian, not as an *upasaka* or lay devotee, that Mitra's passion for Buddhism rested.

In 1877, when Mitra was sent to Bodh Gaya to inspect the ongoing excavations around the Maha Bodhi temple, he witnessed first-hand the effects of time and of, what he felt to be, well-intentioned but misdirected efforts of devotees. The previous year, the Government of India had begrudgingly granted the Burmese king, Mindon Min, permission to repair the temple complex. Britain's relations with Burma were increasingly sensitive, with the two parties having fought two major wars in the past half-a-century and being just years away from a third in 1885, in which the entire kingdom would be annexed as a further province of British India. The Burmese king's emissaries arrived in January, but by mid-year, the government had received reports that their plans of repair were at odds with the types of conservation ideologies implicit in the ASI. Mitra, having already successfully led an archaeological expedition under government jurisdiction in Odisha, was dispatched to the site with explicit instructions to tread carefully and only interfere if their work risked any "serious injury being done to the temple" (letter from Sir Stuart Bayley, Secretary to the Government of Bengal, to Mitra, quoted in Mitra 1878: iii). When the Burmese began rebuilding old sculptures and inserting new ones into the niches along the outer wall of the temple, Mitra penned a message to Calcutta stating that while the Burmese were working "energetically and piously," they had no "systematic and traditional plan". The Burmese, he continued, were "ignorant of the true history of their faith and perfectly innocent of archaeology and history, and the mischief they had done by their misdirected zeal has been serious ... nothing of ancient times can now be traced on the area they have worked upon" (66).

In Mitra's study of the temple, he describes the "demolished" antiquities with a tragic sense of loss and mourning, their memories forever lost to posterity. Yet, as Alan Trevithick (1999) has pointed out, what for Mitra was a matter of loss was to the Burmese a matter of gain. The issue cuts straight to the heart of contemporary debates about Buddhist antiquities as historical, abstract reconstructions whose timelessness must be preserved, and of them as part of a living religious tradition in constant adaptation to the present moment. While for Mitra, the right to manage religious sites was the sole prerogative of modern scholars, not of the zealous devotee, he laid the ultimate blame for the Maha Bodhi temple's decay elsewhere.

Mitra's studies of material remains and Indic literary traditions led him to the conclusion that brahmins were to blame. The Buddha's life, he argued, had been misrepresented and purposefully erased due to sectarian hatred. At Bodh Gaya, "the [Maha Bodhi] temple stood there deserted, forsaken, and dilapidated, and they appropriated it to their own use by giving it and its presiding image new names" (Mitra 1878: 61). The brahmanical bias against the Buddha, he contended, extended far beyond Bodh Gaya and the early tradition. After completing his extensive study of Buddhist remains in Odisha, he concluded, "it is impossible to suppose that they [the brahmins] knew nothing of the ascendancy of Buddhism" (Mitra 1880: 104). Brahmanical silences about Buddhism were not evidence of its non-existence or minimal influence, as some of his colleagues claimed, but deliberate distortions, crafted to suit their socio-political needs. "The omission," he concluded, "can be attributed solely to religious hatred. They would do anything to avoid naming the Jains and the Buddhists; as the old adage has it 'they [brahmins] would rather be eaten up by tigers than seek shelter in a Jaina temple'" (104).[47] While this history of brahmanical antagonism would be repeatedly invoked by Buddhists and their supporters in the coming decades as they attempted to strip the reigning Shaiva mahant of his ownership of the Maha Bodhi temple, Mitra's criticism of brahmins wrongly pegged him as a (sarcastically implied) "enlightened" Anglophile. This too, as his publications evince, was a distortion.

A series of Mitra's writings produced in the late 1870s make clear that he felt some contemporary European scholars were as manipulative as the ancient brahmins in their portrayal of the Indian past. The debate turned sour in 1880 when Mitra and the eminent art historian, James Ferguson, went head-to-head in an ugly exchange. The pot, however, had been simmering for years. Both were legitimate scholars with vastly different interpretations: for Ferguson, the excessive decoration in Indian architecture was a sure sign of its "decadence"; for Mitra, the extensive ornamentation in temple architecture established its "grandeur" (Singh 2004: xiv–xv). Yet, when Mitra charged Ferguson with ignoring the evidence of stone architecture in India in order to categorize the Buddhist motifs at Amaravati as under "Classical" Greco-Roman rather than "Native" influence, the conversation turned nasty. After two anonymous, harshly worded reviews of Mitra's work appeared in the *Indian Antiquary* (Vol. 9. 1880: 113–16, 142–44), Ferguson formally replied in a politically and racially infused diatribe entitled *Archaeology in India with Especial Reference to the Works of Babu Rajendralal Mitra* (1884). In the course of 141 pages, Ferguson (1884) not only attacked Mitra's (unfortunate) iconographic blunders, but in a heavily patronizing tone, accused Mitra of being an "uneducated" Indian incapable of assimilating the "great truths of scientific knowledge" (5):

> Is it that the Babu's eye is so uneducated, that he cannot perceive the obvious distinction between Classical and Native art in India? Or is it that he is so satisfied by his own superficial knowledge, that he has not cared to follow the recent developments of Indian archaeology, and cannot consequently state them with intelligible clearness (99)?

For Ferguson, formerly a resident of India, the real issue at stake surpassed the question of whether early Buddhist art had "classical" (European) or "native" (Indian) origins. Rather, he was questioning the ability of any Indian of even being capable of assessing such a thing. At the time that Ferguson was writing, there was sustained debate in India regarding the passing of the Ilbert Bill, a controversial measure that would allow British residents of India to be tried in a court of law by senior Indian judges and not just by other white Europeans judges, as current law prescribed. For racists like Ferguson, such "equality" was simply outrageous. In his view, if even the most educated of Indians like Mitra—"a typical specimen of one of the proposed class of governors [judges]"—could not interpret history "objectively", how could they be fit to judge whites? (4) While such attitudes were by no means typical of all Indian–European scholarly interactions, the case demonstrates the way that even seemingly abstract or trivial matters regarding the dating of an ancient Buddhist sculpture were tied to the politics of the period.

Sarat Chandra Das and the Study of Tibet

Beginning in the 1880s, students of Northern Buddhism became increasingly familiar with the name of Sarat Chandra Das (1849–1917). Popular newspapers and scholarly journals from India and abroad, including the *Asiatic Quarterly Review, Journal of the Royal Asiatic Society of Great Britain, Open Court*, and *The Academy*, loved telling the story of the Bengali explorer–scholar, who, disguised as a pilgrim, braved icy rivers and Himalayan passes to make it to the holy city of Lhasa. He visited Tibet, first in 1879 and again in 1881, to study Buddhism and explore the Land of Snows. There he met the Panchen Lama, studied Tibetan scriptures, and returned to his Darjeeling home (aptly named Lhasa Villa) with approximately two hundred hitherto little-known Tibetan Buddhist manuscripts. Raised in the port city of Chittagong, Das left to study for a degree in civil engineering at Calcutta University in the early 1870s. After falling ill with malaria—he never finished his studies—he was offered a position by (later Sir) Alfred Croft, the then inspector of schools in Bengal to head a newly established boarding school for Tibetanized hill peoples (Bhutias) in Darjeeling.

Known as the "Queen of the Hill Stations", Darjeeling was perched on a steep ridge in the south-eastern Himalayas rising nearly seven thousand feet above the Bengal plains. For the British, Darjeeling had become a popular "sanatorium" to escape the disease and heat of the plains. Ostensibly, this is why Croft had offered the job to Das. But the nature of the Bhutia Boarding School he was to head was unusual, as was reflected in a classified letter Croft wrote to the government in Simla: "the school is to train up interpreters, geographers and explorers, who may be useful if at any future time Tibet is opened to the British" (quoted in Waller 1990: 93).[48] Since at least the 1840s, the government had begun making efforts "to train intelligent natives of the border ... in the use of instruments by which they might fix the position of the chief cities, the courses of the great rivers and mountains" of nearby lands (letter No. 38/247, 8 May 1862, from Major J.T.

Sarat Chandra Das on a yak crossing Donkhya Pass (Sikkim)

Walker, superintedent, Survey of India, to the secretary of the Government of India, Military Department, quoted in Madan 2004: 13). Concerns about Russian activities in Central Asia, the 1857 uprising in northern India, and the ever-present interest in creating an overland market in China through Tibet saw increased government expenditures for trainings in and along India's northern borders with Tibet and the Himalayas. By the time the Bhutia Boarding School opened in 1874, at least nine pandits, mostly from *pahari* (mountain) Hindu families in the north-western Himalayas (Kumaon), had already been sent to different parts of the Tibetan Plateau, whence they returned months and sometimes years later with reports of rugged landscapes and urban oases rich in resources but fraught with serious danger.

The location of the new school, then, was apt. Set up just six miles from the princely Buddhist kingdom of Sikkim and eleven miles from the Nepal border, it was surrounded by an extraordinary mixture of polyglot peoples and diverse cultures. Although the demographics of the region were quickly shifting, the small population of Buddhists left a decisive imprint on the landscape.[49] The four major towns of Ghoom, Kurseong, Darjeeling, and Kalimpong peopled several thousand Tibetan Buddhists, and were home to the imposing Nyingma (*rnying ma*) and Drukpa Kagyu (*'brug pa bka' brgyud*) monasteries (*dgon pa*).[50] These religious estates and their leaders (*bla ma*) were linked to other monastic institutions and patrons across the trans-Himalayan and inner Asian world via networks of learning and trade crafted over centuries.

When Das arrived at the school in April 1874, he immediately began studying Tibetan with Lama Sherab Gyatso (*sog pa shes rab rgya mtsho*), the Mongolian head of the Yiga Choling monastery (est. 1850).[51] During the first two years of work, Das spent much of his time recruiting local students, studying Tibetan, and exploring the surrounding hills with fellow schoolteacher, Ugyen Gyatso (*orgyan rgya mtsho*). In addition to being a fine scholar, Ugyen Gyatso was a veteran surveyor, having provided intelligence to the British for over a decade (Strahan 1889: 3–7). The two appear to have developed a good relationship, Ugyen Gyatso "the harassed and hard-working surveyor" and Das "the light-hearted observer," as one contemporary put it (Holdich 1906: 250). Nearly all accounts of their journeys to Sikkim and Tibet make it evident that Ugyen Gyatso did the leg work, acquiring the necessary documentation from Tibetan officials, even carrying Das on his back at times over mountain passes, but Das's skills as a linguist, lexicographer, ethnographer, and, importantly, English-speaking babu, brought him the imperial fame. After playing a critical diplomatic role in the 1885 British mission to Peking, the senior government administrator, Colman Macaulay, even penned a poem about:

> Sarat Chandra [Das], hardy son,
> Of soft Bengal, whose wondrous store
> Of Buddhist and Tibetan lore
> A place in fame's bright page has won,
> Friend of the Tashu [Panchen] Lama's line,
> Whose eyes have seen, the gleaming shrine
> Of holy Lhassa, came to show

The wonders of the land of snow

(Macaulay, in Das 1893: Appendix I, iii).

Das's public persona was significant enough for some scholars to contend he was the inspiration behind the Indian spy in Kipling's *Kim* (Waller 1990: 193). While this remains debated, his value to the imperial state is not. Even two decades after his last journey to Tibet, he continued to hold fictitious, but salaried, appointments for the government. His more than a decade of work on the superb *Tibetan-English Dictionary with Sanskrit Synonyms*, eventually published by the Government of Bengal in 1902, had cost the government more than forty thousand rupees (FDSE August 1901, Nos. 31–33). The expenses were justified, Viceroy Curzon wrote in a classified letter (25 July 1901) to His Majesty's Secretary of State in London, because the "employment was semi-political .... [Das's] special knowledge will continue to be available to the local authorities, who are at present entrusted with the duty of collecting intelligence about Tibetan politics and affairs" (FDSE August 1901, Nos 31–33).

Even if the government effectively bankrolled Das's studies of Tibetan Buddhism and his Buddhist Text Society (1892–1907), it was his wonderful storytelling and astute analysis that energized the budding Buddhist interests of the Indian elite. With the completion of the Darjeeling railway in 1881, transforming the previously week-long, 300-mile journey to Calcutta into a two-day affair, Das began visiting the city regularly at the invitation of prominent societies and institutes. At the Indian Museum, the Asiatic Society, the Indian Association for the Cultivation of Science, and the Bengal Students' Association, he enchanted audiences with tales of "High Priests" from the "Holy City" and lucid explanations of "Bodhi Dharma" and "the doctrine of transmigration" (Das 1893). His exploits, like most adventurers' tales, were nearly mythic: the Tibetan companions who guided him over mountain passes are mostly absent, except when they intervened like true Bodhisattvas in perilous moments when his life was in danger.[52] The memoirs may have added a dash of spice, but his analysis of Buddhist doctrines and practices was methodical and incisive, indispensable to scholars as late as the 1960s (Wayman 1966: 778).[53] They opened the door to the Indian public for a more comprehensive understanding of the past, one in which Buddhism was seen as playing a largely positive role in connecting India with the rest of Asia. In his *Journey to Lhasa and Central Tibet* (1902), he explained how he was "transported with joy" when he discovered Sanskrit texts written in Tibetan script inside Shigatse's Tashilunpo monastery (Das 1902: 112). At public lectures, he described dozens of ancient Indian pandits who, one millennium before, spread "Indo-Aryan culture," "Buddhist propaganda" and "civilization" to Tibet, China, and beyond (Das 1893: 45–50). Through Das's influence, the Bengali- and English-speaking public in India were converted to the idea that Tibetans had retained the essence of this ancient Indian dhamma with perfect clarity and utmost reverence. Now, after so many centuries of separation, Indians like him were recovering the Buddha's Word (*vacana*) and bringing it home.

Das's emphasis on Tibetan sources and, in particular, his argument that Tibetan Buddhism was the most faithful replication of late Indian Buddhist developments left a strong imprint in the scholarly and popular world. Das accepted this view without questioning how this lent greater authority to Tibetan practices themselves (Leoshko 2003: 110–15). Although he was not the first scholar to argue that in the absence of Indian sources, Tibetan Buddhist texts and art forms could be used to understand developments in Indian Buddhist history, the contention gained greater specificity in his time, leading to the popular paradigm in which Tibetan lamas were viewed as the unrivaled carriers of "authentic" Indian Buddhist teachings and practices.[54]

Das's privileging of Tibetan sources, and the government support he was able to furnish for it, was an extraordinary intervention considering it came in an era in which scholars of Buddhism, weary of Sanskrit sources, were increasingly convinced that Pali texts represented the only valuable subject of study. Das did not discourage Pali language studies, and one of his most accomplished students (and another secret agent), Satish Chandra Vidyabhusan (1870–1920), became an influential Pali scholar.[55] Yet, the wholesale support Das gave to Tibetan literature changed the way scholars thought about Indian history. It is unlikely he could have accomplished such a feat without the government's support, which rested heavily on geopolitical strategies. In the short term, this led to critical institutional support from Sir Asutosh Mookerjee, the Vice Chancellor of Calcutta University (and a high court magistrate). In the long term, it led later explorer–scholars like Ekai Kawaguchi, Giuseppe Tucci, and Rahul Sankrityayan to Tibet in search of Sanskrit manuscripts housed in monasteries. Das also attempted to intervene in what he saw as the public's romantic and ultimately misguided beliefs about early Buddhism. He argued against the popular idea that the Buddha was a social reformer or opponent of caste (Das 1894) and attacked the idea that the early sangha promoted gender equality (Dharmapala 1908).

Census Commissions and Crypto-Buddhists

During the decennial census of 1901, Sir Herbert Hope Risley (1851–1911), the newly appointed census commissioner and, former president (1897–99) of Das's (renamed) Buddhist Text and Anthropological Society, sent local magistrates in Bengal a printed circular. The memo contained explicit instructions to find evidence of Buddhist practice in the province, along with an outline of *The Discovery of Living Buddhism in Bengal* (1897), a recent text published by the Calcutta University professor and Mahamahopadhyaya (Greatest of Teachers), Haraprasad Shastri (1861–1930).[56] As a frequent consultant for government offices, including the Calcutta High Court and the Bureau of Information and Political Office of the foreign department, Haraprasad's innovative views on Indian history rarely went unnoticed. A former student of Rajendralal Mitra and, in the government's eyes, a "good man" (HDBPB Sept. 1892, Part B: 87–90), felt to be far "too rare" (FDE Apr. 1906: 1–4), Haraprasad was well liked by authorities and had friends in high places.[57] News of his latest "discovery" had begun several years earlier when he published three exploratory essays for the Asiatic Society of Bengal (Shastri 1894; 1895a; 1895b), noting how certain religious practices, symbols, and imagery surrounding a popular Bengali folk deity named Dharmaraj resembled Buddhist rites he had witnessed in Nepal and read about in medieval manuscripts. By 1897, he reported more confidently:

> It is said that the expulsion of [Indian] Buddhism was complete but can this ever be a fact that the religion which counted its votaries by the million should altogether disappear from the soil of its birth and the scenes of its greatest power and influence? One is not disposed to believe such a thing …. With the materials obtained up to this

time, I humbly believe a case has been made out for considering the worshippers of Dharma[raj] to be the ancient Buddhists of India. If further investigation confirms my views, a very large proportion of the population of Bengal will have to be taken out from the list of Hindus and put down under the head of Buddhists. The Census of India will have to be considerably modified and the theory that Buddhism has been swept away from the soil of India will have to be given up ... *with a little care a census of the followers of Dharma[raj] may be taken. The population will be considerable, nay, several millions* (Shastri 1897: 4, 62, 65).

Despite his claims to the contrary, the call to reclassify the "several millions" of Dharmaraj followers as Buddhists was hardly a "humble" gesture.[58] Yet, even after the 1901 Census ethnographers returned from the field with no evidence of that which "savour[s] most strongly of Buddhism" (quoted in Kemper 2015: 275), the search continued. In 1911, census officials, on the basis of further evidence produced by one of Haraprasad's colleagues, reclassified a population of approximately twenty-five hundred *sarak*s (weavers) living in the Cuttack hills of Odisha as Buddhist. The saraks, the Census reported, worshipped a deity named *shunyata* (Emptiness), erected "pseudo-chaityas," and met once a year during the Buddhist festival Vesak in the cave temples of Khandagiri to worship a deity called Buddhadev or Caturbhuja (Risley 1915: 79).[59]

The driving force behind this latest ethnographic "discovery" of Buddhism was the Odia polymath, Pandit Nagendranath Vasu (1866–1938).[60] This "Ocean of Orientalist Knowledge" (*Prachyavidyamaharnava*) was a powerful figure amongst the colonial elite, revered as much for his compilation of the first Bengali and Hindi encyclopaedias (*vishvakosh*) as for his novels, plays, and scholarly works. Beginning in the late 1890s, Vasu took great interest in the Dharmaraj cult, investigating the folk deity's worship in Odisha, particularly the area around Cuttack and the princely state of Mayurabhanj, where he spent several seasons overseeing archaeological excavations with the support of the local Hindu king. The two critical works he produced from these researches, *The Archaeological Survey of Mayurabhanja* (1912) and *The Modern Buddhism and Its Followers in Orissa* (1911), were landmarks in the study of Indian Buddhism. Both are complex and ambitious histories, but like Haraprasad's *Discovery*, they brought a historian's analysis to the ethnographic scene, making provocative and often speculative claims about Buddhism in the present-day landscape.

Vasu and Haraprasad's arguments about pseudo-Buddhist practices in contemporary India shared three especially noteworthy features, symptomatic of the wider context in which Indian scholars understood Buddhism's "end days". First, the "crypto-Buddhists" (as Vasu termed them) that both he and Haraprasad identified were always of lower caste, tribal, or untouchable background, having been cast out by brahmanical leaders for their historical dissent. As Shastri (1897: 20) noted, the Dharmaraj worshippers "rarely if ever, accept the ministration of Bráhmanas". Yet, like the early Buddhists, the "priests of Dharma[raj] ... never oppose Bráhmanas worshipping their deity. The Bráhmana can any time enter a Dharma[raj] temple" (45). Similarly, Vasu's crypto-Buddhists or devotees of Mahima Dharma were tribals (adivasis) and shudras found scattered throughout the Cuttack hills, forced to flee there after systematic persecutions in the sixteenth century (Vasu 1911: cii–civ). Second, the liturgies of the crypto-Buddhists were composed in "impure" and "common" vernaculars like Bihari, Hindi, Bengali, and Odia, the kinds of unrefined linguistic registers which no orthodox brahmin would allow, since according to Shastri, "the formula of meditation among the Hindus is given always and without exception in Sanskrit" (Shastri 1897: 28).[61] Third, the central world views inscribed in the Mahima Dharma and Dharmaraj scriptures held more in common with Buddhist than brahmanical Hindu doctrines. Both groups, for example, believed "that the world sprang from non-existence" (Shastri 1897: 54) and phrased their discussions of the Absolute in terms of shunyata (emptiness) and *saddharma* (the "True Dharma"), common expressions found in Buddhist texts (Vasu 1911: cci-ccv, ccxxxvi).[62]

The idea that Buddhist identities had withered away through a centuries-old process of "Hinduization" was nothing new. Mitra pointed to the Hindu assimilation of Buddhist sites in Odisha and Bihar, and many other scholars have since then identified—sometimes wrongly, sometimes correctly—stupas converted into Shivalingams, or Buddhist images being worshipped as Hindu deities.[63] But just as Mitra claimed to understand Buddhist tradition better than Burmese Buddhist themselves, here too it was argued that only a scholar with "modern credentials" could define who or what a Buddhist is or was. Haraprasad's informants explained to him that Dharmaraj "is either a form of Visnu or a form of Çiva [Shiva]," but Haraprasad couldn't accept such an idea. He believed they were misled, for "in their books he [Dharmaraj] is much above them. He is the Supreme Deity" (Shastri 1897: 21–22). Vasu was equally bold. When a group of caste subalterns and Mahima devotees attempted to enter the Hindu Jagannath temple in Puri in 1881, leading to a riot and the burning of the Jagannath idol, he argued that the movement was orchestrated by the blind poet, Bhima Bhoi (1850–96). According to Vasu (1911: ccxlvi–ccl), Bhima Bhoi proclaimed himself as Buddha incarnate and was hoping to reclaim the (supposedly) Buddhist image inside the temple and re-create a casteless society. The 1881 riots are still poorly understood (Bannerjee-Dube 2009: 69–116), but all accounts agree that several people were arrested, at least one person died, and the celebrated Jagannath image was dragged outside the temple and burned.[64] Conflicting accounts of the event were widely reported in newspapers and magazines, and the once little-known Mahima Dharma group was catapulted into public spotlight. This, of course, would have strengthened interest in Vasu's interpretation of the events since he was one of the few "authorized" scholars who not only possessed their medieval liturgies and scriptures but could also read them. In the end, when the Jagannath riot was investigated in court, Vasu's account of the group's Buddhist origins and beliefs was critical to the litigation (Bannerjee-Dube 2009: 103–04). Thus, we are again presented with a situation in which the "modern" scholar's expertise is privileged above and beyond that of the practitioner or informant.

Buddhism and the Indian Public

Between the 1880s and the 1920s, Indian academic studies of Buddhism grew exponentially. Sarat Chandra Das and Haraprasad Shastri continued their pioneering work in Sanskrit and Tibetan studies, from the 1880s until their deaths in 1917 and 1931 respectively. Fairly comprehensive histories of Buddhist studies in early twentieth-century India have been discussed by P.V. Bapat (1944; 1956: 382–446) and D.C. Ahir (1991: 141–74), among others, but even a small sampling of the most widely read and cited works from the 1900s to early 1930s is suggestive of India's research impact at this historical juncture. This included Satish Chandra Vidyabhusan's English translation and Devanagari transliteration of Kacchayana's Pali Grammar (1901), and his monumental *History of Indian Logic* (1922); Harinath De's editing of multiple Sanskrit, Pali, and Tibetan texts, including a partial English translation of Taranatha's *History of Indian Buddhism (Rgya gar chos 'byung)* in 1911; Beni Madhab Barua's *The History of Pre-Buddhist Indian Philosophy* (1921) and *Prakrit Dhammapada* (1921), the latter with Sailendranath Mishra; Bimala Churn Law's *Life and Work of Buddhaghosa* (1923), *Women in Buddhist Literature* (1927), and magisterial two-volume *History of Pali Literature* (1933); Sukumar Dutt's *Early Buddhist Monachism* (1924); Benoytosh Bhattacharyya's *Indian Buddhist Iconography* (1924); and P.C. Bagchi's early works on Indo–Sino Buddhist relations, such as *Le canon bouddhique en Chine* (2 volumes, 1927–38).

While much of what conditioned these works were wider studies taking place in academic institutions around the world, it was also subcontinental institution building that created the conditions necessary for the rise of Indian critical studies of Buddhism. Take Calcutta University. By the 1910s, the institution was a major center for studying Indian Buddhism thanks to the formidable efforts of its vice chancellor, Asutosh Mookerjee (1864–1924), a renowned jurist and mathematician who also served as the first president of the Maha Bodhi Society until his death in 1924. By 1915, Pali, Sanskrit, and Tibetan were not only languages of Buddhist examination at Calcutta University, but also reflected the institution's modern-day cosmopolitanism. Such linguistic diversity drew scholars and students from across Asia and beyond, all of whom were welcome at the University's three-story Buddhist hostel. Japanese intellectuals, in particular, flocked to this "Oxford of the East" and saw the imperial city as a place of modern learning where they could be trained in Indian languages, be introduced to Orientalist scholarship, and gain access to rare critical texts (Jaffe 2004; 2019).

While Calcutta continued to be a hub for Buddhist studies until the end of the colonial period, western India was not far behind thanks to the liberal support of progressive reformers like Sayajirao Gaikwad III, the maharaja of Baroda (r. 1875–1939). A keen supporter of the Buddhist movement from the early 1900s onwards, Sayajirao commissioned the publication of several Buddhist texts, made several donations to the Maha Bodhi Society, generously supported the work of the Pali scholar, Dharmanand Kosambi, for many years, and even installed a public image of the Buddha at Baroda's Jubilee Square in 1913.[65] Likewise, R.G. Bhandarkar's leadership of multiple Indological initiatives, from his establishment of the Bhandarkar Oriental Research Institute in Pune in 1917 to the organization of the annual All-India Oriental Conference starting in 1919, also provided Buddhist studies a critical space. As vice chancellor of Bombay University, Bhandarkar also tapped Kosambi to establish a Pali curriculum at the University in 1912. Kosambi trained many students who would leave as significant a shape on global Buddhist studies as he did. This included the well-known scholars, N.K. Bhagwat and C.V. Joshi, who produced numerous English and Marathi translations of Pali texts. Kosambi's most influential student, however, was P.V. Bapat, the prolific author of more than a hundred books and essays, including translations and new editions of Sanskrit, Pali, and Chinese texts, as well as a landmark study of the *Vimuttimagga and Visuddhimagga* (1932), based on his PhD dissertation at Harvard.

The geographical and temporal distances between many of these scholars may seem significant, but they were all deeply bound up through trans-regional academic networks that became increasingly well worn even in the midst of enormous political and social turmoil.[66] Many of these figures were close friends, sharing resources and roles on editorial boards, overseeing conferences and academic programs, and sending their pupils to study with peers and noted authorities at institutions across the world, in Pune, Bombay, Calcutta, Colombo, Bonn, London, and Boston. The sheer number of works produced by Indian scholars during this period, and their influence on the international discourse surrounding Buddhism has yet to be fully recognized but it is certain that by this time they were as much the "curators of the Buddha" (Lopez 1995) as their Western counterparts.

While much of this scholarship was mediated through English and other European languages, there were also conscious efforts to make them readily available in local languages. Already by the early 1900s, those who could read Bengali, and possessed the resources to access libraries and reading rooms, could explore the simplest as well as the most opaque aspects of Buddhist doctrine and history. Given his unquestionable love for his western Indian roots, Dharmanand Kosambi published almost the entirety of his scholarly oeuvre in Marathi and Gujarati (see Kosambi [1909–49] 2010: 415–17, for a list of publications). Kosambi's commitments to "democratizing" and "vernacularizing" the knowledge of Buddhism were superseded only by Rahul Sankrityayan, who from the 1930s onwards began addressing his audiences in the supra-regional language of Hindi (Ober 2013).[67]

While scholarly publications often landed in specialist journals, this material was also republished and circulated by propaganda houses and social reform organizations to advance their own agendas. The Buddhist Mission in Rangoon, for instance, published both Bengali-language translations of Pali texts and Pali-language texts in Bengali script (*bangla lipi*). It also helped that many university professors spoke regularly at meetings of the Brahmo Samaj, Theosophical Society, Prarthana Samaj, Maha Bodhi Society, Bengal Buddhist Association, Bombay Buddha Society, Buddhist Text Society, Shakya Buddhist Society, and other such organizations. This ensured that academic arguments were disseminated among a much wider public. Beni Madhab Barua's commitments to Buddhist revival in Bengal and his leadership in academic and non-academic Buddhist programs blurred the lines between scholar, devotee, and activist (Surendran 2013: 123–39). Dharmanand Kosambi was active in multiple social reform associations and regularly delivered talks for non-academic audiences.

This gray area between being a scholar, activist, and popularizer had, in fact, marked the emergence of Buddhist studies in India since the 1880s and was one of the many ways that the academy helped inspire continued interest in Buddhism among diverse Indian publics.[68] In short, formal academic studies of Buddhism were rarely a solitary, private affair. Not only were they considered integral to people's lives, but their dissemination and publicization among the everyday Indian public was also considered paramount, lest the religion become (as many feared) confined to intellectuals bickering amongst themselves. So, at the same time Sarat Chandra Das was dazzling public audiences with his tales of the Land of Snows, Haraprasad Shastri was publishing serialized stories of historical

Buddhist fiction in the popular Bengali-language journal, *Bangadarshan*.[69] Likewise, Raja Sivaprasad's *Itihas* shaped the minds and works of popular Hindu religious reformers like Dayanand Sarasvati. When Sarasvati composed his popular manual, *Satyarth Prakash*, or Light of Truth, in 1875 for the Arya Samaj, he used the *Itihas* as the basis for his arguments *against* Buddhist and Jain world views (Cort 2012: 137–61).

The finer points of scholarly difference may have been confined to the insular life of university and scholarly associations, but the conversations they had were heard across social spheres. From the 1870s to the 1880s, some of the most prolific Indian writings on the Buddha were composed by the predominantly upper-caste Bengalis who made up the Brahmo Samaj, a group whose wealth and activism gave them a much wider influence than their comparatively small membership suggests (Kopf 1979).[70] Even as early as 1882, the Brahmo ascetic, Aghore Nath Gupta (1841–81), published a major Bengali-language study of Buddhism entitled *Sakyamuni-Charitra o Nirbana-tattva (Life of Shakyamuni and the Philosophy of Nirvana)*.[71] Compiled on the basis of both primary and secondary sources—the Asiatic Society's Rajendralal Mitra assisted with materials—Gupta's *Sakyamuni-Charitra* (Gupta [1882] 1957) attempted a reconciliation between the Buddha's purported atheism and Brahmo theism. For Gupta, the Buddha was neither an atheist nor an agnostic, but a "religious humanist" who "found religion in the notion of infinite knowledge" (Gupta, quoted in Kopf 1979: 284).[72]

Among the most influential of Brahmo voices on Buddhism was that of the organization's energetic leader, Keshab Chandra Sen (1838–84). In 1879, the same year that Sen announced his "New Dispensation" to establish the "truth" of all great religions, he also began a more rigorous exploration of Buddhism. That year, he even organized a Brahmo pilgrimage to Bodh Gaya (*Missionary Expedition* 1881: 14–15). As per Sen, the Buddha had perfected the practice (sadhana) of detachment or asceticism (*vairagya*) as well as contemplation (dhyana). He was a model guide for modern living (Sen [1881–82] 1956: 17). He argued that with the Buddha's discovery of the path to nirvana and India's rediscovery of that path, a New Dispensation (*nava vidhan*) could be established. This would give rise to a "nation of enlightened, ascetic race of Buddhists" that transcended the Vedas, brahmanism, and bibliolatry, and which could "save the world and emancipate humanity"

(19). Despite the fact that all Brahmo promotion of Buddhism came through a deeply assimilative lens, their admiration for early Buddhist teachings was deep enough to arouse sustained public interest in the tradition. The names of many Bengalis who popularized Buddhism through plays, dramas, and popular writings—Rabindranath Tagore, Satyendranath Tagore, Dwijiendranath Tagore, Nobin Chandra Sen, Maharaja Jatindra Mohan Tagore, and so on—almost all came from families who were closely associated with the Brahmo Samaj.

Yet, nowhere was the Indian public's tryst with Buddhism more obvious than in their response to Sir Edwin Arnold's (1832–1904) poetic biography of the Buddha, *The Light of Asia* (1879). This immensely popular work, which sold an estimated half-a-million to one million copies in America alone— even outselling, by some accounts, Mark Twain's *Huckleberry Finn*—took colonial Indian publics by storm (Ober 2021; Ramesh 2021). In fact, many of *The Light of Asia*'s first ever translations were in subcontinental tongues: in Bengali (1885, 1887, 1894), Marathi (1894), Tamil (1898, 1918), Telugu (1902), Malayalam (1912, 1914, 1915, 1917), and many others in later decades. By the end of its two-year run as a dramatic performance at Calcutta's Star Theatre from 1885 to 1887, crowds were having to be turned away for lack of standing room. Decades later, *The Light of Asia* would inspire one of India's first-ever black-and-white films, *Prem Sanyas / Die Leucthe Asiens* (1925), produced by the Bengali–German duo, Himanshu Rai and Franz Osten, with a screenplay written by Niranjan Pal, the son of the famed anti-colonial nationalist, Bipin Chandra Pal. While *The Light of Asia*'s literary aesthetics captivated innumerable nationalist elites and intellectuals, like Jawaharlal Nehru, Mohandas K. Gandhi, Swami Vivekananda, Abanindranath Tagore, and Ramcandra Sukla, it also served as an inspiration and tool to advocate for social reform and anti-caste activism among izhavas along the Malabar coast, as seen in the works of the noted Malayali poet, Kumaran Asan.

It is often assumed that these kinds of discourses never seeped beyond the confines of elite social circles and that such ideas never had any impact on the wider masses. But in places like Chittagong, the Terai, and parts of the Himalayas, many subaltern populaces were deeply influenced by the discursive shifts in knowledge that the new Indian elite propagated. By the early decades of the twentieth century, many Tharus in Nepal's Terai began propagating theories about their "original" Buddhist origins, while denouncing their contemporary socio-religious existence as a form of "degenerate Hinduized Buddhism" in need of reform (Guneratne 2002: 154–56)· These self-fashioned identities gave further stimulus to existing discourses of reform from itinerant Buddhist missionaries (*dharmadoot*) across Asia, who called upon diverse populations to return to their "original" Buddhist identities. In Odisha, for example, Vasu's identification of crypto-Buddhism helped stimulate real social change. Tired of the scholarly conclusion that Mahima devotees were "actually" Buddhists, in the 1930s, Biswanath Baba, a prominent leader of a Mahima sect, drew a clear line of separation between Buddhism and Mahima Dharma, in an effort to align the latter with Advaita Vedantic traditions (Banerjee-Dube 2009: 77–78, 122). Meanwhile, other Mahima devotees accepted Vasu's view and attempted to reform and revive their "original" Buddhist identity. By the 1940s, about ten thousand *bauddhatanti*s, or weavers, from Cuttack had even organized a "Bauddha Shravaka Sangha," calling on Buddhist monks living in Calcutta to help them "return to their past" (*MBJ*, Vol. 61/12, 1953: 445; Dash 2002). The weavers, however, were not the only new communities in India attempting to once again live according to the words of the Buddha.

Banyan Tree Buddhism

In the winter of 1885, a fifty-two-year-old wrestler (*pahalavan*)-turned-bhikkhu named Mahavir landed at the ferry dock in Tuticorin, south of Madras. Having made the journey from Ceylon, he had plans to visit the ancient Buddhist sites that his esteemed Buddhist master (*acharya*), Ambagahawatte Indasabha Mahasthavir (1832–86), had taught him so much about during the past four years.[1] Like other pilgrims, Mahavir visited Bodh Gaya, Rajgir, Nalanda, and Sarnath, by foot, train, boat, and other forms of ancient and modern transit. But unlike for most Buddhist pilgrims of the time, the sights and sounds of the open plains and bustling markets were already familiar to Mahavir. He was raised in Bihar and by most accounts, was the "first" north Indian Hindu in modern times to become a Buddhist monk (Kausalyayan 1941: 99–109; Buddhamitra 1999; Lal 2004: 87–93).

Born to a family of rajputs in Arrah (Bihar) in 1833, Mahavir Singh had spent his childhood training to be a soldier. Rumor had it that when his uncle, the famed Kunwar Singh, led a rebellion against the British during the great war of 1857–58, Mahavir was on the front line. When, after months of bloody fighting, it was clear that the British *firangi*s were the victors, Mahavir fled. Left to his own devices, he organized some of the last remaining soldiers into a team of traveling wrestlers, who, moving from one city to the next, earned their keep by competing in tournaments (*dangal*) staged by wealthy Europeans and Indian royalty. By the late 1870s, his career as a wrestler was nearing an end—sarcopenia's inevitable arrival later earned him the name

Mahavir Singh, the wrestler
who became a bhikkhu

Mote Baba, or the Fat Saint—and he journeyed to Ceylon after winning his
last match in Madras.

In Galle, he found employment with a Hindu merchant who helped
him settle in and began teaching him astrological sciences (*phalit jyotish*).
These skills, which were in high demand among the Sinhalese elite, brought
him into close proximity with the sangha. The itinerant wrestler continued
to move from place to place until one day, after suffering from some sort
of dysentery, he fell deeply ill. To his good fortune, a band of monks from
the Ramanna Nikaya took him to Ambagahawatte's monastery and began
nursing him back to health. The Ramanna Nikaya, which Ambagahawatte
had co-founded in 1864, was a reform-minded monastic order known for
its strict adherence to the Vinaya, willingness to ordain individuals from
any caste, and firm rejection of *devapuja,* or popular Buddhist rituals that
propitiated supernatural deities.[2] Under the care of these monks, Mahavir
refused to be served food by a non-brahmin and only through "cleverness,
caring, and tenderness" did Ambagahawatte break Mahavir's casteism and
false views (*shanaih shanaih jat-pat ke mithya-vishvas*) (Kausalyayan 1941:
103). Following his recovery, Mahavir adopted the saffron robe and began
studying Pali, the "True Dhamma" (*saddhamma*), and the history of the

ancient Sakya sage who, like him, was a son of the soil (*bhoomiputra*).[3] Upon Ambagahawatte's request, he took his higher ordination (*upasampada*) in Burma in 1885.

Back in India, Mahavir moved seasonally between country houses (*bagan*) outside Calcutta and Kushinagar, the latter of which had only recently been excavated and identified as the site of the Buddha's *parinirvana*. He was well acquainted with other Buddhist travelers in India, figures like Venerable Kripasaran and Gunalankar, the Chittagong monastics and leaders of the future Bengal Buddhist Association (Bauddha Dharmankur Sabha). By the late 1890s, Kushinagar would become Mahavir's permanent home, leading him to build the ancient town's first modern Buddhist dharamshala–vihara in 1902. The trans-national network that supported him in this endeavor was extensive, but the most significant figure was his patron (*dayak*), the Calcutta jeweler and tobacconist, Khee Zarhee.[4] The latter hailed from Arakan and had amassed a small fortune from his business in gems and stones. He was a well-connected man. In addition to owning shops in Rangoon and Akyab, his rented house, not far from the University of Calcutta, was frequented by businesspeople and monks from all around the Bay of Bengal. He knew Anagarika Dharmapala—their Calcutta residences were only a short walk from one another—but after a group of Arakanese monks were assaulted in Bodh Gaya in 1895, Zarhee and Mahavir distanced themselves from the Maha Bodhi Society, feeling that Kushinagar's Buddhist affairs were best pursued without Dharmapala's assistance.[5]

From the time of his ordination in 1885 until his death in 1919, Mahavir was a critical figure in the new Buddhist milieu beginning to take shape across northern India. His significance is threefold. First, he represented a new face in the development of modern Indian Buddhism: the Indian whose understanding of Buddhism came first and foremost through regimented, monastic curricula and exposure to living Buddhist cultures as opposed to the more common discovery via popular texts, Orientalist writings, and colonial pedagogies. Those who traveled this path were typically few and far between, but it is notable that many of the most influential Buddhist Indians in the early twentieth century derived their understanding of Buddhism from formal, monastic studies, and chose to wear the saffron robe for much, if not all of their lives.[6] Second, Buddhists like Mahavir have been typically ignored in secondary scholarship. On one hand, this is simply a result of his own unwritten record, making it extremely difficult to grasp the scope of his contributions and personality. However, this is also a shortcoming of the Anglo-centric and elite focus of so many studies of colonial-era Buddhism which have tended to highlight globetrotting cosmopolitans like Anagarika Dharmapala, one of the driving forces behind India's Buddhist revival, and the co-founder of the Maha Bodhi Society.[7] Thus, figures like Mahavir rarely appear in the record because they failed to leave written English materials or establish the kind of voluntary organizations that came to dominate urban colonial life and formed the bedrock of innumerable social reform and educational movements. Third, to overlook Mahavir and other figures like him is to miss a critical grass-roots link in the re-establishment of Buddhism in India.

In the case of Mahavir, his absence comes at a great cost, since his primary disciple and companion of more than two decades, the Arakanese bhikkhu, U Chandramani (1875–1972), became one of the most influential Buddhists in modern South Asian history. Not only was U Chandramani the ritual officiant during Ambedkar's public entry into the Buddhist fold (*upadhyaya*), presiding over the conversion of close to half a million dalits in 1956, he also helped spearhead the Theravada movement in twentieth-century Nepal by introducing a new lineage of trained monks and nuns, particularly among traditionally Vajrayana Newar families (LeVine and Gellner 2005: 41–48).[8] Despite the formidable role that Mahavir played in the development of Buddhism at Kushinagar and the cultivation of U Chandramani, his name has been largely lost to posterity.[9] Yet, as will be evident later, Mahavir's native linguistic advantages, his familiarity with north Indian culture, and his monastic links made him a key interlocutor in the web of Buddhist networks and associations forming across India and Asia.

Rebuilding Buddhism: Networks and Associations

Since the early 2000s, there has been an explosion of literature demonstrating how Buddhist ideas, peoples, and objects from the late nineteenth century onwards moved at an unprecedented speed through tightly knit global networks with no apparent center. The shape of these networks and flows were undoubtedly conditioned by political regimes and trans-regional commercial interests, but they were also in large part the creation of several energetic and dedicated Buddhist activists, intellectuals, and missionaries. These individuals did not simply see the nineteenth and twentieth centuries as a period of colonial interference. Instead, they sought opportunities for religious expansion and growth facilitated by empire, through new communication and transportation technologies, such as steamships, railways, and cheap print (Jaffe 2004, 2019; Blackburn 2010; Turner, Cox, and Bocking 2013, 2020; Ober 2013; Kemper 2015; Harding, Hori, and Soucy 2020; Chia 2020).

In late nineteenth- and early twentieth-century colonial India, many of these figures traveled and shaped what is best described as the Buddhist *ecumene* or the lived Buddhist world. The Buddhist ecumene refers to those parts of the subcontinent where Buddhism was studied, practiced, comprehended, and encountered. Viewed from above and with the advantage of hindsight, the ecumene looks like a complex, interconnected web of networks with ever-shifting centers and branches that connected India with the rest of Asia and even distant cities like London, New York, Tokyo, Singapore, Honolulu, and beyond. Any number of features could shift the relations between these disparate points: new urban viharas, rediscovered Buddhist spaces, charismatic leaders, freshly laid railway lines, university institutes, were all constantly transforming the places, people, and pathways in the ecumene. Those who entered this network rarely possessed a comprehensive picture of its breadth and were thus ever pushed and pulled in different directions, forever subject to different ideological currents, migratory flows, and new social movements. While existing networks often defined probable trajectories and delineated the horizons of what was possible at any given juncture, they were never fully determined because some personal agency always remained.

In spatial terms, the Buddhist ecumene is perhaps best likened to a banyan tree, that instantly recognizable mammoth fig native to the subcontinent, whose aerial prop roots regularly spawn into thick, woody trunks resembling their own groves of trees and thereby becoming indistinguishable from the primary trunk. Just like trying to track a single branch of a banyan tree to its core, when Buddhists or non-Buddhists traversed the Buddhist ecumene, they learned of other branches in the web of "complex global loops" (Jaffe 2004: 67) connecting the Buddhist world. In its lived and imagined form, the Buddhist ecumene not only became a significant connective tissue between India and the rest of Asia, but also offered new concepts and practices for understanding Buddhism, in turn transforming what it meant to be a Buddhist both in India and the world more widely.

While these kinds of commercial and monastic networks have long been at the center of Buddhist history, Buddhist social organization in colonial India moved in significantly altered directions. In pre-colonial times, Buddhist social affairs were often organized around the social and economic affairs of nearby monastic institutions (sangha).[10] However, most of these institutions had collapsed in almost all areas of the subcontinent after the fifteenth century, barring an outer ring from the northernmost Himalayas in Ladakh, Spiti, and Kinnaur, south-eastwards through the Kathmandu Valley, Sikkim, and Bhutan, and descending into the Chittagong hills and alluvial floodplains of Arakan. For Buddhist communities in these regions, the sangha played an active role in ritual and social affairs, economic life, and political organization. Their temples continued to be built throughout the second millennium CE. With that also came active networks of patronage and exchange that extended across regions, ethnicities, and languages and were typically characterized by geo-cultural corridors that linked Chittagong, Arakan, Burma, Siam, and Ceylon on one hand, and the Himalayas, Kathmandu, and Tibet, on the other. Yet, in those areas of the subcontinent where a living sangha did not already possess long-standing relations with local communities, Buddhist social organizations tended to follow models that had all the formal trappings of a "modern" urban voluntary organization.

In particular, from the 1880s on, a variety of new spaces were set up in urban India where Buddhists or Buddhist sympathizers could congregate, organize, discuss, and disseminate Buddhist teachings and practices. The first explicitly Buddhist groups to be formed were the Chittagong Buddhist Association (1887) and the Maha Bodhi Society (1891), but other organizations (*sabha, samiti, samaj*) modeled along similar lines soon followed. Near-simultaneous with the founding of the Maha Bodhi Society was the Calcutta-based Bengal Buddhist Association (1892), which continues to manage several branches and viharas across India to this day. In the south of India, the Shakya Buddhist Society (later South Indian Buddhist Association) was founded in 1898, experiencing incredible growth in the next thirty years before collapsing into a fraction of its former self by the time of Indian independence in 1947. Elsewhere, in places like Darjeeling (1907), Lucknow (1916), Agartala (1918), Bombay (1922), and Calicut (1925), many more Buddhist societies were formed before 1925; these too had limited lifespans, with some more enduring than others. By the time of Independence and Partition, there were well more than a hundred such organizations and affiliated branches scattered across West Pakistan, India, Nepal, East Pakistan, Sikkim, Bhutan, and Burma.

The brick and mortar of these voluntary associations—membership subscriptions, letter writing, editing, weekly meetings, and regularly scheduled events—was demanding work. Their leaders were often products of the new British schools, and like Max Weber's "notables" (*honoratiores*), they could typically "count on a certain level of provision from private sources" and "hold office by virtue of the members' confidence" (Weber 1978: 290). Participation in these associations had various interlocking components. Joining a Buddhist association, as Alicia Turner (2014) argues in her study of Buddhism in colonial Burma, was a fundamentally "modern" way of being Buddhist, although not entirely disconnected from the past. With their community events and even larger readerships—made possible through new print technologies—these organizations provided individuals a purpose and place within a wider imagined body of "unseen, unknown" Buddhists (A. Turner 2014: 144). Joining a Buddhist association, regardless of whether one's objectives were explicitly "religious" or not, could also be socially and economically pragmatic.[11] The most well-known Buddhist organizations in India, like the Maha Bodhi Society and the Bombay Buddha Society, provided valuable connections abroad and among the upper echelons of Indian society. Bright, hard-working members could rise through the ranks as treasurers, secretaries, vice presidents, and so on, learning critical managerial and secretarial skills easily transferable to other arenas of urban civil society. It is not surprising then that many such

Buddhist societies in India, particularly the Maha Bodhi Society, Bombay Buddha Society and, to a lesser degree, the Bengal Buddhist Association, were led by prominent national elites.

Yet, just like the other associations that formed the basis of urban civic life for Hindus, Muslims, Jains, Parsees, and Christians elsewhere in India (and the globe), Buddhist associations also helped flatten some long-standing social hierarchies. In the new milieu, religious authority was no longer just the providence of royal patrons, ritual specialists, and esteemed monastics. The powerful actors now were government clerks, editors, and educators who could compose an essay and have it printed on a paper, knowing that it might be read by thousands in just a matter of days.[12] Nonetheless, it is telling that most of these organizations arose according to clear class, caste, and demographic designs: just as reading societies and lending libraries developed primarily in urban centers, urban, English-educated, upper-caste Indians tended to dominate the new spaces where one could glimpse aspects of the dhamma. While there were exceptions, rural market towns and villages, while never entirely off the map, were slower to establish the kinds of spaces where locals or visitors could access Buddhist reading materials or encounter scholars and practitioners willing to teach them something of the Buddhist path. In many cases, as the following pages will make clear, these associations were not always so much Buddhist as they were enthusiastic about Buddhism.

Theosophical Currents

The professionalization and popularization of nineteenth-century Orientalist scholarship and archaeological studies stimulated public interest in the history and practice of Buddhism. Some of the most concerted efforts to promote awareness of Buddhism came from non-Buddhist organizations, like Keshab Chandra Sen's Brahmo Samaj. When Keshab's relative, Norendronath Sen, took over the popular Calcutta daily, the *Indian Mirror* in 1879, the paper became, as Steven Kemper (2015: 190) puts it, "a vehicle for propagandizing the Buddhist cause". Norendronath was not a Brahmo but a staunch proponent of theosophy, the latest religious movement to profess the unity and fusion of all the world's "Wisdom Traditions". In April 1882, when Norendronath opened Calcutta's first Theosophical Society branch, the American and German-Ukrainian founders of theosophy had been in India for barely three years. The American, Colonel Henry Olcott (1832–1907), was a retired officer, spiritualist, journalist, and prominent New York lawyer, who had served as a primary investigator in the Abraham Lincoln assassination case (Prothero [1996] 2011). His colleague, Helena Blavatsky (1831–91), was cut from different cloth (Johnson [1994] 1997; Washington 1993: 1–104). Born to German nobility, Blavatsky spent much of her youth living among the Kalmyk Buddhist tribes of eastern Russia, where her grandfather was a distinguished military commander. After marrying the vice governor of an Armenian province, Blavatsky moved among the imperial aristocracy in Tbilisi and Cairo. Around 1874, the duo met in New York for the first time and one year later founded the Theosophical Society in a Manhattan apartment.

With its ad hoc conglomeration of Darwinian science, phenomenalism, chemistry, mesmeric healing, and much, much more, this nineteenth-century hybrid religion can be challenging to define. For American and British working classes, theosophy's "do-it-yourself" (Cox 2013b: 173–74) form of spiritualism offered direct experience of the divine without priestly mediation; to "renegade Protestants" (177) it was a refuge from the prying eyes of the Church; to the eclectic and highbrow, it could be religious, scientific, neither, or both. On paper, the charter was simpler: the society sought the union of divine (*theos*) wisdom (*sophia*). Olcott was its "ethicist" and "organizer," and Blavatsky its "esoteric philosopher" (Prothero [1996] 2011: 51). Theosophy emerged at a time when Darwin's *The Origin of Species* (1859) had prompted many intellectuals to believe that materialist science would finally lead humanity away from religion and create a true heaven on earth. Although deeply influenced by Darwinian thinking, spiritualists like Blavatsky and Olcott believed that neither science nor Christianity could ever completely satiate human needs. Instead, one had to uncover the ancient wisdom traditions that underpinned all scientific and religious thought.

For the theosophists, the progenitors and keepers of this perennial wisdom tradition were a group of cryptic figures known as the Masters or Mahatmas. The identity of the Masters remains deeply contested. Some claim they were nothing more than figments of imagination. Others argue they were real human beings, or modeled after contemporary historical figures, at the very least. (For a review of the nearly century-and-a-half-long debate, see Washington 1993; Johnson [1994] 1997.) To understand theosophy and its pervasive role in the late nineteenth- and early twentieth-century world, two important features must be recognized. First, communication with the Masters was limited to Blavatsky, Olcott, and later, a small but growing number of "spiritual adepts" capable of accessing the "astral plane" where the Masters were said to sometimes dwell.[13] In other words, Blavatsky and Olcott, for all purposes, were the (un)official spokespeople of the Masters, and therefore, of the nineteenth-century theosophy more widely. Second, despite theosophy's theoretical universalism and appreciation for all Wisdom Traditions, the perennial truths the Masters expressed were deeply shaped by Hindu and Buddhist teachings. Moreover, the Masters themselves were almost invariably believed to be residents of Tibet, India, or Ceylon, and these lands were seen as the founts of universal wisdom. Needless to say, all Hindus or Buddhists did not agree with the theosophists' interpretation of their doctrines. But the theosophists argued that their understandings of those traditions were the "real" and "authentic" versions.

In a critical study of the Masters, as represented in theosophical literature, Paul Johnson ([1994] 1997) notes that this "cosmic hierarchy of supermen" (40) were most often portrayed as males wearing "Buddhist robes" or "dressed in Rajput fashion" (196). One of the most prominent Masters, Morya—or in theosophical parlance, "M"—was typically imagined as having one of three different identities: a Hindu ruler of central India, a Buddhist in Tibet, or a Nepalese Buddhist living in Ceylon. Other Masters, like the famed Koot Hoomi or "K.H.", were also widely believed to be Buddhists living in Tibet. None was likely to have been a real person but when Indian theosophists claimed to have met the Masters in the 1880s, they described the latter as wearing "Buddhist gowns" and living in Buddhist kingdoms (typically, Tibet, Sikkim, or Bhutan).[14] It is easy to scrutinize many of these encounters, but their historical value lies less in their factual basis than in their adoption and popularization of Buddhist imagery. For, not only was theosophy incredibly popular in the western hemisphere, it had a tremendous bearing on Indian national politics, leadership, and religious movements (Bevir 2003). Theosophical literature was widely distributed among elite Indian classes, and the fact that the Masters were often seen as Buddhist was of no small consequence. In theosophical circles, Indian "Brothers" and "Fellows" (as members of the organization were called) were instructed to dress in Buddhist robes and even take on Buddhist identities. In other words, there was a visceral component to the Masters' identities that located ancient wisdom and modern science—the fusion of which was theosophy's call to arms—in the idea of Buddhism. As Laurence Cox (2013b: 176) puts it, "not all Theosophists became Buddhists; but any serious member had to engage with Buddhism".

In India, the Theosophical Society (TS) found long-term supporters among a primarily urban, educated Indian elite. The institutional headquarters was always at Adyar, a leafy suburb of Madras where Olcott and Blavatsky built lodges, multi-denominational temples, and an outstanding library amidst a vast campus of banyan trees.[15] For Indians, who, by 1893, formed roughly three quarters of the organization's 3,500 members at more than eighty chapters (Datta 1904: 10; *Theo* Vol. 13, 1892: 20–33), the TS had two primary attractions: its anti-Christian missionary rhetoric and its message of Asian revival. The first of these themes, articulated everywhere from public platforms to Blavatsky's "textbook" on theosophical thought, *Isis Unveiled* (1877), allowed the TS to forge several unions with local associations that opposed the Christian missionary presence.[16] The second theme, of Asian revival, was framed in terms of what Olcott called a "National Samaj of Aryavarta" for India and a "United Buddhist World" for the rest of Asia. With the help of the TS, Olcott promised, "the ancient trunks of Indian Brahmanism and Buddhism" could be re-fertilized, "causing their hoary crowns to be once more covered with luxuriant leafage" (Olcott 1890: 2). Herein lay the primary difference between the theosophists and the Orientalists. Whereas (post-Anglicist) Orientalists saw in Asia's past a grand tradition of learning and excellence, they wished to preserve it in museums and believed the primary way forward for India was to adopt European modalities and epistemologies.[17] The theosophists, in contrast, were as Cox (2013b) describes them, "dissident Orientalists," who argued that a modern future lay in the *combination* of "Eastern" spiritual truths and "Western" material technologies.[18]

While theosophy's anti-Christian rhetoric and devotion to "Oriental wisdom" was able to mobilize broad levels of support, the devil, as always, was in the details. To begin with, many Indians resented the fact that Blavatsky and Olcott presented themselves as ultimate authorities on Indian traditions. As the Arya Samaj leader, Dayanand Sarasvati, asserted in a letter to Blavatsky less than one year after her arrival in India, "you had come here to become disciples, now you wish to become teachers" (Sarasvati 1987: 68). There were also internal differences and scandals (Washington 1993). Olcott envisioned a broad, inclusive society committed to a liberal theory of religious unity and social reform. Blavatsky, meanwhile, advocated for a small private body where a chosen few would be inducted into the mysteries of the occult. In her eyes, Olcott's activism among the poor masses was nothing short of a distraction. As Prothero ([1997] 2011: 117) writes, Blavatsky's idea of spiritual life was "individual rather than social: one labored to uplift *oneself,* not to uplift *others.*"

A more enduring issue was the complex set of international alliances that held together the TS's truly global enterprise. Theosophy looked different in different places, reflecting the outlooks and needs of its various constituencies. In Ceylon, for example, there were two main theosophical factions: the more popular Buddhist Theosophical Society (BTS), whose membership was mainly Sinhala and interested in Buddhism, and a smaller, "scientific" branch whose interests were mostly "occult" (Malagoda 1972: 246).[19] The Indian branches were also as diverse. In the Punjab of the 1880s, the TS was closely linked to the Sikh reformist organization, the Singh Sabha, whereas in Benares, it was led by a group of conservative brahmin pandits. Likewise, the first theosophical branch in Chittagong (est. 1887) was founded in conjunction with the Chittagong Buddhist Association and led by a coalition of Buddhist monks and laymen. The global composition of theosophy would have long-term effects on its Indian membership, allowing its Fellows from across the globe to transcend cultural divides in a fusion of anti-colonialism and appreciation for non-Christian traditions. Unlike the Brahmos, whose membership rarely included non-Indians, the theosophical commitment to universalism was made plain by its incredible linguistic, religious, and cultural diversity.[20]

Despite the TS's public commitment to pluralism, Olcott's private identity as a Buddhist and his prominent public reputation as a "defender" of Buddhist interests in Ceylon meant that the religion always possessed a cherished place. Articles on Buddhist doctrine were regularly published in *The Theosophist*, the monthly periodical (still running) "devoted to Oriental philosophy, art, literature and occultism" launched in 1879 with a circulation that reached six continents. In the journal's first two decades, numerous Indians debated fine points of Buddhist doctrine—albeit through their own theosophical lens—but with the belief that studying the "Arhat Path" of early Buddhism was essential for mankind.[21] Discussion on the Arhat Path was always relational, in comparison and conjunction with other religious paths. However, under Olcott's editorial control, the number of articles on Buddhism, including translations of Buddhist suttas, was always robust. While the commentary on these sources often came with limited or no understanding of the cultural context in which they were produced, their sheer availability and presence in the marketplace was a significant departure from the decades before. Theosophical writings were largely dismissive of contemporary Buddhist practices, perpetuating the view that present-day Buddhism was but a "brutalization" (Olcott 1890: 2) of its imagined original state. Nevertheless, these "scripturalist" attitudes often appeared alongside the writing of eminent Buddhist monks, who wrote not as outsiders but from firmly within the center of centuries-old Buddhist scholarship.[22]

When Olcott and Blavatsky first traveled to Ceylon in 1880, they were accompanied by approximately twenty companions, most of whom were Hindus and Zoroastrians from Bombay. At Galle, the entire party took *panchshil* ministrations from the erudite Buddhist monk–scholar, Hikkaduve Sumangala (1827–1911).[23] How these individuals understood their taking of panchshil under a Buddhist cleric and whether it entailed a change in identity, religious or otherwise, is difficult to assess. The writings of some of these figures make clear that there were differences between the various traditions, although the harder edges are often blurred. Although critical studies of individual Indian theosophists are lacking,[24] it appears that, for the theosophists, moving between religious identities was not problematic. All religions, in their view, were incomplete expressions of the truth. After all, the theosophical motto went, "there is no religion higher than truth" (*satyan nasti paro dharma*). Therefore, external identities like Buddhist, Hindu, and so on, were in principle secondary to the higher identity of a theosophist or one who seeks divine wisdom. Of course, these idealistic expressions of earthly transcendence were always theoretical, and the this-worldly logic of cultural politics and emerging religious nationalisms posed a grave challenge to the notion that theosophists could be both Buddhist and Hindu at the same time.

For the Maharashtrian brahmin, Damodar Mavalankar (1857–?), Hindu–Buddhist theosophy was as transformative as it was tragic. One of the earliest and most respected of all the Indian *chela*s, Mavalankar accompanied Olcott and Blavatsky on their travels across South Asia. After taking panchshil in Ceylon, he began calling himself a Buddhist, later adding the vows of a sannyasi and becoming a prolific writer of theosophical thought. Although Buddhist scholars would undoubtedly cast a scrutinous eye at Mavalanakar's interpretations of "Arhat philosophy," with its thick theosophical filter and Vedantic overtones, his writings on Buddhism remain valued among theosophists.[25] However, Mavalankar's theosophical journeys also cost him dearly, both in family and in life. In exchange, he found universal brotherhood in the international family of wisdom seekers. Yet, his ceaseless search for the Mahatmas led to his ultimate demise, and he disappeared in the winter snows of Sikkim in 1885.[26] Not all Indian chelas were so unfortunate. In Manohar Lall, a Hindu doctor from Bombay *mofussil*, who translated Olcott's *Buddhist Catechism* (1881) into Hindi and Gujarati no later than 1888, the organization found an energetic and enthusiastic promoter of Buddhism. "True" Buddhism, the text explained, did not admit differences of schools, sects, or beliefs. It was based solely on "scientific laws" and a "universal brotherhood" with "no taint of selfishness, sectarianism or intolerance" (Olcott [1881] 1897: 60).[27] This moral, scientific philosophy, in other words, was the *only* religion for the modern age.

By the mid-1880s, a considerable number of TS chapters in India housed images of the Buddha in their meeting rooms, as did some members in their offices. If Buddhism in colonial India was truly seen, as David Kopf (1979: 283) argues, as "a foreign religion," now, its most potent symbol, the Buddha himself, was returning to the soil. The TS secretary in Bombay, Tukaram Tatya (1836–98), for instance, kept an image of the Buddha in the Oriental Life Insurance office he managed, as did other theosophists in Nellore and Madras (*IM* 3 March 1885: 2; 7 March 1885: 2–3).[28] It is not entirely clear how these images were utilized—were they bathed according to Buddhist conventions, dressed with tilak according to Hindu customs, or simply commodities kept bare for aesthetic pleasure? Whatever the case, their possession and public display was a radical intervention in the material culture of India's religious marketplace. Some theosophists, like Kesava Pillai, a police inspector in Nellore, even began to don Buddhist robes and organize pilgrimages to Buddhist sites. After being instructed in a letter from Master "K.H." [Koot Hoomi] to dress in the yellow cap and robe of the Tibetan Buddhist Gelukpas, take the name "Chandra Kusho" (the latter being a term of respect in Tibetan), Pillai departed for a two-month journey in 1885 with similarly dressed theosophists through Sikkim and Bhutan. His reports from the journey published in the *Indian Mirror* show that neither he nor his companions were interested in learning from the Drukpa Kagyu monks, who, in the narrative, appear as little more than dangerous architects of "Black Magic" (*IM* 7 March 1885: 2). While Pillai's account fits well with common colonial travelogues of "exotic Lamaism," it must also be recognized that his account—printed in one of the most popular English-language newspapers in the country—must have created a kind of ethnographic curiosity about Himalayan Buddhism. At the worst, it may have led to further sneers and rumors about the "degraded practices" of the "Buddhist Bhotias" (although Pillai praised the Gelukpa for their use of "White Magic"). It could even have inspired readers to pick up more informed ethnographic accounts by intrepid scholars like Sarat Chandra Das or seek out Hindi- and Bengali-speaking scholar–monks like Lama Ugyen Gyatso.

The fact is, from the late 1880s until the mid- to late 1890s, there was a sense among Indians, be they TS members or not, that, were one to get involved in theosophy, one would have to get involved in Buddhism, for better or worse. That belief stemmed from three major factors. First, Olcott's personal preference for Buddhism over other religions intensified over the 1880s, and the almost legendary, Bodhisattva-like stories of the "White Buddhist," that circulated across South Asia, augmented that perception. Olcott's Buddhism became increasingly pronounced after Blavatsky set sail for Europe in 1885—she never returned to India—leaving the organization's administration entirely in his hands. Although she continued to contest Olcott's leadership, the TS was hereafter firmly under his control. With Blavatsky's effective exit, Olcott steered the organization towards his campaign for a "United Buddhist World", fashioning himself "into someone resembling Buddhism's Paul" (Prothero [1996] 2011: 130). Although Prothero is adamant that Olcott's personal commitment to Buddhism never interfered with his public activism on behalf of other religious groups, many of his contemporaries did not see it that way. The Hindu reformist organization, Arya Samaj, even circulated pamphlets in 1882 accusing Olcott of being an atheist, a Buddhist, or both, and instructed their followers to lead "street-corner denunciations" of these "faithless Feringhees" (quoted in Johnson 1995: 107).

Second, the nearly back-to-back publications of two major theosophical works, Olcott's *Buddhist Catechism* (1881) and Alfred Sinnett's *Esoteric Buddhism* (1883), only helped spread suspicions that theosophy was a covert form of Buddhism. The fact that Olcott traveled with an official document from leading Sinhalese Buddhist monks authorizing him to "register interested people" as Buddhists would not have helped ease religious anxieties.[29] Third, and perhaps most importantly, was theosophy's short-lived alliance with, and in many ways, creation of the Maha Bodhi Society.

Replanting the Bodhi Tree: Anagarika Dharmapala

Almost all histories of Buddhism in colonial India begin with the founding of the Maha Bodhi Society's Calcutta chapter. However, this was not India's first Buddhist organization. Instead, it was a society established in Chittagong, the breezy port city in today's south-eastern Bangladesh, that came first. When Krishna Chandra Chowdhury (1844–1910), a businessman and government inspector (*nazir*) in the Chittagong Land Reforms Office, established the Cattagram Bauddha Samiti, or Chittagong Buddhist Association, in 1887, he was working from within a social milieu touched as much by the Theosophical Society as it was by a resurgent monastic movement stemming from the Arakanese bhikkhu, Saramedha (1801–81/2).[30] With state support from Burmese kings desperate to stretch their influence over a quickly shrinking political orbit, Saramedha had made tremendous inroads among the Bengali-speaking Chakmas and Maghs (also spelt Mogs) of Chittagong (Charney 1999: 259–61; Charney 2002: 218–21). Krishna Chandra Chowdhury hailed from one such Barua community. Saramedha's Sangharaja Nikaya (est. 1846) and its supporters felt that Chittagong Buddhists—especially their "quasi-Buddhist" monastics (*rauli*)—were failing to uphold the moral precepts (*dasa-sila*) of the faith, worshipping the wrong deities, and desperately in need of "purification". Their "Buddhism" was at odds with the Pali-text-inspired modes of praxis propagated by the Sangharaja Nikaya and its Burmese supporters. When the Sangharaja Nikaya reformers gained the support of the most powerful native ruler in Chittagong, the Chakma queen (rani), Kalindi (r. 1844–73), Saramedha began organizing annual fairs honoring Shakyamuni Buddha, installing replicas of the famed Mahamuni image, and building the area's first Pali-language "model schools".

These events came to have significant influence on the Indian Buddhist world. From her royal court, Kalindi sponsored the translation of several Burmese and Pali scriptures into the Bengali language (Barua 1978: 273–74; Chaudhuri [1982] 1987: 32–36).[31] With Kalindi's death in 1873, these efforts to vernacularize the dhamma were taken up by figures like Krishna Chandra Chowdhury, who used the revenues and connections from his business offices in Calcutta, Chittagong, and Burma to build modern schools and sponsor the education of monastics and laity alike. Among his most successful dependents was Bhikkhu Dharmaraj (1860–94), a monk from the small Buddhist village in Raozan upazila, who studied Pali in Siam and Ceylon. After returning to Chittagong, Dharmaraj published more than eight Bengali translations from the Pali canon, including the *Sutta Nipata* of the *Khuddaka Nikaya* (1887), the *Sigalovada Sutta* (1889) and the *Digha Nikaya* (1889). These works were widely known among Bengali elites and Orientalists, and one of his most well-known works, a compendium of Buddhist rituals, *Hastasara* [*Handbook of Essence*] (1893), served as the Nobel laureate Rabindranath Tagore's introduction to Buddhism (Dash 2007: 84). Much of Krishna Chandra Chowdhury's success in bringing these texts to light and in securing funds for their publication was a result of not only his intimate connection to the Chittagong Buddhist world but also his

Anagarika Dharmapala at
the Parliament of the World's
Religions in Chicago, 1893

ability to navigate the wider colonial Buddhist scene.

When Henry Olcott visited Chittagong in 1887 on behalf of the TS, it was Krishna Chandra Chowdhury who paddled him upriver in an open canoe to Pahartali. There, Olcott delivered a lecture, while Chowdhury translated (*Theosophist* Vol. 12/3, 1890: 158). Two years earlier, Chowdhury had launched the first Indian journal aimed specifically at Buddhist audiences, the *Bauddha-Bandhu* [Buddhist Friend], published in Bengali and English. And right around Olcott's arrival, he established the Chittagong Buddhist Association, better known today as the Bangladesh Buddhist Association. Taking a two-year sabbatical from his government posting, Chowdhury followed in Olcott's footsteps, traveling across Bengal, Burma, Siam, and Ceylon in a grand venture to raise "voluntary subscriptions towards his very laudable object of raising his people through education" (158). Sadly, verbal support failed to translate into material gains, and within two years, the magazine went under. "Sympathy he received in abundance," Olcott said of him, "but shekels he could not get, even for the love of Lord Buddha" (158).

Despite these shortcomings, Chowdhury remained a pivotal figure among Buddhist revivalists. He was an honorary member of the first governing body of the Maha Bodhi Society in 1892 and participated in the famous Buddhist conference Olcott convened in 1891 in order to formulate his "Fourteen Buddhist Principles". Yet, just as these ventures were taking off, Chowdhury, and the Chittagong Buddhist community more widely, were eclipsed by the emergence of Anagarika Dharmapala. In May 1891, Olcott and a group of Buddhist leaders, including Hikkaduve Sumangala and Dharmapala, established the Buddha-Gaya Maha Bodhi Society [later, Maha Bodhi Society]. Its goals were explicit: to establish Bodh Gaya as a sacred center and pilgrimage site for all of the world's Buddhists and to gain control over the Maha Bodhi temple complex. Although Olcott was signed on as its director and chief advisor, with Sumangala as its president, the organization was effectively Dharmapala's fief. Under his management, the organization quickly replaced the TS and the Chittagong Buddhist Society as the new face of Buddhism in India, particularly for English-speaking publics.

Born as Don David Hevavitarana, Dharmapala (1864–1933) was the product of Ceylon's new upwardly mobile, globalized urban elite. The son of a wealthy businessman and philanthropist, Dharmapala attended Christian missionary schools despite his family's close relationship with leading Buddhist priests involved in Ceylon's Buddhist revival movement.[32] When the theosophists first came to Ceylon in 1880, Dharmapala was taken by their message. He joined the organization (against his parent's wishes), eventually gaining employment through their Colombo offices and traveling with Blavatsky to Adyar for the 1884 Theosophical Convention. It was during this journey that Dharmapala began studying Pali and vowed, "henceforth my life should be devoted to the good of humanity" (*MBJ* Vol. 41/4, 1933: 158). Other TS members viewed Dharmapala as a promising "Brother" on account of his elite social connections in Ceylon and commitment to the organization as the general secretary of Colombo's Buddhist Theosophical Society. By the 1890s, Dharmapala's dynamism and regular attendance at the boisterous Adyar conventions made him one of theosophy's most ardent activists, a role he played as Olcott's partner and protégé during meetings abroad in Asia, Europe, and North America.

Theosophical Society Fellows at the Adyar Convention, December 1884. Seated second from left in the front row, Norendronath Sen; fourth from the left, S. Ramaswami Iyer; to his left, Tukaram Tatya. Seated in the back row, third from the left, T. Subba Row; to his left, Damodar K. Mavalankar; and beside him, H.P. Blavatsky. Standing to the right is Col. Henry Olcott

The catalyst that set Dharmapala in a different direction was his first visit to Bodh Gaya in January 1891. Accompanied by two Japanese Theravadin "converts," Kozen Gunaratne and C. Tokuzawa, who had come to Ceylon to study Pali, he visited Sarnath and Bodh Gaya after attending the annual Adyar convention. Having read Edwin Arnold's quintessential lamentation of Bodh Gaya's degradation in *India Revisited* (1885), Dharmapala set off with preconceived notions about the mahant's callousness and mismanagement of the temple complex. Upon arriving at the seat of enlightenment, he refused to accept the mahant's hospitality, moved into the Burmese rest house that had been constructed during the Burmese Buddhist king Mindon Min's restorations in 1877, and left three months later. Back in Ceylon, Dharmapala devised a plan in consultation with Olcott and Sumangala to purchase the land surrounding the Maha Bodhi temple, restore the site as a non-denominational Buddhist shrine, and then draw Buddhist representatives from around the world to nearby rest houses. Bodh Gaya would become to Buddhists, he planned, "what the holy sepulcher is to the Christians, Zion to the Jews and Mecca to the Mohammedans" (*MBJ* Vol. 19/2, 1911: 349).[33]

The differences between Olcott's International Buddhist League and Dharmapala's Maha Bodhi Society were subtle, but significant. Olcott's Fourteen Point Buddhist Platform reached almost exclusively English-speaking elites and was representative of his Protestant emphasis on scripture and belief. Although Dharmapala's concerns were equally scripturalist, given the influence of both Christian missionaries and monastic scholars of Pali, his focus on Bodh Gaya, and India more widely, shifted his concerns away from text towards space. This move may have stemmed from his exposure and awareness of earlier efforts in Ceylon to "maintain and protect" Buddhism by restoring Buddhist sites that had experienced decline or were abandoned during Portuguese, Dutch, and British occupations. Furthermore, while Olcott's idealism envisioned a united Buddhist world, Dharmapala was more pragmatic, realizing that uniting Buddhist publics divided by sectarian, ethnic, caste, and class-related divisions would be a Herculean effort. Nonetheless, he settled for the still monumental goal of reviving Buddhism in India.

In the Maha Bodhi Society's first five years, Olcott and Dharmapala traveled widely to raise money and enlist support for their project. In Chittagong, Arakan, Japan, Burma, Darjeeling, and Ceylon, they found ready ideological allies, but the funds they collected frequently fell short of their goals. The Maha Bodhi temple movement was occasionally a rallying point in these regions, particularly in Ceylon. But local, not international, Buddhism was the mainstay here, except in moments of cultural crisis. In India, Bengalis, and Theosophists in particular, were the Maha Bodhi Society's first supporters, but like the situation abroad, most of the support came from a few well-connected individuals.

Three Bengali theosophists were especially important. Dharmapala's closest supporter was Norendronath Sen, the successful lawyer who acquired the Brahmo-owned *Indian Mirror* in 1879. Norendronath supported Dharmapala and the many Buddhists who passed through Calcutta in innumerable ways, lending his weight as a founder of the Indian National Congress, executive member of the India Association, representative in the Bengal Legislative Council and the proprietor of one of India's most popular English dailies. Then there was the Mukherjee family, led by the father, Neel Comul, and his only son, Neerodh Nath. Neel Comul was the secretary of the Bengal Theosophical Society and heir to a major petroleum company, and both he and his son generously provided housing and support to Dharmapala in the first two decades of his work in India. Such Bengali theosophists lent support almost unequivocally, despite having no interest in becoming Buddhists themselves. This stemmed more from a growing civilizational and national pride in the Buddha's "Indian-ness" as well as from the wider Theosophical, Brahmo, and Orientalist fetish with early Indian Buddhism.

Yet from early on, dissent was in the air. As early as 1892, many Calcutta theosophists began voicing concerns about their parent organization's connection with the Maha Bodhi Society, fearing that it was too closely linked to Buddhist politics and Buddhism more widely. Olcott and Dharmapala both tried to mollify these fears, delivering lectures on the kinship between Hindus and Buddhists.[34] Two Indian newspapers, the *Behar Times* and *Indian Mirror*, of Gaya and Calcutta, respectively, consistently supported Dharmapala, delicately highlighting the "Buddhist viewpoint" on critical issues, and encouraging readers to welcome Buddhists at Bodh Gaya. However, the friction between the two organizations only grew worse as the decade wore on. The first significant rupture occurred in 1896 when Olcott resigned from the Maha Bodhi Society and withdrew his support from the legal case that Dharmapala had by then raised against the Shaiva mahant of Bodh Gaya. Reports of Buddhist monks being attacked at the temple and antagonism from the Hindu press had made Olcott uncomfortable with the legal proceedings, which clearly pitted Buddhists against Hindus. While the Bengali press launched a vitriolic campaign against Dharmapala, castigating him as a missionary intent on destroying Hindu–Buddhist ties, his relationship with the theosophists also soured with the British orator, Annie Besant (1847–1933), rising as its newest star.

Besant's arrival in India in 1893 marked the beginning of a new tone for Indian theosophy, one where the differences between Buddhism and brahmanism were increasingly minimized and the Buddha's teachings took a backseat to the Vedas and Upanishads. In public lectures and popular essays, she asserted the superiority of the Vedas over the Pali *Tipitaka* and argued that the Buddha promoted caste divisions and the notion of an atman. A prominent freethinker and socialist, Besant's impassioned calls for Hindu revival earned her a tremendous following. She was even elected as president of the Indian National Congress in 1917, the political party that came to dominate Indian politics for the rest of the century. As president of the Theosophical Society from 1907 to 1933, her exuberant praise of "Hindu sciences" reinvigorated theosophy's place among the caste Hindu leadership; accordingly, her stance that Buddhism was "unsuited to India" was disastrous for Dharmapala's Maha Bodhi Society (Besant, in *MBJ* Vol. 16/9 1914: 144). By July 1898, Dharmapala was threatening Olcott that he would drop the word "Theosophical" from the Colombo Buddhist Theosophical Society if Besant did not change her tune. Olcott refused Dharmapala's demands, and the friction between the two men only worsened, eventually degenerating into a litany of slanderous articles regarding each other's organizational failures, character flaws, and faulty views. The final blow came in September 1905 when Olcott's abusive attack on the authencitiy and worship of the Tooth Relic in Kandy—one of Ceylon's most sacred Buddhist sites—effectively decimated the support he previously held in the island. Although Olcott continued to work on Buddhist affairs up through the early 1900s, particularly among the paraiyars, an "untouchable" caste in south India,[35] the TS–Maha Bodhi Society alliance was effectively rent in two.[36]

Venerable Kripasaran and the Bengal Buddhist Association

Like the Maha Bodhi Society, which struggled to maintain Indian support for its cause, other Buddhist organizations in India were experiencing similar fates. In October 1892, just thirteen months after the Maha Bodhi Society established its first Calcutta office, a twenty-six-year-old bhikkhu from Chittagong named Kripasaran launched the Bauddha Dharmankur Sabha or the Bengal Buddhist Association (BBA).[37] According to its charter, the BBA had five primary goals: "(1) to improve the social, intellectual, and religious status of Indian Buddhists, (2) to spread education among Buddhist boys and girls, (3) to promote a wider knowledge of the tenets of Buddhism, (4) to foster the study of Pali and Sanskrit Buddhist literature, and (5) to remove the difficulties and disadvantages into which pilgrims are put on their way to and from Gaya, Kusinara, etc." (*BBA* 1912–1913, frontispiece).[38] On the surface, these objectives were hardly different from those of the Maha Bodhi Society. In a similar vein, membership in the BBA was "open to all persons irrespective of their religious beliefs and does not imply any more than an interest in one or other of the objects of the Sabha or in its publications or other portions of its work" (*BBA* 1912–1913, 3). They also shared many of the same Indian patrons and, intellectually, they both projected Buddhism as more of a "science" than "religion". The two organizations were even located a short walk from one another in north Calcutta.

Nevertheless, there were distinct differences between them. Language and ethnicity were the most obvious ones. The BBA published almost all of its literature in Bengali, and its monthly journal, *Jagajjyoti* (Light of the World), launched in 1907 and still published today, was in many respects a Bengali-language version of Dharmapala's *Maha Bodhi*. The journal's target audience, however, was less the elite Bengali public in Calcutta than the Bengali-speaking Buddhists from Chittagong who had migrated across the subcontinent and were closely linked to the nineteenth-century reforms of the Sangharaja Nikaya in Arakan.

The group's founder and fountainhead, Kripasaran (1865–1926), embodied the clear differences between the two organizations.[39] Raised in a small village outside Chittagong city, Kripasaran was orphaned at a young age and placed under the care of local monastics. His parents were Barua "Maghs," the contested name given to those Bengali-speaking Arakanese who had migrated north of the Naf River into southern Chittagong after Burmese armies conquered Arakan in 1785.[40] As these populations resettled across Chittagong and other parts of Bengal, many Arakanese women married Bengali men, and the descendants of these families were known as rajbansis or, more commonly, Barua Maghs (*Census of India*, Vol. 6, Part 1, 1901: 156). Colonial administrators were long familiar with the Maghs— the Portuguese had immortalized them as pirates and slave traders—and in British eyes, they were hard workers, noted for their excellent cooking

Venerable Kripasaran,
the 'other' propagator of
Buddhism in Calcutta. The
Chittagongian founder of the
Bengal Buddhist Association

and egalitarian nature, which led them to be employed in cantonments as distant as Simla and Lucknow (*Imperial Gazetteer of India,* Vol. 6, 1886: 167–69; Vol. 10, 1886: 305–10).[41] Later, when the BBA expanded, their branches serviced these scattered Barua populaces.

When Kripasaran turned twenty (in 1885), he took his higher ordination (upasampada) under Candramohan, a respected elder of the Sangharaja Nikaya who had studied in Ceylon for four years and was well acquainted with northern India, having lived in Calcutta in the 1850s. A year after Kripasaran was ordained, he followed his preceptor to Bodh Gaya, where his biographers all proclaim that in a Dharmapala-esque moment, the young monk gazed at the Bodhi tree and swore to work for the glory of Buddhism both in Chittagong and elsewhere in the subcontinent.[42] By the early 1890s, he was renting a small house named the Mahanagar vihara in Calcutta, where the BBA was founded. The location of the office in Bowbazar was apt: a house occupied by Arakanese Buddhists, including Mahavir's wealthy sponsor Khee Zarhee, was located close by, as was a community of several hundred Baruas who could provide alms for the small monastic body.[43]

The early years of the BBA are murky, with reports that Kripasaran spent much of his time traveling across the subcontinent, often with Mahavir, visiting sacred sites in India (Chowdhury 2015: 34–38), collecting funds for his plans to build a vihara.[44] However, by the end of the century, the activities of the Chittagong Buddhists were well known to Calcutta's "worthy people" (bhadralok). When the BBA held its third annual Buddhist Assembly (bauddha sammilani) in Calcutta during 24–25 October 1902, Buddhist monks, lay Baruas, and caste Hindus gathered together "to promote the cause of Buddhism ... establish a universal brotherhood among the Buddhists," and "reform social conditions among them" (MBJ Vol. 11/7, 1902–03: 127). The nearly four hundred attendees heard recitations of various Pali suttas (such as the Mangala Sutta, Ratna Sutta, Jayamangala Gatha), commentaries in Bengali on the Dhammapada, Buddhist devotional songs (kirtan), and short lectures by local businessmen and Calcutta University faculty. Large-scale events like these only appear to have increased the stature of the BBA, and soon it was hosting the colonial state's diplomatic envoys from Buddhist countries. In 1905, when the colonial government orchestrated the Panchen Lama's state visit to India, the BBA's newly constructed Dharmankur vihara (completed 1903) played host to the Panchen's elite entourage of British officials, Indian scholars, Tibetan aristocrats, and incarnate lamas (Tibetan, sprul sku). Five years later, the Thirteenth Dalai Lama's name would be added to the list of major Buddhist dignitaries who had visited the society's headquarters (see Huber 2008: 268–90). To put this in historical context, this was fifteen years before the Maha Bodhi Society had even built its first temple in India. The BBA, in other words, was a centerpiece of Indian Buddhism, and its global importance was only later un-archived by subsequent generations of scholars fixated on Dharmapala's legacy.

Unlike the Maha Bodhi Society, which between 1906 and 1930 received more than three hundred thousand US dollars in donations from the wealthy Hawai'ian theosophist, Mary Foster, alone (Karpiel 1996: 184), the BBA possessed neither that kind of capital nor an international donor network.[45]

By contrast, in almost the same timespan, Kripasaran raised twenty thousand rupees through his preaching tours in India, Burma, and Ceylon (*BBA 1916–1917*: xvii).[46] A respectable amount, but paltry in comparison to the single donation of two-and-a-half times that came from Foster to the Maha Bodhi Society in just 1913.[47] While Dharmapala sailed around the world, delivering lectures, building schools and colleges, establishing relief funds for famine-struck areas of Bengal, and employing the country's best lawyers for his Maha Bodhi temple case, Kripasaran and his close colleague, the vice president of the BBA, Bhikkhu Gunalankar, approached local zamindars, Hindu royalty, and Buddhist merchants in north and north-east India. Comparisons aside, the BBA's fundraising was enough to purchase a small plot of land (five *katha*s, at a cost of about four thousand five hundred rupees) and construct the Dharmankur vihara in 1903, the *first* major Buddhist temple to be built in Calcutta since the Panchen Lama's Bhot Bagan (est. 1776).[48] They added a reading room, the Gunalankar Library in 1909, and a school, the Kripasaran Free Institution, in 1912, the latter of which offered free daytime classes for boys and girls, and night classes for day laborers. The temple complex still remains the headquarters of the BBA, and its new travel hostel has led it to recently join the rank of Calcutta's international backpacker scene, even being featured in *Lonely Planet*.

Many of the BBA's activities were supported by the provincial government and the many colonial officers who frequented the society.[49] Sir Harcourt Butler (later, governor of the United Provinces and lieutenant governor of Burma) and Asutosh Mookerjee, the high court magistrate and vice chancellor of Calcutta University, were both on the society's official list of patrons. Butler helped them acquire a free plot of land in Lucknow, where the BBA built the Bodhisattva vihara in 1907. Mookerjee, who proclaimed, "it is due to his [Kripasaran's] association alone [that] I was attracted to Buddhism and Buddhist literature," used the BBA's connections to Pali scholars abroad to bolster Calcutta University's program (*Hundred Years of the Bauddha Dharmankur Sabha* 1992: 23).[50] Under his watch as vice-chancellor (1906–14, 1921–23), which also coincided with his presidency of the Maha Bodhi Society (1911–24), Calcutta University developed a Pali language department (1907), making it the first university in India to do so, constructed a three-story hostel for Buddhist students (1915), and further developed the university as an international center for critical Buddhist scholarship. Kripasaran's links with governmental elites proved especially fruitful when the state offered a coveted scholarship for "the scientific study of Pali in Europe" to the organization's most promising member (DEEB, August 1914, Part A, 99–109). The honor went to the brilliant Beni Madhab Barua (1888–1948) of Chittagong. Barua used the grant to become the first Asian to earn a DLitt from the University of London, where he read Pali with the eminent scholar, Thomas Rhys Davids (1843–1922), founder of the Pali Text Society. Upon returning to Calcutta in 1918, Barua was appointed a full professor at Calcutta University, edited the BBA's monthly organ, *Jagajjyoti*, and established a reputation as an individual who could move between critical scholarship and religious practice with little problem. As the pride of the BBA, Barua's achievements very much became the society's achievements.

The question that has perplexed many scholars is why the BBA and the Maha Bodhi Society did not form a closer relationship when their goals were so seemingly identical.[51] Dharmapala and Kripasaran first met by happenstance, in February 1891 at Bodh Gaya, just months before the founding of the Maha Bodhi Society. Dharmapala was impressed by the young monk's ascetic devotion. According to his diary (DpD, 27 and 28 February 1891), Kripasaran cut his finger while making a vow to the Buddha, and sold his sandals and umbrella in order to purchase oil to light lamps at the shrine. Months later, while disembarking from a steamship in Calcutta, Dharmapala, again by chance, ran into him and some of his monastic colleagues. This time Kripasaran guided Dharmapala to his rented home, the Mahanagar vihara in Calcutta. "I came in his trap," Dharmapala reported in his diary (DpD, 15 July 1891), "and the priests walked down to a so-called Temple in Warris Bagh Lane," where Kripasaran coaxed Dharmapala "to purchase sundry articles for the priests". In the years that followed, the two had an off-and-on relationship. They attended each other's functions, shared the same Bengali Hindu patrons, and before Dharmapala acquired his own property, the BBA even hosted Maha Bodhi Society meetings. Yet, there were tensions.

One major falling out was regarding Kripasaran and Gunalankar's joining of the Buddhist Shrines Restoration Society (BSRS) from 1906 to 1910, which Dharmapala (justifiably) interpreted as a betrayal of his confidence. The BSRS was founded in 1906 and was the product of an incredible collaboration between European officers, Bengali Hindu elites, Sikkimese aristocracy, Japanese military officers and Buddhist priests, Tibetan lamas, and Chittagong Buddhists.[52] As the original prospectus, submitted to the Government of India on 6 February 1906, makes clear, the BSRS was nothing short of an intervention in the Maha Bodhi Society campaign in Gaya:

> You are no doubt aware of the fact that the state of affairs prevailing at Buddh Gaya has for many years past been a cause of dissatisfaction to Buddhists throughout the East … for some years past negotiations of a kind have actually been in progress … [they] have been conducted chiefly through the medium of a certain Mr. Dharma Pala, the President of that [Maha Bodhi] Society. But I must say here that Mr. Dharma Pala has prejudiced his own case by his *violent and uncompromising attitude* and by the *ill-judged nature* of his proceedings .… Mr. Dharma Pala continues his campaign, but he is discredited by Hindus and Buddhists alike ("Letter from Captain W.F. O'Connor to Secretary to the Government of India in the Foreign Department," 6 February 1906, FDE, April 1906, Nos. 104–06, emphasis added).[53]

As the minutes of the more than three dozen meetings held in Calcutta, Rangoon, Darjeeling, and Mandalay over the next four years recount, this was less a "secular society" than a broad movement of Asians and Europeans, Buddhists and non-Buddhists, who had lost faith in Dharmapala's leadership.[54] Both Kripasaran and Bhikkhu Gunalankar were working members of the association.[55] The BSRS continued to work independently of Dharmapala up until January 1909, when a final judgment was delivered in the court of the subordinate judge of Gaya, declaring that the mahant was the sole owner of the Maha Bodhi temple complex, thus bringing to a (temporary) close Dhamapala's fourteen-year legal case.[56] Significantly, just four days after Dharmapala received news of his devastating loss, the BSRS, in what must be considered a conciliatory gesture, invited him to join the society in what was to be their last-ever meeting.

The spirit of forgiveness appears to have prevailed, and in 1911, Kripasaran visited Ceylon on Dharmapala's invitation, and three years later, returned the favor, hosting Dharmapala in Chittagong during Vesak. Yet, behind the facade, class and cultural differences lingered. After leaving a function at the BBA in 1915, Dharmapala scribbled in his diary (DpD, 27 October 1915): "Came away disgusted seeing the utterances of the Bhikkhus there. They bring shame on the religion .... The low born Bhikkhus are responsible for the destruction of the Sasana." Dharmapala would later compare Sammana Punnanada, the BBA's resident monk, to Devadatta, the Buddha's murderous cousin (16–17 April 1917). Perhaps the only exception to his tirades was Bhikkhu Gunalankar, the vice president of the organization, whom Dharmapala eulogized as a "most amiable kindhearted man .... In his death Bengal Buddhists lose the best Bhikkhu" (27 March 1917). But when it came to Kripasaran, Dharmapala was more ambivalent. He (wrongly) called him "illiterate" but acknowledged that he is "respected": "He is a tower of strength. He does not know a word of Pali but he has got an active temperament" (7–10 September 1915). There was clearly an admiration for Kripasaran's accomplishments, but the immensely different worlds they had been raised in were likely too much to overcome. Kripasaran was the child of migrants and cultivators, raised among monastics on the fringes of Burman and British Empires. He spoke rudimentary English, the lingua franca of the cosmopolitan colonial elite, and it was his charisma and asceticism that earned their respect, not his social origins. Dharmapala, on the other hand, was part and parcel of the global elite, more comfortable in the imperial urbanity of Calcutta and London than among the "low born Bhikkhus" who made up the BBA.[57]

Iyothee Thass, Lakshmi Narasu, and the Shakya Buddhist Society

Dharmapala's ambivalent attitude towards the "low born" was equally visible in south India where the Banyan tree grew in directions radically different than in the north. Until the turn of the century, the region's Buddhist publics were centered around Madras, where organizations like the Theosophical Society, Government Museum, and Madras Literary Society hosted discussions on Buddhist doctrine and history. Most of these conversations, however, were filtered through the lens of romantic nostalgia and were scarcely interested in reinvigorating the *sasana* as a living force.[58] But in 1898, four years after Henry Olcott founded the Panchama Free Schools to educate the "depressed classes," he was approached by a teacher, P. Krishnaswamiar, from one of the schools, with a request.[59] Krishnaswamiar and his colleague, Iyothee Thass (1845–1914), a native doctor (siddha) born into a so-called untouchable caste (paraiyar), explained to Olcott that they were "originally" Buddhists and that if he helped build them a Buddhist temple "where they could worship according to their ancestral rules," several hundred persons would join (Olcott 1902: 24; Olcott 1900: 338–45).[60] By returning "to our old Buddhist Faith only in its primitive purity," Thass explained in an open letter, "we hope to restore our self-respect and to gain that right, to win by our own exertions, domestic comforts and untrammelled personal liberty of action, which are denied us in the Hindu social system of caste, under the weight of which we are now and for many centuries have been crushed into dust" (*MBJ* Vol. 7/3, 1898–99: 23–24).[61]

After some debate as to whether this would violate his oath as president of the Theosophical Society to not engage in proselytization, Olcott agreed[62] and by summer's end, he set sail for Ceylon, joined by Thass, Krishnaswamiar, Dharmapala, and the Sinhalese monk Gunaratna. In Colombo, the group was welcomed by the island's senior Buddhist authority, Ven. Hikkaduve Sumangala, and a large group of other Buddhists "highly excited" by the idea "that these two black men were the chosen delegates of an outcaste community numbering five millions of people" (Olcott 1900: 345).[63] Amidst cries of "Sadhu! Sadhu!" Hikkaduve administered the Five Vows (panchshil) and told them (in Olcott's rendition), "to remember that although they had been degraded to the lowest social level under the caste system of India, at the moment they became Buddhists all these arbitrary social distinctions were stript [sic] off their shoulders; they became freemen, entitled to their own self-respect" (Olcott 1900: 345).[64]

Returning to India, Thass and his colleagues started the Shakya Buddhist Society at Royapettah, a neighborhood in central Madras.[65] Like Thass, the other leading lights of the organization were part of a minority within oppressed caste groups whose social livelihoods had benefited from the new educational and economic schemes implemented under the British Raj. That is, for this small group of educated Tamils, the liberal promises of colonial modernity offered some vestige of hope through increased access to public spaces, employment, education, new technologies, and political representation. There were limits to these opportunities no doubt, but access to them helped give rise to new social publics where untouchables could more easily imagine a past, present and future that transcended conventional narratives of them as poor, polluted, expendable labor.[66] Thass, for instance, was an experienced organizer who long before turning to Buddhism had used a combination of journalistic publications, organizational bodies, and juridical practices to demand dalit access to education, public offices, and public wells and ponds.

In terms of its structure and mechanics, the Shakya Buddhist Society was not unlike other modern voluntary organizations (sabha, samaj) in South Asia: members held meetings and public lectures, oversaw Buddhist "conversions" (by administering panchshil), constructed temples, schools, and care facilities, conducted charitable work, led educational programs, and ran a publishing house. In its first thirty years, the Shakya Buddhist Society spread rapidly outside Madras in ways that can be clearly traced to the migration patterns of the marginalized castes it served: branches were opened alongside railway workshops in Hubli (1913), military bases in Bangalore (1907), mining camps in the Kolar Gold Fields (1907), and laboring fields in Burma (1909), South Africa (1911), and Ceylon (1924).[67]

Like all of India's new Buddhist societies (sabhas, etc.), the functions of the Shakya Buddhist Society were often held in conjunction with traveling Buddhists' arrivals from abroad. In 1908, the Irish bhikkhu, U Visuddha, officiated at the conversion of "1,000 workers and their families" (*Ceylon Observer*, 7 November 1908, quoted in Cox 2013b: 255–56) and installed a Buddhist statue inside the Kolar Gold Fields temple (Tamil, *viyaram*). At the nearby Champion Reefs branch, established in 1916, the Burmese monk U Kantha opened a Young Men's Buddhist Association Library in 1921 to instill "the habit of reading Buddhist works and journals and to inculcate good habits" (quoted in Perumal 1998: 536). Scores of other Buddhists from India, such as Dharmanand Kosambi, Bhikkhu Gunalankar (of the BBA), and U Tezzavamsa of the Burmese vihara in Sarnath, passed through its offices, teaching Buddhism and officiating at conversion ceremonies.[68] The German-American philosopher and Open Court publicist, Paul Carus

(1852–1919), even served as the organization's first president.

While its transnational presence is noteworthy and should be seen as part of the Shakya Buddhist Society's clear integration into global Buddhist networks, caution should be exercised in overestimating their influence. The nuts and bolts of these societies—management of properties and finances, drafting resolutions, etc.—were the domain of local Tamil functionaries and, therefore, largely outside the capacities of foreign monastics and other Buddhist enthusiasts who could rarely speak Tamil and were generally less commited to its radical hermeneutics, and fight against casteism. Nonetheless, the presence of monastics from distant lands played an important ceremonial and symbolic role, "authenticating" the activities of the Shakya Buddhist Society by linking them to unbroken lineages (*parampara*) that could be (purportedly) linked to the Buddha.[69]

Unlike those Indians who had joined Olcott in taking *diksha* (initiation) under Hikkaduve in 1879, the Shakya Buddhists were not theosophists and appear to have cared little, if at all, for the theosophical mission. They understood Buddhism to be fundamentally rational, humanistic, and egalitarian—standard fare in the colonial marketplace of ideas—but they also drew upon other intellectual developments in southern India, including the emergence of radical freethought and atheism.[70] Of equal importance was the fact that they did not see their turn to Buddhism as something new. Like the Cuttack weavers, and the izhavas and mahars of later decades who also "returned" to their "original" Buddhist faith, they understood their own (re)turn as a revival and restoration of a glorious Dravidian past, one in which the stigma of caste had yet to be pressed upon them. In reframing Tamil or Dravidian Buddhist identity in this way, Thass and his colleagus created what was in effect a collective identity and history for a people who had until then been understood as having no history.

To uncover the meanings of this rediscovered Dravidian Buddhist identity, Thass launched a highly original research project that challenged the "authorized" versions of history and reclaimed the past for the caste oppressed.[71] His methods involved a comprehensive and at times highly speculative rereading of sources in Tamil, Sanskrit, Pali, and English. On the basis of these works, he argued that paraiyars were the original inhabitants of India and that Buddhism was the pre-Vedic "indigenous" religion. Flipping the dominant colonial theory of the Aryan invasion on its head, Thass pushed the origins of Buddhism back several thousand years and argued that the mleccha (Tamil, *milechar),* an ancient term typically denoting foreigners or non-Aryans, were actually brahmins.[72] When the brahmins came to India, they violently supplanted the then reigning Buddhist kings, colonized their sacred spaces, and brahminized the histories to make it appear as if the Vedic traditions were the true autochtones. For their resistance, the "indigenous" Dravidian Buddhists were punished with the stigma of caste. The argument had some antecedents in the thought of other anti-caste intellectuals working in different linguistic registers, like Phule, as well as among some competing Tamil Shaivas and Jains. But this particular articulation of a Buddhist past derived largely from Thass's deep readings of ancient Tamil literature (Sangam) and his solid grounding in Sanskrit and Pali texts. His central thesis that caste arose due to the conflict between Buddhism and brahmanism would become the cornerstone of twentieth-century dalit Buddhist thought.

Thass communicated his ideas through his weekly Tamil-language periodical, *Oru Paisa Tamilian* (One Penny Tamilian) or *Tamilian,* founded in 1907.[73] The *Tamilian* covered diverse topics, but its core attractions were Thass's astute and shrewd essays on politics, etymology, sociology, philosophy, ethics, and history, nearly all in service of reconstructing Buddhism through a radical historiography. In serialized articles, the *Tamilian* argued that the Vedas were originally Buddhist ethical books, that many Hindu heroes had in fact been Buddhists, and that many popular Hindu celebrations, like Diwali, were actually appropriations of Buddhist festivals (Ayyathurai 2011: 101–27). At times, his writings were deeply polemical. In a four-part series he published in 1913, Thass asked rhetorically how Indian society could venerate books and gods that celebrate the rape of women (in reference to Krishna), the stealing of food (Ganesha), a property dispute that results in mass murder (Mahabharata) and the destruction of a nation (Ramayana). Hindu scriptures, he declared, "not only foster laziness and destructive qualities but make one live like a beast, not a human being" (*Tamilian,* 9 July 1913, quoted in Ayyathurai 2011: 29).

Thass's pointed criticisms of caste Hindu beliefs and practices were consistent with his political activities. He had long been engaged in the emerging swadeshi movement and was critical of the role Hinduism played in it. At a Congress convention in July 1891, he struck out at the hypocrisy of the so-called "Brahmin Congress" after they refused to pass his ten resolutions for the removal of caste distinctions. Having lost faith in the Congress, he cast his lot with the ruling British government, believing that the marginalized stood a better chance under them.[74] The political thrust that Thass instigated in the dalit Buddhist movement left an enduring mark, with its most obvious descendent being Ambedkar's Buddhist movement of the 1950s. Its politics also circulated widely among the urban poor of Lucknow and the izhavas of Kerala. For these figures, Buddhism possessed the potential to spark liberation and not just emancipation, to use Suraj Yengde's (2019) distinction. "Emancipation," Yengde writes, "puts all the onus on the oppressor ... [and asks the] oppressed subject to stand [pleading] before the doorsteps of emancipators" (87), while liberation has the capacity to free not only the oppressed, being generated out of their own self-will and determination, but also the oppressors from the trap of the artificial ideologies underpinning their exploitative practices (85–88). The liberatory message was spread via many other luminaries in the Shakya Buddhist Society, including M.N. Singaravelu (1860–1946) and Pandit G. Appadurai (1890–1961), but after Thass's death in 1914, the organization's leadership turned to the professor of science, P. Lakshmi Narasu.

Narasu (1861–1934), unlike Thass, was a product of colonial schools and the son of a prominent advocate in the Madras courts. He studied physical sciences, graduating from Madras University, and was appointed assistant professor of chemistry at Madras Christian College before moving to Pachaiyappa College in 1908 where he taught until retirement in 1924.[75] When Narasu became the president of the Shakya Buddhist Society, he augmented its broader social stature, opening new branches, delivering lectures at national conferences, all the while presiding over conversions and brahmin-free "reformed marriage" ceremonies (Aloysius 1998: 112–16; Narasu 2002: 210–23). He shared the gauntlet with Thass from the early days of the association, but, according to the sociologist G. Aloysius, their differences were significant. Although both men came from "backward" communities, Narasu's family had "made it to respectable positions in then colonial society" (Aloysius, in Narasu 2002: xv). He also knew English and

P. Lakshmi Narasu, the rationalist president of the Shakya Buddhist Society

French well, and his mastery of science "gave him access to the world not only of dominant knowledge but also the circle of men of consequence in the emerging metropolis" (ibid). These qualities lent a new edge to the Society's articulation of Buddhism.

A prolific writer, Narasu's English-language works were as well known internationally as they were among the Shakya Buddhist Society members. His *The Essence of Buddhism* (1907) was republished with a foreword by Dharmapala in 1912 and with a preface by Ambedkar in 1948, who called it "the best book on Buddhism that has appeared so far" (Ambedkar's 1948 preface, in Narasu 1976: ix). His other works, like *What is Buddhism?* (1916), had more than fourteen editions in addition to German, Japanese, and Slovak translations.[76] With his rational commitment, Narasu's interpretations of Buddhism were incisive and inventive, making the Buddha sound less like an antiquated sage and more an urgent solution to the world's problems. In thirteen quick-witted chapters, Narasu's *The Essence of Buddhism* ([1907] 1976) explained why the "Shakyamuni is not a supernatural founder" (xiii), how "moral ideas have nothing to do with supernatural beings" (23), and why caste is "quite noxious and therefore disregarded by Buddhism" (xiv).

Undergirding Narasu's gentlemanly demeanor and clear inheritance from European scholarship was a determination to not submit to anyone but himself.[77] Indeed, part of his attraction to Buddhism appears to have been its epistemological foundations, which, as famously expressed in the *Kalama Sutta*, emphasized reasoning and experience as the only source of knowledge and therefore set aside "all recourse to authority or revelation as worthless" (Narasu [1916] 2009: 21).[78] While some of his Shakya colleagues found his interpretations too "strange" and "scientific," his "alarmingly materialistic" interpretations of karma and rebirth did not sit well with the Maha Bodhi Society (Valisinha's 1946 "Introduction" to Narasu [1916] 2009: 14).[79] Writing from the perspective of the marginalized, Narasu refused to accept the idea that one's rebirth is a result of one's previous station in life, arguing, on the basis of the *anatta* (non-self) and *anicca* (impermanence) doctrines, that a sentient being's karma passes on to others in this life alone and remains preserved in them until that person's death (see, for instance, Narasu 2002: 119–26). For many Buddhists, such an idea reeked of nihilism.

Narasu reserved his harshest words for Hindus, but he did not spare the sangha either, seeing in it the same "obscurantism" and "dogma" he despised in other religions "unsuited" to the modern world. The criticisms were a constant source of strain on his relationship with the Maha Bodhi Society, which, through Mary Foster's generosity, continued to make donations to the Shakya Buddhist Society, including providing extensive funds for their construction of the Perambur Viyaram (vihara), completed in 1920 (*MBJ* Vol. 29/6, 1921: 218–22). By that time, the content of Narasu's "materialistic" and "sectarian" Buddhism was so at odds with the Maha Bodhi Society's mission that in its reporting of the Shakya Buddhist Society's second general conference, held in Bangalore that year, it censored key aspects of Narasu's presidential message. To give just one example, the *Maha Bodhi* omitted Narasu's declaration that, "Even the words of a Buddha are to be rejected, if they do not accord with reason."[80] Such literalist interpretations of the *Kalama Sutta* were too much for the Maha Bodhi Society to handle.[81]

Tensions had simmered for decades. Not long after helping establish the Shakya Buddhist Society in 1899, Olcott had quietly withdrawn his support, unconvinced of the "scriptural proofs" that Thass provided for his "original" Buddhist identity. Dharmapala was equally ambivalent, unable to find common ground with a social movement whose anti-caste commitments were a direct challenge to the network of caste Hindu supporters he had carefully cultivated over the past decade. Thass too had serious misgivings about the Maha Bodhi Society and even published a scathing critique of the organization in 1911 in which he accused it of promoting casteism (*Tamilian* 17 May 1911, in Aloysius 1999: 168–69).[82] In the four years prior to Narasu's death in 1934, the rift was palpable, and finances, as often in life, became the straw that broke the camel's back. In a civil court case filed against Narasu (only resolved sixty years later in the Madras High Court!), the Maha Bodhi Society claimed that the former had illegally occupied the Perambur vihara premises, that it was actually Maha Bodhi Society property, and that they deserved financial compensation for their losses.[83]

Colonial India in a Buddhist World

With their diverse origins, constituencies, and goals, it is tempting to see these different Buddhist associations as representing self-contained worlds. In some respects, this is a fair assessment and can also explain the many fractures in early twentieth-century Indian Buddhism. The Buddhist project at Kushinagar was effectively led by two Arakanese and one Indian, all of whom intentionally distanced themselves from the more boisterous, Anglo-centric approach of the Maha Bodhi Society. Similarly, both the Shakya Buddhist Society and the BBA were largely confined to their own ethnolinguistic spheres, mediated first and foremost by language, then by ethnicity and caste. For the BBA, the critical links were the Bengali language and the Buddhist Baruas of Chittagong. As in Chittgong, its primary aim was not to convert non-Buddhists to Buddhism but rather to cultivate and preserve a reformed Pali-language Buddhism among Chittagongian diasporas. For the Shakya Buddhist Society, the aim was the revitalization of an imagined egalitarian Tamil Buddhist identity. When these societies spread, their growth could almost always be traced along the migration patterns of their independent diasporas: those groups (either Tamil dalits or Baruas) who had been either involuntarily relocated by colonial plantation policies (Tamil dalits) and Burmese aggression (Baruas) or who had migrated as indentured or free laborers out of their own self-determination.

Despite the many divisions, whether of caste, ethnicity, language, class, and so on, their activism and interpretation of Buddhism stemmed from a common desire to revitalize the buddhadhamma. Like a banyan tree, whose different branches appear as separate trees while still stemming from a single trunk, India's early twentieth-century Buddhism was linked to a much more extensive web of changes across the globe. The period ushered in expanding education systems, international commercial networks, globally itinerant pilgrims, mass-produced copies of ancient Buddhist scriptures and original works, all of which penetrated deeply into everyday Indian life. It is sometimes assumed that dalits and other marginalized communities were not privy to this world, but the voices of the *Tamilian* and the emerging Buddhist world of the urban poor in other Indian cities is evidence to the contrary. International Buddhists may not have exercised much authority in the shaping of certain localized traditions, but they fulfilled an important function, creating the impression, imagined or real, that the beliefs and practices of disparate groups were part of a larger, unseen global Buddhist community.

Throughout the period that these societies were working to revive Buddhism among their respective locales, there was a current of communication, sharing, and borrowing across cultural and geographical boundaries. White Europeans and Americans, from both colonizing and colonized nations (such as Ireland), were flocking to India in search of alternative religiosities and bringing with them their own presuppositions and ideologies. Many of them were poor working-class "beachcomber bhikkhus," like the Irish Buddhist radical, U Dhammaloka (c. 1850–1914), and other cast-offs of empire—"the beggars, tramps, itinerant seamen, confidence tricksters, invalids, and ex-prisoners" (Turner, Cox and Bocking 2020: 157–58). Making up the bottom half of white colonial society, their engagement with Buddhism and other Indian religions alongside their substantial racial and ethnic intermixing with native populaces was a source of anxiety for colonial authorities (Fischer-Tiné 2009). Similarly, in Japan, there was an incredible surge of interest in the Pali scriptures that Southern Buddhists regarded as the purest form of Buddhism but which, for centuries, had been contemptuously dismissed by Japanese Buddhists as a "Lesser

Vehicle" (Hinayana). Some Japanese responded by calling for a return to "original Buddhism" (*genshi bukkyo*) or "fundamental Buddhism" (*kompon bukkyo*), and by the early 1900s, there were dozens of Japanese intellectuals studying in Calcutta and in Ceylon in order to revive the "purest, truest form of Buddhism" (Jaffe 2004: 87). At the same time that Buddhists from other lands looked to an imagined Buddhist India for inspiration, Indian artists and writers were seeing their own Buddhist past as a link to the rest of Asia.

The Nobel laureate, Rabindranath Tagore (1861–1941), and his nephew, Abanindranath (1871–1951), the "founder" of the Bengal School of Art, were both deeply shaped by the discovery of India's Buddhist past and East Asia's Buddhist present. In Buddhism, they saw a vessel through which to revitalize and redefine contemporary Indian art forms. While many factors guided their works, Buddhist ideas and historical art forms invigorated their artistic output. Through their friendship with the Japanese art historian, Okakura Kakuzo (1862–1913), the Tagores began working towards a pan-Asian artistic tradition that blended the shared aspects of "Eastern" spiritual and artistic culture (Bharucha 2006). In early works like "Buddha and Sujata" (1902), Abanindranath drew heavily on stylized representations of the Buddha in Japan and ancient India, and connected them to visceral scenes richly described in Sir Edwin Arnold's popular book, *The Light of Asia* (Ober 2021: 3). At the alternative college Rabindranath built in Santiniketan, he established a Buddhist studies department in 1922, inviting the French scholar, Sylvain Lévi, to head it and the Bengali artist, Nandalal Bose, to paint Buddhist murals on its museum walls.[84]

Yet it was Rabindranath's prodigious output of poems and novels, as the late Eleanor Zelliot (1979) argued, that, more than anything else, "placed the themes and legends of early Buddhism before the modern [Indian] public" (391). Beginning in the 1890s, he incorporated Buddhist suttas in his works, contrasting Buddhism's openness with brahmanism's vertical hierarchies and rigid mores. For Tagore, the teachings of the Buddha inspired a great sense of universality and were of tremendous relevance to what he saw as the modern malaise of greed, corruption, and wealth. Buddhist stories and themes permeated his writings. This included his popular collection of poems, *Katha* (1900), and the drama, *Acalayatan* (1912), inspired by the *Divyavadana*, to his late-period dance dramas, *Shapmocan*

(1931) and *Shyama* (1939), based on stories from the *Mahavastu Avadana*. For many Indians, particularly Bengalis, the Tagores were the pride of the land, and when Rabindranath and others talked of Buddhism with either the paintbrush or the pen, the nation listened. Their depictions, literary and visual, were mass-produced in their tens of thousands by lithographic printers and then distributed through bazaars. Like this, the ancient spaces of Buddhabhoomi entered ordinary homes and businesses, guiding modern India's Buddhist place-making.

Yet, the subtle fissures within these publics were notable. In one of Tagore's most famous performative works, *Candalika* (1938), based on a story about Ananda and an untouchable girl in the *Divyavadana*, the theme of the play revolves around gender and sexuality. But when, nearly two decades earlier, the esteemed Malayali litterateur, Kumaran Asan (1873–1924), retold the same story in his famed poem, "Candala Bhiksuni" (1922), the emphasis was on the oppressiveness of caste and the social prejudice against the young untouchable girl. Asan, an izhava of so-called "lower caste" origin, drew on Buddhist narratives to critique caste Hindu norms, while Tagore minimized themes of caste difference in order to accentuate themes of patriarchy and misogyny (Ober 2021: 12). Indeed, when Indians spoke of Buddhist revival, the question that was frequently raised was what kind of Buddhism this would be. Why Buddhism had disappeared was of equal importance, for, if it was so "ludicrously false" and "at war ... with the approved principles of the modern age," as one Bengali critic named Ram Chundra Bose (1886: 65) argued, then there was no reason to even consider its revival at all. The contemporary fetish for all things Buddhist, Bose declared, was "one of the queerest freaks of the nineteenth century" (65).

There were many who criticized Buddhist revivalism, but among those who supported it, its global currency was obvious. Although the term Theravada had not yet come into full provenance (Perreira 2012), the influence of Theravadin or "Southern" traditions, on the debate was profound. In their selective reading of the past, that still holds sway in much of the world today, Buddhist apologists and a battalion of Orientalist scholars argued that Pali traditions, on account of their antiquity, were more faithful to the original teachings of the Buddha and thus represented the purer, more "scientific" and rational aspects of the tradition. While dissenting Mahayana voices, like those of the Japanese scholars Nanjo Bun'yu (1849–1927) and D.T. Suzuki (1870–1966), argued otherwise, Indian Buddhist enthusiasts largely privileged a selective Pali canon. Pali scriptures were considered a "garden of aesthetic delight" (*MBJ* Vol. 25/5 1917: 105), far superior to the netherworld of deviant tantriks and mystics awash in the "Mahayana mist," as P.C. Bagchi called it (*MBJ* Vol. 37/10 1929: 509–10).[85] After India lost its knowledge of "pure" Buddhist teachings, science and morality had decreased: it had become a topsy-turvy place, "a vast insane asylum" where "boys of twelve years are married to young girls of two years; and girls of fourteen years are married to men of fifty years" (*MBJ* Vol. 13/5–6, 1904–05: 45). From Thass and Narasu to Dharmapala and Kripasaran, all believed that the Buddha was the only doctor who could treat India's sickness. The problem was that they often disagreed about the nature of his prescription.

According to the anthropologist Arjun Appadurai (1990), globalization's inherent tension between homogeneity and heterogeneity is only resolved through local agency. When locals lose control, problems emerge. Local agency, therefore, is what prevents that tension from rupturing. If Appadurai is right in this contention, it explains well the differences within the Indian Buddhist ecumene. What pressed on Kripasaran's mind were the serious nikaya divisions cutting across Ceylon, Burma, and Siam. Born and bred in the monastic world, this was an issue dear to him, and in 1924, he called a major meeting (*bauddha mahasammelan*) of two hundred monastic leaders to attempt a reconciliation of Vinaya differences and bring unity to the sangha.[86] But such issues mattered less to men like Thass. What drove his activism was the desire to eradicate the inhumane violence of caste in which so many of his peers languished. His vision, although cosmopolitan at heart, was trans-regional in its aim and defined largely by the cultural and linguistic "meaning-making enterprises" of the Tamil hermeneutic tradition (Rajangam 2018). For Dharmapala, the problem was the very divisive past that underlined contemporary Buddhism as a global unit or "world religion". Sri Lankan Buddhism, in his time, was riven by nikaya and caste-based divisions. In Japan, he witnessed how sectarian differences had led to unresolvable cleavages in the sangha. Like Olcott before him, he never gave up his vision of a united Buddhist world, forging ahead with a new International Buddhist Union in 1920. Although its members included representatives from more than twenty-nine countries, the "bond of union ... between all existing societies and individual Buddhists throughout the world" (*Buddhist Review* Vol. 12/1, 1922: 2–7) collapsed in less than three years. A decade later, the Chinese intellectual and monk, Taixu, would travel the globe in his own grand venture to unify Buddhism (Pittman 2001).

For many colonial-era Indians, the deep history of Buddhist tradition, while grand and admirable, also seemed burdened by its unique complexities. To revive it, it had to adapt to contemporary conditions. Narasu believed the sangha had to change and become more socially engaged. Dharmapala proposed a new semi-renunciate order of lay people, the "Order of Homeless Ones" (*anagarika*), to expand its social footprint. The Bombay Buddha Society (est. 1922), still living in the shadow of theosophy, attempted to circumvent the monastic sangha altogether by redefining the Three Refuges it recited at the beginning of chapter meetings: they proclaimed: the "human race is one family," and the sangha was any "brotherhood of man" (*MBJ* Vol. 36/8, 1928: 400–05).[87]

The most glaring absence in the new Indian conversations and encounters with Buddhism is the lack of women. It is possible that the membership of the various Buddhist associations was less exclusively masculine than the archives indicate, but female Buddhist leaders or writers in India were few and far between. The Bombay Buddha Society was for some time led by Sophia Wadia (1901–86), a Colombia-born naturalized Indian theosophist, who moved to India after marrying B.P. Wadia, a prominent labor activist and theosophist.[88] Likewise, the annual reports of the BBA note special meetings convened by the "Buddhist women of Bengal" and describe the formation of a Buddhist Women's Society (Satbaria Bauddha Mahila Sammelani) in Chittagong in 1917, but their ideas and activities are obscure (*BBA* 1916–17).[89] Similarly, among the members of Shakya Buddhist Society of southern India, there was a "Buddhist Women's Association" in Champion Reef (Aloysius 1998: 94). Thass's *Tamilian* ran an exclusive "Ladies' Column" in which men *and women* wrote on topics like education, child marriage, sex, and widowhood. One of its leading contributors was C.S. Ambal, the editor of a women's magazine, *Tamil Maadu,* and manager of a widow's home (Ayyathurai 2011: 73–74, 196–204). Signing off as Swapneswari, this self-proclaimed "Universal Sister" (*sarvajana sakotiri*) encouraged "women to become their own agents of change" and "to pursue creative living that would make them happy and inspire young girls" (74). A critic of Indian patriarchy, she alerted readers to society's double standards, stating plainly that "men get away with no reprimand irrespective of the damages of their actions, whereas women even if their action is equal to a mustard seed, the society makes a mountain out of a mole hill" (198). Although the *Tamilian* promoted women's educational achievements, printing news of women's scholarships and lamenting pitiable data on widows and on child marriage, its advocacy of female education, like Swapneswari's herself, was always within the framework of being a homemaker and making women's lives more tolerable, rather than equal (197). By today's feminist standards, this may fall far short, but it can also be said to have opened up the floor for later critical feminist takes on Buddhist misogyny and Indian patriarchy.

These fleeting records do make clear that strong women were able to move beyond normalized gender roles. Without further digging in the archives, however, one can only speculate as to why women were not more active. Civil society in colonial India reproduced patriarchal practices, and women were typically barred from holding major public roles (Sangari and Vaid [1990] 1999). Not only did this pose significant challenges for women attempting to enter already male-dominated voluntary associations, but it must also be acknowledged that the social costs of public conversion or affiliation with Buddhism would have likely been more severe for them. The public, then as now, was far more rigorous in policing women's lives than men's, as the "Universal Sister," C.S. Ambal, bravely pointed out. Ambal was, of course, not alone. Other early Indian "feminists" include Savitribai Phule (1831–97) and Pandita Ramabai (1858–1922). But for any Indian woman, regardless of caste, class or religion, the penalties for affiliating with an alternative religion (dharma) like Buddhism were considerable.

Women's voices may have been largely absent, but men, as usual, attempted to speak of and for them. Narasu ([1907] 1976) admitted that while "theoretically man and woman are placed by the Buddha on the same footing of equality ... in practice the latter stands much lower" (92). He blamed the situation on later brahmanical influence, arguing that works like the *Therigatha,* or poems of the ancient *bhikkhuni*s (nuns) were evidence not only of the "high intellectual achievements" of women, but also the early Buddhist revolt against gender inequality (89–96).[90] Like many Buddhist apologists of the period, Narasu resorted to contemporary tropes about women in Burma, and to a lesser degree Japan, as evidence of what could have transpired had India only *remained* Buddhist. For decades, colonial officials had waxed eloquent on how women in Burma appeared more "refined" and possessed greater social status than women in European countries (A. Turner 2014: 46–49). Although much of this was based purely on sentiment, reports filed by colonial statisticians and ethnographers were music to the ears of Buddhist revivalists. For many Indian Buddhists, what was of considerable importance was the role of Burmese women in these tabulations as opposed to Hindu women. According to the General Report of the Census of India in 1911 (published 1914), Burmese Buddhist women did not marry, on average, until between the ages of twenty to thirty as compared to more than two-thirds of Hindu women who would be married by the age of ten (276). After reading figures like these, polemicists like Narasu would proclaim, "[In Burma], women do not hide behind veils and shun the street as a pest. The Buddhist law favours equality with the sexes, while the Hindu law enjoins the complete subjection of the wife to the will of her husband .... Infant marriage and enforced widowhood are eating the very vitals of Hindu society" (Narasu [1916] 2009: 82). In an environment where issues like child marriage, widow remarriage, education, and caste discrimination were the pressing concerns of social reformers, Buddhism in its idealized, imagined form ruled the roost.[91]

While men's comparisons of women's bodies in Buddhism with other religious traditions never ceased, it was only a single intersection in what was a much larger discussion about the relationship between Hinduism and Buddhism. Such conversations had existed for centuries, but with the rise of anti-colonial Buddhist politics in Asia and anti-colonial Hindu politics in India, the discussion took on new tones.

4

Brahmanizing Buddhism

During the Seventh Session of the All-India Hindu Maha Sabha [hereafter, Maha Sabha] at Benares on 19 August 1923, the Sinhalese Buddhist founder of the Maha Bodhi Society, Anagarika Dharmapala, explained to a crowd of six thousand people why "Buddhists were also Hindus". Established in 1915, the Maha Sabha was a right-wing nationalist outfit that aimed to unify the disparate Hindu organizations across India. The audience that heard Dharmapala's speech in August 1923 was by all accounts thrilled. The event was widely covered in the national press. As the Calcutta newspaper, *Amrita Bazar Patrika,* reported:

> Mr. Anagarika Dharmapala of Ceylon … [said] the Buddhists … were all Hindus (cheers). Some might call them un-Aryan ("no", "no",) but Buddhists crossed the seas, taking Hindu civilization with them to Japan and China and made them Aryans … 90 percent of Hindus and Buddhists were converted into Mussalmans ("shame"). They must all be brought back into Hinduism ("hear", "hear"). In Kashmir, several Buddhists have become Mussalmans and they must all be reconverted ("hear", "hear") (*ABP*, 31 August 1923, in HDPB, File no. 198, Part B).[1]

After Dharmapala finished his speech, the Hindu publicist, Congress politician, and recently elected president of the Maha Sabha, Pandit

Madan Mohan Malaviya (1861–1946) reaffirmed Dharmapala's sentiment: "Buddhism, Jainism and Sikhism were only separate sects of this great religion [Hinduism] ... Buddha did not preach a separate religion, but only emphasized some aspects of Hinduism according to the needs of the time" (*The Leader*, 22 August 1923, in HDPB, File no. 198, Part B).

Since establishing the first Indian branch of the Maha Bodhi Society thirty-one years before, Dharmapala had offered a wide range of propositions regarding Hindu–Buddhist relations. In his first public lecture at Calcutta's Albert Hall on 25 October 1891, he argued there was no difference between the two systems of thought (Kemper 2015: 191). In the late 1890s, he wrote several essays arguing that the great scholar of Vedanta, Shankara, was in fact a Buddhist (Dharmapala 1898–99, 1899–1900a, 1899–1900b). A decade later he recanted, asserting that Shankara burned Buddhist scriptures and massacred Buddhist bhikkhus (*MBJ* Vol. 18/3, 1910: 412–15). That same year, his essay, "The Creed of Buddha", concluded that, "the philosophy of the Upanishads has no more to do with Buddhism than the principles of Evolution with the Mosaic Bible and the Synoptic Gospels" (*MBJ* Vol. 18/5, 1910: 462–65). Only a few years after taking the stage at the Maha Sabha convention, he would argue that there was no such thing as Hinduism at all (*MBJ* Vol. 33/6, 1925: 284–87). In the grand scheme of things, Dharmapala's views on Hindu–Buddhist relations reveal no underlying rationale. Rather, he was closely attuned to cultural winds and exploited every opportunity, either towards amity or antagonism, as he felt would best strengthen his case to reclaim the Maha Bodhi temple. A pragmatist to the end, Dharmapala "presented a distinctive Buddhism for every constituency" (Kemper 2015: 30).[2]

The great Indian minds that Dharmapala encountered in his lifetime also offered similarly complex representations of Hindu–Buddhist relations. However, in the nineteenth century, there was a palpable shift in the popular Indian attitude towards the Buddha. This is best illustrated by the difference between Subaji Bapu's polemical response to the *Vajrasuchi* in 1839 where he castigates Buddhist doctrines for their anti-brahmanical impulse, and Sivaprasad's *Itihas* in 1874, where the same anti-caste, anti-brahmanical ethos is praised, and the Buddha appears as a liberator of the downtrodden. At the end of the nineteenth century, the idea that Buddhism was antagonistic to the brahmanical world, became less relevant, and a new interpretation and understanding of Buddhist–brahmanical (Hindu) relations emerged. As the Bengali historian, R.C. Dutt (1893), argued at the Buddhist Text Society of India in 1893: "the cardinal tenets of Buddhism, the doctrine of *nirvana* and the doctrine of *Karma* were directly derived from Hindu ideas and Hindu practices and Buddhism was the offspring of Hinduism" (ix). The notion that Buddhism was a branch of Hinduism remains entrenched in popular Indian culture, and only in recent decades have some Indologists been more forceful in the argument that *shramana* traditions, like early Buddhism, developed in a place and time largely free of brahmanical influence.[3]

To many scholars writing today, the question of the Buddha's "Hindu-ness" may seem absurdly anachronistic. After all, the word Hindu did not register as part of a more common South Asian vocabulary until some 1,800 to 2,000 years after the historical Buddha's death. Even today, the idea that the historical use of the term had any specific religious implications remains a matter of intense debate (Lorenzen 2006; Bloch, Keppens and Hegde 2009; Nicholson 2010). In many ways, the question can be seen as a product of the colonial era, inextricably tied to the birth of the modern nation and intellectual assimilation of the subcontinent's religions into the world religion paradigm. That paradigm, which crystallized in the late nineteenth century through initiatives like the World Parliament of Religion in Chicago in 1893, established new avenues for thinking about the historical relationships between religion—itself a socially constructed category—but while it made important steps to include non-Christian traditions, it ultimately remodeled them according to Protestant Christian values (Masuzawa 2005). The urgency and seriousness with which modern Indian thinkers dwelt on these matters however, cannot be solely reduced to the wider intellectual apparatus of colonial modernity and its attempt to make sense of a vast history through new umbrella concepts like Hinduism and Buddhism. The issue of the Buddha's "Hindu-ness" was also driven forth by the politics of the moment. There were domestic concerns, the rising tide of internationalism, transnational religious networks, and the desire—perhaps even need—to craft a space, a home, for India in an Asia that was so often imagined in a Buddhist guise. But before attending to those issues, it is useful to set aside our insistence on historical accuracy and ask ourselves in what ways we can understand the Buddha's "Hindu-ness"? All labels, it should be remembered, are inexact, and like in Borges's (1948: 325) story, the only accurate label is the one which is exactly as broad as the territory it maps. Nevertheless, it is useful to think through such problems.

Historians tell us that the popular usage of the term "Hindu" began only in the middle centuries of the second millennium (Lorenzen 2006). Earlier uses were largely geographical or cultural in sense, suggesting that anyone who is born and lives in Hind or Hindustan (India) was a "Hindu". For some, the term was used to distinguish between those residents of the subcontinent who were Muslim and those who were not (kafir), between those who were of Turkic or Persian heritage and those who were not. Although it is an anachronism, in this purely geographical mode, the Buddha can be called a Hindu. But the use of a socio-religious term, which is how the modern-day issue of the Buddha's "Hindu-ness" is most often posed, for geographical indication is deeply problematic. Even as late as the nineteenth century, there were many prominent Indians who opposed the use of the term "Hindu" to identify themselves, seeing it as of mleccha origin and less meaningful than terms like Sanatan Dharma, Vaidika Dharma, or Arya Dharma. But by the beginning of the twentieth century, the religious sense of the term Hindu had gained widespread currency, used primarily to denote those who followed the Vedic brahmanical tradition, that is, the followers of Vaishnavism, Shaivism, Shaktism, or a mélange of different traditions shaped by Puranic or Vedic elements.[4] What do these "Hindu" traditions have to say about the Buddha or Buddhists?

In the main, it is rare to find the Buddha praised as a master of any major Hindu tradition, be it Vaidika, Vedantika, Shrauta, Smarta, Vaishnava, Shaiva, or Shakta (Joshi 1983). Only some thousand years after the Buddha's death do arguments regarding his "Hindu-ness," or perhaps something akin to that notion, begin to surface.[5] By the fourth and fifth centuries CE, works like the *Vishnu Purana* begin claiming the Buddha as an avatar of Vishnu, an incarnation that descends to the earthly realm as a teacher of false propaganda. He deceives the demons (daityas) that have been wreaking havoc in the universe as a purveyor of delusion (mayamoha). By accepting his false teachings, they become weak and fragile, vulnerable to the next

Vishnu incarnation, Kalki, who is to descend to the earth to annihilate them. Some later Hindus appear to have been more concerned with rehabilitating this loathsome picture of Vishnu's Buddha avatar. Jayadeva's *Gita Govinda* (tenth century CE), for instance, praised the Buddha-avatar for his loving kindness and non-violence towards animals. But in most brahmanical Hindu literature, the Buddha was stigmatized as a destructive misfit and a menace to society. Along the same lines, Buddhists were seen as no different from other materialists and nihilists (nastika, Vainashika, Lokayata, Carvaka), all of whose teachings were to be avoided. Buddhists, it appears, were considered, by orthodox Hindus at least, as disavowers of the Vaidika Dharma or Sanatan Dharma.

At the time that Europeans began unearthing Buddhist ruins and commissioning pandits to translate Buddhist texts and read ancient inscriptions, this adversarial attitude towards the Buddha and Buddhists was still part of living Hindu discourse. In many areas, the word Buddhist even appears to have become a term of colloquial insult and derision (cf. Rao 2008: 96; Pullapilly 1976: 30).[6] And yet, a rather extraordinary shift in this nearly two-and-a-half-thousand-year-old attitude towards Buddhism occurred in the late nineteenth and early twentieth centuries. By the time of Indian independence in 1947, most Hindus would no longer see the Buddha or Buddhists as separate from their own esteemed tradition, but as integral to it, a fundamental thread in the fabric of the imagined Hindu nation. This change coincided with the meteoric rise of Buddhist studies in late nineteenth century India, which happened in the context of emerging global debates about the importance of ethics, the creation of world religions, and the place of India in world history, especially vis-à-vis a purportedly superior and more civilized Western world. The political stakes of India's rediscovery of Buddhism, in other words, was high. It offered a radically new vision of the subcontinent's past, of what the modern nation might symbolize, and of what it meant to be modern in the first place.

As Indian elites began rethinking the Indian past through the lens of discrete religious entities like Hinduism and Buddhism, they put forth a variety of theories on the relationship between the latter two. While the first generation of Indian Orientalists like Rajendralal Mitra and Haraprasad Shastri tended to see Buddhism and brahmanism in opposition to one another, by the turn of the century, a new generation of scholars saw brahmanism in all things Buddhist. These theories were actively supported by a number of prominent European scholars. T.W. Rhys Davids, the founder of the Pali Text Society, for instance, saw brahmanical and Buddhist histories through the prism of the Judeo–Christian past. Dismissive of the notion that the Buddha had been raised in a non-brahmanized culture, Rhys Davids cast the Buddha as a Jesus-like figure who was born a Jew (read: Hindu) and utilized his Jewish (Hindu) religious inheritance to formulate a distinctive vision of the Kingdom of Heaven (moksha), leading him to famously declare, "The Buddha was born, and brought up, and lived, and died a Hindu" (1877: 83).[7] While the scholarly verdict on the Buddha's Hindu-ness was very rarely one-sided with much of the debate hinging upon the dating of critical texts, many popular Hindu leaders were less agnostic about the matter. As is so often the case, the popularizers and politicians dominated public discourse.

The beginnings can be traced to the Brahmos and theosophists, but at the turn of the century the Hindu Buddha found his most charismatic champion in the immensely popular Hindu mystic, Swami Vivekananda (1867–1902). In Vivekananda's eyes, the Buddha was one of the greatest teachers of Hinduism's universal thought and the very pinnacle of human compassion, with his loving kindness radiating in all directions. "The Lord Buddha is my Ishta—my God. He preached no theory about Godhead— He was Himself God. I fully believe it" (Vivekananda 2016: 227). During a decade-long love affair with the Buddha, Vivekananda pitched him as the ideal *karmayogi*, the only real vedantin, a great Hindu reformer, the greatest teacher of Hinduism, and most famously, its "rebel child," all the while appropriating Buddhist teachings as part of his universalizing Hindu mission, arguing that Buddhists themselves had corrupted the message of the Compassionate One (Joshi 1983; Holt 2005; Sharma 2013).[8] As Vivekananda's intellectual footprint expanded over the coming decades, his refashioning of the Buddha into the mold of the "ideal Hindu" gripped the imaginations of Hindu thinkers and the nationalist elite across India.

Nationalizing Hinduism and Hinduizing Buddhism

In the early decades of the twentieth century, the Hindu–Buddhist conversation gained new relevance as archaeological discoveries, relic diplomacy, and Dharmapala's public campaigns to gain ownership of the Maha Bodhi temple elevated Buddhism's profile at national and imperial levels (Ray 2014). While these factors alone helped arouse the interest of Hindu intellectuals, there were also more systemic issues related to the emergence of Hindu nationalism and modern Hinduism that were equally important in their engagement with Buddhism. The wider context for these new developments was the rise of Hindu organizations (sabha, samaj, etc.) as the premier means through which "representative communities" accessed the state and voiced "public interests" (Jaffrelot 1996; Hansen 1999; Jones 2006). Although these organizations had made up Indian civic life for more than a century, they truly blossomed after the 1910s when constitutional reforms introduced by the colonial government instigated a new "politics of numbers" (Hansen 1999: 44). Popular franchise was expanded at the local and provincial levels and electorates based on religious identities became crucial in political governance. Under this new scheme, Hindu leaders quickly realized that demographic majorities based on census classifications were key to amassing political power. This major shift in governance left Hindu organizations shuffling to expand their base, and unify and organize those communities that did not fit neatly into existing religious boundaries.[9] One outcome was the reformulation of "Hindu tradition," which by the 1920s was being articulated through terms like Sanatan Dharma, or the "Eternal Religion". When Hindu scholars and activists used the term "Sanatan Dharma," they implied more than just an ancient religion. They meant "[the] religion in or behind all religions, a kind of 'metareligion', a structure potentially ready to comprise and reconcile within itself all the religions of the world, just as it contains and reconciles the so-called Hindu sects, such as Saivism or Vaisnavism and their subordinate 'sectarian' formations" (Halbfass 1991: 51).

Using the term Sanatan Dharma as a catch-all for all things "Hindu" was one thing, but putting it into practice was another. In the midst of such immense diversity, Hindu leaders experimented with different measures and arguments. For reformist groups like the Arya Samaj, modern Hinduism's unity rested in its doctrinal centrality in the Vedas (Jones 1976). For organizations like the Maha Sabha, however, doctrine was less vital than social practice. They argued that all Hindus have an organic role in society and therefore deserve respect, although not a change in their caste or sectarian status (Zavos 2001: 117–20). The Maha Sabha's promotion of cow protection and of the Devanagari script, their service to widows and, later, shudras and untouchables—although, again, without changing their status—were supposed to reflect the unity and consensus of modern Hinduism. As the Hindu ideologue, M.S. Golwalkar (1906–73), contended, "diversities in the path of devotion did not mean division in society. All were indivisible organs of one common *dharma* which held [Hindu] society together" (quoted in Bapu 2013: 75).

The argument meshed well with the most powerful new symbol of Sanatan Dharmi Hinduism: the Hindu nation.[10] For the Maha Sabha, the term Hindu was essentially synonymous with "Indian-ness". Under the influence of intellectuals like Vinayak Damodar Savarkar (1883–1966), "Hindu-ness" or *Hindutva* came to represent a combination of territorial, racial, religious, and cultural characteristics.[11] To a large degree, Hindutva was defined by one's racial and religious relationships to the Aryavarta (India), the sacred territory (*punya bhoomi*) of the Aryans. In this view, Indian Muslims and Christians were not "real" Indians, for although they may have been born in India and even lived there for their entire lives, their purported allegiances to sacred spaces outside India, namely Palestine and Arabia, made them imposters whose loyalties to the nation would always be questioned.[12] Buddhists, on the other hand, were still Hindu, for, despite being unmistakably "heterodox" (nastika), their presumed allegiance was to the Aryavarta, the land where Gotama Buddha lived and died.

The Maha Sabha's emphatic stress on Hinduism's orthopraxy (practice) and not orthodoxy (belief) was evident in the new *Hindu rashtra mandirs*, or Hindu nation temples, they constructed. One such was the Mother India temple in Benares, inaugurated by Mahatma Gandhi on 25 October 1936, in which the inner sanctum contains a massive, thirty-foot by thirty-foot, three-dimensional map of "Mother India" (Bharat Mata) carved in marble.[13] The map, which includes all the territories from Burma to Afghanistan and from Sri Lanka to eastern Tibet, is itself suggestive of the aggressive posturing of the new Hindu nationalist movement. Its territorial vision is not the only novelty here. In addition to being open to anyone, regardless of caste, class, sex, or race, which made it somewhat of a spectacle in Benares's rigid caste landscape, the temple was also constructed on top of the "sacred books of all Aryan religions including Nastik ones" (*ISR* Vol. 47/10, 1936: 153–54). The idea of including the scriptures of Buddhists, Jains, Sikhs, and all the other "troublesome" indigenous critics (nastika) of Vedic authority within a brahmanical complex was a radically new way of conceiving of Hinduism. This was a profound break from a more scriptural Puranic Hinduism that spurned any brahmin who entered a Buddhist temple.[14] For some, the initiative to include Buddhists and other nastikas into the Hindu fold may have indeed been borne out of a genuine sense of common fellowship, but Savarkar's landmark text, *Hindutva: Who is a Hindu?* (1923), better captures the prevailing sentiment: "the Buddha—the Dharma—the Sangha. *They are all ours*" (Savarkar [1923] 1938: 27).

The Hindutva vision of India, as current political events indicate, continues to be incredibly influential. But scholarly discussions of its ideology have tended to stay focused on its exclusionary aspects within the context of the Indian nation state. Even so, key aspects of the Hindutva ideology, particularly as it related to Buddhism, went far beyond the confines of Mother India. Although Dharmapala was not the only Buddhist delegate at the Maha Sabha convention in 1923, he was the only Buddhist to take the stage and was largely perceived by the Indian public as representing an imagined pan-Asian or even global Buddhism. Newspapers in Pune and Madras construed Dharmapala's statement as evidence of the Maha Sabha's ability to "reorganize" Hindu society (*Maharatta* (Pune), 19 August 1923) and "make Hinduism a living force that can mould the destiny of mankind" (*The Hindu* [Madras], 22 August 1923).[15] The popular Bombay weekly, the *Indian Social Reformer* (25 August 1923), argued that it proved "Hinduism is not a kingdom but an Empire. It is not one religion but every religion which answers to certain general characteristics" (*ISR* in HDPB File no. 198, Part B).[16] *The Times of India* (24 August 1923, in HDPB File no. 198, Part B) was less impressed by Dharmapala's appearance but accurately surmised that the inclusion of Buddhists at the convention was evidence that the Maha Sabha was on a "warpath".

Arya Samajis who only decades before were publishing treatises ridiculing Buddhists now attempted to make the "Buddha's *gita*" known to "every household in India" (Satyadevaji 1923: iii). In cross-country lecture tours and through his 1923 Hindi translation of the *Dhammapada* as *Shribuddha Gita,* the prominent Arya Samaji, Swami Satyadevaji, explained why the Buddha was a cultural hero whose wonderful organization, the sangha, converted the whole of Asia to an Indian dharma. Just one year later, the Hindu maharaja of Darbhanga commissioned a network of pandits and sadhus from various Hindu sabhas to confirm once and for all Buddhism's debts to Hinduism. The outcome was the semi-scholarly *Buddha-mimansa,* published in 1924 in both Hindi (Maitreya and Mishra 1924) and English (Maitreya and Yogiraja 1924). Circulated widely among administrators, publicists, and scholars in India and Nepal, the work's thesis was that the Buddha was a "friend of fire" (*arkabandhu*) who performed the Vedic fire sacrifice (yajna) and taught the one Upanishadic reality (*Advayavada*).[17] Drawing on an impressive range of materials in Sanskrit, Pali, German, French, English, and Hindi, the Gaya mahant, Yogiraja, and his disciple, Maitreya, argue that nearly every facet of early Buddhism was derived from brahmanical works like the Bhagavad Gita and the *Grihya Sutras.*[18] Taking T.W. Rhys Davids's expression—made popular by the former Indian president, S. Radhakrishnan, decades later—the authors proclaim that the Buddha was born, lived and died a Hindu, and was honored as such through ritual mantras and in temples for many centuries after his death.[19] Only when the Buddha's followers became increasingly degenerate and composed of foreigners (mleccha) and outcastes (*achoot*) was Buddhism transformed into an anti-Vedic teaching. For this reason, the authors contend, India rejected Buddhists but not the Buddha (Maitreya and Yogiraja 1924: 56–67).[20] The views of the *Buddha-mimansa,* with slight variations, remained dominant among many Hindus well into the second half of the century.

One of the strongest advocates of this reinvented Buddha-dev or "Hindu Buddha," and a persuasive voice no less, was none other than Mahatma Gandhi. After Gandhi's release from prison in 1924 for his leadership in the Non-Cooperation Movement of 1920–22, he made his first major public appearance at the Bombay Buddha Society for Vesak celebrations organized by philanthropist and the Society's founder, Dr Anandrao Nair. Here, Gandhi praised the Buddha's ahimsa but made explicit his conviction that "Buddhism is a part of Hinduism" (Gandhi, 18 May 1924, in *CWMG* Vol. 27: 447–49). Exactly one year later, while speaking at the Vesak celebrations in the Maha Bodhi Society's Dharmarajika vihara in Calcutta, he ridiculed the Buddhist effort to take control of the Maha Bodhi temple: "what does it matter whether we go to a little temple and worship his [the Buddha's] image or whether we even take his name ... it is not necessary for millions to associate themselves with one man who seeks for truth" (*MBJ* Vol. 33/6, 1925: 312).[21] In subsequent decades, Gandhi frequently affirmed the Buddha's "Hindu origins". On multiple occasions, he even had the audacity to explain, to what must have been dumbfounded Buddhist crowds, how Hindus were more Buddhist than they were and how not only had the teaching of "Gautama, the Enlightened One" been "incorporated in Hinduism" after his death, but was also "best preserved in India" (Gandhi, 4 October, 1933, in *CWMG* Vol. 61: 452–53).[22] Gandhi's saintly aura and national presence gave his words a particular potency, but they were just the beginning of what was nothing less than a full-fledged assault on the idea that Buddhism was somehow separate from Hinduism.

Servants of the Arya Dharma: J.K. Birla and the Hindu Maha Sabha

By the late 1930s, the majority of the modern Buddhist organizations in India had some degree of contact with the Maha Sabha. When the latter was first founded in 1915, Buddhism was nowhere in its agenda. It mostly emerged as a reaction to the Muslim League with a mandate to provide an organizational and political basis for the innumerable provincial and local Hindu organizations (sabha, samaj, etc.) that mushroomed across the subcontinent after the constitutional reforms of the 1910s. In theory, this meant that the Maha Sabha was tasked with representing "Hindu interests" at the pan-Indian level. In practice, its social base, leadership, and ideals were largely north Indian and brahmanical in character.[23] Cow protection and Devanagari drove much of its early political programming as did an unequivocal commitment to making manifest the popular slogan "Hindi, Hindu, Hindustan". While it drew heavily from the reform-minded Arya Samaj networks in the Punjab and conservative Sanatan Dharma organizations in the United Provinces, most of its key supporters were educated upper-caste Hindu professionals—brahmins and banias—who lived in the large trading cities like Allahabad, Kanpur, Benares, and

Lucknow.[24]

Initially, Buddhist communication with the Maha Sabha largely involved discussions of the possible transfer of the Maha Bodhi temple to Buddhists, for which the Maha Sabha organized several meetings from the 1920s onwards. The more conservative elements within the organization grimaced at the idea of Buddhist management, contending that since "Bhagwan Buddha preached the religion of the Upanishads," the temple authorities should profess the Vedic dharma and Lord Buddha as their personal deity (*ishta devata*) (Letter from Sri Pratap, secretary of the Sanatana Dharma Sabha, Kashmir, to the editor of the *Ananda Bazaar Patrika,* reprinted in *MBJ* Vol. 33/5, 1925: 233). In the end, the more progressive elements within the organization prevailed. In a major resolution passed along with Congress party members in 1926, it was agreed that the temple was *in actuality* Buddhist and should therefore be managed by an equal number of Hindu and "Hindu–Buddhist" delegates.[25] Just as in past resolutions, further negotiations stalled, and only in 1949, some twenty-three years later, was a near-identical resolution turned into law. In the intervening years, the Maha Sabha became increasingly linked to the Maha Bodhi Society, which remained the dominant force behind the Maha Bodhi temple negotiations.

With Dharmapala's death in 1933, the Sinhalese anagarika, Devapriya Valisinha (b. 1904), took over as the Maha Bodhi Society's general secretary, a position he held until his death in 1968. Valisinha was an astute and passionate networker who continued Dharmapala's courtship of the Congress and Maha Sabha elite. The degree to which this was successful is evidenced by the fact that the president of the Maha Bodhi Society from 1942 to 1953 was none other than the Bengali finance minister, Dr Syama Prasad Mookerjee (1901–53).[26] Best known for founding the Bharatiya Jana Sangh (BJS), the rightwing Hindu political party that metamorphosed into India's largest political party, the Bharatiya Janata Party (BJP), Mookerjee's tenure as the Maha Bodhi Society president coincided with his presidentship of the Maha Sabha (1944) and his work among the Hindu paramilitary group, the Rashtriya Swayamsevak Sangh (RSS).

The real mechanics of the Hindu–Buddhist courtship, however, began more than a decade before, when resolutions at the Hindu Maha Sabha called upon the "servants of Arya Dharma" to form an "Aryan cultural

Jugal Kishore Birla at Buddha Jayanti celebrations in New Delhi's Buddha vihara, 1951.
From left to right: Rajendra Prasad, then president of India; J.K. Birla; S.K. Patil, then mayor
of Bombay (seated); and L. Ariyawansa Thera, then manager of the Buddha vihara

brotherhood" of Hindus and Buddhists "to enlighten the present age of materialism with the message of peace" (*MBJ* Vol. 41/12, 1933: 530). The Arya Dharma, which literally means the "noble law" or "noble [collection of] moral and religious duties" was the broad category that many Hindutva ideologues used when refering to all religious paths that originated in India. The term signified an imagined unity between Hindus, Jains, Buddhists, Sikhs, and other "branches" of the Sanatan Dharma. But its use in Buddhist publics had a special kinetic appeal since South Asian Buddhist modernists also used the term to refer to the Buddha's own teaching.[27]

In the context of Hindu–Buddhist relations, the most important Hindu protagonist was the famed industrialist and philanthropist, Seth Jugal Kishore Birla (1883–1967). During the early to mid-twentieth century, Jugal Kishore (hereafter, JK) constructed dozens of new temples aimed at reformulating the subcontinent's past as part of a singular Hindu landscape. Through a sustained engagement with Buddhists, both living and dead, JK and the Maha Sabha worked to rewrite the history of the Buddha and his sasana as part of a Hindu nationalist vision of India.

JK was the eldest son of the wealthy marwari entrepreneur, Baldeo Das Birla (1863–1956). Born in Rajasthan, JK joined the family business in Calcutta in the 1890s, initially trading in cotton and hessian before moving into opium speculation. These pursuits, along with what were then novel ventures, like importing Japanese cloth to Calcutta, reaped huge profits, making the family one of the wealthiest in India, a status it still holds today.[28] More than just astute businessmen, the Birlas were also devout Hindus who well understood the influential role Hindu institutions could possess if financed properly. Like most Hindu trading communities, they were early supporters of the Nagari and cow protection movements that were the unifying principles of disparate Hindu sabhas.[29] The Birlas were particularly close with the Congress and Maha Sabha leader, M.M. Malaviya, who "enjoyed the status of a learned guru" for the family, providing them advice and guidance (Kudaisya 2003: 67). In return, Malaviya's various educational and religious projects in the name of Hindu revival, from managing the Banaras Hindu University (BHU) to running several major newspapers, were largely due to JK and his father's generosity (61–75). As Malaviya's son, Padam Kant, put it, when Malaviya wished to get something done, "Jugal Kishore became his right hand" (Malaviya 1968: 70).

While the Birlas were unquestionably loyal to Gandhi, effectively bankrolling his political campaigns and calls for Hindu tolerance and inclusivity, they were also firm supporters of a more muscular, militant Hinduism. Wrestling gyms (*akhara*s), military schools, RSS training camps, and Hindu propaganda training centers—these were all seen as integral to the Birlas' vision of a twentieth-century pan-Hinduism (Kudaisya 2003: 255, 269–70).[30] As the ideological divide between the Hindu Maha Sabha and Gandhi's Congress widened, the Birlas' own position in this relationship became increasingly complex. While Ghanshyam Das (GD), JK's younger brother, sided with Gandhi and the Congress, JK and his father, considered to be the more conservative members of the family, continued their firm support of the extreme Hindu right (although they never stopped supporting Gandhi either).[31]

While all the Birlas attended Buddhist events during the colonial period, JK's involvement in India's modern Buddhism was most pronounced. His first public intervention occurred in 1920 during the opening of Dharmapala's

Dharmarajika vihara in Calcutta, when he donated five thousand rupees for its expansion.[32] For much of the next decade, he was silent, but from 1933 onwards, his reputation as a modern-day Anathapindika, the Buddhist patron par excellence, becomes well deserved. In addition to funding the construction of more than fifteen major Buddhist temples, rest houses, schools, and academic institutes in India alone, JK also sponsored the printing of more than five thousand copies of the Hindi translations of different Pali scriptures, such as the *Dhammapada*, the *Digha Nikaya*, and the *Majjhima Nikaya*. He also provided handsome fellowships to Buddhist monastics for conducting missionary work (*dharmadoot ka kam*) in India.[33] Supported by one of India's wealthiest and most well-connected households, the figures involved in the many construction projects were the best that money and political influence could buy. These were undertaken at well-known Buddhist pilgrimage centers like Rajgir (1936), Sarnath (1937), Bodh Gaya (1938), and Kushinagar (1939), and also in new centers of urban Buddhist activity, including Calcutta (1935, 1937), Calicut (1937), Bombay (1937, 1940), and New Delhi (1939) (see table).[34]

Major Buddhist constructions financed by J.K. Birla, 1920–40

Year	Name of vihara/ Dharmashala	Location	Notes
1920	Expansion of Dharmarajika vihara (Maha Bodhi Society)	Calcutta	Rs 5,000 donation
1934	Buddha Mandir	Ranchi (Jonha Falls)	Opened by Seth Jamnalal Bajaj (of the Bajaj Group)
1935	Siva–Buddhist temple	Calcutta	Further information lacking (see *MBJ* 1935, 607)
1935	Saddharma vihara	Calcutta	Nipponzon Myohoji temple built for Nichidatsu Fuji. Inaugurated 16 February 1935, by JK, Fuji, U Ottama, and the mayor of Calcutta
1936	Oshajo vihara	Rajgir	Nipponzon Myohoji temple built for Nichidatsu Fuji

1937	Maha Bodhi Mission vihara	Calicut	Partially financed by J.K. Birla (property provided by C. Krishnan). Inaugurated by Dhammaskanda, Kottai Kumaran (secretary of Maha Bodhi Mission)
1937	Arya Dharma Sangha Dharmashala	Sarnath	Foundation laid 1935. Opened on 10 January 1937, by Chen Chang Lok (consul general, China), M.M. Malaviya, Devapriya Valisinha and Tan Yun Shan (professor, Visva Bharati University)
1937	Maha Bodhi Vidyalaya [College]	Sarnath	Foundation laid on 29 April 1937, by Pandit Hriday Nath Kunzru (president, Servants of India Society)
1937	Construction of Bhikkhu accommodations at Ananda vihara	Bombay	Donation of Rs 500 to Bombay Buddha Society to provide lodging for resident monastics
1937	Bahujan vihara	Bombay	Inaugurated on January 1937. Dharmanand Kosambi served as preceptor until 1939
1937	Construction of three-story Arya vihar at Bengal Buddhist Association	Calcutta	Inaugurated 11 December 1937 by J.K. Birla, Sarvepalli Radhakrishnan (later president of India), and S.P. Mookerjee (later founder of Bharatiya Jana Sangh)
1938	Arya Dharma Dharmashala	Bodh Gaya	
1939	Bhagavan Buddhdev ka mandir and Arya vihar	Kushinagar	Financed at the cost of Rs 30,000

1939	Buddha vihara (part of the Lakshmi Narayan Mandir or the Birla temple)	New Delhi	Foundation laid 31 October 1936, by J.K. Birla, Devapriya Valisinha, Bhai Parmananda (VP of Maha Sabha), K. Yonezawa (consul general, Japan). Opened 18 March 1939 by Mahatma Gandhi, Valisinha, JK and G.D. Birla, Acharya Kripalani, and more than a dozen Buddhist monks
1940	Nipponzon Myohoji temple	Bombay (Worli)	Semi-complete in 1940, but the advent of WWII delayed completion. Inaugurated in 1956 by J.K. Birla and Fuji

When one considers JK's concurrent involvement in Maha Sabha politics and practices, it is clear that his championing of Buddhism was also a careful socio-political strategy to contain the new Buddhist threat to Hindu orthodoxy. This point was made as early as 1950 by Rahul Sankrityayan in his characteristically provocative manner when he described the new Birla Dharmashala at Kushinagar: "Maybe some knuckleheads (*aundhi khopariyon*) thought that if you threw twenty-five [or] fifty-thousand rupees at the site, you could turn the anti-caste, atheist, self-supporting Buddhists into Hindus" (Sankrityayan [1944–63] 2014, Vol. II: 192). In Sankrityayan's view, Hindu leaders (*neta*) were fearful that the "thousands of [Buddhist] people" (*hazaron admi*), who visited Kushinagar each year after Chandramani and Mahavir's arrival, might inspire the untouchable (achoot) populace to embrace Buddhism (191). Birla's actions, which always need to be considered within the context of those of the Maha Sabha, were without a doubt marked by this kind of religious positioning.[35] But it was not just the idea of Buddhism as an exclusive entity that made Hindu leaders like Birla uneasy; increasingly, Buddhism's anti-caste and anti-brahmanical characteristics were being marked as integral to it and therefore apropriable by the anti-caste movements of the period.

Three interrelated developments were especially germane. First were the temple-entry movements of the 1920 and 1930s (Jeffrey 1976) that further catapulted the "caste problem" and questions of "untouchable uplift" into the center of nationalist debates around social reform. Second, in the aftermath of the Round Table Conferences (1930–32), the Gandhi–Ambedkar debates, and the resulting Poona Pact, Congress leaders and other Hindu parties began taking the dalit threat to political power more seriously, especially when led by someone of Ambedkar's stature (Rao 2009: 138–40; Rawat 2011: 167–80; Guha 2018: 421–47). The third was Ambedkar's public declaration in Yeola in 1935, when he announced his decision to leave Hinduism and called upon fellow dalits to do the same. Birla's vihara-building activities—apart from the singular donation to the Calcutta vihara in 1920—all occurred in the wake of these events. They also happened in tandem with the activities of the Harijan Sevak Sangh, the organization Gandhi founded just days after the Poona Pact in order to eradicate untouchability and which JK's younger brother, Ghanshyam Das (GD), served as president.

The network of Hindu sabhas across northern (and to a lesser degree, southern) India kept Maha Sabha leaders well informed of the Buddhist "missionary" (dharmadoot) activities among the working classes in 1930s Lucknow and Kanpur, as well as among a more diffuse population along the Malabar Coast between the 1920s and 1940s.[36] By the 1930s, thousands of Buddhists from across Asia and the western hemisphere were visiting India, carrying with them the message of Buddhist social emancipation and rationality that was said to be a "solution" to India's "untouchability problem" (cf. *DD* Vol. 1/8, 1935–36: 71; Kausalyayan 1940, 1941; *MBJ* Vol. 59/9, 1951: 336–37). In the midst of all this, the Maha Sabha made frequent attempts to curtail or, at the very least, control the way that Buddhism was being presented. When missionaries and intellectuals, Buddhist or otherwise, contended that Buddhism was independent of Hinduism, Maha Sabha leaders quickly shot back, passing a number of resolutions stating that Hinduism and Buddhism were one and the same and that "Buddhists are as much Hindus as Protestants are Christians" (*HO*, 25 May 1940: 3).[37]

A visceral example of such an effort to stave off Buddhist threats occurred in Kushinagar, the ancient site of the Buddha's parinirvana in present-day Uttar Pradesh. Surrounded by fields of sugar cane and dotted with Buddhist ruins dating back some two thousand years, Kushinagar was one of the remotest sites in the growing Buddhist pilgrimage circuit. Yet, despite its economically impoverished surroundings and general lack of accomodations for travelers, the small temple town underwent a vast transformation during the early twentieth century under the guidance of the Burmese–Arakanese monk, U Chandramani. Visitors began flowing in and with the support of donors and pilgrim donations, Chandramani gained ownership of large tracts of land both within and outside the town vicinity. On the main street, he established a school, clinic, and temple rest house, all adjacent to the major cluster of ancient Buddhist sites, including the eighteen-foot-long sandstone statue of a reclining Buddha, believed by the devout to be positioned exactly as the Buddha was when he passed. Sculpted out of sandstone some 1,500 years ago and managed by the Archaeological Survey of India, the iconic sculpture was undoubtedly the most popular Buddhist pilgrimage site in Kushinagar. Under Chandramani's leadership, the once desolate Buddhist ruins were reborn as a living Buddhist space marked by daily ritual activities and seasonal festivities. The ownership of land and the reconsecrecation of Buddhist sites were sometimes a source of strain with local communities. This was compounded by growing numbers of local Hindu youths as well as Newars and Europeans who came to Kushinagar to take diksha and receive monastic ordination under Chandramani's guidance (Hla 2002: 53–63).

Meanwhile, the Birla family began sponsoring their own projects in the small town, including the construction of a "Hindu–Buddhist" temple–dharmashala (*Bhagavan Buddhadev ka mandir tatha arya vihar*) across the road from Chandramani's sprawing complex. This new structure had the distinctive red-and-yellow plaster which other Birla temples across India also shared. It was built with large chaitya arches reminiscent of the Buddhist caves at Ajanta, hanging bell motifs, and miniature shikharas. Inside the central hall of the the Hindu–Buddhist rest house is a lone statue of the Buddha. Hindi-language plaques outside the rest house explain to visitors that "Hinduism and Buddhism are branches of the same tree" (*baudh aur hindu dharm ek hi mool ki do shakhae*).

As discussed in detail by the art historian Padma Dorje Maitland (Ober and Maitland, *forthcoming*), the Birlas also funded the construction of a temple dedicated to the Hindu god Shiva on a property adjacent to the Hindu–Buddhist rest house. Although again sharing the same red and yellow plaster as other Birla constructions, the Shiva temple is distinguished by its large dome representing a Shivalingam, an aniconic symbol of the deity. Unlike the colossal Lakshmi Narayan Mandir the Birlas built in New Delhi in 1939, in which the Buddha is imagined as an avatar of Vishnu, the Shiva temple in Kushinagar reflects a more concerted effort to establish Buddhism and Hinduism as two branches of a singular Arya Dharma. This is made explicit in the three plaques inside the inner sanctum of the temple. The first two plaques depict Shiva and the Buddha. Both are rather standardized images, and are labeled explicitly ("Bhagavan Shankar" and "Bhagavan Buddh"). The image on the third plaque is more ambiguous. A corresponding label is conspicuously absent, although just below it is a series of quotes in Hindi, Sanskrit, and English, all denoted as "The Words of the Buddha." Read this way, the image appears to be that of the Buddha at the moment of his enlightenment in the *bhoomiparsha mudra*: seated with his right hand reaching towards the ground with the palm inward, calling the earth to witness his victory over the temptations of the demon, Mara. But the conventional Buddhist characteristics end here. The figure's lips are also painted a bright red, closely resembling the image of Shiva on the accompanying plaque, while its hair lacks the tightly cropped, curly *ushnisha* (topknot) of conventional Buddha images. Instead, it is tied into a loose, swirling topknot reminiscent of Shiva.[38] Rather than depicting the Buddha or Shiva, the plaque presents a vision of both figure as symbols of a singular tradition.

These kinds of appropriative efforts were reinforced in many temples and rest houses built by the Birlas for Buddhists, Sikhs, Jains, and Hindus throughout India. Some might contend that JK's support for Buddhists and other "dharmic" minorities stemmed from the long-standing tradition of giving alms (*dana*) in Indian cultures. Contrarily, when the future president of India, Sarvepalli Radhakrishnan (1946: 1), described the Birlas as men "who know not only how to earn but what is more important, how to spend," what he really meant was how to spend on Hindus (in the Hindutva sense of the term).[39] His was a generosity that, publicly at least, extended only to Hindus, which to him, included all "Aryanized" populations.

When speaking at Buddhist events, JK most often articulated his support for Buddhism through the lens of Hindu devotion. According to his children and peers, he was a deeply religious man who followed a strict regimen of ritual practices. He started each day at five in the morning with prayers, regularly consulted astrologers, and hired brahmins to "ward off suspected obstacles and neutralize evil influences" (Kudaisya 2003: 191). As the eldest son in the family, his decisions were considered "binding on all"; he instructed other household members to memorize verses from the Ramayana and the Gita, chant prayers, and "carry on with *bhajans, kirtans,* and *havans*" (191). In speaking of the Buddha, he was thoroughly Vaishnava in orientation, understanding Buddhadev to be the avatar of the current age and the dharmic protector of the current era (Kalelkar 1968: 48). "Changes take place with change of time and in language, dress, and social rites and practices," Birla declared at the opening of the Birla-funded Japanese Buddhist temple (Nipponzon Myohoji Saddharma vihara) in Calcutta in February 1935:

> But they have no great bearing upon the true spirit of religion ... after long centuries, things have again changed and the reign of injustice pervades the entire world. The downfall of those professing Arya Dharma in India has reached its limit on account of mutual jealousy. If for this reason anybody says that Indians have forgotten Lord Buddha, then it must be admitted that that is true in one respect, for had we kept in our minds the teachings of Lord Buddha, this great nation of India would not have welcomed the state of subjection and slavery by quarreling with one another for mean, selfish ends and would not have hurt their co-religionists in a spirit of contempt. There is yet time to get wide awake .... This is my prayer to Lord Buddha that with such strength as He may vouchsafe to us—the followers of the Arya Dharma—we may succeed in benefitting the whole world by benefitting ourselves (*MBJ* Vol. 43/3, 1935: 111–14).

JK's speech here, which more or less mirrored those he gave at other Buddhist functions, is remarkable for a number of reasons. First, it challenged the popular notion that early Buddhism and, particularly, Buddhist non-violence was responsible for India's conquest by foreign peoples. Even as Gandhi's Congress championed satyagraha and ahimsa as the twin pillars of political success, the historical nature and consequences of Buddhist non-violence had become important matters for Indian intellectuals and politicians.[40] In Gandhi's eyes, Buddhist non-violence proved to be one of the few aspects of Buddhism that he routinely supported: "It is my unalterable belief that India has fallen not because it accepted Gautama's message [of non-violence], but because it failed to live up to it" (*MBJ* Vol. 32/7, 1924: 273). Many prominent scholars of Buddhism, like Dharmanand Kosambi, supported Gandhi's thesis, but others like the Lahore professor, Gulshan Rai, felt strongly that it was because of Buddhist non-violence that India "became slaves of a foreign [Islamic] culture and civilization" (*ISR* Vol. 44/40, 1934: 633). Rai's view, foreshadowed in Sivaprasad's (1874: 118) *Itihas Timir Nashak*, was amplified by Hindutva hardliners like Savarkar, Golwalkar, and Moonje, who all stressed repeatedly and loudly that Buddhist non-violence destroyed Indian society.[41]

It may seem odd that JK aligned himself with Gandhian Hindus, rather than hardliners like Savarkar and Moonje, when it came to the utility of non-violence. But his understanding of ahimsa appears to have been more about the *absence of hatred* than the absence of physical violence. In this Gita-esque, karmayogic interpretation, physical acts of violence performed without motivations of anger and attachments to the result could be deemed acceptable (Robinson 2006: 64–68). JK's support for Buddhist ahimsa was also mediated through his own principled commitment to vegetarianism, which was a product of his rigid brahmanical orthodoxy. Birla's vegetarianism was not just a private, dietary matter but also a way of being and living in the world.[42] In 1938, when JK learned that his nephew's profitable pharmaceutical company processed animal glands, he forced the latter to close the business (Kumar 1994: 31–32). A second incident, more central to the Buddhist context, is recalled in the memoir of Gose Lama (Thub-dlan 'Byung-gnas), the founder of the first Tibetan Buddhist temple (est. 1955) in Sarnath. Gose Lama recounts that throughout the 1940s and 1950s, JK "used to give monthly stipends to the members of the Tibetan Bodhgaya monastery [est. 1938]," but once "he came to know about our meat consumption," he cut off all support for the carnivorous monastics (Shastri 2005: 126). When read in conjunction with JK's public expressions of support for Buddhist ahimsa, both of these stories, despite being anecdotal in nature, reveal an important component of how he understood the role of non-violence in the Arya Dharma.

Greater India's Empire of Dharma

The motto: "Hinduism and Buddhism are branches of the same tree" (*baudh aur hindu dharm ek hi mool ki do shakhae*) was inscribed on plaques on the outer and interior walls of most Buddhist structures financed by JK. Other inscriptions make even more explicit his vision of Hindu encompassment. At the temple rest house dedicated to Buddhadev in Kushinagar, a plaque on the outer wall reads: "All Hindu pilgrims (including Harijans [dalits]), i.e., followers of Sanatan Dharma, Arya Samajists, Jains, Sikhs and Buddhists, etc. are accommodated in the Dharamshala subject to the standing orders of the Dharamshala committee." Another marble plaque at the opposite end of the building goes on to explain that "Arya Dharmists" (*arya dharmi*) include Buddhist peoples from China, Japan, Siam, Burma, Tibet, Lanka, Indochina, etc. For students of the Hindutva ideology, the idea that Indian Buddhists were Hindus is nothing unusual. However, the idea that Buddhists *outside* India were also Hindus is rarely discussed. Even so, a slight derivation of that idea was widely popular among leading scholars of the period.

In the early decades of the twentieth century, a variety of Asian thinkers began drawing up pan-Asian cosmopolitan histories with India and Buddhism at the center (Sarkar 1916, 1922; Liang 1924; Chung 1999; Tsui 2010). While these visions were anything but unified, they drew from and dovetailed into common pools of thought—from the Eastern spiritualities invoked by the theosophists and the "swadeshi internationalism" (Manjapra 2012) of early twentieth-century India, to the pan-Islamic and pan-Asian cosmpolitanisms, emerging in Turkey and Japan respectively (Aydin 2007). In 1920s India, these visions gained a systematicity through the Greater India Society, a Calcutta-based organization established in 1926. The core thesis of the Greater India Society was that ancient India had played an active role in the cultural and religious development of South-east Asia. As Susan Bayly (2000, 2004) has shown, leading Greater India scholars were keen to demonstrate that ancient India was home to a highly developed civilization that pre-dated most of Europe, one that possessed the same drive and aggressiveness as Muslim and Christian "colonizers". India, as the influential Indian historian and Greater India ideologue, R.C. Majumdar, wrote, was "the home of a master-race" that had brought the "heterogenous

mass of [southeast Asia's] barbarians within the pale of civilization, a task
which the Chinese, their next-door neighbours, had hitherto failed to
accomplish" (Majumdar 1927, quoted in Bayly 2000: 601). Many Greater India
Society scholars had close links with the Maha Sabha and the Maha Bodhi
Society, and figures like Malaviya were major sponsors of their work.[43]

While Sanskrit, Indian architecture, and the arts were seen as central
to this civilizing process, Buddhism, as India's premier "missionary
religion," was often credited as being the primary agent in the spread of
"Indo-Aryan" civilization.[44] As members of the so-called reformist wing of
Hinduism, Buddhist missionaries were seen as conduits of Hindu culture.
The prominent Greater India Society scholar, S.C. Mookerjee (1921), argued
in 1921 that "Higher Hinduism" and Buddhism were "built of the same flesh
and blood," with the latter being no "-ism" at all, but an "Arya Dharma ...
a stirring exhortation of [Indian] Culture" (245). For Mookerjee, reading
the archives of Greater India made the solution to India's contemporary
problems simple: only by resuscitating this ancient Arya Dharma could
India regain its cherished place in the world (Mookerjee 1921, 1923, 1924).

As the Greater India geo-imaginary of a singular Hindu–Buddhist
Asia was translated from academic publications into the popular sphere,
it permeated diverse social circles, even those that otherwise had little
penchant for Hindutva ideologies. For instance, in mid-1935, the self-exiled
revolutionary, Mahendra Pratap, published a hand-drawn map of the world
in the magazine, *World Federation*. In this rendering, the world was divided
into five main "provinces": Asia was "Buddha," while Europe and Africa
were labeled "Christ" and "Mohemmod" [sic] respectively. According to the
historian, Carolien Stolte (2016), Pratap appears to have had no immediate
interest in the Hindu–Buddhist networks being cultivated by Maha Sabha
ideologues or in reconciling Hindu–Buddhist thought. His vision of a
singular Asia united by the Buddha, however, is telling. For Pratap, like
many Asians, it was the primary way in which a broad pan-Asian union
could be envisioned.

By the 1930s, the vocabulary, syntax, and grammar of a singular Hindu–
Buddhist Asia became common parlance not only for the members of
the Maha Sabha, but also for those who petitioned the organization with
agendas of their own. In India and Nepal, bodies like the All-India Buddhist

Society drew on the language of Arya Dharma to forge alliances with right-wing Hindu groups in order to encourage Buddhism's spread in the subcontinent, while in Japan, Indian revolutionaries like Rashbehari Bose wrote to Savarkar arguing for the need of "a Hindu bloc extending from the Indian Ocean up to the Pacific Ocean ... creating solidarity among the Eastern races" (quoted in Stolte 2016: 67). JK's invocation of the Arya Dharma was symptomatic of these larger discourses. Buddhists, in his eyes, were Aryanized Hindus who had left their Bharat Mata (Mother India) long ago and were now returning after a painful separation of many centuries. Dharma or moral duty demanded he welcome them back.

The Maha Sabha also used the trope as the basis of its active networking with Buddhist organizations across Asia. As early as 1933, the Hindu Maha Sabha passed major resolutions calling on the "servants of Arya Dharma" to form an "Aryan cultural brotherhood" of Hindus and Buddhists who could "enlighten the present age of materialism with the message of peace" (*MBJ* Vol. 41/12, 1933: 530). In the following years, it sent "Hindu–Buddhist" ambassadors abroad to Buddhist conventions in Penang (in Malaya), Burma, Japan, and Indochina. Its greatest success appears to have been with the Japanese, who themselves had long "sought to bolster ties with other Asians by stressing their shared Buddhist past" (Jaffe 2019: 244). In 1934, at the one-thousand-strong meeting of the Pan-Pacific Young Buddhist Association in Japan, the Maha Sabha representative, Pandit Visvabandhu Shastri, emphasized the importance of "Arya Dharma" or "the unity of spirit underlying the different Asiatic peoples in Indo-China, Manchuoukuo [sic], Japan, Penang, Siam, Burma and India" (*MBJ* Vol. 42/11–12, 1934: 570). The Maha Sabha's close ties to the Maha Bodhi Society proved beneficial, and it is notable that the only other Indian representative at the week-long event was the former Arya Samaji-turned-Buddhist bhikkhu, Anand Kausalyayan.[45] Shastri and Kausalyayan came to Japan together and left together, being touted as evidence of the Hindu–Buddhist alliance that was possible if only their "superficial" differences could be transcended (*MBJ* Vol. 42/2, 1934: 71–76; *MBJ* Vol. 42/11–12, 1934: 535–39).

Efforts at fomenting an "Asiatic Brotherhood" between India and Japan were particularly pronounced in the 1930s, when several prominent Japanese Buddhist (Nichiren) monks settled in India. Led by Nichidatsu

Fuji (1885–1985), Tadao Okitsu (dates unknown), and Daisaburo Maruyama (dates unknown), the Japanese renunciates were inspired by Nichiren's (c. 1222–82) prophecy that in the final Dharmic age (Japanese, *mappo*), Japanese Buddhists would return the True Dharma (saddharma) to India. Making India their field of action for the next several decades, the Nipponzon Myohoji monks traveled through the country, chanting the Lotus Sutra mantra *"namu myoho renge kyo"* to the beat of hand-held fan-shaped drums. Through their own assertions of pan-Asianism and intensive ascetic practice (Kisala 1999; Stone 2003; Nichidatsu [1972] 1975), they found themselves in the vicinity of Hindu–Buddhist political action, living with Gandhi at his ashram at Wardha in 1933 and gaining the support of the Birlas. The Japanese trio made a strong impression, and to this day, daily prayers at Gandhi's ashram in Sabarmati begin with the *daimoku* (Lotus Sutra mantra) while Fuji's drum is displayed publicly inside the main hall of the Birla Mandir in New Delhi. With JK's financing, Fuji constructed three major Nipponzon Myohoji temples in colonial India: in Calcutta in 1935, in Rajgir in 1936, and in Bombay in 1940.[46] At the grand opening of Calcutta's Saddharma vihara, or Temple of the True Dharma, on 16 February 1935, the spirit of unity between Hindus and Buddhists worldwide was the dominant theme. JK emphasized the need of followers of the Arya Dharma to unite against the materialist forces (read socialism and Western capitalism) at rise in the world, while the Arakanese–Burmese monk, U Ottama, prayed for an Indo-Japanese fellowship "under the deep reposefulness of the Buddhist banner of love and Ahimsa" (*MBJ* Vol. 43/3, 1935: 137).

While deeply invested in the Japanese Buddhist sangha in India, the Birla family also sponsored projects for other international Buddhist communities. These included the construction of a rest house in Benares in 1942 for pilgrims from Burma, as well as the Chinese Buddhist temple in Sarnath, established in 1939. Both of these sites were designed with the same kind of Hindu revivalist architecture that marked other Buddhist construction projects in India funded by the Birla family. All of these temple-building activities helped assert and amplify India's claim as being Buddhism's homeland and of Buddhism being part of a singular Hindu or Arya Dharma tradition (Ober and Maitland, *forthcoming*).

Honoring Lord Buddha, "a Hindu of Hindus"

The prized place that Buddhism held in the Maha Sabha's vision and the importance of integrating foreign Buddhist leadership into its fold is evident in two major events that occurred in the next five years. The first happened just two months after the opening of the Japanese vihara in Calcutta when Bhikkhu Ottama was elected president of the Maha Sabha.[47] The decision came at the behest of Malaviya and JK, who felt it would demonstrate the all-embracing attitude of the Hindus to the Buddhist world. During Ottama's tenure (1935–36), which preceded the partition of Burma from India in 1937, he used the pulpit to protest the proposed separation and argue for the ancient unity of Buddhists and Hindus, Burmese and Indians. "Lord Buddha was a Hindu of Hindus," he explained in his presidential speech, and since all Buddhists of Burma "look upon India, where he [the Buddha] was born and preached his gospel, as their holy land," its separation was nothing less than the "dismemberment of the great Hindu nation" (*ISR* Vol. 45, 27 April 1935: 548). This was a Buddhist cause that Hindutva ideologues could rally around. As history demonstrates, Ottama's demand to stop the Burma–India partition failed, but his calls for Hindu–Buddhist unity were more enduring. The Maha Sabha accelerated its rhetoric of a singular Arya Dharma uniting all of Asia, electing Buddhist heads to regional chapters, decorating general convention platforms with Buddhist motifs and symbols, and petitioning monastics to chant *paritta* (protective verses) during temple inaugurations.[48] An article published in the Maha Sabha's weekly organ, *The Hindu Outlook,* in 1938, demonstrates this tendency. On one hand, there is the standard fare of an ancient prince who "brought a renaissance of the rationalistic ideals in religion" (*HO*, 18 May 1938: 9). Yet, further in the text, it explains how the Buddha "enriched the vedantic doctrines with [a] wealth of ethical refinement," and how "His *Nirvana* was the assimilation of the *Jiva* [soul/life] with the *Siva* [God]" (10–11). So much for the central Buddhist teaching of non-self (*anatman*).

While the Birlas built temples, schools, and rest houses for all Aryan religions across India, none of these structures garnered the nation's attention like the Lakshmi Narayan Mandir on Reading Road (present-day Mandir Marg) in New Delhi. Better known as the Birla Mandir, this grand temple complex, which sprawls across seven acres and continues to be one of the most visited Hindu temples in the capital city, was one of the first "pan-Hindu" temples or Hindu Rashtra Mandirs built in the twentieth century. The impetus to build such massive structures had come from the prominent Arya Samaji, Swami Shraddhananda (1856–1926), who argued that every city in India needed grand pan-Hindu temples to contend with competing Islamic spaces like Old Delhi's monumental Jama Masjid (Jaffrelot 1996: 19–25). Had Shraddhananda survived his assassin's bullet in 1926, the New Delhi Birla Mandir may have fulfilled his dream. While the complex is Vaishnava in orientation, it contains the full constellation of "Aryan" seers, gods, and saints with separate enclosures and wall paintings honoring Vedic rishis, Sikh gurus, Jain tirthankaras, bhakti poets, lower-caste and outcaste sants, and virtually any other revered "Aryan Hindu". In the first corridor outside the north-west corner of the sanctum sanctorum is a small enclosure with an image of Bhagavan Buddha and several short Sanskrit and Hindi passages detailing his teachings (*vani*), their similarity to the Bhagavad Gita, and their singular origin (*ek hi mool ki*) in India. In comparison to other sections of the temple, the Buddha quadrant is relatively small, and with good reason. In the property adjacent to the Birla Mandir and connected to it by a short walkway is a large Buddha vihara whose *shikhara* (top) rivals that of the main complex.

The Buddha vihara was also financed by JK and designed by the nationalist architect, Sris Chandra Chatterjee, in consultation with Pandit Vishwananda Shastri, a member of the Maha Bodhi Society and author of a major text on the Buddha avatar.[49] When the two temples were consecrated in a joint Hindu–Buddhist celebration on 18 March 1939, nearly fifty thousand people crowded the roadway to see Mahatma Gandhi oversee the ceremony. At the Buddhist temple, monks chanted paritta while in the Hindu complex brahmin priests recited Vedic *stotras* before a fire. The crowds were so overbearing that the microphone arrangements broke down and all of the planned speeches by Gandhi, the Birlas, and Devapriya Valisinha had to be called off ("Opening of Sri Lakshmi Narain Temple," *HT*, 19 March 1939).[50] The speeches that were later released to the press dwelt largely on the contributions of the Birlas to Hindu revival and the reformative role that Buddhism had played in removing the stigma of untouchability. As in the speeches delivered during the laying of the foundation stone three years prior,[51] here too there was discussion of how "We [Hindus and Buddhists] are brothers and we should live like brothers" (*MBJ* Vol. 44/11, 1936: 555–56). The Japanese consul general, Konezawa, explained how he spoke on behalf of "forty-one million" Japanese Buddhists who "are thankful to you [India] for giving them their religion" (*MBJ* Vol. 44/11, 1936: 552). He stressed the chaos and strife in the world, blaming it on "selfish materialism," and the need for Buddhism to perform its "great mission ... not only in Asia but also the whole world" (552). There was no discussion on how Buddhism was being currently used by imperial Japan to justify its aggression and military conquests in eastern Asia (Victoria 2006; Ives 2009), only how in this moment of great uncertainty Hindus and Buddhists alike needed to live up to their solemn duty of remembering that this was the age of the Buddha and only the Buddha could eradicate suffering.

Being Buddhist in a Hindu World

The expansive network of guest houses and temples built by the Birlas in the twentieth century were part of a wider religious and commercial circuit, one that tied together Hindu, Jain, Sikh, and Buddhist sites. In the context of Buddhism, such networks encouraged pilgrims from other countries to visit the Hindu holy sites as well as Buddhist ones, and to see them as linked through a single, curated experience of traveling across India.

With the help of the Birlas, the Maha Sabha came to dominate Indian Buddhist affairs and public spaces. The very nature of the colonial state, in which political representation was based on demographic figures, obliged Buddhist organizations to cast their lot with the Maha Sabha, which was the only major political organization in India to recognize Buddhists as a community of significance (*DD* Vol. 1/1, 1935: 13). In this sense, the Maha Sabha's dominance could be construed as coercive since there were few other options. Nearly all of the urban Buddhist associations founded in colonial India, from Dr Anandrao Nair's Bombay Buddha Society (est. 1922) to B.M. Barua and Aditya Dharmacharya's All-India Buddhist Society (Akhil Bharatiya Bauddh Maha Sabha), established in 1927, drew on networks of support derived from the Maha Sabha.[52] Those Buddhist organizations that pursued other paths in order to attain their educational, social, and cultural goals, like the Bharatiya Bauddha Samiti, or the Indian Buddhist Society (est. 1916), of Lucknow, were almost exclusively driven by an anti-caste activism that was anathema to the Maha Sabha's caste Hindu leadership. The Maha Sabha did manage to make some inroads into these organizations, such as in the Malabar Maha Bodhi Mission of the Kerala Buddhist Association (est. 1925). But by and large, anti-caste Buddhists proceeded independently, most powerfully under the leadership of Ambedkar. Ambedkar's Buddhism was later reflected in the design of new Buddhist spaces as well, most notably at Nagpur's Dikshabhoomi and Bombay's Chaityabhoomi, both of which drew inspiration from the great stupa of Sanchi as a symbol of Buddhist religious and political autonomy.[53]

By the 1940s, many Hindus had come to accept the notion that the Buddha was not only a Hindu but had been one of the greatest figures in Indian history, and therefore deserving of the nation's respect and admiration. They had no qualms in worshipping the Buddha since, according to their logic, "all the qualities of Buddhism were absorbed into Hinduism" and the Buddha had in fact "lived and died a Hindu" (Jagadiswarananda 1941: 298–99). Venerating the Buddha, in their view, did not make one a non-Hindu. On the contrary, leading a "Buddhist way of life," a phrase often invoked throughout the period to mean the inculcation of righteous behavior, self-reflection, compassion, and reason, was the mark of being a "cultured Indian" (Radhakrishnan 1950). Reviving Buddhism then was not a threat to the social norm, but rather "another name for our resuscitation of our national culture" (*BI* Vol. 1/1, 1927: 53). Buddhism, the argument went, was both "Aryan" and "Sanatan," and therefore part of Hinduism's modern destiny. As one Hindu–Buddhist campaigner declared at the All-India Buddhist Conference in 1927, without Buddhism, "India will be like milk without butter or cream" (*BI* Vol. 1/1, 1927: 3).

Those Hindus who publicly challenged that view typically came from political, sectarian, or intellectual quarters. When in 1956, the scholar of Madhva philosophy, Dr Nagaraja Sarma, asked how a modern state composed primarily of Hindus could support the Buddha's teaching which "stands at the very antipodes of Hinduism" (Sarma, foreword in Neminath Maharaj 1956: 4), the Indian vice president and Oxford scholar,

S. Radhakrishnan, deflected the criticism with his characteristic argument that the Buddha was a Hindu and his teachings were derived from the Upanishads. Sarma, like many other scholars, saw things differently, recognizing the clear distinctions between early Buddhism and its "Hindu" interlocutors. The kind of generalized Hindu animosity towards Buddhists is equally evident in the memoirs of S.N. Goenka (1924–2013), the famous Buddhist master of meditation who was raised in a devout Hindu family of banias in Burma. When Goenka first traveled to India as a young adult in the 1940s, Hindutva narratives that demonized Buddhism gave profound shape to his thinking, leading to a "strong distrust of Buddhism" and later provoking a "major internal conflict" when he encountered the Burmese Buddhist traditions of vipassana that he went on to master (Stuart 2020: 34). Such ideas always remained in vogue but in the Indian marketplace of ideas, the Radhakrishnan–Sanatan Dharma view of Buddhism came to dominate. Today, many Hindus adore Gotama Buddha, the royal prince turned ascetic, who in their view was a great Hindu reformer. His actual teachings are largely ignored, purposely misconstrued, or synthesized on rather fragile foundations.

The modern Hindu assimilation of Buddhism, and in particular of the Buddha, had a variety of consequences. For the most part, it was effectively an appropriation of the Buddha and Buddhism for its own ends, just as the brahmanical castes had done more than a millennium before. Even if the intentions may have been similar, the substance of the argumentation was fundamentally different. During the medieval appropriation, the Buddha was one of the delusive avatars of Vishnu, a figure so stigmatized in Indic thought that even centuries after Buddhism's decline, he continued to be remembered with disdain. In the twentieth century milieu, the Buddha's place in the Vaishnava pantheon was regularly touted as evidence of a pre-modern ecumenicalism without discussing the real content and nature of the Buddhadev incarnation. Occasionally, Hindu swamis, poets, and intellectuals acknowledged the elephant in the room. As the *chayavadi* poet, Mohanlal Mahto Viyogi (1901–1990), asked rhetorically, "when this Buddhagaya temple was still half buried under the earth [until the nineteenth century], where was the proof of our devotion (*MBJ* Vol. 43/7, 1935: 336)?"[54]

Other strata of Hindu society felt strongly that there was no reason to "make amends". When Gandhi asked the Hindu Congressman, B.G. Kher, to oversee J.K. Birla's donations to Kosambi's Buddhist Bahujan vihara in Bombay, Kher penned a letter to Gandhi declaring that he could not be involved in the temple once it was complete: "How am I to work on a Buddhist Vihar committee? Are they all going to become Buddhists? Where is the need" (24 August 1936, in *CWMG* Vol. 69: 318fn2)?[55] In the early 1930s, when Jagdish Kashyap (then Jagdish Narain) began studying Pali, the authorities at the Arya Samaji gurukul in Deoghar barred him from associating with his Pali teacher, Bhikkhu Seevali (Ojha 1986: 83). After leaving the gurukul for Ceylon where he too became a bhikkhu, Kashyap returned to India but his promotion of Buddhism in places like Sarnath so inflamed the local contingent of brahmins and banias that one night a gang of locals attempted to kill him by setting fire to his home while he was sleeping inside (*DD* Vol. 3/8, 1937: frontispiece). Just a few years later, Kashyap returned to Benares at the invitation of JK, Malaviya, and Radhakrishnan to take a distinguished posting at Banaras Hindu University as an instructor of Pali. While their support helped protect Kashyap from further violence, the presence of an Indian Buddhist bhikkhu on the orthodox campus was not always welcome.[56] Even in this new milieu, the centuries-old brahmanical tradition of stigmatizing a demonic Buddhist other continued to be crucial to the political imaginaries and strategies of some Hindu elites. The repercussions of being outwardly and inwardly Buddhist were even more severe for the marginalized castes.

Despite the enduring stigma of being a Buddhist in India, the support of elite Hindu organizations and liberal leaders helped ease such caustic animosity. Gandhi explained to B.G. Kher that there was no reason to fear Dharmanand Kosambi's Bahujan Buddhist temple in Bombay. In his eyes, it was no different from a temple to Rama or Krishna, just a part of the Hindu revival (Gandhi 1936, in *CWMG* Vol. 69: 318–19). Similarly, the Birla viharas–dharmashalas at all the major Buddhist sites contain plaques explaining to visitors that Buddhists are their brothers and sisters, no different than anyone else passing through this world of suffering (*samsara*). Yet, naturally, Hindu support was a double-edged sword. By calling Buddhism as Hinduism and Buddhists as Hindus, Buddhist traditions were denied their intrinsic identity and autonomy, and, in effect, falsified. Since modern Hindu ideals (*adarsh*) were said to already be in accord with Buddhist values and ways of life, there was little reason to study Buddhism on its own terms. This made Buddhism something incidental, unnecessary, and trivial, effectively disregarding the ways that Buddhist teachings can structure real human lives.

Still, there were unusual counter-trends. J.K. Birla, for instance, did not just support Buddhist activists that toed the Hindutva line. This was the case with Rahul Sankrityayan, Jagdish Kashyap, Dharmanand Kosambi, and Anand Kausalyayan, all of whom benefited from Birla's support in the 1930s, at a time when they were writing stinging criticisms of Hindu scriptures, doctrines, and the Maha Sabha.[57] The Nipponzon Myohoji monastics in India were not as aggressively anti-Hindu as these figures, but JK was certainly aware of their desire to "convert" India to Mahayana Buddhism. Even then, JK supported them, and the Birla Temple Japan Trust continues to support eight Nipponzon Myohoji centers in India to this day.[58] Likewise, at the Maha Bodhi Mission that JK supported along the Malabar Coast in modern-day Kerala, the monks and activists, led by the Malayali bhikkhu, Dhammaskanda, and C. Krishnan, espoused a rhetoric that was clearly at odds with the hard-line Hindutva agenda. Whether this should be taken as a sign of Hindu confidence that the Buddhist revival did not constitute a major threat or was simply due to JK's private interests is unclear.

While it would be careless to underestimate the hegemonic and ultimately assimilative role of the Maha Sabha in Buddhist affairs in the post-1940s era, allying with the Maha Sabha also provided brief, short-term gains for some Buddhist communities. When Ottama founded the Burmese Bengal Buddhist Association in Barisal (in modern-day Bangladesh) in 1936, the fact that he was simultaneously the president of the All-India Hindu Maha Sabha must have helped ease fears about Buddhist proselytization. After all, he had already declared, just like Gandhi, that the Buddha was "a Hindu of Hindus". So, it was not just the conservative elements of the Maha Sabha that benefited from the Hinduization of Buddhism, but also the Buddhist leaders who used the Maha Sabha's national positioning to augment their own efforts in spreading Buddhist teachings.

Lastly, calling Buddhism as Hinduism was also a rhetorical strategy that allowed many Hindus to explore the dhamma without being seen as having "abandoned" one's culture (of which Indian Christians and Muslims were often unjustly accused). For people like the Punjabi advocate, Rai Bahadur Pandit Sheo Narain (c. 1860–1936), who was one of colonial India's most ardent Buddhist propagandists, following Lord Buddha did not mean one had "to shelve their great Indian Heroes" (Narain 1923: 259).[59] In Narain's view, the Buddha's teachings were to be studied in the spirit of comparative religion, alongside those of Rama and Krishna, Christ and Muhammad, in order to determine the true spirit of religious brotherhood. "If people imbibe it [Buddhadharma] even in spirit and act accordingly it ought to make no difference whether they call themselves Buddhistic or not" (260). Similarly, for Anandrao Nair, the object of his Bombay Buddha Society was not to "convert people to Buddhism," for if they did that "they could not be called moral in their purpose. Their object was to study the life of Buddha and translate his preachings [sic] into action" (*ISR* Vol. 28, 21 May 1927: 603). To some, this appeared to be a watered-down version of Buddhism, but it is significant that some of the most influential Buddhist activists in India began their studies in this context and only later became convinced of Buddhism's autonomy. For those who did dissent from this liberal Hindu view, being Buddhist was often enmeshed within a much larger sociocultural vision of being neither brahmin nor Hindu.

The Snake and the Mongoose

On 14 October 1956, Dr "Babasaheb" Bhimrao Ramji Ambedkar (1891–1956) and his wife, Savita (1909–2003), took refuge in the Three Jewels (*triratna*), promised to observe the Five Precepts (panchshil), and then, in a novel venture, commited to uphold twenty-two additional vows emphasizing moral conduct and a rejection of Hindu beliefs and rites. Alongside Ambedkar sat several Indian and foreign Buddhist monastics, of which the senior-most bhikkhu, U Chandramani (1875–1972), initiated the recitation of the Three Refuges and Five Precepts.[1] Conversion ceremonies like these, barring the twenty-two vows (which were Ambedkar's invention), had been a regular feature of the Buddhist revival in India since at least the early 1900s.[2] What made this event far grander than other ceremonies were two additional components. First, the figure taking initiation (diksha) was one of India's most well-credentialed citizens (he held two PhDs and a law degree), a former law minister, the chief architect of the Indian Constitution, and the undisputed national leader of India's dalits. That last fact was brought home by the sea of bodies, dressed in white, and estimated at up to half a million, who had traveled from across the region to join their beloved Babasaheb in repeating the Three Refuges, Five Precepts, and the newly invented "Twenty-two Vows". In the following months, these ceremonies were repeated across western and northern India as hundreds of thousands of dalits, primarily mahars of Ambedkar's own caste (jati), renounced Hinduism, declared themselves Buddhists, and replaced the Hindu images in their temples

Ambedkar and his wife Savita being administered the Three Refuges and Five Precepts by Bhikkhu U Chandramani during the historic mass conversion ceremony in Nagpur, 14 October 1956. Ambedkar (to the right), Savita (far right), Chandramani (seated, far left), and Devapriya Valisinha (to Chandramani's left)

with those of Gotama Buddha (Beltz 2005).[3] By 1961, Ambedkar's Buddhist intiation (*dhamma diksha*) was being hailed as the largest mass conversion movement in history with nearly three million of his followers having publicly declared themselves Buddhist. Six decades later, the number has nearly tripled, and the Ambedkarite Buddhist movement remains a vibrant force in Indian society.[4]

To many of Ambedkar's followers, he was a living Bodhisattva, and the accounts of his life often possess hagiographic traits. But the standard narrative tracking his journey to Buddhism loosely adheres to the following chronology: He was first introduced to Buddhism at his high school graduation when one of his former teachers gave him a Marathi-language biography of the Buddha (*Buddhacarita*) (Keer [1971] 2009: 19–21).[5] Due to his mahar background, Ambedkar's graduation was an unusual event, and with the support of several progressive Hindu reformers, he went on to attain scholarships to study in the UK and the US. Here he earned two doctorates in economics, from the London School of Economics in 1923 and New York's Columbia University in 1926, as well as a law degree from London's prestigious Gray's Inn in 1923. Despite his education, his caste continued to make him the object of ill repute, prejudice, and even physical abuse when he returned to India. He retaliated with socio-political mobilization and the launching of several print journals that gave a rare public voice to the downtrodden and, by extension, earned Ambedkar a well-deserved reputation as an acute social critic and firebrand activist. Then, in the two decades after Ambedkar's famous Nashik statement of 1935, where he declared he "would not die a Hindu," he began studying other religions "as if it were a massive research project" (Queen 1996: 51).[6] Gradually, he turned to Buddhism, after considering all other major religions, seeing it as the only possibility for a just and egalitarian Indian society.

One of the central questions in studies of Ambedkar's conversion is why a man committed to secularism and progressive jurisprudence would turn to religion and in particular Buddhism. A survey of the most important studies on the subject (Zelliot 1992, 2013; Rodrigues 1993; Queen 1996; Vishwanathan 1998; Beltz 2005; Jaffrelot 2005; Rao 2009) points to several interlocking themes. These include his desire to: 1) combat brahmanical norms and hegemony with equally powerful anti-caste Buddhist symbols and ideas; 2) build a new moral order based on equality, justice, and fraternity; 3) protect dalits from continued oppression by giving them a new personhood and way of life that neither the state nor caste Hindus could strip away; 4) provide dalits with a "national" (as opposed to de-nationalizing) identity, rooted in ancient India and yet respected by the world; and 5) exploit the non-existence of a powerful local Buddhist community capable of challenging his leadership.

All of these issues—the failures of the state to protect dalits, the anti-brahmanical thrust of Buddhism, its Indic heritage, and so on—had undoubtedly major influences on Ambedkar. However, what is rarely discussed is Ambedkar's links to other Indian Buddhist movements of the period. That is, many scholars still take it for granted that Buddhism was dead in India, and that Ambedkar, as one prominent scholar wrongly put it, built this "new Buddhism from scratch" (Vajpeyi 2012: 231). Ambedkar's dhamma was indeed a monumental intervention in the Indian Buddhist marketplace, but to fully grasp its significance, one needs to not only consider the reinventions of Buddhism that had been going on in South Asia since the mid-nineteenth century, but also those conversion-based Buddhist movements in India that preceded the mass conversions of post-1956 India.

Buddhism among the Bahujan and the Bahujan in Buddhism

Before proceeding, it is necessary to discuss some terminology surrounding caste and caste politics. The term "bahujan," which literally means a mass or majority of people, has acquired a strong political connotation in contemporary India due to the rise of the prominent political party, the Bahujan Samaj Party.[7] However, the word also had a strong Buddhist flavor during the middle decades of the twentieth century, when adherents popularized the ancient Pali expression, *"bahujana hitaya, bahujana sukhaya,"* or "for the good of many, for the happiness of many".[8] From this expression, various uses of the term "bahujan" emerged to refer to the majority of the population, but more particularly the downtrodden and marginalized. A typical example of its use by Buddhist scholars at the time was in Dharmanand Kosambi's Bahujan vihara in Bombay, inaugurated in 1937, and aimed primarily, as its name suggests, at the laboring castes in Parel. During that time and since, "bahujan" became both a popular slogan in mobilizing so-called "lower caste" (shudra) and outcaste (dalit or "untouchable") communities on a unified platform (as in dalit–bahujan), as well as a point of resistance for some dalit thinkers who felt that the singular category of bahujan obscures the distinctive struggles of dalit communities (Rawat 2011: 16–17). While recognizing the contested nature of the expression, I use the term as a sociological catch-all, as it was used by many Buddhist thinkers of the late colonial period, to refer to the large bulk of the Indian populace, with a particular emphasis on those communities who fell under two ever-shifting categories.[9]

The first category refers to the group of people once widely described as "untouchables," but more commonly known today as dalits. In contemporary political sociology, dalits are often understood as a discrete historical agent and were variously described in the governmental parlance of the period as scheduled castes, depressed classes, and "pariahs".[10] All of these terms were, in the period under study, used interchangeably in different regions, although each one, along with other common expressions like *ati-shudra*, achoot and harijan, evokes mixed feelings from various audiences (Rawat 2015: 335–55).[11] Differences aside, the terms all pointed, in that historical moment, to the community that fell outside of the *chaturvarna*, or the brahmanical system of four major castes. Dalits were the *avarna* groups (literally, "without caste"), who, in the brahmanical view, were essentially sub-human and whose touch, visible presence, and in some cases even shadow was considered polluting by caste (*savarna*) Hindus. What caused these groups to be treated with such grotestque inhumanity remains contested, but in the early twentieth-century colonial context, dalit livelihoods were often based in or represented by scavenging, rubbish removal, street cleaning, leatherwork, and other forms of menial labor deemed "ritually impure" by brahmanical standards (Rawat 2011; Gupta 2016; Jangam 2017).

The second group was classed under various governmental terminologies, but after the 1930s, most commonly as the Hindu "backward classes". Like the depressed classes, this category was composed of hundreds (if not thousands) of sub-castes (jati) linked to specified hereditary occupations (such as laborers and service providers). In the fourfold brahmanical theory of caste, the backward classes were seen as shudras, and although they were "touchable" (*choot*) and possessing of caste (savarna), they were not "twice-born" (*dvija*) and therefore were barred from the central ritual activities and religious affairs of the three upper castes.

While the precise origins of caste remain nebulous, its basic organizing principles are not.[12] Caste theory is centered on power and serves as the basis for systematic political and economic servitude. It functions according to a vertical, sliding scale of privileges and obligations, and purity and pollution. The top of the caste hierarchy is deemed pure, possessing numerous privileges over the rest of society. The bottom, on the other hand, has no shortage of obligations, yet lacks privileges (except the right "to serve" the higher castes). From the perspective of personalities like Ambedkar, the whole system functions as an "ascending scale of reverence and a descending scale of contempt" (quoted in Keer [1971] 2009: 150).

It is important to recognize that there are many variations and sub-hierachies within each of these broad categories and they have varied widely depending on time and geography. There have been fierce contestations over the classifications of many sub-castes (jati) within each of the varnas, and in many regions of India, the fourfold varna matrix holds less weight or is observed in significantly altered fashion. In spite of these disputes and variations, these two general broad categories of shudra and dalit, or backward class and depressed class, held then, as they do today, a profound ideological bearing. As the late sociologist Gail Omvedt (2003: 220) explains: "India represented on the whole a 'three-strata' society: the 'twice-born', comprising the birth-defined elite as contrasted with the 'masses' [Bahujan]: but within the 'masses' another significant category divided ... the 'clean' Shudras ... from Dalits (the 'unclean')."

The penetration of Buddhist ideas and symbols among the bahujan was not uniform, and barring Malabar, the United Provinces, and the Madras Presidency, it was not significant enough to spur on a social movement anywhere until the early 1940s. Moreover, in those areas where bahujan leaders actively engaged Buddhism, as practice or theory, it was almost always limited to a small minority who through a combination of determination, mental acuity, and sheer chance were able to receive a "modern" education in new urban settings. The incisive social critic and anti-caste educator, Jotirao Phule (1827–90), illustrates this well. A contemporary of Ambedkar's father and a mali (gardener) by caste, Phule was exposed to modern epistemologies through an education provided by Scottish missionaries in Pune. Inspired by the radical works of Thomas Paine's *Age of Reason* and *The Rights of Man*, Phule founded his own Society of Truth Seekers (Satyashodak Samaj), aimed at educating dalits and shudras (whom he wished to unify) and challenging theories of brahmanical superiority through alternative histories of India (O'Hanlon 1985: 111–12). Although Phule penned a harsh critique of British colonial governance in 1882, like many other bahujan leaders he welcomed European attacks on brahmanism. It is not surprising, then, that when

Orientalists and Christian missionaries alike began publishing materials contrasting the "high-mindedness" and "glories" of Buddhism with the "superstition" and "demagoguery" of Hinduism, figures like Phule took to the new Buddhist message. As early as the 1860s, he and his colleague, Tukaram Tatya Padwal (1838–98), published a Marathi translation of Ashvaghosha's *Vajrasuchi,* the scathing Buddhist criticism of caste first published in the 1830s that left many caste Hindus up in arms.[13]

Despite this early subaltern intervention, Phule's grasp of Buddhism appears to have been elementary at best. In his provocative Marathi-language work, *Shetkaryaca Asud* or The Cultivator's Whipcord (1882), he contended that the ancient teaching was started by "four disinterested holy wise men" (Omvedt 2003: 233). Yet, he knew enough to exploit its anti-brahmanical symbolism, naming it a campaign "to free the ignorant shudra farmers from the noose of the Aryabhats [Aryan brahmins]" (Phule 1882, quoted in Omvedt 2003: 233). Phule said little more about Buddhists, but it should be remembered how closely this idea resembled the one found in the influential trilingual (Hindi, Urdu, English) schoolbook, *Itihas Timir Nashak* (1864–74).

Phule's use of modern print technologies and Buddhist texts to directly challenge brahmanical authority was rare among the Indians of his day. However, by the turn of the century, a powerful undercurrent of anti-caste Buddhist egalitarianism was under way in south India. When the members of the soon-to-be Shakya Buddhist Society of Madras (est. 1898) joined Henry Olcott in Ceylon to return to their "ancestral faith," restore their self-respect, and free themselves of caste by becoming Buddhists, two important arguments were framed. First, Shakya Buddhist Society leaders like Iyothee Thass argued that the "original inhabitants" of India were (Dravidian) Buddhists and that when "foreign" Aryans migrated to the subcontinent, they conquered the "indigenous" Buddhist dynasties and punished them with the stigma of untouchability. Second, they argued that Buddhism's progressive outlook and egalitarian ethos could solve what was then being called "the pariah problem". These two notions, of an ancestral dalit Buddhist lineage and of Buddhist equality and freedom, not only spread far beyond Thass's Shakya Buddhist Society, but became the intellectual and political cornerstone of later bahujan Buddhist imaginaries. In doing so, they reversed the conventional gaze of caste society and synthesized the perspective of two historical "others"—the stigmatized outcaste and the stigmatized Buddhist. Drawing from their own literary reserves, folk narratives, myths, and histories, these Buddhist groups from Lucknow and Kanpur to Calicut and Madras promulgated new meanings of human dignity and launched a social project that was as much political and ethical as it was historiographical.

Soldiers of the Sasana

Before turning to the bahujan Buddhist publics, it is worthwhile reflecting on the wider Buddhist context at the time. In addition to the emergence of a small, educated, and highly motivated minority among the bahujan that worked against tremendous odds to spread Buddhism among their peers, there were other currents in the cultural landscape transforming the Indian encounter with Buddhism. As the ancient Buddhist spaces in north India continued to develop as sites for travelers, pilgrims, and scholars, a growing number of missionary monks (dharmadoot) began congregating there, establishing small but often boisterous hubs of Buddhist activity. At some spaces, such as Kushinagar and Shravasti, but most importantly at Sarnath, the new Buddhist communities were vigorous in preaching the dhamma among local communities.

From the 1930s onwards, Sarnath was the de facto center of India's international Buddhist activist scene. This was led by Sinhalese and Indian monastics and laity associated with the Maha Bodhi Society, the International Buddhist College, and the Missionary Training Institute. In addition to the several Indian-born Buddhist bhikkhus and upasakas from across western UP and Bihar who regularly visited Sarnath, foreign Buddhist activists came primarily from Ceylon. Some, like Bhikkhu Sangharatana (1912–84) of Sarnath and Shravasti, moved to India not long after taking their preliminary monastic vows and studied at Indian schools. They were, in other words, well equipped linguistically and culturally to adapt the Buddha's message for a local Indian audience. Most, however, were products of Dharmapala's last attempt to bring dozens of Buddhist missionaries to India. The first significant contingent came in the winter of 1929 when eight "soldiers of the Sasana," as Dharmapala called them, led by Bhikkhu Dhammaloka of the Lankan Missionary Society (Dharmadoota Sabha), came to India (*MBJ* Vol. 37/12, 1929: 578–83). Initiating a cycle that would be repeated over the following decades, most of these monastics first settled in Calcutta, from where they then traveled to Tagore's university at Santiniketan, studying local languages, history, and culture, before dispersing to Buddhist centers at Sarnath, Bodh Gaya, Shravasti, Bombay, Calicut, and beyond.

Not all Buddhist monastics traveling and working in India conceived of themselves as soldiers there to convert the *pashanda* or impious. Many were like the Chinese Theravadin bhikkhu, Suriya, known popularly as the "Chini Baba" (1886–1971), who built a hut inside an ample banyan tree at the Ramabhara stupa outside Kushinagar, dwelling in meditation, and gathering a cult following for his saintly behavior (Bauddh 2008: 191). Others, like the Tibetan savant, Gendun Chopel (1903–51), combined their Buddhist scholarship with a curiosity for travel and worldly delights, imparting their socio-political messages not to audiences in India but back home (Stoddard 1986; Chopel 2014). Moreover, as the story of Bhikkhu Ottama, the Arakanese–Burmese anti-colonial agitator and president of the All-India Hindu Maha Sabha in 1935, indicates, even those who saw the saffron robe as the missionary's vestment were far from being radical anti-caste activists.

The fact that many of these monastics were affiliated with the Maha Bodhi Society, which was closely linked to the Hindu Maha Sabha, warrants further discussion. On the surface, it is obvious that the Sarnath Maha Bodhi branch's more rigid Buddhism was regularly at odds with the general ambience of its headquarters in Calcutta, where Bengali upper-caste Hindus dominated the society. For instance, after Ambedkar explained to ten thousand leaders of the depressed classes gathered at Nashik that the only solution to their problem was to "change your religion," the Sarnath branch telegraphed Ambedkar promising their support if he were to become a Buddhist (*TOI*, 18 October 1935, quoted in Zelliot 2013: 159). The Calcutta leadership, which also managed the English-language *Maha Bodhi* journal, was less enthusiastic, explaining that they disagreed with "his intended apostasy, but if, however, he is determined to leave Hinduism, Buddhism has all the requisites which he looks for in his religion" (*MBJ* Vol. 43/11, 1935: 557–58).

The juxtaposition between these two Maha Bodhi Society trends is further highlighted in a special "Harijan Conference" (Harijan Sammelan) attended by roughly five hundred people held on the third and last day of the Mulagandhakuti vihara celebrations in Sarnath on 12 November 1935. The event came at a moment when Hindus of all stripes, from Gandhi and Birla to Moonje and Malaviya, were frantically trying to tamp down the threat of dalit conversion, following Ambedkar's recent speech and the wider fallout from the Poona Pact. Standing before the crowd, Bhikkhu Bodhananda, a major leader in the anti-Congress Adi-Hindu movement of western UP and the author of a popular Hindi-language book denouncing Hindu culture, explained that now was the time for India's Buddhist revival (*punarutthan*) and that if freedom (*azaadi*) was to be attained, Hindus could not represent the dalits, only dalits could represent themselves (*svadhinata*) (*DD* Vol. 1/8, 1935–36: 71).[14] Following Bodhananda, the Punjabi Buddhist bhikkhu, Anand Kausalyayan, explained that Buddhism offered dalits complete equality (*samanta*) and that "if they wanted to abandon Hinduism in which caste is an integral part, they are welcome to embrace Buddhism" (*MBJ* Vol. 43/12, 1935: 604). After the speeches, J.K. Birla and Baba Raghava Das—the latter a prominent Congress leader and brahmin head of a Hindu ashram in Deoria—handed out clothes, sweets, and fruits to dalit youth. The juxtaposition between Birla and Raghava Das on the one hand, and the speeches of the bhikkhus on the other, is striking. The former group represented a Hindu Congress platform that opposed conversion and the self-representation of dalits, while the latter was fiercely anti-Hindu and anti-Congress. These were strange bedfellows.

By the 1940s, the Hindu–Buddhist tension within the Calcutta branch of the Maha Bodhi Society was palpable. As Bhikkhu Sangharakshita's (1991, 1996) accounts suggest, finding a suitable compromise between these two parties was a constant balancing act for Devapriya Valisinha, the Sinhalese general secretary in Calcutta. How was Valisinha to explain to his caste Hindu Bengali patrons why Maha Bodhi monks in Sarnath—from the British anagarika, Priyardarshi Sugatananda (né Francis Story) to the "Ambedkar of Burma," U Oliyar—were traveling the country urging India's downtrodden to "return to their own ancestral religion" and enter "the democratic fold of Buddhism" (*MBJ* Vol. 59/9, 1951: 336–37)?

The intellectual habitus of these "soldiers of the Sasana" is most clearly seen in the Sarnath monthly, *Dharmadoot*, or The Buddhist Messenger (or Missionary). This Hindi-language journal, the first of its kind to focus solely on Buddhism, was published by the Sarnath branch of the Maha Bodhi Society beginning in 1935.[15] Like its English-language counterpart, the *Maha Bodhi*, *Dharmadoot* published essays by well-regarded scholars of the day, including Har Dayal, Rahul Sankrityayan, Vidhushekar Shastri, Jagdish Kashyap, P.C. Bagchi, and Acharya Narendra Dev.[16] Despite its Buddhological emphasis, the journal was a curious mix of voices, ranging from prominent leftists in the Progressive Writers' Association and anti-caste activists (like Chandrika Prasad Jigyasu) to Hindu pandits and mainstream Indian Buddhologists with advanced degrees from Western universities. While the journal's core emphasis was on clarifying doctrinal positions, publishing Hindi translations of Buddhist scriptures, and reporting Buddhist news, it also had a substantial focus on social and political issues. Vicious denunciations of brahmanical scriptures were the norm, attacks on Gandhi's political and religious views were not unusual, and the adoption of Buddhism was (not surprisingly) regularly advocated as a solution to India's woes. Sometimes these arguments were explicit, being the subject of entire articles; but, even in those essays more explicitly concerned with ostensibly "religious" matters, the ethos was obvious. In an eighteen-part series that ran from 1935 to 1938 entitled "Letters of a Monk" (Bhikshu ke patra), readers entered the intimate world of a conversation that took place between Anand Kausalayayan (the author and "the monk") and one of his disciples ("Yogendra"), a recent Hindu convert to Buddhism. Through topics like the need for rationalism and sources of authentic knowledge, Kausalyayan clarifies Yogendra's doubts about Buddhism and provides his own confessional account of why any "rational, intelligent man" could see the immutable flaws and problems in Hinduism and other religions (Kausalyayan 1940).[17]

It is unclear how widely known *Dharmadoot* was among the bahujan populace in north India. Distribution and funding were both recurring problems for the journal, but the network of monastic centers across western UP and Bihar may have helped its circulation in these regions. The space it gave to both Chandrika Prasad Jigyasu and Bhikkhu Bodhananda, two of the most well-known writers in the Adi-Hindu movement at the time, may have not only helped augment its profile among bahujan communities but also created a sense that the new Buddhist presence was an "ally" in a common cause.

While the soldiers of the sasana unleashed their intellectual weapons in the war against caste and brahmanism, groups like the Hindu Maha Sabha and Arya Samaj were intent on purging Hinduism of untouchability. The problem for them, from the viewpoint of Buddhist activists (and others), was that they were unwilling to give up ideas about caste as important signifiers of difference. Arya Samaji activists, for instance, argued that caste was a real ontological category, but that it was not determined by birth but by worth (*guna*) and actions (karma). Prominent Hindu reformers saw similarities in this notion and the Buddhist critiques of caste (Eltschinger 2012). From this platform, caste Hindus like Syama Prasad Mookerjee (1901–53), who during his long tenure as president of the Maha Bodhi Society also led the Hindu Maha Sabha, propagated Buddhism as a "higher form of Hinduism". Gandhi's support for Dharmanand Kosambi's Bombay Bahujan vihara hinged on a similar logic. For Gandhi, temples honoring the Buddha were integral to Hindu "reform" and "revival" (Ober 2013: 140). In places like Kerala, Maharashtra, and UP, several leading Buddhist advocates were also of this "Hindu–Buddhist" persuasion.[18] The varied Hindu–Buddhist tensions that manifested in the Maha Bodhi Society's branches and in other spheres, then, were clearly as much about caste as they were about other dimensions of the Buddha's teachings. Similarly, the interventions of the Maha Sabha, like those of Gandhi, Birla, Savarkar, and other Hindu leaders, were clearly aimed at abating these tensions, not so much as part of a calculated plot to control Buddhism but because of their own insecurities about the unraveling of Hindu-ness. Such anxieties would drive Hindu actions in Buddhist spaces in far-flung parts of the subcontinent for decades to come.

South Indian Currents: Seeking Equality in the Malabar Mission

The Tamil-led Shakya Buddhist Society (est. 1898) or South Indian Buddhist Association never completely collapsed. The organization was known well enough that Ambedkar met with Shakya leaders in Madras in 1944 (Keer [1971] 2009: 367), as did the Panchen Lama and Dalai Lama during their visit to India for the Buddha Jayanti in 1956 (*MBJ* Vol. 65/1, 1957: 27–30). However, in 1936, when a sympathetic Bombay journalist visited several of their branches, he lamented the disorganized leadership of the Society and its failure to ably follow in the footsteps of either Iyothee Thass (d. 1914) or Lakshmi Narasu (d. 1934) (*Bombay Chronicle*, 22 August 1936, in *BP* Vol. 4/4, 1936: 708–10). Although the organization persists to this day in the temples of Chennai and among the railway workers of Hubli, the rising tide of the Dravidian Self-Respect movement diminished its coherence, and it was soon co-opted by leaders like E.V. Ramasamy Naicker "Periyar" (1879–1973), who also drew on Buddhism as a form of cultural resistance and representation (Aloysius 1998: 191–93; Aloysius 2006).[19]

Apart from Tamil Nadu, the most organized social movement towards Buddhism occurred in the 1920s and 1930s among the Malayalam-speaking izhava community along the south-west coast of India. Izhavas, sometimes referred to as thiyas, were typically classified as a "lower caste" (shudra) community, and were scattered across British Malabar and the Hindu kingdoms of Travancore and Cochin in present-day Kerala. Although colonization was far from being a uniformly liberatory force for the subcontinent's subordinate castes, the British annexation of Malabar in 1800 enhanced occupational opportunities and social mobility for a large number of izhavas (Pullapilly 1976). Their caste status led them to endure much humiliation from the region's empowered namboodiri brahmin elites; but they were not "untouchable" or "unapproachable" and therefore able to function as important intermediaries between the new British authorities and the generally conservative priestly caste. This social flexibility became essential in the improvement of the conditions of the izhava community in the nineteenth century, allowing them to play an important role in governance and administration. As the historian Cyriac Pullapilly (1976: 34) writes, within only a few generations, "practically all the Indian-born higher officers in the administration of the province until the second quarter of the twentieth century came from the Thiya [izhava] community".[20]

By the early 1900s, this new generation of relatively well-to-do izhavas had joined forces with other caste reformers to agitate for the removal of social inequalities. Most threw their support behind the prominent Hindu ascetic and social reformer, Swami Narayana Guru (1856–1928), and his non-dualist (advaita) message of "one caste, one religion, one God" (Chandramohan 1987). This protest mantra, which is branded on buildings across Kerala to this day, found its social basis in Narayana Guru's popular organization, the Sri Narayana Dharma Paripalana Yogam (SNDP). Early SNDP ideologues, like the polyhistoric poet–translator, Kumaran Asan (1873–1924), drew on Buddhist literary works in Tamil, Sanskrit, Malayalam, and English to propagate Narayana Guru's message of love and compassion. Whether in his Malayalam-language translation of Edwin Arnold's *The Light of Asia*, serialized between 1915 and 1924, or his celebrated adaptation of the canonical story of Ananda's encounters with a young untouchable girl in *Candala Bhiksuni* (1922), Asan reworked the central narratives to highlight Buddhism's historical protest against the violence of caste (Ober 2021: 13–15; Das [1995] 2006: 306–08).

While Asan saw Buddhism primarily as a literary device, the public conversation about Buddhism changed directions around 1920, when a Hindu swami wrote a letter to Narayana threatening to convert to Buddhism if the SNDP did not eradicate caste discrimination immediately (Joseph 2008: 245–70). Although conversion to other religious traditions, primarily Christianity and Islam, had long been part of regional debates, the idea of conversion to Buddhism was more novel. In line with many other brahmanized regions of the subcontinent, the popular view of Buddhism in Kerala was based on a hodgepodge of negative assumptions. Even the word "Buddhist" in colloquial parlance was a synonym for "idiot" (Pullapilly 1976: 30). As the debate about Buddhist conversion escalated, several leaders within the SNDP began to voice their support.

The driving force was C. Krishnan (1867–1938), a former advocate in the high court and editor of a popular Malayalam newspaper, *Mitavadi*. Born to a family of thiyas (izhavas) in British-controlled Trichur, Krishnan was educated in a government program that funded schools for "Backward Hindu" classes like his own. Like most izhavas, he was an early devotee of Narayana Guru, and his home even functioned as the Calicut branch of the SNDP. In 1903, Krishnan began serving as a high court vakeel in Calicut, but he soon gave up the practice and turned his attention to public activism and journalism, using the funds he made from the Calicut Bank, which he founded in 1908, to finance his activities. According to his biographer, K. Sabukuttan (2002: 48–50), Krishnan's interest in Buddhism was sparked in 1907 after reading Paul Carus's *Gospel of Buddhism*—a book he felt should be kept in every home. He spent the next years reading as much Buddhist literature as possible and traveling to sacred Buddhist sites like Bodh Gaya and Sarnath. These experiences led Krishnan to see Buddhism as a refuge for izhavas and to build Calicut's first Buddhist temple, inaugurated on 16 May 1927, in a colorful function at Paran Square.[21]

By the early 1920s, newspaper columns were increasingly debating the possibilities of izhava conversion, and Krishnan's *Mitavadi* projected itself as a pro-Buddhist voice in opposition to the *Matrubhoomi*, the other major Malayali newspaper, whose upper-caste ownership leveled sustained criticism against calls for conversion of any kind (Joseph 2008: 245–46). Despite growing opposition, especially from within the SNDP, in February 1925, Krishnan and his colleagues organized a large gathering at Paran Square to discuss the possibility of switching to Buddhism. The two-day conference, formally touted as the All-Kerala Buddhist Conference, was attended by a few dozen delegates from across the Malabar Coast along with a contingent of Buddhist monastics from Ceylon. The speeches delivered were primarily concerned with "how thousands of Hindus had really no place in their religion as the Samskaras [life-cycle rituals] and other privileges of a Hindu were confined to the first three varnas and not to shudras" (*MBJ* Vol. 33/3, 1925: 143). Others imagined more provocatively the "social advantages which Buddhism could confer on the ill-treated and oppressed classes of Malabar" (144).

Throughout the Kerala conference, theosophy was writ large. One of Krishnan's closest colleagues, a brahmin by the name of Manjeri Ramier [also spelled Rama Iyer] (1877–1958), who had been a major leader in temple-entry movements in the early decades of the century, was also the head of the local Theosophical Society branch. Presumably, it is through Ramier's Theosophical Society networks that the large contingent of Sinhalese Buddhist monastics attended the event. On the second day, the Sinhalese bhikkhu Jinavamsa administered panchshil to "Brahmins, Nairs, Thiyyas [izahavas], Christians, men, and women,"; the conference president, former

Leaders of the Malabar Buddhist Movement. Seated (from the left):
Dr. V.I. Raman, Bhikkhu Dhammaskanda, Bhikkhu Ananda Maitreya, a Buddhist
novice, and C. Krishnan, Member Legislative Council. Standing: P.C. Amat,
Kottai Kumaran, Manjeri Ramier, K.R. Achuthan and P.C. Gopalan

bhikkhu, and globetrotting theosophist, Jinarajadasa (1875–1953), then clarified how the Buddha was antagonistic to no religion (*MBJ* Vol. 33/3, 1925: 144).[22] He explained how anyone—Hindus, Muslims, Christians, savarnas, avarnas, females, males—could take panchshil. It was fundamentally about living an ethical, upright life. In this orientation, which would be emphatically rejected by Ambedkar thirty years later, you could be both Buddhist and Hindu, as long as you were moral. But for Ambedkar, Hinduism was anything but moral.[23]

An important feature of the conference, which resulted in the formation of the Kerala Buddhist Association, was the argument that izhavas were "originally" Buddhist. Articulated carefully, this meant that becoming Buddhist was not simply a "conversion," but rather a "reversion" to an ancient tradition. There were subtle differences between this claim and those made by the Tamil Shakya Buddhists. For Shakya Buddhists, Buddhism was part of an ancient "indigenous" Dravidian culture that preceded the "foreign" Vedic tradition. In the Kerala Buddhist Association view, the theory of ezhavas "originally" being Buddhist was based on the idea that they were Buddhist migrants from Ceylon who had come to India in the early centuries of the Common Era. Support for these claims was evidenced using a diversity of sources, both concrete and speculative. Some pointed to archaeological findings, like the Buddhist statues at places like Mavelikkara and Bharanikavu that were now being worshipped as Hindu deities. Others reconstructed migration patterns by tracing linguistic similarities. The caste name "izhava" or "ezhava," for example, was said to derive from "Eelam," the Tamil word for Sri Lanka, while the caste name "thiya" or "thiyan," as enunciated in north Kerala, was argued to be an adaptation of "dvipan" or islander. Variations of these theories abounded, but most centered on the following historical narrative, described by the historian, P.C. Alexander (1949: 134–35):

> When Buddhism declined in Kerala those who followed that faith, contemptuously called as "Bauddhas," became the victims of social degradation. The vast number of Buddhists along with the Ilavas [izhavas] now constituted a new class of "Bauddhas" whose position was little better than that of the untouchables. When Buddhism completely disappeared from Kerala these "Bauddhas" were received back into the Hindu fold, but they had to be content with the lower rungs of the social ladder.[24]

Alexander's argument bore the stamp of academic approval and helped cement izhava claims to an "original" Buddhist identity. But the argument had been circulated in various forms throughout the Malabar Coast, for more than two-and-a-half decades by izhava Buddhist leaders themselves. By declaring themselves Buddhists, izhavas were not only identifying themselves with a universal religious community but also one whose history stretched deep into the Indic past.[25]

Like the Shakya Buddhist Society, the Kerala Buddhist Association worked closely with a variety of monastic institutions and new Buddhist societies from elsewhere in South Asia. From the 1930s on, "soldiers of the sasana" from Sarnath circulated in and out of the Kerala Buddhist branches, but the latter's early network was more connected to the Maha Bodhi–Theosophical institutes of Ceylon. In 1925, the Lanka Dharmadoota Sabha or Lanka Buddhist Missionary Society sent the highly respected meditation master and scholar, Bhikkhu Ananda Maitreya (1896–1998) to live with Krishnan.[26] By the early 1930s, the Hindu Maha Sabha was also working its way into, what was by then self-consciously dubbed, the Malabar Mission of Great Awakening (Malabar Maha Bodhi Mission) (*DD* Vol. 1/5, 1935: 55). J.K. Birla, as always, picked up the bill. He sponsored the construction of a Buddhist vihara in 1937; a reading room, dispensary and expansion of the headquarters in 1938; and in 1941, a Buddhist school named Vidyodaya Vidyalaya after the well-known Buddhist college in Colombo (*MBJ* Vol. 49/10, 1941: 392).[27] In 1935, Birla, Krishnan, and Ramier also sponsored Bhikkhu Maitreya, another unnamed Sinhalese monastic, and the Malayali bhikkhu, Dhammaskanda (dates unknown), to spread the "Arya Dharma" during a three-month tour of the Malabar Coast. As the Maha Bodhi Society reported quite cryptically, the "all-Aryanizing doctrine of metta and compassion alone can make them [shudras and ati-shudras] Aryans, as it has made in the case of so many Buddhist countries" (*MBJ* Vol. 33/3, 1925: 165).

With Krishnan's death in 1938, the bhikkhu, Dhammaskanda, became the face of the Malabar Mission. Details on Dhammaskanda's life are skeletal but he appears to have been one of the few izhavas who donned the saffron robe. Around 1925, he left for Ceylon, where he took his ordination and studied Pali and *Abhidhamma* before returning to Kerala ten years later. He was an extremely active figure whose fluency in local languages and in Pali doctrines must have helped his own effort "to return" the izhavas to their ancestral faith. Within his first two years back, he established at least four branches across the state and led some six hundred people to "embrace Buddhism" (*DD* Vol. 2/2, 1936: 22; *MBJ* Vol. 46/10, 1938: 461–62). One woman "convert" (*upasika*) explained during the Buddha Jayanti of 1937 that she became a Buddhist because Hindu, Islamic, and Christian religions were "means devised by clever men to suppress and oppress womenfolk" and "it was only Buddhism that gave freedom to women" (*MBJ* Vol. 45/6, 1937: 278). Beyond rare passages like these, most of those who became Buddhist appear to have upheld the theosophical and "Arya Dharmik" position that being Buddhist did not require any rejection of central Hindu rituals or religious or caste identity. By 1961, only seventeen people in the Calicut district identified as Buddhist in that year's census (*Kerala District Gazetteers: Kozhikode Supplement* 1981: 25).

A definitive answer as to why the Malabar Buddhist movement failed awaits further study, but at least four reasons are apparent. First, after the Temple Entry Proclamation of 1936, when state-owned temples were legally opened to all caste groups, including untouchables, the momentum for conversion (to any religion) was significantly weakened (Pullapilly 1976: 42). Second, since the early 1920s when the question of Buddhist conversion was first raised, the SNDP, and even Narayana Guru himself, had tactfully undermined its very basis (Sabukuttan 2002: 51–52). From the very first All-Kerala Buddhist Conference in 1925, when a Narayana devotee explained how "there was no difference between the higher teaching of Hinduism and the higher teaching of Buddhism" (*MBJ* Vol. 33/3, 1925: 144), to the SNDP's veneration of the Buddha during major gatherings (*MBJ* Vol. 45/6, 1937: 277), there was a concerted effort to contain any possible fragmentation triggered by the Buddhist movement.

Third, and less obvious, was the critical effort made by Gandhi to both ridicule conversion and challenge claims of Buddhist equality. Gandhi's views on conversion, especially in light of the conversion of the dalit masses whose votes he needed for the Congress to succeed, were ones of antipathy. After Ambedkar threatened conversion in 1935, Gandhi replied, "religion is not like a house or a cloak, which can be changed at will" (*The Hitavada*, 16 October 1935, in *CWMG* Vol. 68: 65).[28] Even earlier, when the general secretary of the Maha Bodhi Society, Devapriya Valisinha, published an essay advocating that dalits convert en masse to Buddhism, Gandhi responded, "it is my conviction that there is no occasion whatsoever for Hindus to change their faith" ("Letter to Devapriya Valisinha", 18 March 1933, *CWMG* Vol. 61: 86). Gandhi was well aware of the izhava interest in Buddhism, having visited Krishnan's home in 1918, meeting him several times thereafter, and kick-starting the temple entry campaign in Malabar, the citadel of Hindu orthodoxy, a central part of his campaign to reform Hinduism. The timing of these events should not be underestimated. After his five-and-a-half-week tour of Malabar in the fall of 1927—at the height of the Malayali Buddhist movement—Gandhi left for Ceylon. During his three-week trip across the Buddhist-majority island, he used the pulpit to condemn, again and again, the adherence of Sri Lanka's Buddhist populace to caste ("Speech at Ananda College, Colombo," 15 November 1927, and "Speech at Nalanda Vidyalaya, Colombo," on 15 November 1927, in *CWMG* Vol. 40: 365–67).[29] After pointing out the endemic caste rift within the Sinhalese sangha, Gandhi then invoked his own moral righteousness and argued that he was more Buddhist than his audience.[30] Gandhi's positionality here, of using moral rather than knowledge-based claims to speak on behalf of all religions, was not an unusual tactic. This was one of his most characteristic political strategies. The timing, especially, of his criticism of Buddhism is crucial, though. He was an astute political leader and well understood the cultural capital that Buddhism carried in addition to the radical alternative it promised for India's bahujan. It was a dangerous combination. As the speeches he delivered during the Ceylon tour and afterwards demonstrate, in his view, there was no reason to convert to Buddhism at all. For one, not only was the Buddha a Hindu (and therefore the idea of conversion did not really make sense), but then also, why convert to a religion that was as much in need of "reform" as Hinduism?

While Gandhi's charisma and personal appeal did much to ward off considerations of conversion, the fourth and final element that undercut the Malabar Buddhist movement was the very nature of its support system. As discussed in the previous chapter, Birla's lofty rhetoric of Arya Dharma dismissed the notion that Buddhists possessed any independent, autonomous identity, making explicit that Buddhism was just another Hindu sect, albeit a very important one. Furthermore, the Hindu Maha Sabha's involvement in the Malabar movement, channeled through Birla's funds, always sent mixed messages. While many members of the Maha Sabha clearly saw Buddhists as Hindus and therefore part of the "Aryan faith," others continued to be wary of this nastika path.[31]

"Original Indians" and Lucknow's Urban Poor

Like African-American communities in the United States, and peasant and working classes worldwide, dalits and other oppressed castes in India have, until recently, been largely excluded from institutional histories and narratives. Their stories remained untold because they could not be easily integrated into the upper-class, upper-caste Hindu nationalist narratives that shaped both colonial and postcolonial scholarship. This does not mean they were inactive. In the early twentieth century, bahujan Buddhist groups voiced their demands, played critical roles in shaping debates, and like marginalized groups the world over, shaped their struggles as a fight for both recognition and difference, to be an equal on the world scale but understood and valued for their own cultural outlook. While the syndicated "Hindu–Buddhism" of the Kerala Buddhist Association was mostly alien to the social emancipation project that Ambedkar later envisioned, there was a concurrent Buddhist conversion effort in the United Provinces whose influence on Ambedkar is more easily traceable.

That influence stemmed from Bhikkhu Bodhananda (1874–1952), the founder of Lucknow's Bharatiya Bauddha Samiti or Indian Buddhist Society (est. 1916) and the Risaldar Park vihara (est. 1924). Bodhananda was a powerful voice in both the Indian Buddhist ecumene and among the Adi-Hindu religio-political movement that galvanized the bahujan public in western UP. He also was something of an anomaly: he was a brahmin-born Bengali who spent the last four decades of his life living as a Buddhist bhikkhu among the Hindi-speaking urban poor of Lucknow.[32] After being orphaned at a young age, Bodhananda, born Mukund Prakash Lahiri, moved to live with his aunt in the holy city of Benares. Restless, he set off for the "four quarters" of India, flirting with Brahmoism, the Arya Samaj, theosophy, and Christianity, before taking initiation as a Vaishnava sadhu in Sindh and adopting the name Nil Bodhananda. But, his initiation brought him anything but salvation. He became increasingly distressed by caste discrimination and the workings of a society that he felt had failed its most vulnerable members. During the devastating famines of the mid-1890s, his life took another turn when, just as he was on the verge of "taking shelter under the shadow of Jesus Christ" (Sankrityayan, quoted in Jigyasu 1965: 29), he encountered several Sinhalese bhikkhus on pilgrimage to Sarnath. They explained to him that in the *Vasala Sutta*, the Buddha refutes caste-based views of humanity and that he need not look to Christ as his savior.

Moving to Lucknow to manage a Vaishnava temple in Ameenabad Park, Bodhananda continued to learn what he could about Buddhism. His interest in the Buddha's teachings were not always appreciated, and after he installed a Buddha image inside the temple complex in 1907, he was expelled from the property along with several of his followers. Not far from there, he met the Chittagong Buddhist bhikkhu and founder of the Bengal Buddhist Association, Kripasaran, who in that same year established Lucknow's first Buddhist temple (Bodhisattva vihara, est. 1907) on La Touche Road (today Gautam Buddha Marg) with the support of Sir Harcourt Butler, later the governor of the United Provinces. As a Bengali, Bodhananda had no problem immersing himself in the rich world of Bengali Buddhist scholarship and, seven years later, he traveled to Calcutta to take full monastic ordination (upasampada) in a Ramanna Nikaya water ceremony (*udakukkhepsima*) orchestrated by Kripasaran, Bhikkhu Gunalankar, and according to some accounts, Anagarika Dharmapala.[33] Those who knew Bodhananda closely described him as a compassionate, well-read, and fiery intellectual. As his colleague Rahul Sankrityayan put it:

> [W]henever something good was said about the caste system (*varna-vyavastha*) or caste-relations (*jat-pat*) [in front of Bodhananda] … it appeared as if a sleeping lion had been awakened. From then onwards, quoting shlokas and quadrant verses (*caupai*), from Manu to Tulsidas, he would annihilate the caste system (Sankrityayan, quoted in Jigyasu 1965: 29).[34]

Back in Lucknow, Bodhananda founded the Bharatiya Bauddha Samiti, or the Indian Buddhist Society (hereafter "Samiti") in 1916. According to his biographer (Jigyasu 1965: 4), the Samiti had nine principal goals:

1. To treat the sufferings of others as one's own and to make efforts for their welfare
2. To remove casteism (*jati-bhed*) and feelings of hierarchical differences for the sake of awakening ideals of humanity (*manavata*) by

propagating equality (*samata*) and cooperation in public life

3. To study various philosophical principles of Buddhism in a coordinated manner

4. To place emphasis on the specialties of Buddhism through a comparative study in relation to present-day science and other non-Buddhist religions and philosophical views

5. To publish ancient Pali, Prakrit, and Sanskrit texts, modern research works, and their translations

6. To organize the Indian Buddhist Society, propagating a feeling of brotherhood (*bhaichara*) within it and safeguard its members' general welfare and cultural rights (*hiton evam samskrtik adhikaron ki raksha karna*)

7. To prepare capable teams of Buddhist teachers and missionaries

8. To provide assistance to Buddhist schools and cultural centers

9. To cooperate with other Buddhist institutions having identical aims and activities.

On paper, many of the goals and values of the Samiti were aligned with other Buddhist associations of the period, from the stress on cultivating compassion, friendship, equality, restraint, and selfless service, to the interest in publishing Buddhist works and research. Beyond this, central to the Samiti's ethos was its anti-caste commitment.

By the early 1920s, a small but influential group of educated leaders, most of whom were conventionally seen as "low caste" and/or "untouchable," had begun to gather around Bodhananda. With their support, he purchased a plot of land in 1924 or 1925 adjacent to today's Risaldar Park in Lucknow. The property, which soon housed a modest one-story Buddhist vihara (two more stories were added post-Independence), is only a short walk from what was then the city's only other Buddhist space, the Bodhisattva vihara (est. 1907) of the Bengal Buddhist Association. The Bengali and Chittagong Buddhists clearly played a significant role in the early years of the Samiti, and major Buddhist celebrations, like the Buddha Jayanti, were often held jointly at the Bodhisattva vihara.[35] Even then, the differences between the two organizations were clear. While the Bodhisattva vihara catered primarily to the small Barua Buddhist community of domestic servants and cooks

The Risaldar Park vihara in Lucknow, c. 1940.
Bhikkhu Bodhananda, as a silhouette in the doorway

Inside the Risaldar Park vihara, Lucknow, 2015

भदंत बोधानंद महास्थविर

Bhadant Bodhanand Mahasthavir

Buddh Bihar, Risaldar Park, Lucknow.

गंगा-फ़ाइनआर्ट-प्रेस, लखनऊ

Bhikkhu Bodhananda, on the frontispiece of his biography of the Buddha, co-authored with
the Burmese monk, Bhikkhu Ottama, and anti-caste publicist, Chandrika Prasad Jigyasu

in Lucknow, the principal audience of the Samiti were poor, working-class migrants—oilmen (*teli*), ropemakers (*barai*), betelnut sellers (*tamboli*), shepherds (*gariya*), porters (*kahar*), boatmen (*mallah*) and potters (*kumhar*) —who had migrated to urban areas of north India in recent decades (Jigyasu 1965: 5).[36] It is also notable that despite the society's generally subaltern membership, it also included individuals belonging to elite circles. Visitors to the Samiti included the head of the Sanskrit department at Lucknow University, a principal of the Islamic Shia College, European Buddhist travelers, and several professors from Tagore's university at Santiniketan.

In addition to holding Buddhist events, the Samiti distributed Buddhist literature and pamphlets on both political and religious topics. Due to a debilitating injury that Bodhananda suffered on his hand, writing was a difficult endeavor, and it was due to this injury that he became acquainted with the famed anti-caste publicist and writer, Chandrika Prasad Jigyasu (1885?–1974).[37] "With the thoughts of Bodhanand and the pen of Jigyasu" was the calling card of many of Bodhananda's works (Hunt 2014: 39). Throughout their decades-long collaboration, Jigyasu absorbed Bodhananda's Buddhist dialectic and began propagating Buddhism in his own popular writings (Khare 1984). Two of Bodhananda's first major works were a Hindi translation of the *Dhammapada* (c. 1928) and a biography of the Buddha (*Bhagavan Gautam Buddh*, 1933). In the latter work, which draws on Pali and Sanskrit sources and the Orientalist scholarship of Rhys Davids, the Buddha is viewed through a humanistic–historical lens, paralleling other modern biographies of the Buddha being produced globally at the time. Yet, far from being a dull adaptation, the text peppers conventional Buddhist vocabulary like compassion (*karuna*), friendship (*maitri*), equality (samata), and peace (*shanti*) with the more contemporary phrasing of the Buddha's human pragmatism (*manushya mapavad*) and global friendship (*vishva bandhutva*) (Bodhananda [1933] 2012).[38]

The text that brought Bodhananda's Buddhism to the wider Hindi-speaking bahujan public, however, was his 1930 publication, *Mool Bharatvasi aur Arya* (The Original Inhabitants of India and Aryans) (Bodhananda [1930] 2009). To grasp the full significance of the text, it is necessary to understand its place within the Adi-Hindu movement. The Adi-Hindu (literally, "original" Hindu/Indian) movement refers to a broad spectrum of lower-caste touchable (choot) and outcaste, untouchable (achoot) groups that formed an influential socio-political bloc in opposition to the Congress and other closely-allied Hindu reformist organizations during the late 1920s and early 1930s. Three main features of the Adi-Hindu movement are especially pertinent (Rawat 2011: 147–48; Gooptu 2001). The first is the Adi-Hindu argument that untouchables were the original inhabitants of India who after the Aryan conquest were reduced to the contemptuous category, as punishment for their resistance. This narrative, of brahmanical outsiders conquering indigenous peoples, possessed striking similarities to those advanced by Phule, Thass, and izhava intellectuals like Krishnan. Indeed, the gambit of having one's own indigenous history and society governed by its own social mores and values is found across the subcontinent from the Adi-Dravida, Adi-Andhra, Adi-Karnataka movements of the south to the Ad Dharma and Ravidasi movements in the Punjab (Juergensmeyer [1982] 2009; Ram 2012; Kumar 2014). Second, Adi-Hindu leaders were adamantly opposed to caste reform organizations like the Arya Samaj and the Hindu Maha Sabha, seeing their efforts to Sanskritize and "purify" the "unclean" castes as deeply demeaning and patronizing. They were also notoriously anti-Congress and contended that if the Congress ever gained unbridled political power, its upper-caste leadership would not make any systematic effort to improve the lives of non-twice-born Hindus. Third, the Adi-Hindu movement drew heavily on the religious symbolism and values of the sants, those esteemed medieval poet–saints, like Kabir, Nanak, Dadu, and Namdev, who espoused a message of absolute equality before god's eyes, thereby de-emphasizing caste differences (Hawley and Juergensmeyer 1988). When *Mool Bharatvasi* was published in 1930, the Adi-Hindu movement's popularity was at its peak, with Bodhananda joining Swami Achutanand (1879–1933) at its helm.

At its core, *Mool Bharatvasi* is concerned with the tragic state of India's caste-oppressed populaces. It offers a threefold solution for their liberation. The first is political mobilization, independent of the Congress, and the second is education (Bodhananda [1930] 2009: 145–55). While these two components are only briefly alluded to at the end of the book—Bodhananda's daily activism in the Adi-Hindu movement, Scheduled Caste Federation, and Samiti spoke to these activities more directly—the third solution is the revival of their ancient past. The thesis is simple: shudras and dalits,[39] as the original inhabitants of India (*mool bharatvasi*), followed an ancient pre-Aryan shramanic tradition that was crystallized to perfection in early Buddhism. Only by returning to their original Buddhist identity, to the one true religion (*satya dharm*), will they be able to regain the human rights (*manushik adhikaron*) that have been stripped from them by an oppressive brahmanical order (*arya-brahmani-vyavastha*).[40]

The first several chapters of *Mool Bharatvasi* explore the history of contemporary Hindu society, focusing on how Aryans spread brahmanism (*brahman hindu-dharm*) and caste (varna) among India's "original inhabitants" (*mool nivasi*). The colonial theory of Aryan invasion figures heavily in this narrative, and he highlights the terrible suffering that Aryan–brahmins meted out to the peace-loving, egalitarian "indigenous" populace (Bodhananda [1930] 2009: 39–51). Quoting from Pali Buddhist sources (with his own Hindi translations), Bodhananda argues that the Buddha, the *jagadguru* or "World Teacher," embodies the high point of this culture. It is only because of him, the "Light of Asia," that "India's head is held high before the entire world" (57).[41] Yet tragically, the "true religion" (satya dharm) that the Buddha founded, in which there "is no exaltation or degradation due to caste distinction," was "completely destroyed" (*nashta-bhrashta karke*) by Aryan outsiders (56). With the combination of Orientalist scholarship and original research, Bodhananda formulates elaborate arguments on how the brahmins erased and appropriated almost every aspect of Buddhist culture and history, thereby plunging it into "the ocean of non-remembrance" (*samarpan*, dedication page). He argues that anything admirable in Upanishadic–Vedantic scriptures (*Prasthan Trayi*) was stolen from Buddhists, but that even then the innately "decadent" (*bhogaishvarya*) nature of brahmanism has left these noble teachings "float[ing] detached like ghee placed in water" (83).

One of Bodhananda's most distinctive arguments is that whenever India's original inhabitants have been on the verge of total defeat and slavery, Bodhisattvas take birth in the world to help them regain their humanity and find freedom from suffering (60–61). He includes the sants in his list of Bodhisattvas, dedicating a full chapter to their poetic verses and "compassionate mode of living" (83). Their work, he argues, is of benefit to the world, and he describes them as direct heirs to the Buddha's doctrine of non-violence, equality, friendship, and peace. The argument was brilliant, for it created a seamless continuity between the Buddhist world, whose revival he desired, and the cherished, familiar religious setting of his bahujan audience.

Although the intended audience of *Mool Bharatvasi* are literate shudras and dalits, several sections in the text call upon Hindu ascetics (sadhu–sannyasi) and upper caste Hindus (*dwijati*) to pay heed to his message. In this "age of freedom" (*svadhinata-upasi yug*), a clear reference to the anti-colonial nationalist movement, "how can you speak of freedom and rights when you knowingly keep the shudras and dalits crushed under your feet?" Bodhananda asks rhetorically (148–55). If you want freedom, he explains, you need to abandon the brahmanical order that is "devoid of humanity" (*manushyatva-shunya*) (55).

In her study of Hindi dalit literature, Sarah Beth Hunt (2014: 39) argues that Bodhananda's *Mool Bharatvasi* "became the most important historical text of the Adi Hindu movement". Through the influence of people like Bodhananda and his prominent disciples, especially Jigyasu, the Adi-Hindu movement devised "a new language of 'belonging' which was no longer about an association with middle-class [Hindu] Indian society, but rather, rearticulated new claims to indigeneity and cultural authority" (40). From an organizational perspective, Bodhananda's movement was largely a failure, for it never mobilized any more than a small group of dalit intellectuals. Yet, many of these figures later became the engine that drove dalit cultural activity and political thought in the post-Independence era.[42] Even though the Adi-Hindu movement's political base effectively collapsed by the late 1930s—much of its energies were later absorbed by Ambedkar's Scheduled Caste Federation in the subsequent decade—its greatest contributions lay in creating a wider bahujan consciousness (Gooptu 2001: 143–84). For Bodhananda's part, this is not only evident in the pervasive influence of Buddhist themes and language in modern-day dalit literature concerning the sants (Bellwinkel-Schempp 2011), but in his direct links to Ambedkar.

Bodhananda's relationship with Ambedkar goes as far back as 1920 when the two met in Kolhapur (Maharashtra) at the famous Non-Brahmin Conference organized by Maharaj Shahuji (Singh, in Bodhananda [1930] 2009: 183). Yet it was in the late 1920s and early 1930s, when the Adi-Hindu movement was at its peak and Bodhananda was one of its major leaders, that he and Ambedkar became more closely acquainted. They met several times throughout the 1930s and 1940s at scheduled caste conferences, and Ambedkar also visited the Lucknow vihara on several occasions looking for Buddhist literature.[43] In fact, according to the late Shanti Swarup Bauddh, the prolific writer and owner of a prominent anti-caste publishing house in New Delhi, when Ambedkar began planning his public conversion to Buddhism in the 1950s, he had hoped Bodhananda would oversee the diksha ceremony (Bauddh, "Preface" (*prakashakiya*), in Bodhanand [1930] 2009: 5).

The Doctor and his Dhamma: the Dalit Buddhist Revolution

This was the lay of the Indian Buddhist world when, in 1933, Ambedkar entered the fray and began hinting to friends that he was, "at that juncture inclined to Buddhism" (quoted in Keer [1971] 2009: 240).[44] The comment came just months after the Round Table Conferences and the Poona Pact, when the British government accepted Ambedkar's argument that the depressed classes constituted a political body separate from Hindus. Gandhi, who opposed the decision, threatened suicide by starvation unless Ambedkar recanted. In the end, as Gandhi inched closer to death, Ambedkar was forced to submit, having been put in one of the most precarious positions in his life: support his political constituency or be held responsible for "killing" India's most beloved leader and thereby risking almost unforeseeable violent retaliation against his followers. For Ambedkar, it was a critical turning point. Now, he viewed Gandhi as a wolf in sheep's clothing and Hinduism as a religion incapable of reform. As he put it only two years later to a crowd of ten thousand depressed class leaders in Nashik:

> If you want to gain self-respect, change your religion.
> If you want to create a cooperating society, change your religion.
> If you want power, change your religion.
> If you want equality, change your religion.
> If you want independence, change your religion.
> If you want to make the world in which you live, change
> your religion (quoted in Keer [1971] 2009: 255).

In Ambedkar's view, most saliently outlined in his undelivered speech published as *Annihilation of Caste*, if the caste system was to be destroyed, so too must Hinduism. The religion, he asserted, had its foundation in the Vedas and shastras, and these two bodies of literature were nothing but a set of immoral codes and unjust mores "legalizing" caste discrimination. "If you wish to bring about a breach in the [caste] system, then you have got to apply the dynamite to the Vedas and the Shastras .... You must destroy the Religion of the shrutis and the smritis" (Ambedkar [1936] 2014: 303–04). As Hindu leaders of the Congress and the Maha Sabha panicked, others recognized Ambedkar's dissent as a monumental opportunity. The nizam of Hyderabad responded by offering Ambedkar forty million rupees "to lead" the untouchables to Islam (*TOI*, 14 April 1936, in Jaffrelot 2010: 159). At one point, it looked as if Ambedkar would become a Sikh (Meadowcroft 2006). Buddhists were equally eager for him to join the fourfold sangha. Burmese Buddhist merchants mailed literature, Sinhalese Buddhists offered missionary support, American bhikkhus traveled to his home in Bombay, and in an essay on "The Future of the Harijans," Sir Hari Singh Gour, the leader of India's Nationalist Party—and Ambedkar's old Round Table Conference nemesis—urged Ambedkar to lead his flock to Buddhism (Gour 1936).[45]

It is difficult to say with absolute certainty the extent of the influence of these interventions from afar.[46] But it is clear that Ambedkar was already working on his Buddhist project in Bombay. Reaching out to the Bombay Buddha Society in 1936, he met with Dharmanand Kosambi (1876–1947), the organization's honorary president, former bhikkhu, and noted Pali scholar. Ambedkar told Kosambi that Bombay needed a Buddhist vihara (*BP* Vol. 5/2, 1937: 770).[47] After the meeting, Kosambi met with Gandhi and J.K. Birla, explaining Ambedkar's interest in Buddhism, and requesting Birla's help in acquiring funds to build the temple. Within months, the foundation stone was laid, and less than a year later, on 26 January 1937, Kosambi inaugurated the Bahujan vihara, or "Temple of the Masses," a small structure topped with an elegant stupa modeled after the ancient Karli cave chaitya.

Located in the middle of the millworker-dominated area of Parel, Kosambi worked as the temple manager, prescribing his heady brew of Buddhist rationalism, non-violence, and democratic socialism to the temple's working-class parishioners. Although Kosambi's Buddhism had nothing in common with the "Hindu–Buddhism" that Ambedkar despised, strangely, Ambedkar does not appear to have ever participated in any of the vihara's events.[48] The reasons for this are unclear, but it could have stemmed from both an unwillingness to support anything financed by the Birlas, the foremost sponsors of the Hindu Maha Sabha and Congress, as well as from the fact that Kosambi was brahmin and a dedicated Gandhian.

Whatever the reasons behind Ambedkar's distance from the Bahujan vihara, by the mid-1940s, his movement towards Buddhism was increasingly obvious. When he started his People's Education Society in 1945, the first college he founded in Bombay the following year was named Siddhartha, after the common Sanskrit name given to the Buddha. Ambedkar's second college, inaugurated five years later in Aurangabad, was named Milinda, after the famous Indo-Greek king "converted" by the Buddhist monk, Nagasena, in the second century BCE. Images of the Buddha were placed behind Ambedkar during Scheduled Caste Federation conferences, and references to Buddhism grew more common in his writings and speeches.[49] An article published in the Marathi-language journal, *Janata*, for the Buddha Jayanti of 1941, makes evident his vision:

> The educated class amongst the Hindus desires to establish democracy in politics based on Hindu culture and for the Hindus. They are striving for this. We pity the intellect of such people … [for it is] clear that Brahmanism and democracy are two opposite things. For the establishment of democracy, there is a need to eradicate the Chaturvarna Dharma [brahmanical teaching of four castes]. In order to kill the germs of Chaturvarna, there is no medicine [more] powerful than the Buddha Dhamma.
>
> Politically India is like a sick man. When we remember India, we imagine a picture of a man whose belly is big, his hands and feet reduced to mere bones, face paled, eyes deeply buried in the socket and a skeleton. He has no power to run the democracy but he has a great desire to run it. In order to satisfy this desire, power is important. This power cannot be achieved without medicine. But what use is medicine! Everyone knows that in order to take medicine, it is necessary to clear the stomach. All the impure elements should be removed. Without this, medicine will have no effect. The stomach of Hindus is not clean.

The filth of Brahmanism is stored in their stomach for a long time. The doctor who can wash this filth will help in establishing democracy in India. That doctor undoubtedly is the Buddha. The lifeblood of Hindus can not be purified by celebrating Rama Jayanti, or Krishna Jayanti or Gandhi Jayanti. Rama, Krishna, and Gandhi are the worshippers of the Brahmanism. They are useless in the establishment of democracy. The Buddha can only help in establishing democracy. Therefore it is important to remember the Buddha and take his medicine for cleansing the political and social lifeblood of the Hindus. Therefore we think that people should chant this greatest mantra for the establishment of democracy:

Buddham Saranam Gacchaami! [I take refuge in the Buddha] Dhammam Saranam Gacchaami! [I take refuge in the Dhamma] Sangham Saranam Gacchami! [I take refuge in the Sangha]

(Ambedkar, "Buddhjayanti ani tice rajakiya mahatatva" [Buddha Jayanti and Its Political Significance], 17 May, 1941, *BAWS* Vol. 20: 327–35).[50]

In this remarkable statement penned more than fifteen years prior to his public conversion in 1956, the contours of Ambedkar's Buddhism are already taking shape: it was an ancient tradition that had fought bitterly against brahmanism and was to be admired for its rationality and democratic social ethos. Despite widespread accusations leveled then (and still today) that his interest in Buddhism was purely political "opportunism," the private, more intimate Ambedkar possessed the very same convictions.[51] In a rare moment of vulnerability, disclosed in a private letter (dated 8 February 1948) to Dr Sharda Kabir, his soon-to-be second wife (later Savita Ambedkar), he explained that, "the only person to whom I owe all my being is Gautama Buddha" ("Letter 137b," in Ambedkar 1993: 205). During the Buddha Jayanti of 1950, he led a procession out of the Buddha vihara in New Delhi for the Scheduled Castes Welfare Association (*Hindustan Times*, 3 May 1950) and later that year, attended the first meeting of the World Fellowship of Buddhists in Ceylon to experience first-hand a living Buddhist culture. Although he was deeply skeptical of the sangha, when he returned from Ceylon he formally announced at Nachidatsu Fuji's Japanese (Nipponzon

Myohoji) temple in Bombay that, "he will dedicate the rest of his life to the revival and spread of Buddhism" ("Dr. Ambedkar at Worli," *TOI*, 1 Oct 1950; "Dr. Ambedkar in Bombay," *HT, 4* May 1950).

Ambedkar's praise for the Buddha was having effects further afield as well. In the Saurashtra region of Gujarat, several Ambedkarite dalits began integrating Buddhist symbols into their common life-cycle rituals. By 1945, brides and grooms sought the blessings of the Buddha, and "on wedding cards ... Lord Ganesh gave way to Lord Buddha," and "parents named their children according to the Buddhist tradition" (Gurjar, "Appendix 2: Dalit movements in Gujarat," in Franco, Macwan and Ramanathan 2004: 365). Likewise, in Nagpur, during the late 1940s, Ambedkar's Samata Sainik Dal or Corps for Equality (est. 1926) was actively propagating Buddhism as an alternative to Hinduism, staging plays based on Dharmanand Kosambi's *Buddhalila* (1914), holding Buddhist study groups, and even attempting to build their own Buddhist temple (Moon 2001: 127–33).

When viewed in this context, Ambedkar's most concerted movement towards Buddhism appears to have occurred in the mid- to late 1940s. This was also the period when he moved to New Delhi to serve in the Viceroy's Council as the secretary of labour (1942–46) and where he stayed on as independent India's first minister of law (1947–51) in Nehru's cabinet. These were transformative years both politically and intellectually. What is less well known is that during this time Ambedkar undertook the serious study of Pali under Ishwardatt Medharthi (1900–71), a Pali–Sanskrit scholar and principal of a "Hindu–Buddhist" school for the backward classes in Kanpur. Born to a dedicated Arya Samaji and doctor in the British military, Medharthi had been educated in the Arya Samaj's gurukul at Haridwar. When Medharthi returned to Kanpur in the early 1930s, he befriended Bodhananda and eventually fell under his sway, transforming his father's school into a major transit spot in the Buddhist ecumene, installing Buddhist images inside it and teaching Pali.[52] Although Medharthi eventually recanted his Buddhist identity, choosing to spend the 1960s reciting Vedic stotras in "flawless Sanskrit" (Bellwinkel-Schempp 2011: 206), in the decades before that he was a critical intermediary in the north Indian Buddhist world. More significantly for our purposes, he began visiting Ambedkar in Delhi during the weekends to tutor him in Pali (210–11).

Ambedkar (seated in the center with a cane) with his wife Savita at the
World Buddhist Conference in Burma in 1954. With them are members of
the Andhra Schedule Caste Federation who attended the conference

Through Medharthi, Ambedkar not only encountered the world of
Pali Buddhist literature but was also introduced to the tightly knit world
of Indian-born Buddhist bhikkhu converts and other soldiers of the sasana.
Ambedkar also met the Arakanese monk, U Chandramani, and his Indian
pupil, Bhikkhu Dharmarakshita (b. 1923) in Kushinagar. Chandramani—a
disciple of the rajput wrestler-turned–Buddhist monk, Mahavir—oversaw
Ambedkar's conversion in 1956, while Dharmarakshita, the editor of the
first Buddhist journal in Hindi, *Dharmadoot*, arranged for Ambedkar's
journeys to the World Fellowship of Buddhists in Burma in 1954, and to
Indian Buddhist sites in 1956 (Ahir 1989: 103–04).[53] This also marked the
beginning of Ambedkar's meetings with Anand Kausalyayan, the Punjabi
bhikkhu who later performed his funerary rites in front of more than half a
million people in Bombay.[54]

The influence of these figures is most evident in Ambedkar's 1948
publication, *The Untouchables: Who Were They and Why They Became
Untouchables* (*BAWS* Vol. 7: 233–381). Similar to Bodhananda's and Thass's
earlier works, Ambedkar's thesis is that untouchables were "broken men,"
the scattered survivors of "original Indians" conquered by Aryan–brahmin

invaders. When the brahmins settled in India, the broken men worked as laborers on the outskirts of their villages. They were deeply despised because they were Buddhists, which was in complete opposition to brahmanical morals and regulations. For Ambedkar, the critical moment in this grand confrontation between two alien cultures was when the brahmins realized they were losing control over the religious landscape. To combat the rising tide of Buddhist supremacy, they adopted Buddhist ethical codes and, significantly, gave up animal sacrifice, becoming vegetarians and declaring the cow sacred. These later elements dealt a severe blow to the Buddhists, who although against animal slaughter, were not vegetarians (311–22).

In Ambedkar's view, it was these two features in particular that were responsible for the origins of untouchability: 1) brahmanical contempt and hatred of the broken men's Buddhist identity, and 2) the broken men's continued consumption of the carcasses of dead but now sacred cows. With these two traits, the broken men became polluted outcastes, forever stigmatized as untouchables (242). Despite its speculative nature, Ambedkar's argument was both astute and sensitive.[55] It not only dovetailed similar theories widely prevalent among Adi-Hindu groups across India and thus could easily reach this audience, but also projected dalits as the true indigenous populace while berating brahmins as the foreign pollutants. Moreover, in what the anthropologist Owen Lynch (1969: 143) rightly called a "stroke of genius," Ambedkar defined Buddhist culture in terms that were almost synonymous with his vision of modern, democratic Indian culture. Being a modern Indian citizen, in other words, meant just being one's "original" Buddhist self.

In the last five years of his life, Ambedkar spent much of his time encouraging Indians to stop treating "religion as something that is handed over from father to son," and to closely consider the differences between brahmanism and Buddhism ("Birth Anniversary of Buddha: Ambedkar's Address," *HT*, 3 May 1950). As he argued in "The Buddha and the Future of His Religion" (Ambedkar 1950), the great strength of Buddhism was that the Buddha "wished his religion not to be encumbered with the dead wood of the past ... this is why he gave liberty to his followers to chip and chop as the necessities of the case required" (118). Fourteen years earlier, in his hugely popular pamphlet, *Annihilation of Caste*, Ambedkar had alluded to the necessity of ridding society of this "dead wood". Quoting his former instructor at Columbia University, the esteemed American philosopher, John Dewey (1859–1952), he wrote:

> Every society gets encumbered with what is trivial, with dead wood from the past, and with what is positively perverse … as a society becomes more enlightened, it realizes that it is responsible not to conserve and transmit the whole of its existing achievements, but only such as to make for a better society (Ambedkar [1936] 2014: 313).[56]

For Dewey, those principles were enshrined in the liberal democratic traditions of the Western world. Ambedkar, however, felt the same principles were latent in many early Buddhist scriptures. The Buddha, he contends, was the "earliest and staunchest upholder of equality," a man who emphasized inquiry, investigation, and rationality, not dogma and blind adherence to tradition (Ambedkar, *The Buddha and His Dhamma,* in *BAWS* Vol. 11: 302). Like nearly every other modern Buddhist rationalist, he was taken by those famous passages in the *Kalama Sutta* where the Buddha explains that reason and logic are the foundations of his teaching. In Ambedkar's eyes, these proved that one can be a Buddhist and be "free to modify or even to abandon any of his teachings if it was found that at a given time and in given circumstances they did not apply" (Ambedkar 1950: 118). When Ambedkar restructured central Buddhist doctrines like nirvana, dukkha and dhamma, he did so on the basis that historically conditioned interpretations of these were dead wood.[57] His Buddha was a champion of morality whose deep-seated rationality would not have approved of those interpretations that privileged dogmatic or immoral views. He showed the way (*margadata*) to salvation, but he did not deliver it himself (*mokshadata*) (Ambedkar 1950: 117).[58]

Ambedkar's Buddhism was based on what he saw as universal, moral values. Carving out a Buddhist identity, separate from Hindus, was central to this project. The most explicit component of this identity is visible in nine of the twenty-two additional vows Ambedkar read out during the dhamma diksha ceremony.[59] These stipulate in explicit terms that the new Buddhist identity is fundamentally a non-Hindu identity and that to become a Buddhist, one must renounce Hinduism. These vows, like Ambedkar's historical works, reinforced the differences between brahmins and Buddhists, a difference that for nearly two millennia Sanskrit grammarians and philosophers had compared to the antagonism between a mongoose and a snake.[60] As someone who had been at the sharp end of caste discrimination, Ambedkar felt that Buddhism's revival in modern India would require a litany of vows, rituals, ideologies, and texts to defeat its great nemesis. In a letter to Devapriya Valisinha, the general secretary of the Maha Bodhi Society in early 1955, Ambedkar explained why rituals were so important for the new Buddhist laity. Buddhism's historical shortcoming, he contended, was its failure to develop external initiation ceremonies for lay and not just monastic Buddhists. To combat this weakness, Ambedkar invented a new formula (dhamma diksha) for conversion and added that those who don't partake in it "will not be regarded as a Buddhist" ("Letter to D. Vali Sinha [sic]," 16 February 1955, in Ambedkar 1993: 217). By the next year, Ambedkar had even created a new marriage ceremony for Buddhists, distinct from customary Hindu rites.[61] Similar life-cycle rituals had been invented and adopted by bahujan Buddhist groups in Lucknow, Malabar, and Tamil Nadu for decades.

In choosing Nagpur as the site of initiation (dikshabhoomi), Ambedkar was bringing the Buddhist past into the present. Although he may have been motivated by a desire to directly confront the city's strong bastion of RSS supporters, the Vidarbha–Nagbhumi region was also a noted center of ancient Buddhism, as evidenced by the mammoth pre-Mauryan stupa excavated at Pauni and the exquisite sandstone pillars of the Naga Mucalinda protecting the Buddha. During the conversion ceremony, Ambedkar spoke of returning to the religion of their ancestors, the Nagas. He argued that the Nagas were an ancient tribe that had fought the Aryans and had been followers of the Buddha. Even as he provided his own caste group of mahars a direct link to the Buddhist past, he also had more universal ambitions. In a speech with the press that took place just after his conversion, Ambedkar explained, "I want the whole of India to be converted to Buddhism. It should not become only a Harijan[62] religion. It is, after all, a universal faith" (*MBJ* Vol. 64/11, 1956: 504).

This vision is also apparent in Ambedkar's concurrent effort to expand the platform of his failed Scheduled Caste Federation into a broader political body, independent of caste relations. Just months before his formal conversion and death, he began reaching out to prominent leftist politicians in the hopes of mobilizing a larger populace or "federation of oppressed populations," composed of not just dalits but workers and peasants, shudras and other non-brahmins (Zelliot 2013: 198–202). The groundwork for this party, aptly named the Republican Party of India, after the quasi-democratic republics of the Buddha's time, was laid in Ambedkar's last months, but his sudden death left the organization headless and it never developed a large presence outside of Maharashtra and, to a lesser degree, Punjab (Ram 2012) and Uttar Pradesh (Lynch 1969: 129–65). Like the Republican Party of India, Ambedkar's vision of Buddhist conversion largely remained a caste-based phenomenon. Not only were the new converts almost entirely dalits, but the vast majority were mahars, the numerically dominant dalit group in Maharasthra into which Ambedkar had been born.

Situating Bahujan Buddhism

In recent decades, there has been an explosion of scholarly research debating the history and legacy of anti-caste activism in modern India. Much of this literature takes it almost as a fait accompli that Ambedkar is the only anti-caste philosopher whose thought has relevance to contemporary politics. While the growing work on Dravidian ideologues, Self-Respect activists, Adi-Hindus, and others has drawn a more complex picture, there has been comparatively little acknowledgement of the critical role that Buddhism played in anti-caste activism prior to the events of 1956. This has also led to a mischaracterization of Ambedkar's interpretation as a revolutionary and radical remodelling of Buddhism. While this was undoubtedly true in the longue durée of Buddhist history, in India's modern Buddhist moment it was far less so. Ambedkar had long been connected to Indian-born Buddhist monastics and scholars who preached and practiced Buddhism along similar lines. In fact, it is clear that Ambedkar was far less willing to break with tradition than has been commonly believed (Fuchs 2001: 266). That Ambedkar desired acceptance from both the Indian Buddhist and the international Buddhist community is evidenced in the Nagpur conversion ceremony itself. According to Bhikkhu Sangharakshita ([1986] 2006: 136), Ambedkar had originally voiced resistance to "taking refuge in the sangha," the third of the Three Jewels of the faith: Buddha–Dhamma–Sangha. Yet in the end, he consented to the authority of the tradition, for as Devapriya Valisinha explained to him, without it, he would never be considered a Buddhist. Throughout the last years of his life, Ambedkar regularly consulted with India's leading Buddhist authorities, and the presence of the monastic body during the great dhamma diksha was an indication that he recognized the importance of the past.

Scholars have often pointed to a single hostile review printed in the *Maha Bodhi* journal that criticized Ambedkar's book, remarking that it should have been called "Ambedkar and His Dhamma," as evidence that the Maha Bodhi Society strongly condemned his conversion.[63] Likewise, years earlier, the British bhikkhu, Sangharakshita (1952), then working as an editor for the *Maha Bodhi* journal, had raised concerns about Ambedkar's call for "a Buddhist bible". Yet neither of these two critiques represented any enduring resistance to Ambedkar's Buddhism. For example, Sangharakshita's Trailokya Bauddha Mahasangha Sahayaka Gana (TBMSG) remains an important organization in contemporary dalit Buddhist life.[64] The resistance within the Maha Bodhi Society did not stem from the central Indian Buddhist leadership but from its upper-caste Hindu supporters and, in particular, its Calcutta-based organizing body. For instance, just months after the conversion, the scholar Rahul Sankrityayan ([1957] 1978: 18) penned an approving pamphlet, comparing Ambedkar's conversion to that of Kublai Khan in the thirteenth century. Bhikkhu Anand Kausalyayan dedicated the remainder of his life to work among the dalits. In Kausalyayan's own scholarly estimation of *The Buddha and His Dhamma*, which he translated into Hindi and annotated with further Pali references, the text was a "new orientation, but not a distortion" of Buddhism (quoted in Queen 1996: 57). When dalit converts to Buddhism lost the rights afforded to them on the basis of their scheduled caste identity, the Maha Bodhi Society's general secretary submitted a memorandum to Prime Minister Nehru asking him to rectify this "great injustice" (*MBJ* Vol. 65/7, 1957: 343). The Maha Bodhi Society's *Dharmadoot* also quickly adapted to the new scene, dedicating a portion of its Hindi journal for articles in Marathi, the mother tongue of the new Buddhist populace. By the end of 1957, the society's new "Indian Buddhist Fund" to support the dalits had even distributed fifty thousand copies of Bodhananda's Buddhist ritual manual

(*Bauddha Pujavidhi*), half in Marathi and the other half in Hindi (*MBJ* Vol. 65/12, 1957: 487–88). As all of these actions indicate, the working body of the Indian Buddhist community—the so-called soldiers of the sasana—were fully invested in Ambedkar's movement.

While many foreign Buddhist monastics came and attempted to work among the new Buddhists, linguistic and cultural divides were major obstacles. They were more successful in forging links with the educated and urban mahar Buddhists, but in villages, where most mahars lived, the difficulty of working among an impoverished and unlettered population incapable of supporting the monastics in the way they were accustomed to in their own societies was insurmountable (Fitzgerald 1999: 79–104). Further complications arose when the foreign Buddhist donors, and most importantly, the Birlas, that had for so many decades bankrolled the revival of Buddhism, effectively closed their coffers on the Ambedkarite Buddhist revolution. Precisely why the former group did so is unclear but it may have stemmed from both their political alliances with the Hindu national leadership and their resistance to Ambedkar's articulation of Buddhism, which was deeply dismissive of other Buddhisms.[65] The Birlas' negative reaction is easier to discern: Ambedkar's Buddhism was sectarian, anti-Hindu, and politically charged. In the end, the Maha Bodhi Society's Indian Buddhist Fund raised a measly Rs 5,676 in the first fourteen months after Ambedkar's conversion.

In a talk broadcast on BBC in May 1956, just months before his death, Ambedkar explained, "why I like Buddhism". Buddhism, he argued, taught three principles that no other religion does: "*prajna* (understanding as against superstition and supernaturalism), *karuna* (love), and *samata* (equality). This is what man wants for a good and happy life. Neither god nor soul can save society" (quoted in Keer [1971] 2009: 490). He then quickly added that, "Marxism and Communism have shaken the religious systems of all the countries" (ibid), and went on to explain how Buddhism answered Marx and was the only solution to the bloody revolutions taking place across the globe. Ambedkar had long toiled with Marxist ideologies and in the last months of his life, he devoted much of his energy to comparing the two universalisms.[66] Marx's revolutionary ideology, he argued, came closest to Buddhism as a liberating force. In his view, Buddhism also advocated the abolition of private property, aligned poverty with social exploitation, and offered tangible solutions in the present moment. But then, Ambedkar was not the only Indian intellectual to see the similarities between the two.

When the Buddha Met Marx

On 1 May 1923, the thin strip of beach across the street from the Madras High Court became the venue of India's first ever May Day or International Workers' Day celebration. The organizer of the event, a sixty-three-year-old grey-haired lawyer named M.N. Singaravelu (1860–1946) also used the occasion to announce the formation of his new political party, the Labour Kisan Party of Hindustan, or Workers and Peasants Party of India. For those who followed working-class movements in India, whether as critics or adherents, Singaravelu was a familiar face. In 1918, within a year of the Russian Revolution, he and his colleague, B.P. Wadia (1881–1958), formed the Madras Labour Union, the first labour union in modern India and one of the first in all of Asia. During the time, Singaravelu's national profile was on the rise, especially after he shocked his colleagues by declaring himself a communist at the annual Indian National Congress convention in Gaya in 1922 and was then charged by the British for inciting revolution against the Crown in the infamous "Cawnpore Bolshevik Conspiracy Case" of 1924.

A century hence, Singaravelu's legacy as one of India's first communists and the "godfather of Indian labour" has been memorialized through city signs across southern India, government stamps, and even a life-size statue on the streets of Pondicherry (Murugesan and Subramanyam 1975; Vasanthakumaran 2003). What is less well known is that at the same time Singaravelu was organizing workers' unions, he was also one of the driving forces behind the Tamil Buddhist movement and the Shakya Buddhist

Society. Born to a family of well-to-do fishermen outside Madras, Singaravelu had gained the best education that colonial Madras could provide, earning degrees from Madras Christian College, Madras University's Presidency College and Law College [now Dr Ambedkar Government Law College]. It is unclear when he first took an interest in Buddhism, but by the time Iyothee Thass reached out to Henry Olcott and Anagarika Dharmapala, Singaravelu was an active partner. As early as 1899, he was managing both the Royapettah branch (est. 1899) of the Maha Bodhi Society as well as the Shakya Buddhist Society headquarters (*MBJ* Vol. 8/4, 1899–1900: 31; Vol. 8/6, 1899–1900: 51). He was well connected with Dharmapala, regularly traveling to his home in Colombo through the first two decades of the twentieth century, and through commercial activity in the rice trade, he traveled further afield, even as far as London where he is said to have attended a "World Buddhist Conference" in 1901 or 1902 (Murugesan and Subramanyam 1975: 8). Although Singaravelu concurred with the Shakya Buddhist Society's emphasis on caste inequalities, his relations with Thass and P.L. Narasu appear to have been strained, perhaps due to his cozy relations with Dharmapala and early involvement in the Indian National Congress.[1] Whatever the reason for these tensions, Singaravelu's smooth transition from a Tamil Buddhist to a labour activist and communist provides an early glimpse into the ongoing negotiation between Buddhism and Marxism as a liberating force in the colonial period. Even by the time that Singaravelu had launched his Workers and Peasants Party, he still did not see any contradiction in signing his political manifesto as "M. Singaravelu (Indian Communist), President, Madras Maha Bodhi Society" (quoted in Ralhan 1998: 119). Records indicate that Singaravelu had no qualms in arguing that "Communism is as old as history" and "was taught by Buddha in a form and practiced by his disciples" (Singaravelu's presidential address at the First Communist Conference in Kanpur, December 1925, in Murugesan and Subramanyam 1975: 206).[2] It is not known how personally invested Singaravelu was in trying to riddle out a dialectical materialism in tune with Buddhist teachings, but as the decades wore on, he would be joined by numerous figures in India and beyond who saw Buddhist teachings as broadly compatible with Marxist thought.[3] These people brought the philosophical lens of the dhamma in line with emergent progressive ideological currents, which in turn provided a new way of imagining Buddhism, both past and present.

In reading the archives of modern Buddhism, most scholars have understood the encounter between it and Marxism to be a post-1950s phenomenon, marked by events such as the Chinese communist invasion of Tibet in 1950, the Cambodian King Sihanouk's "Buddhist Socialism of the late 1950s," Ne Win's "Burmese Way to Socialism" in the early 1960s, or the pseudo-Marxist rhetoric of Pol Pot's Khmer Rouge in the 1970s. However, in recent years, a number of scholars have shown how the dialogue between Buddhism and Marxism actually began several decades earlier in places like China, Mongolia, Russia, and Japan (Ling 1979; Shields 2012; Yu 2016). As the life of Singaravelu illustrates, the encounter between Buddhism and Marxism had an equally formative role in colonial India, with several of the country's most influential Buddhist leaders publicly advocating strands of Marxist ideology either as close alternatives to Buddhism or in conjunction with it. Most of these efforts developed as attempts to resolve the social and political problems of the day. That is, they had shared roots in the reaction against both the British rule, and long-standing systems of inequality and caste oppression. Like other Indian "leftists"—a term used here to denote those Indian individuals or organizations whose ideologies were oriented towards a socialist world view, and in which the writings of Marx were the primary influence (Chandavarkar 1997; Roy 1988; Habib 1998; Chowdhuri 2007)—many Indian Buddhists operated inside the Indian National Congress led by Gandhi and Nehru or as part of the international communist movement. Others, like B.R. Ambedkar, were alien to both.

To illuminate these shifting intellectual and social terrains, this chapter examines the lives of two prominent north Indian Buddhists, Dharmanand Kosambi (1876–1947) and Rahul Sankrityayan (1893–1963), who took strongly to the Buddhist–Marxist ecumene and went to painstaking lengths to dissect and unravel the connections between Buddhist and Marxist doctrines. The close reading of their thought in the context of their wide-ranging travels through India, Ceylon, Russia, America, Tibet, and beyond reveals significant patterns of global commonality and interconnectedness in India's and Buddhism's modern history.

Marx and the Buddha: Early Indian Manifestations

While Indian discussions on "Buddhist Socialism" only became more pronounced in the early 1930s, there were much earlier strands of thought that may have inspired the language and idioms later used to propagate the view of the Buddha as a Marxist-like revolutionary intent on transforming Indian society. Popular nineteenth century school books like *Itihas Timir Nashak* treated the Buddha as a liberator of the oppressed, even comparing him to Tsar Alexander II and Abraham Lincoln. In equally provocative terms, the Hindu mystic Swami Vivekananda (1863–1902) described the Buddha as Hinduism's "rebel child" (Joshi 1983), while anti-caste intellectuals like Singaravelu, Thass, and Narasu portrayed early Buddhism as a religion of the oppressed in an endless struggle against landowning brahmins. While these arguments provided a subtle layer of continuity to the emerging vision of the Buddha as a Marxist, the images, assumptions, and strategies upon which this "Buddhist liberation" was constructed made no explicit reference to Marxist doctrine.

Instead, it was the cathartic and bloody events of the Russian Revolution of 1917 that prompted the imaginary encounter between the Buddha and Marx. Historians generally agree that a sustained and widespread engagement with socialist doctrine and organizations did not emerge in India until after the October Revolution and the making of the Soviet state (Habib 1998: 5; Chowduri 2007: 26). From the 1920s on, the new Soviet government was widely perceived as an anti-colonial and anti-imperial force that had liberated the Russian peasantry from "the yoke of Tsardom" and was committed to the right of all nations (including India) to self-determination. Many Indian revolutionaries, from Nehru to Periyar, began perceiving the Soviet state as a model for their own visions of a modern India. They watched eagerly, with both anticipation and admiration, as the Soviet policies of the 1920s to 1930s transformed Russian society, instituting a new era of social equality, rapid industrialization, and low unemployment. At the same time, they expressed both horror and fear at the bloody events of the Revolution, the draconian turn under Stalin, and the purges of the mid- to late 1930s. The possibility that these same events could occur in India had a profound impact on the Indian national leadership.

Dharmanand Kosambi and the "Remarkable Revolution"

By the time Dharmanand Kosambi died in 1947, he was one of colonial India's most eminent scholars of Buddhism and the author of more than thirty books on various aspects of Indian history, almost all of them in the Marathi and Gujarati languages.[4] But his life was anything but that of a sterile academic. Born to a family of gaud saraswat brahmins in the Portuguese colony of Goa and raised to manage a coconut grove, Kosambi was from an early age disillusioned by his surroundings. After being inspired by a biography of the Buddha, in the Marathi-language children's magazine *Balbodh*, and by a Marathi-language adaptation of Sir Edwin Arnold's *The Light of Asia,* he left home at the age of twenty-three in search of a "knowledge of Buddhism" (Kosambi 2010: 73–74).[5] For the next several years, he traveled across India, Nepal, Ceylon, and Burma, by foot, rail and ocean liner, studying Sanskrit with pandits and shastris in Pune, Gwalior, and Benares, before moving to Ceylon in 1902 to study Pali at the Vidyodaya Pirivena. Under the tutelage of Ceylon's senior monastic authority Hikkaduve Sumangala—the same figure who oversaw Iyothee Thass's ritual conversion to Buddhism in 1898—Kosambi became a Buddhist monk and developed a masterful comprehension of Pali scriptures and doctrines. Further travels to Burma, where he practiced meditation alongside the German convert, Nyantiloka Mahathera, and to India, where he lived with the Indian wrestler-turned-bhikkhu, Swami Mahavir, eventually led Kosambi to Calcutta, where he finally entered a new stage of life aimed at making "some effort to propagate knowledge of Buddhism" in India (Kosambi 2010: 186).

While no single narrative could do justice to Kosambi's peripatetic life, wide-ranging social engagements, and prolific intellectual contributions, it is also fair to state that much of his life was consumed by modern Buddhist scholarship and, ultimately, its vernacularization for Marathi-speaking publics. Editing texts, collecting manuscripts, translating scriptures, undertaking writing and teaching assignments at universities in India, America, and Russia—Kosambi's career was mostly consumed by such pursuits. He was as much a product of the anti-colonial, social reform, and Indian nationalist movements as of the modernist programs of Buddhist social service he learned while living as a bhikkhu in Burma and at the

Vidyodaya Pirivena in Ceylon (Ober 2013).[6] He was also an early colleague of Thass, Narasu, and Singaravelu, having lived at the Shakya Buddhist Society rest houses in Madras for several months while traveling between there and Ceylon from 1902 to 1904. These all informed the making of Kosambi's and, ultimately, modern India's Buddhism. However, it was the discovery of socialism that caused, as he put it, a "remarkable revolution" in his thinking (Kosambi 2010: 221).

The "remarkable revolution" began when Kosambi's talents in Pali and Sanskrit came to the attention of the Harvard Sanskritist, James Woods (1864–1935), who invited Kosambi to the US to work on a critical edition of Buddhaghosa's *Visuddhimagga*.[7] When Kosambi arrived in Cambridge, Massachusetts, the socialist and progressive movements in America were at the pinnacle of their national influence (Kipnis [1952] 2004: 335). The Socialist Party of America and the American Federation of Labor's sensitive portrayals of working-class conditions had a profound impact on his thinking (Kosambi 2010: 205–19). It was not just the solutions that the socialists proposed, however, that Kosambi found so compelling. As he studied them more closely, he became convinced that their ideas paralleled those of the early Buddhist scriptures and living monastic communities he knew so well. In his view, there were two major similarities (313–14). First, just as democratic socialists stressed collective decision making, so did monks within the sangha when reaching decisions about assembly or punishments. Second, the socialist argument for the nationalization of property was akin to the monastic rules forbidding the individual ownership of property (minus the eight items a monk is allowed). Eager to share his "discovery," Kosambi published an essay in the nationalist Marathi-language journal *Kesari,* contending that the idea of democratic-socialist governance was born in the early Buddhist sangha, and therefore was not of modern European origin. Using passages from the *Mahaparinibbana Sutta* and *Samyutta Nikaya* as evidence, Kosambi declares:

> The structure of the sangha of monks—through which the Buddha conducted the task of uplifting the people—was based upon the principle of collective ownership which is the highest stage of democracy. And in Burma the Buddhist Sangha still observes this

Dharmanand Kosambi, who established the Buddhist Bahujan vihara from which Ambedkar kept his distance

principle. Those who propound the principle of collective ownership are known as "socialists" in this country [the USA] and in Europe ... the chief principle of socialism is "to establish national ownership over privately owned property, and to induce all citizens to work in a manner conducive to the collective good without falling prey to the temptation of personal gain under the guise of trade or anything else" (314–15).

Kosambi's idea that early Buddhism operated according to democratic socialist principles was to become one of the most persuasive and enduring arguments about modern Indian Buddhism. At this time Kosambi's support for this "democratic Buddhist socialism" was delicately stated, but in the ensuing decades it was a position he and many others around the globe fervently defended. Placed in a wider context, Kosambi's argument needs to be read alongside similar propositions made by religious modernists and dissident scholars attempting to withstand the colonial and scientific assault on religion. Kosambi's predecessors, like the Hindu reformer Dayanand Sarasvati, had long been arguing that all of the discoveries of modernity, such as chemistry, physics, and engineering, could be found in the Vedas, if only approached with the right eyes (van der Veer 2001). Similarly, Erik Hammerstrom (2015) has shown how many Chinese intellectuals in the early twentieth century boldly proclaimed that Buddhism had transcended the discoveries of modern science. Clearly, Kosambi's own argument that Buddhism was a kind of precursor to Marxism shared similar agendas. By showcasing its "modernity," Kosambi was molding Buddhism into a religion of reason, one that could withstand scientific critiques and refute colonial discourses of Asian "backwardness" and "superstition". At the same time, it is important to recognize that unlike some of his colleagues Kosambi did not romanticize the past to the extent of claiming that the Buddha already possessed all knowledge, scientific, spiritual, or otherwise, or that it lay deposited in the *Tipitaka*. He undoubtedly was nostalgically drawn to history and accepted the common narrative of Asia's decline from its great cultural past; yet, even in his most provocative historical works, he remained adamant that Buddhism was neither identical to nor superseded Marxism.

Following his return from the USA and during a decade of teaching at Indian universities in the 1910s and 1920s, Kosambi's belief that "real political strength is concentrated in the union of workers" grew more adamant, and he continued to publicly advocate the Marxist ideology of "equality of status and power" as solutions to India's socio-political misfortunes (Kosambi 2010: 221). During the early 1920s, when Gandhi's calls for non-cooperation led to the first nationwide political action, Kosambi went through a phase of profound Gandhian influence, quitting a profitable research position to work at Gandhi's nationalist college in Ahmedabad, Gujarat Vidyapith (est. 1920). This was also the period when communism began to make its first serious inroads within the subcontinent.[8] By the mid-1920s, there were several independently organized communist groups across the subcontinent's major urban centers, whose leading comrades were in correspondence with one another, working tirelessly to organize the working classes. During this time, Kosambi's former colleague, the Tamil Buddhist Singaravelu, was using his private newspaper, *The Hindu*, in concert with other Indian Marxists as a cover to avoid the British interception of communist ideas, a ploy that came to a sudden end in 1924, when Singaravelu was charged in the Cawnpur Bolshevik Conspiracy case for attempting "to deprive the King Emperor of his sovereignty of British India, by complete separation of India from imperialistic Britain by a violent revolution" (Overstreet and Windmiller 1959: 48–79). While Kosambi remained unsure over the universal applicability of the Soviet model and, most importantly, its advocacy of violence and class conflict, there were other developments in the Soviet Union that had a powerful impact on his thinking.

During the first decade after the Russian Revolution, the Soviets had not only implemented radical social and economic policies but also taken, what the historian Vera Tolz (2011: 160) calls, a "pragmatic" or "tolerant" position towards its religious minorities. One result of this policy was that many of the most prominent Russian "scientists" (*akademik*s) in imperial Russia's "Rozen School" of Orientalism had been deemed essential to the new Soviet bureaucracy. Similar to the role of anthropologists and Orientalists in the European colonization of Asia, their knowledge of national Buddhist minorities and neighboring Buddhist nations was praised by Soviet leaders, including Lenin himself (Hirsch 2005: 58–61). Two of the most important of these "scientists," Sergei Oldenburg (1863–1934) and Fyodor Stcherbatski (1870–1942), were widely known in Russia and abroad for their scholarly contribution to India's Buddhist history. They were the founding editors of the major academic series, *Bibliotheca Buddhica* (est. 1897), and with Aghvan Dorjiev (1853–1938), the Buryatian monk and ambassador to the thirteenth Dalai Lama, they established the first Buddhist temple in St Petersburg (est. c. 1909).[9] During the immediate post-revolution period, these akademiks set about establishing Buddhist exhibitions, international conferences, and museums, all of which promoted the compatibility of Buddhism and Bolshevism. The idea that Buddhism could help facilitate the spread of Enlightenment values had much older roots, but under the auspices of the Leningrad Academy of Sciences, "Bolshevik Buddhism" became a real possibility. At events like the Buddhist exhibition in Petrograd in 1917, Russian Orientalists argued that Buddhism was extraordinarily close to the modern scientific world view and a religion of the oppressed that had the potential to advance the brotherhood of nations (Stcherbatski 1970: 11–18).[10]

It was in the midst of these developments that Kosambi—by now an internationally respected Pali scholar—was invited by Stcherbatski to work at Leningrad's new Institute for the Study of Buddhist Culture (est. 1927). Kosambi's work among the Russian Orientalists, from 1929 to 1930 and again in 1932 or 1933, coincided with two distinct moments that would have a long-lasting influence on his later thought. On one hand, he was working alongside scholars, in particular Stcherbatski, widely recognized by American and European scholars alike to be one of the greatest scholars of Buddhism at the time (Nakamura [1980] 1999: 301). In this context, it is important to recognize that the statements they made regarding Buddhism's purported affinity to Marxism were not crackpot theories of rogue scholars but claims made by "scientists" at the vanguard of Buddhist thought. Naturally, the ideas they held about Buddhism as a progressive, liberal force in the modern world only served to strengthen the ideas that Kosambi already held about its compatibility with socialism. On the other hand, Kosambi's travels in Russia overlapped with the beginning of the draconian turn under Stalin, his campaigns against religion and "dispersal" of those communists who did not fall in line with Soviet orthodoxy. These were the precursors to the horrendous purges of the mid- to late 1930s, events that disillusioned Kosambi as they did the mainstream Indian leadership.

Shortly after Gandhi inaugurated the Civil Disobedience movement in 1930 by picking up a handful of salt on the Dandi seashore in Gujarat, Kosambi returned to India to join the anti-colonial effort. Despite his interest in the Communist Party of India and their steady growth among the subcontinent's urban trade unions, he remained loyal to Gandhi's Congress, confident that it still provided the best avenue for eradicating Indian poverty and gaining political freedom. In the period between April and October, he was arrested twice: first, during a salt satyagraha at Shiroda, and a second time in October when he was sentenced to a year of hard labor. Most of his political efforts during this time were focused in Parel (Bombay), a densely populated neighborhood of millworkers and stevedores that formed the metropolitan underbelly of the workers' movements of colonial Bombay (Chandavarkar 1998: 266–305).

While Kosambi's memoirs are particularly silent about these events, daily reports furnished by intelligence officials and the Bombay Presidency Police provide important glimpses into his activities. In the reports and intelligence abstracts furnished by the police commissioner, Kosambi's name appears more than fifty times for those entries dating between April and October of 1930 (Chaudhari 1990). They report that he regularly delivered speeches, amidst crowds of up to five thousand people, on the "Workers Duty to the country," "The fight for Bread," and the "happy and contended [sic]" (186) history of India before British rule. In handbills and pamphlets written and signed by Kosambi, "white officers with fat salaries" (55) and their "callous and heartless capitalist" (314) cronies are condemned for protecting the "faithless pledges of a dying Empire" (403).

After Kosambi's release from jail, he grew increasingly disillusioned with Gandhi's Congress and its failure to address the grievances of India's peasant and labor movements. It was in this context that in 1934 the most powerful leftist political party in India was born. As an organization formed within the Congress rather than in opposition to it, the Congress Socialist Party (CSP) aimed to "change the content and policy of the Congress so that it might emancipate the masses both from foreign power and the native system of exploitation" (Chowdhuri 2007: 155).[11] While teaching in the mid-1930s at Kashi Vidyapeeth, an institution then under the guidance of the CSP president and budding Buddhologist, Acharya Narendra Dev (1889–1956), Kosambi wrote his most significant work of political theory, *Hindi Samkrti ani Ahimsa* [*Indian Civilization and Non-violence* (1935)].[12]

Indian Civilization is a creative and ambitious work, covering several thousand years of Indian history, from the Vedic era to the rise and fall of shramana cultures up through the present day. The text demonstrates Kosambi's mastery over Sanskrit and Prakrit sources. At the same time, its Marxist undertones are obvious: the reader is taken on an evolutionary journey following the classical Marxist historiography of primitive communism, slavery, feudalism, capitalism, and finally, communism. While a Marxist focus on private property shapes the text, the thread that pulls the entire narrative together is Kosambi's argument that Buddhist (and Jain) non-violence (ahimsa) has and will be central to the progress of Indian civilization. In the last chapter, Kosambi makes his thesis explicit. The premise is simple: as non-violence advances, so too does civilization; when violence ensues, civilization declines. But then, in his assessment of the present state of Indian affairs, Kosambi makes clear that Gandhian-style non-violence alone is not enough:

> India's Hindu middle class is agitating for independence. It wants independence—whether through non-violence or violence. A sickly man thinks little of whether a medicine [aushadhi] contains the pure essence [pavitrata] of plants or impure essence [apavitrata] of meat and such things. He only wants good health [arogya, literally "absence of disease"] and the sooner it comes the better. The medicines of the Arya Samaj, Lokamanya [Tilak's] Ganesh festival, and Mahatma Gandhi's non-violent and constructive project have been tried, but none have brought the cure [labh]. If the Bolsheviks have freed the working classes [mazdoor-varg] in all of the Russian Empire by destroying the aristocrats [sardar] and landowners [zamindar] all the while fighting the entire world, then why are we not able to free India of her suffering by taking the same path? (Kosambi [1935] 2010: 168)

Kosambi then outlines his own revolutionary strategy that avoids the unnecessary bloodshed of the Bolsheviks by welding the Buddha's doctrine of non-violence, the Marxist wisdom of socio-economic reform, and the tactical brilliance of Gandhi's satyagraha. This socialist dharmic remedy should be understood as part of what scholars like David Scott (2004) have described as the modern "longing for total revolution". According to Scott, the modern conception of revolution is based on "distinctive ways of defining the problem to be overcome ... so as to achieve satisfaction" (64). For Kosambi, the problem is not just Indian independence, but human suffering (dukkha) more widely, and his solution is clearly a blend of Buddhist and Marxist strategies.

Only towards the end of the book, when dealing with the contemporary period, does Kosambi depart radically from Marxist historiography to begin his own rigorous Buddhist critique. He contends that while the

Marxist criticism of capitalism as an alienating and exploitative force is correct, it is better understood through a Buddhist lens. Using a series of passages from the *Tipitaka*, Kosambi explains how existential suffering (dukkha) is created by three types of cravings (Pali *tanha*, Sanskrit, *trishna*): for sensual pleasures (*kam*), for experiences (*bhav*), and for non-experiences (*vibhav*) (Kosambi [1935] 2010: 176). Pursuing these pleasurable but ultimately temporal experiences, he explains, will lead only to decay and further suffering. Having established this point, he then argues that Marxists conceive of suffering primarily through the lens of servitude and bondage as relating to the ownership of private property. This too, Kosambi explains, is linked to the Buddhist conception of craving. For according to Kosambi, the sangha's eventual demise in India stemmed from its desire for and accumulation of private property—in the form of land (*zamin*), women (*stri*), and slaves (*dasa*) (182–83). Thus, he concludes that religion, including Buddhism, has indeed been an opiate for the masses.

The craving of modern-day nations, he adds, is an equally deadly addiction. If religion is an opiate, "nationalism is liquor" (Kosambi [1909–49] 2010: 354). While Buddhist scriptures point to collective and personal craving as sources of suffering, Kosambi envisions a new criterion of suffering in the modern world, a feeling he calls "nationalist craving". Echoing Marx, but couched in a uniquely Buddhist idiom, he recounts how the nationalist craving for "profitable trade" among the upper classes of England drove them to conquer the world, from the Americas to Asia to Africa. "The national good, that is, bringing into the country the wealth of other countries, turned every evil deed into a praiseworthy one! .... [I]nstead of feeling disgusted by craving, England developed greater greed. The result was the last world war" (339). Warning that Britain's "imperial greed" will only lead to further violence and exploitation, Kosambi concludes that the foremost solution to "national craving" is the same as suggested for other forms of craving: the doctrine of *aparigraha*, or "avoidance of possessions". Here again, as in his earlier writings, he draws a parallel with the nationalization schemes theorized by democratic socialists. However, this time, Kosambi cleverly equates the revolutionary call to nationalize property with a verse he translates from the *Bodhisattvacaryavatara* in which Shantideva proclaims: "Nirvana is giving up everything, and that is what I wish for. If I have to give up everything, it is best to do so for the welfare of all creatures" (353fn12). He wonders: "By abandoning their great and small estates for the good of mankind, would our wealthy people not share in such unparalleled joy" (ibid)?

Having shown that Buddhism and Marxism propounded similar views for the "welfare of mankind," Kosambi prescribes his new tonic: the practice of "true wisdom" (prajna) and non-violence (ahimsa). Marx, in Kosambi's vision, was a dispenser of the former but "suffered from the narrow-mindedness of Europeans" (355). That is, while his scientific knowledge of social evolution was instrumental in the advancement of mankind, it has been ultimately destructive because it was not accompanied by non-violence. Turning Marx's historical sociology back at him, Kosambi calls Marx a product of his culture, a culture that "demands an adversary" and believes that "civilization will not advance without such competition" (356). According to Kosambi, the Marxist solution to nationalism and capitalism was to unite the entire working class and oppose the bourgeoisie with the premise that the hostility between the two would wane after the struggle was over. This, he argues, simply transfers the hostility between nations to a hatred between bourgeoisie and workers.

The only viable way to free man's cravings from the mundane agonies of daily life, he proposes, is an eclectic blend of ahimsa, socialist wisdom, and Gandhian political strategy (satyagraha):

> In our country, Parshwa [the Jain Tirthankara] and the Buddha turned the current of non-violence towards the good of the masses. But it did not get into the political sphere and was, as a result, mired in a puddle of religious sectarianism. Around it grew the forest of the puranas [Hindu myths]. Mahatma Gandhi's attempt to give that further impetus and turn it to the political sphere is truly to be congratulated. But it was obstructed midway and suffered a loss of direction. This was good, in a way, because if it had continued it would have fallen into the ditch of nationalism and proved detrimental. Only if non-violence is accompanied by the wisdom of socialists will this current [the looming threat of war] turn in the right direction, and lead to the welfare of mankind (357).

Kosambi was no doubt aware that a similar political critique had been formulated two decades earlier by those communists who went on to found the Third International or the Comintern. What is original in Kosambi's argument, however, is his rather eclectic articulation of his point in indigenous Indic terminology which was much more likely to precipitate his Marathi-reading audience into action. The spectrum of global voices in Kosambi's philosophy of history—Gandhi, Tolstoy, Marx, Ashvaghosha, Voltaire, Shantideva, Lenin, the Buddha—indicates the ideological conventions that intellectuals like Kosambi had to depend on to give Buddhism a respected place in the modern Indian conscience. The loom upon which Kosambi's philosophy is set is undoubtedly Marxist, but the final weave is most clearly a modern democratic Buddhist socialism designed to clothe the poor, the oppressed, and the left-leaning, non-violent revolutionary. As is clear in *Indian Civilization*, the role of Buddhist non-violence always took precedence over not just the core Buddhist doctrine of suffering, but also the Marxist thrust on exploitation. The World War I, the Soviet purges, and the experience of witnessing lives "being reduced to corpses" at the Shiroda satyagraha had cemented Kosambi's dedication to Gandhi's non-violent tactics (230). Although never losing sight of the Marxist emphasis on social exploitation, even his penultimate work, a play on the life of Gotama Buddha (*Natak: Bodhisattva,* 1949), depicted the Buddha's renunciation not as a result of the experience of witnessing sickness, old age, and death, but the imminent warfare of the Sakya and Koliya clans.[13]

Indian Civilization was Kosambi's last major written attempt to influence political developments. His later works continued to bear the stamp of leftist thought, but it was his son's scholarship during the next decades that enduringly associated the Kosambi name with Marxism.[14] At the same time that Kosambi's efforts to explicitly synthesize socialism and Buddhism began to wind down, one of Kosambi's distant colleagues and an equally influential scholar began espousing his own revolutionary dhamma.

Rahul Sankrityayan and the Marxist Reform of Buddhism

If Dharmanand Kosambi forged a Maharashtrian Buddhist public, the radical scholar and intrepid explorer, Rahul Sankrityayan (1893–1963), did the same for the Hindi-speaking world. Unlike Kosambi, however, Sankrityayan's engagement with Marxism was more forceful, his Buddhist vision couched in the language of Marx, rather than being Kosambi's socialism couched in the language of the Buddha. Before becoming a globe-trotting bhikkhu and manuscript hunter in the 1930s, and communist propagandist from the 1940s onwards, Sankrityayan had lived the life of a Vaishnava sadhu, an Arya Samaji social reformer, and Congress politician (Chudal 2016). Yet writing was always his primary domain and source of income. While his roughly one hundred and fifty published books and more than seventy published articles speak of the breadth and depth of his intellectual engagements, it was his prolific research as a scholar that gained him fame in Buddhist circles.[15]

Sankrityayan's own reading of Buddhism was deeply shaped by Pali scriptures like the *Kalama Sutta*, which were widely seen by Buddhist modernists as expressing Buddhism's scientific tendencies. In his memoir, *Meri Jivan Yatra* [My Life Journey], Sankrityayan writes of the first time he encountered the text:

> When in the Kalamas, I discovered the Buddha's teaching—do not accept the teaching of any book, any tradition, out of concern for your elders, always decide for yourself before you take it on principle—my heart suddenly said, listen, here is a man whose unswerving faith in truth [*satya*], understood the strength of man's independent reason [*buddhi*] (Sankrityayan [1944–63] 2014, Vol. 2: 19).

As his study of the Three Jewels intensified throughout the 1920s and 1930s, it began to coalesce with the wider message of social equality and political liberation that he encountered both in India and abroad.

Like Kosambi before him, Sankrityayan took his full ordination (upasampada) in Ceylon in 1930.[16] The Buddhist atmosphere that he encountered there was extremely cosmopolitan, studying alongside Chinese, Sinhalese, Indian, and European monastics. Yet, in other ways, his experience of Sinhalese monasticism was significantly different from Kosambi's nearly thirty years before. While Kosambi had studied at Vidyodaya Pirivena, Sankrityayan had been sent to that college's sister institution, Vidyalankara Pirivena. The contrast between the two institutions was stark. Vidyodaya—Kosambi's alma mater—advocated a "sober" and "conservative" program of Buddhist social service and economic policies. Sankrityayan's garden of enlightenment, Vidyalankara, on the other hand, was groomed in an "indigenous anti-imperialism" by a new generation of Marx-inspired Sinhalese Buddhist nationalists (Seneviratne 1999: 131fn2; 56–188).[17] Indeed, the writings of Sankrityayan ([1944–63] 2014: 1–28, 106–10, 124–28) along with other Indian Buddhist monks studying at Vidyalankara Pirivena in the 1930s, including Kavi Nagarjun (1911–1988, a.k.a. Vaidyanath Mishra), Anand Kausalyayan, and Jagdish Kashyap, describe a vibrant atmosphere in which Pali manuscripts, Sanskrit literature, and Orientalist scholarship was circulated alongside the writings of Marx and American freethinkers like Robert Ingersol.[18]

While the intellectuality of these institutions may disrupt the sanitized visions of Buddhist monasticism imagined by many, this was not just a facet unique to British Ceylon. Elsewhere, Sankrityayan's global encounters with Buddhism were peopled by individuals acutely aware of, and keen to discuss, the politics of de-colonization and the rise of the Marxist paradigm. During his four major research expeditions in central Tibet from 1929 to 1938, rumors of a new "Buddhist dialectics" pervaded the air. As early as 1929, his Mongolian tutors informed him of the Soviet-instigated "renewal movement" to restore Buddhism to its "primitive form, which has no friction with atheism, communal ownership of property ... [and] Marxism". "Buddha and Marx are not antagonistic," he was told, "but complementary to one another" (Sankrityayan 1984: 137). When serving as a missionary (dharmadoot) for the Maha Bodhi Society in London and Paris from 1932 to 1933, these ideas were further confirmed by European Orientalists who all pointed to the Soviet akademiks as being at the cutting edge of this new scholarship (Sankrityayan 1957: 195).

Sankrityayan spent most of the 1930s on the move, traveling through Asia and devoting himself to a painstaking reconstruction of the past from original manuscripts in Sanskrit, Tibetan, Apabhramsha, and other languages.[19] In between travels to Europe, Tibet, and elsewhere in Asia, Sankrityayan continued working closely with Indian scholars whose own lives were being transformed by the political revolution transpiring in India. This network of scholars was by no means limited to Buddhologists with leftist leanings or leftists with Buddhological interests, but it is notable that the two often went hand in hand. The union was not created overnight, but was a slow and steady tug of war between the competing universalisms taking root in Indian soil.

There were men like Rammanohar Lohia (1910–67), J.P. Narayan (1902–79), Acharya J.B. Kripalani (1888–1982), and Acharya Narendra Dev (1889–1956), all of whom theorized the parallels between Buddhism and the progressive socialist movements they were attempting to uphold. Take for instance, Narendra Dev, the prominent educator and founding president of the Congress Socialist Party. Dev was also an exceptional scholar of Buddhism and his 1956 Hindi-language *Bauddha-dharma-darshan* (Dev [1956] 2011) is still considered a monumental study of Buddhist philosophy.[20] He and Sankrityayan translated the *Communist Manifesto* into Hindi in 1931, and in the next two-and-a-half decades, they met often at Buddhist celebrations, scholarly conferences, and at leftist political platforms.

In 1935, Sankrityayan made his first journey to Russia. At the time, Buddhism was, in his view, a teaching based on reason (*buddhi*), human pragmatism (*manushya mapavad*), and atheistic humanism (*nastik manaviyata*). These were the same qualities, which David Scott (2004) has argued, in the context of Marxism's global rise in the 1930s, that gave Marxist revolutionaries "a new idea of the rhythm of history, a new conception of historical agency, and a new idea of how to self-consciously wrest the future from the past" (68). But by the time Sankrityayan was finally granted permission to work for an extended period with Fyodor Stcherbatski in Leningrad in 1937–38, the Soviet attitude towards Buddhism had changed, moving from tolerance to outright condemnation and persecution. Stcherbatski's works on Buddhist logic were condemned as part of the "ideological struggle against Leninism," a deliberate slandering of "the logic of dialectical materialism," and his well-known series *Bibliotheca Buddhica* was shut down for being "a mouthpiece of the Buddhist-Lamaist religion" (Tolz 2011: 18–19). Such "revisionist" ideas had grown so prominent that Stalin himself felt it necessary to publicly ridicule "the absurd theory of the identity of the Communist and Buddhist doctrines" (Snelling 1993: 234). Six of Stcherbatski's closest colleagues at the Institute of Buddhist Culture (where Kosambi had also worked) were arrested, denounced as "counter-revolutionaries," and one was even executed. In Soviet Mongolia, the Stalinist turn against Buddhism was even more catastrophic when the state instigated the killing of "approximately eighteen thousand lamas and a similar number of other people and the physical destruction of the monasteries" (Kaplonski 2014: 32–33). In Stalin's Russia, such were the consequences of equating the Buddha to Marx.

Yet, throughout the 1930s, Buddhist intellectuals around the world grappled with the possibly complementary visions of modernity prescribed by Buddhism and Marxism. As China's future became increasingly divided along Guomindang and communist paths, "progressive Buddhists" like Master Juzan (1908–1984) argued that the study of Marxist thought could be of immense help to Chinese Buddhist traditions by removing "superstitions" and "feudal elements" (Yu 2016). Across the sea, the Japanese monk Seno'o Giro (1889–1961) adapted and appropriated the language of Marx in his own struggle to reform Japanese Buddhism (Shields 2012: 343–44). Back in Russia, Sankrityayan pondered Buddhism's downfall in India by approaching the problem from the context of his own training in Indian philosophical traditions and Marxist historiography. There were distinct cultural differences among all of these figures, yet they drew from common pools of thought—in this case, Buddhist and Marxist—to solve the problems that lay before them.

By the time that Sankrityayan left Russia in 1939, his perspective on Buddhism had moved past Kosambi's "Buddhist socialism" to be more proximate to the strict Soviet orthodoxy. Like Juzan in China or Seno'o in Japan, he began arguing that if Buddhism could be purified of its links to the landed classes and returned to its "primitive" or "original" state of "atheistic humanism" (nastik manaviyata), it could once again act as a dynamic and progressive force in society. However, while he remained supportive of the Buddha's atheism, dynamic thought, and call for social equality, he was now convinced that the teachings of the Buddha were incapable of doing what Marxism could. Buddhists had learned how to understand the world, to accept change and impermanence (*anitya*/anicca), but they had failed to change situations for their own ends, in accordance with their own desires. In Sankrityayan's view, that program had been enunciated only by Marx.

Imbued with a newfound commitment to the forces of international communism, Sankrityayan renounced his monastic vows, married Stcherbatski's student, the Tibetologist, Ellena Narvertovna Kozerovskaya (dates unknown), and left Russia to join the peasant movements in Bihar. There, he worked among the kisan sabhas (peasant associations) and the Communist Party of India for the next decade. Along with J.P. Narayan and Swami Sahajanand Saraswati (1889–1950), Sankrityayan quickly emerged as one of the foremost leaders of the organization, working on their behalf to fix the "agrarian problem" through the mobilization of peasants on radical Marxist platforms.[21] While fighting *zamindari* or landlordism was primary to the movement, so too was the destruction of institutionalized religion, or the "illusion of dharma," as Swami Sahajanand (1995: 133) called it. So, it is not difficult to see how the early Buddhist impulse against the Vedas and brahmanical interests could be easily invoked as part of the movement's wider political theology. Equally important was that rootedness of ancient Buddhist teachings in the soil of the Bihari peasants themselves. While working for the kisan sabhas, Sankrityayan was jailed for a total of twenty-nine months on three separate occasions with his third and final arrest as part of the British government's "exceedingly drastic" measures to "cripple the Communist machinery" during the spring of 1940 (Overstreet and Windmiller 1959: 183–84).

In the two decades after his release from prison in 1942, Sankrityayan's writings took on a much more rigorous Marxist tenor. Although much of this literature dealt with Buddhism and Marxism independently, it is in his novels and popular books where the relationship between the two is most explicitly addressed. In two of his more popular non-fiction works, a short English essay, "Buddhist Dialectics" (Sankrityayan [1956] 1994)[22] and a Hindi-language biography of the Buddha, *Mahamanav Buddh* (Sankrityayan [1956] 2011), he provides a clear synopsis of his views. To begin with, the Buddha's critique of caste, as also his teaching of self-dependence or reliance (*atmavalamban*) and intellectual freedom (*buddhisvatantrya*) was far ahead of its time, on par with Marxist thought. Echoing Kosambi, he applauds the Buddha for trying to introduce "absolute communism [*poorn samyavad*] inside the sangha" and points to the early Buddhist preference for democratic republics (*gana*) (Sankrityayan [1956] 2011: 35, 104–09). The Buddha's rationality, criticism of revealed scriptures, and atheism—all qualities shared by Marx, he adds—allowed him to recognize that "the origin of monarchy did not lie in any divine source but ... was the product of the growth of private property" (Sankrityayan [1956] 1994: 4). Furthermore, the Buddha's doctrine of "bahujana hitaya, bahujana sukhaya," or "the good of many, the happiness of many," he contends, rivals Marxist ethics.

On the economic and social fronts outside the sangha, he paints a more complex picture. Although the Buddha was to be praised for advocating universal brotherhood, preempting the Marxist ideology of humanity, he was to be criticized for failing to abolish caste in society at large. Like most Marxists, including Singaravelu (presidential addresss at Kanpur Communist Conference, December 1925, in Murugesan and Subramanyam 1975: 203), Sankrityayan viewed caste from a class perspective. "The caste system originated in economics," he argued. "The high castes owned property, whereas the low castes were deprived of it. One could only be abolished by abolishing the other" (Sankrityayan [1956] 2011: 103). Had the caste system not been based on wealth (*sampatti*) and had the Buddha allowed debtors (*rni*), slaves (dasa), and soldiers (*rajsainik*) into the sangha, thus undercutting the strength of the landed classes, caste inequalities could have been eradicated. Instead, the Buddha barred these groups from taking ordination for fear of reprisal from the merchants and kings that the sangha relied upon. In Sankrityayan's historiography, this had profound consequences.[23] As in Engels's history of Christianity (Boer 2014), Sankrityayan argued that although Buddhism possessed the will of the people, this characteristic made it a tool of the status quo, thereby undercutting its ability to revolutionize the masses.

Despite these shortcomings, Sankrityayan believed that Buddhist philosophy continued to shape the foundations of Indian history in ways similar to what Hegel and Marx had done in Europe. And just as Marx is said to have turned Hegel's theories on their head, Sankrityayan saw in the eighth-century Buddhist philosopher, Dharmakirti, a figure close to Marx. Dharmakirti argued that reality was defined by "that which is capable of objective action" (*artha-kriya-samartham*) and that we must learn to accept "objects as our guide." In this, Dharmakirti had touched on the fundamental principle of modern empirical science (Sankrityayan [1956] 1994). Sankrityayan calls this a "big weapon," but laments that it was "not used." By Dharmakirti's lifetime, Buddhism's ties to the status quo had forced it to "soften its sharpness" (Sankrityayan 1942: 105). The failure to utilize Dharmakirti's knowledge of the conditions necessary to change objective reality with the "rational and heart-stirring" (105) message of the Buddha was, in effect, the failure of Buddhism as religion. In an evocative passage, he outlines his solution to revitalizing the Buddhist revolution through a radical revision of the Buddha's Four Noble Truths:

[1] Suffering is to be found in the world;

[2] it is caused by exploitation;

[3] suffering will cease to exist if exploitation is done away with, that is, [if the] road to communism is followed;

[4] and communism is the way to the cessation of suffering (quoted in Bhattacharya 1994: 119).

What Marxism can provide Buddhism, it is argued, is the revolutionary praxis to free Buddhists from the bondage of their own historical failures.

Despite Sankrityayan's commitments to reforming Buddhism through Marxism, his sympathies for Buddhism were often too much for more hard-line colleagues, who attacked him as a "revisionist" (Chudal 2016: 239–41). Nowhere were these sympathetic gestures more evident than in his fictional writings. Among the seventeen novels Sankrityayan wrote in the last two decades of his life, several touch on themes or events connected to the ancient Buddhist world. These works, which need to be read as part of the Progressive Writers' Movement and its theory of "purposive art" (as opposed to "art for art's sake"), largely subscribe to the ideals of socialist realism and were intended as propaganda pieces.[24] In his novel *Jay Yaudheya* (1944), for instance, the reader is taken on an imaginary journey to Yaudheya, an ancient Indian state that embodies the absolute communism of the Buddha's sangha, where there are neither masters nor slaves, and equal rights are offered to all. Likewise, in his most famous piece of historical fiction, *Volga se Ganga* or *From the Volga to the Ganges* (Sankrityayan 1942)—which underwent multiple editions in fourteen different languages—Buddhism rarely comes under severe critique. Through most of the text, the suffering of slaves and working classes is often at the hands of corrupt brahmin priests, greedy banias (merchants), belligerent mullahs, and Christian capitalists. In stark contrast to these images, Sankrityayan describes the Buddha as a man who "wanted a revolution (*kranti*), one that would make the world a better place" (138); his dhamma is compared to "a sort of communism" (174) and his sangha as "a kind of model for a world of tomorrow" (142). The Buddha, it seems, was indeed the heart of a heartless world.

Reconsidering the Buddha and the Left

The attempt to unify Buddhism and Marxism prior to the 1950s was short-lived, based on an intense but ultimately superficial understanding of one another. In most parts of Asia, Buddhist dialogues with Marxism were typically based on rather simplistic notions of Marxist thinking. As Agehananda Bharati (1976: 107) suggested long ago in the case of Sri Lanka, the term Marxism was more a twentieth-century buzzword capable of inciting terror and uniting the masses than a sophisticated appreciation of its competing discourses. Trevor Ling (1979: 91) has argued similarly regarding the collaboration between Buddhists and Marxists in Burma and Cambodia. The early Buddhist appeal to Marxism, Ling suggests, was less a doctrine of historical materialism than its criticism of the materialistic capitalism of the West. That is, in most Asian Buddhist case studies, Marxist doctrines were used strategically as rhetorical tools in the fight against imperialism and colonialism, forming a central part of a sustained ideological alliance only on rare occasions.

Rather than thinking of Marxism's influence on Buddhism as a unilateral diffusion of ideology from the "West" to the "East," it is more accurate to think in terms of linked global networks where conversations and encounters between intellectuals produced a number of parallel outcomes, disjointed chains of influence, and creative interpretations. The intensity and speed with which these encounters and conversations occurred were due in large part to the widespread participation of Buddhists and Marxists in the major transformations of the twentieth century, namely, the expansion of state power, international commercial interests, and the death of long distance— the communications and transportation revolutions in printing, telegraph, steamships, railways, etc. Nor can the connection between Buddhism and Marxism be solely reduced to modern political alliances and/or desperate attempts by Buddhists to survive communist regimes. In the late 1940s, the

French belletrist, André Migot, asked rhetorically whether "the words of Engels might not equally well have been those of the Buddha" (Migot, quoted in Ling 1979: 167). A decade later, the famed structural anthropologist, Claude Lévi-Strauss, dedicated an entire chapter of his monumental work, *Tristes Tropique* (1955), to exploring the links between Buddhism and Marxism. The two systems, he proposed, are each "doing the same thing as the other, but on different levels." Buddhism, he concludes, "has achieved something that, elsewhere, only Marxism has brought off: it has reconciled the problem of metaphysics with the problem of human behavior" (Lévi-Strauss, quoted in Shields 2012: 334–35).

In India, the intersections between Buddhist and leftist ideologies gave rise to animated discussions, new ways of thinking and being. It is undeniable that the Praja Socialist Party's popular platform of "social humanism" in the 1950s and 1960s was deeply influenced by its founder Narendra Dev's deep studies of Buddhist philosophy. Similarly, for the "people's poet," Kavi Nagarjun (1911–1988), who moved to Ceylon to study Pali and don Buddhist robes before returning home to Bihar's peasant movement, one could be both modern and traditional, a progressive thinker and a Buddhist bhoomiputra, or "son of the soil" (Jha 1999). Ambedkar was no less cognizant of the Buddha's relationship to the left, even delivering a major speech at the World Fellowship of Buddhists in 1956, in which he argued that the two "–ism's" were nearly the same. Like Kosambi and Sankrityayan, he praised the Buddha for his communist-like sangha and equated Buddhist dukkha with the Marxist emphasis on poverty and exploitation. The only fundamental difference between Marxism and Buddhism, he argued, was in their methodology. While the Buddha used persuasion, moral teachings, and love, Marx advocated power and violence. In Ambedkar's logic, this was Marxism's fundamental error. Unlike Russia's communists, he remarked, "the wonder of all wonders is that the Buddha established Communism so far as the Sangha was concerned without dictatorship" (*BAWS* Vol. 3: 471).[25]

The enduring influence of these idioms and images in South Asia and beyond demonstrates that modern Buddhism was shaped as much by Marxist ideas about property, economic organization, and the sources of political authority as it was by the Orientalists who "discovered" India's "lost" religion. Remarkably, the role of Marxism on the socio-cognitive conditions of modern-day Buddhists is greatly under-theorized. In several of the most important scholarly works on Buddhist modernism (McMahan 2008; Lopez 2012, 2013), the influence of Marx and/or Marxism is almost completely absent. While claims about ancient Indian Buddhist communism may be dubious in historical detail or, at the very least, they may be greatly misplaced anachronisms, they were powerful as modern myth. The importance of these images for understanding modern Indian Buddhism, then, is not in their historical truthfulness but in the way in which they speak of the revolutionary world that modern Indians inhabited. In fact, with the birth of the new nation in 1947, India's first prime minister, Jawaharlal Nehru, drew on Buddhism's emotional appeal and revolutionary rhetoric precisely to forge a new ethos for the independent nation.

The Buddha Nation

In the months leading up to Indian independence in August 1947, there was a growing consensus among India's political elite that the future of the nation would look to its ancient past for inspiration. Among the many meetings convened by the country's top political brass in the weeks just prior to Independence were those of a subcommittee whose only duty was to finalize the design for the new national flag.[1] In a resolution approved by the Constituent Assembly on 22 July 1947, just three weeks prior to formal independence, the Gandhian charkha, or spinning wheel, was replaced by the Buddhist dhammachakra as the flag's central symbol. The Constituent Assembly minutes of that day make clear that the interpretations of the flag's meaning and its connections to the Buddha and Ashoka differed widely among its members (*CAD* Vol. 4, 22 July 1947). But this diversity of views was an illustration of the profound manner in which India's Buddhist past had come to permeate nearly all quarters of Indian society and nationalist thought. When the Constituent Assembly approved the decision, there was little dissent. On the eve of Independence, just three weeks later, a delegation of seventy-two women led by the prolific writer and social activist, Hansa Mehta (1897–1995), unfurled the national flag in the Constituent Assembly.[2] Indeed, it was just the beginning of early postcolonial India's fetish for the images and ideals of an imagined Buddhist past. Less than a year later, the Lion Seal of Sarnath, the ancient symbol of the Buddhist king Ashoka's Mauryan Empire, was adopted as the state

A homecoming for Buddhism. Buddhist delegates with Jawaharlal Nehru at the Buddha Jayanti in Delhi, 1956. In the first row from left to right are, Prince Palden Thondup Namgyal of Sikkim; Burmese prime minister, U Nu; His Holiness the fourteenth Dalai Lama; Indian prime minister Jawaharlal Nehru; His Holiness the tenth Panchen Lama; Tashi Namgyal, the king of Sikkim; and Chini Dorji, the queen of Bhutan

emblem to be used on all official government documentation. When the new constitution outlawing "untouchability" was unveiled later that year, the Maha Bodhi Society could not resist linking the act with the symbols that now represented the new nation: "Sometimes, truly, the road forward is the road back, in this case a return to the high level of consciousness attained in India when Buddhism prevailed and caste discrimination was condemned" (*MBJ* Vol. 56/12, 1948: 413). By January 1950, when Rajendra Prasad was sworn in as the first president of India beneath a mammoth sandstone image of the Buddha carved in Mathura some eighteen hundred years ago, the Central government's new leanings were clear.[3]

Public spaces took on names with Buddhist overtones—Gautama Hall, Buddha Park, Kanishka House, Lumbini Lane—while the state and Central governments poured substantial funds into restoring and revitalizing India's (and Nepal's) ancient Buddhist sites at Bodh Gaya, Sanchi, Shravasti, Lumbini, and Nalanda.[4] Apart from the restoration of ruins, new state-sponsored Buddhist institutes and educational centres were also set up.

The government made large contributions to publish Buddhist texts in local languages, including the forty-six-volume series of the complete Pali *Tipitaka*, or Words of the Buddha, in Devanagari script.[5] By 1956, the Ministry of Information and Broadcasting had even produced a full-length feature film, *Gotama the Buddha,* on the life of the Buddha that later won an award at the Cannes Film Festival for its "exceptional artistic and moral beauty" (quoted in Bakker 2009: 161). This was an age when, as one writer put it, "the Buddha spirit swept the nation" (Ahir 1994: 137). The pinnacle of this new-found confidence in Buddhism was the grand Buddha Jayanti celebration of 1956, a more-than-a-year-long event of festivals, conferences, art exhibitions, and international gatherings to mark the 2,500th anniversary of the Buddha's birth.

All of this activity constituted the Nehruvian state's promotion of Buddhism for secular purposes. Nehru's projects had two ambits: one concerning Buddhism's domestic consumption by citizens of the new nation, and one concerning its uses as an instrument of foreign policy. Although not averse to using Buddhist symbols to generate emotional appeal, Nehru's Buddhism was a modern "religion of reason," a scientific, moral code that did not require any formal, institutional commitment. This is visible in two remarkable statements made by Nehru, first in his early writings and later in front of a crowd of international leaders. In *The Discovery of India,* he declares:

> Buddha had the courage to attack popular religion, superstition, ceremonial, and priestcraft ... he condemned also the metaphysical and theological outlook, miracles, revelations, and dealings with the supernatural. His appeal was to logic, reason and experience, his emphasis was on ethics, and his method was one of psychological analysis ... it is remarkable how near this philosophy of the Buddha brings us to some of the concepts of modern physics and philosophic thought (Nehru [1946] 1985a: 120, 129).[6]

Nearly a decade later, during a grand Buddhist ceremony in Sanchi, where Nehru presided over the installation of Buddhist relics in a new vihara constructed with state funds, he added: "All that is necessary is not this Vihara in stone and brick but some kind of a temple in each one's mind and heart which will enshrine those eternal truths and which will guide us along the right path which we forsook so long ago" (*MBJ* Vol. 61/1–2, 1953: 5). The "truths" which Nehru and other state leaders regularly invoked were by no means unique to Buddhism, but they were adamant that the Buddha was the first great universalist, an undeniable proponent of reason, non-violence, and ethics. They took great pride in the fact that the Buddha was an Indian and that an *Indian* tradition had given so much shape to the world.[7] Buddhism was, as Nehru put it before the Constituent Assembly in 1947, proof that India was not just "a tight little narrow country," but once an "international centre" that guided the world (*CAD* Vol. 4, 22 July 1947).

Despite this, only in rare cases have scholars recognized what an important role Buddhist symbols and rhetoric played in the making of the Nehruvian state. For instance, in an otherwise insightful essay on the transformations of the Indian national flag, the political scientist, Srirupa Roy (2006: 511–12), has argued that "the replacement of the [Gandhian] charkha with dharmacakra is a literal indication of the wider reorientation of political and economic philosophy under way at the time, as Gandhi's vision of a decentralized, economically self-sufficient India of village republics was replaced by the Nehruvian commitment to an industrialized and centralized polity." Roy's analysis is astute, but her vision of the symbol as tied to a purely mechanical enterprise underestimates the historical and aesthetic significance of the revitalized Buddhist symbol. It is not just the bureaucratic modes of production that demonstrate state authority, but also the "poetics of power" (Geertz 1980: 123) or theatrical performances that serve political interests as well. Political success has always relied upon strong, emotional public appeal, and members of Nehru's new government, from B.R. Ambedkar and Sarvepalli Radhakrishnan to Rajendra Prasad and S.P. Mookerjee, recognized well the latent potency of Buddhist symbols and ideas. Nehru's use of Buddhism may be best understood as an attempt to provide a model of modern, civilized existence, similar to Clifford Geertz's idea that the act of invoking an "exemplary center ... [such as the Buddha or Ashoka's India] ... creates not just a center of power ... but a standard of civilization" (15). When Nehru took charge of the cremated remains of Buddhist saints and passed them on to neighboring rulers, who installed them in their own royal halls and constitutional assemblies, he was linking these different polities to India's history and modern mode of being, both in the past and in the present. It sent an unequivocal signal: love the Buddha, love India.

When the 2,500-year-old remains of Sariputta and Mogallana, two of the Buddha's most respected disciples, arrived in Calcutta in January 1949, more than half a million people sitting in "utmost reverence and orderliness," watched Nehru receive two reliquary urns and touch them to his forehead (*Maha Bodhi Centenary Volume* 1991: 188). Surrounded by a sea of Buddhist monks adorned in red and yellow robes, Nehru's arrival on the twenty-foot-high platform, where the relics rest, coincided with a shower of yellow rose petals. Throughout the day, foreign delegates and government officials gave speeches, broadcast live on All India Radio, on why Buddhist teachings were necessary for India and the world's well-being. Nehru himself stressed the importance of the Buddha's teachings on reason and compassion alongside Ashoka's ideals of tolerance. He described Buddhism as "a bond of the spirit" that did not require political attachments and called on the audience to once again renew that "silken bond" (187). One speaker compared Nehru to the esteemed Ashoka himself (*dharmika dharmaraja*), arguing that the government was following the same "lofty principles" of "righteous rulership based on benevolence and equality of rights .... You have given the followers of all religions and all denominations the opportunity not only to enjoy freedom of religious belief but also to live together in harmony and take an equal share in promoting the national welfare" (186). Many speeches given that day linked the Buddha to Gandhi, sending a clear message that like Bapu, the Buddha too was the father of the nation, capable of healing the wounds of the country following the former's tragic assassination.[8]

Over the course of the next month, an estimated four hundred thousand people visited the Maha Bodhi Society's Shri Dharmarajika vihara where the relics had been placed for public viewing (darshan). Celebrations of India's Buddhist heritage and speeches on the contribution of Buddhism to world peace continued throughout the month at select sites across the city. While sporadic violence in Calcutta canceled several of the planned public processions, most continued unabated in private spaces like the Bengal Buddhist Association, Japanese Buddhist temple (Saddharma vihara), Burmese temple, and Ramakrishna Mission. Photos and descriptions reveal military guards of the Gurkha Rifles standing attentively alongside long processions of military bands, Buddhist monks, decorated elephants, canopies of white silk, Rolls Royces and the latest model from Hindustan Motors. Amidst the highly charged communal atmosphere following the Great Calcutta Killings of 1946 and the Partition, associating India with the moral sovereignty of Ashoka and the Buddha was, as several scholars have noted, a "safe" means to heal and unify the nation (Jaffrelot 2010: 12; Brown 2009: 293–315). Besides, it was also about invoking the assumed rational core of religion, "the common faith of mankind" (Dewey [1934] 2013: 80), a secular religion liberated from dogma and hate. "For the sake of national interest," the governor of West Bengal proclaimed at a public speech, "Buddhist morality should spread in the country" ("Bengal Governor's speech," *HT,* 4 May 1950). When state officials praised Buddhist doctrines in India, they rarely discussed its soteriological or deeper philosophical dimensions. Instead, they focused on its ethical spirit and historical significance. As Nehru explained at Sanchi, there were two paths ahead: "the way of the sword and the way of Buddha and Mahatma Gandhi ... we have to remember ... the lesson of equality and service of society and compassion that Buddha taught" (*MBJ* Vol. 61/1–2, 1953: 3).

In the Cold War world, a pan-Asian unity based on Buddhist principles and Indian civilization was the theme of the day. In a letter congratulating Sri Lanka on its independence in 1948, Nehru recalled that the seed of Buddhism that "has flourished in Ceylon ... [is] a symbol of *that great gift which India gave to Lanka and the world* so long ago ... [it] is therefore a symbol of India and Lanka being together, for our mutual advantage and for the freedom and advantage of the world" (SWJN Vol. 5: 535, emphasis added). A decade later, these ideologies permeated foreign affairs. At the Buddha Jayanti celebrations in 1956, Nehru invited more than two hundred royal dignitaries, heads of state, foreign ambassadors, and Buddhist leaders from across the world to celebrate "twenty-five hundred years" of Buddhism. During the state-sponsored celebrations, helicopters and airplanes showered villages and towns with lotus flowers and government pamphlets praising Buddhist non-violence, while Nehru and other officials stressed the ancient connections between India and the rest of Asia. Non-violence, religious tolerance, pan-Asianism, and Indian civilization: these were to be the ideological bearings for the future. The underlying ethos was implicit. The teachings of Lord Buddha were capable of transcending any differences—cultural or political—that existed between India and the rest of Buddhist Asia.

In February 1956, when the government was considering the transfer of Buddhist relics to Burma, the Indian ambassador in Rangoon wrote a letter to Nehru explaining that, "I am convinced that nothing brings us so close to the Burmese as concrete evidence of our common spiritual heritage ... it would be a fine gesture on our part if we send the relics to Rangoon by a special plane accompanied by some of our high-ranking monks in the Buddhist hierarchy" (Letter from R. R. Saksena, 21 February 1956, in MEB File no. 40/3). Nehru followed through, and in an elaborate ceremony attended by several thousand Burmese and Indians, the Burmese prime minister, U Nu (1907–95), received the relics despite having attended his father-in-law's funeral the same day. In a classified document on how to improve India's image in Ceylon, composed by the Indian high commissioner in Colombo just one year later, the same thinking was explicit, only now equated with demographic figures:

> India is the land of the Buddha. The Buddhists of Ceylon who number more than 60 percent of the population look to India for religious inspiration. It is said to be the dying wish of every Buddhist to be reborn in India, the land of the "Dhamma" ... friendliness can be strengthened by emphasizing cultural and religious affinities. The press generally attaches tremendous importance to material on Buddhist activities in India ... the Mission can, whenever possible, cull out all such comments from the Indian press and hand them out unofficially for local consumption ("Annual Reports on Ceylon," MEARIB File no. 3/8, 1957).

The high commissioner went on to recommend the development of a "Cinema-cum-Library van" or a "mobile film unit" that could screen popular documentaries in all accessible parts of the island. As is apparent by these examples, the desire to promote Buddhism was deeply enmeshed in the culture of the governing elite.

The first cabinet of independent India. B.R. Ambedkar, seated to the far left. Jawaharlal Nehru, fifth from left; to his left, Rajendra Prasad; and S.P. Mookerjee, seated to the far right

The Nation's Tryst with Buddhism

In postcolonial India, the lives of several state-level leaders were closely intertwined with the revival of Buddhism, with its most critical leadership found in four members of Nehru's cabinet. The first was President Rajendra Prasad (1884–1963), a trained lawyer from Bihar. Prasad had served as the chairman of the controversial Maha Bodhi temple case from the early 1920s until its resolution in 1949. Despite being a conservative politician allied with the Hindu wing of the Congress, Prasad was instrumental in the negotiations that granted partial management of the temple to Buddhists in 1949 (Trevithick 2007). Besides Prasad, there was the vice president (and later second president), Sarvepalli Radhakrishnan (1888–1975), a figure whose reputation as an intellectual outweighed that of any other member in the cabinet. A former professor at Oxford, Radhakrishnan's works on Indian philosophy remain central source books for scholars today. He published widely on Buddhist thought, and just three years after Independence, he produced an influential English translation of the *Dhammapada*, where he argued that the Buddha's teachings were derived from the Upanishads (Radhakrishnan 1950). As with his *Dhammapada,* Radhakrishnan's interpretation of Buddhism was encoded through Vedantic philosophy. Radhakrishnan's philosophical assimilation of Buddhism into Hinduism coincided with his frequent public declarations that Buddhism was simply an "offshoot of Hinduism" and that the Buddha "was born, grew up and died a Hindu" (Radhakrishnan 1956: ix).

The third figure was Syama Prasad Mookerjee (1901–53), a former finance minister of Bengal and veteran of the rightwing Hindu paramilitary group, the RSS. Mookerjee's brief tenure as the Union minister of industry and transport (1947–50) was marked by serious tensions with Nehru and the Congress. A former president of the All-India Hindu Maha Sabha (1944), Mookerjee's links with the Hindu political right came under increased scrutiny after Gandhi was murdered by a Maha Sabha ideologue in 1948, leading Nehru to jail thousands of its members and sympathizers. Relations between the two worsened over the crisis in Kashmir, and in 1951, Mookerjee resigned from the cabinet to start the Bharatiya Jana Sangh, the political party that later morphed into the Hindu nationalist Bharatiya Janata Party (India's current ruling party). In line with the wider Hinduization of Buddhism transpiring throughout the first half of the twentieth century, Mookerjee's militant Hinduism had not prevented him from serving (like his father, Ashutosh Mookerjee) as the president of the Maha Bodhi Society. He held that position from 1943 until his death ten years later. This made him indispensable to Nehru's Buddhist programming, particularly during the late 1940s and early 1950s when Mookerjee himself traveled to Cambodia, Burma, and Ceylon to deliver Buddhist relics on behalf of the Indian government and the Maha Bodhi Society. Despite their severe differences, the two nemeses often held the rostrum together at Buddhist events jointly organized by the Maha Bodhi Society and the Central government, even after Mookerjee resigned from political office.

The fourth member of Nehru's cabinet, and undoubtedly the most vocal Buddhist voice of them all, especially after 1950, was B.R. Ambedkar. Although Ambedkar's Buddhism shared the same rationalistic interpretation as Nehru's, the latter's version possessed a sharper edge and was not easily assimilable to Nehru's vision. Like Mookerjee and many others, Ambedkar was also a political oddity in Nehru's cabinet, having opposed the Congress for almost his entire political career.[9] Ambedkar, however, was a pragmatist, particularly when it came to championing the cause of dalits and women, and in 1947 he agreed to take on the role of India's first minister of law and create India's Constitution as chairman of the drafting committee. The Constitution had all the characteristics of Ambedkar's social reform agenda. It prohibited discrimination based on sex, religion, and race, abolished untouchability, guaranteed the right to freedom of religion, and enshrined a system of reservations or affirmative action for scheduled castes (dalits) and scheduled tribes (adivasis). Even so, in Ambedkar's eyes, the document did not go far enough and, in 1950, he turned his energies to the controversial Hindu Code Bill, aimed at ensuring the legal rights of women in matters pertaining to marriage, inheritance, adoption, etc. He hoped the bill would implement more far-reaching and necessary reforms in Indian society, but Nehru withdrew his support, not so much for lack of approval of the proposed initiatives but for fear of alienating and antagonizing the more conservative elements of the Congress (Jaffrelot 2005: 5–6). When the Hindu Code Bill failed to pass in 1951, Ambedkar resigned from Nehru's cabinet. The political divorce that ensued did not so much sever Ambedkar's and Nehru's relationship as it drew it out in a torturous fashion. When Nehru organized the much-publicized Sanchi restoration ceremonies in 1952, Ambedkar did not receive an invitation despite being India's only national leader to have publicly declared himself a Buddhist.[10] Four years later, when Ambedkar finished his magnum opus, *The Buddha and His Dhamma,* to coincide with the nationwide Buddha Jayanti celebrations, Nehru dismissed Ambedkar's plea for financial assistance in distributing the book (See, "Letter 168: from Ambedkar to Nehru, 14 Sept 1956" and "Letter 169: from Nehru to Ambedkar, 15 Sept 1956", in Ambedkar 1993: 191–92).[11]

Taken as a whole, the national leadership's support for and interest in Buddhism was multi-pronged and emphatic but it was hardly uniform. This was not a cabinet with a singular vision of the religion but one whose members spoke of competing *Buddhisms*—disparate interpretations that catered to different audiences. While the gathering of so many Indian politicians invested in Buddhist discourses may appear to be a conscious decision, it should not be read in such a manner. Instead, this was largely a symptom of a colonial age when Buddhist thought and history had a profound influence on the Indian populace, whatever one's political affiliations, caste, class, religion, or gender.

Placed within this wider context, Nehru's interest in Buddhism was hardly different from that of other Indian elites. Indeed, considering Nehru's early exposure to a wider world and intellectual development in Western liberal traditions—he studied at an elite boarding school in England before moving on to Cambridge and Gray's Inn in London—it is not surprising that he possessed the modernist's appetite for a "de-culturalized" Buddhism. Still, because of the power and authority Nehru came to exercise, a discussion of the way he understood Buddhism is a necessary prelude to the evaluation of how it informed his politics. Nehru, as many biographers have noted, was notorious for being skeptical, if not downright hostile, to religion. So the idea that he could have been personally attracted to and influenced by Buddhism should raise eyebrows. "Religion," in Nehru's own words, was "closely associated with superstitious practices and dogmatic beliefs, and behind it lay a method of approach to life's problems which was certainly not that of science" (Nehru [1946] 1985a: 26). In contrast, the Buddha and his dhamma, Nehru wrote in 1936, "has always had a great appeal for me. It is difficult for me to analyse this appeal, *but it is not a religious appeal, and I am not interested in the dogmas that have grown up round Buddhism.* It is the personality that has drawn me" (Nehru [1936] 1941: 197, emphasis added).

Even prior to his studies in Europe, Nehru had learned of Buddhism from his childhood tutor, the theosophist, F.T. Brooks. At the age of thirteen, Nehru was initiated into the Theosophical Society by Annie Besant and although he was deeply skeptical of theosophy, in later years he described the experience in positive terms.[12] His interest in Buddhism continued through his childhood years and he recalls that "the Buddha story attracted me even in early boyhood, and I was drawn to the young Siddhartha who, after many inner struggles and pain and torment, was to develop into the Buddha. Edwin Arnold's *The Light of Asia* became one of my favorite books" (Nehru [1946] 1985a: 130). As Nehru grew older and his political responsibilities began to take him across the subcontinent, he began incorporating visits to "the many places connected with the Buddha legend, sometimes making a detour for the purpose" (130).

Nehru's "detours" led to several sustained encounters with Indian Buddhist scholars and prominent foreign Buddhists. When the Maha Bodhi Society inaugurated the construction of a new Buddhist temple in Sarnath on 11 November 1931, by re-enshrining Buddhist relics found at Taxila nearly two decades before, Nehru, along with his wife and sisters, attended the functions. The cosmopolitan ceremony—it drew no less than nine hundred distinguished visitors, more than half of whom came from outside India— must have brought firmly to reality both the intellectual and devotional appeal of Buddhism's modern-day revival.[13] In fact, a Buddhist exhibition of its size and grandeur would not be repeated in India until almost exactly two decades later in 1952 when Nehru, then prime minister of an independent India, orchestrated his own re-enshrinement of relics at the newly constructed Chaityagiri temple in Sanchi. Those, however, were different days. This early experience clearly left an impression. Six weeks later, he mailed a full-size flag of the Congress to the Maha Bodhi Society, with a short note reading: "I trust this flag will be a perpetual reminder to you of the good will of the Indian Nation towards the *great cause* you represent" (*MBJ* Vol. 40/1, 1932: no page number, emphasis added).[14]

Over the next decade, as Nehru grew in political stature, he regularly presided over and appeared at Buddhist functions at Santiniketan, Bodh Gaya, Sarnath, Bombay, and beyond.[15] These events, while not as grand as the one at Sarnath, continued to provide exposure to a wider Buddhist world and served as springboards for several important post-colonial relationships. Nehru even used Buddhist events to facilitate meetings with Taixu (1890–1947) and Tan Yun Shan (1898–1983), two of the most influential Chinese Buddhists in the mid-twentieth century. Both Taixu, a Guomindang-allied reformist Chinese monk trying to make "humanistic Buddhism" (Chinese, *renjian fojiao*) the "meeting place for all races" (*MBJ* Vol. 37/7, 1929: 357), and his lay disciple Tan, a noted professor of Chinese history and director of the Cheena Bhavan in Santiniketan, were driving forces in the push to reconnect India and China. At the height of European hegemony, when Japan began its violent incursions into Chinese territory, these figures sought out Nehru and the Congress, hoping to ally India and China through the medium of

Buddhism. Tan, who had joined Tagore's Visva-Bharati at Santiniketan in 1928, not only organized several meetings between high-profile Guomindang and Congress officials, but also arranged Taixu's pilgrimage to India and meeting with Nehru in 1940 under the auspices of "Ashoka Day" celebrations. The day after their first meeting, Taixu visited Nehru at home and spoke of how the "future collaboration among the Buddhist countries of Asia" rests upon "the revival of Buddhist pilgrimage sites in India and the establishment of an international Buddhist university" (Sen 2016: 313). Seeds were being planted in the future prime minister's mind.

Of equal importance were the relationships Nehru forged at these events with other Indian scholars of Buddhism. Throughout the 1930s and the 1940s, when several Indian savants saw traces of socialism in early Buddhist teachings and organization, Nehru was part and parcel of the ideological current. He was close to Acharya Narendra Dev (1889–1956), the leader of the Congress Socialist Party and a respected scholar of Buddhist thought. In the early 1940s, when both men were imprisoned together for their involvement in the Quit India movement, they spent their days discussing Buddhist philosophy, in particular the *Abhidharmakosha,* which Dev was in the process of translating into Hindi (Nehru [1946] 1985a: v, 165). Through these experiences, Nehru began to see Buddhism as a cosmopolitan and modernizing force with pan-Asian appeal, something that could be blended with other world views that shaped his thinking: Tagore's swadeshi internationalism, Marxist and Fabian-inspired democratic socialism, and theosophical spiritualism. When he became head of the world's largest democracy, he drew on these intellectual and human resources to forge diplomatic connections abroad and a new nation at home.

The simplicity and single-mindedness with which Nehru spoke about Buddhism gave his vision a clear and coherent form. His relationship with the Buddha appears to have been remarkably personal (Nehru 1941: 198; Pryor 2012: 112–13). There is strong evidence to suggest that as Nehru's political responsibilities set in, he felt closer to the Mauryan emperor Ashoka (Vajpeyi 2012: 168–207), the world conqueror, rather than Shakyamuni, the world renouncer. Throughout his writings, Nehru celebrates Ashoka's conquest of other nations through the propagation of morality (dharma) and non-violence (ahimsa). He took Ashoka, the "great son of India," to be the philosopher-king par excellence, a just and non-violent ruler, a model to be emulated. In a letter written from prison in 1932 to his daughter and future prime minister, Indira Gandhi, he tells her how Ashoka's "way of thought" led him to preside over one of the most powerful empires the world has ever seen, "nearly the whole of India, except a tiny tip in the south, was under him" (SWJN Vol. 9: 63).[16] Writing again from jail in the 1940s, in a climate tinged by communal violence, Nehru makes special reference to the fact that Ashoka, "ardent Buddhist" that he was, "showed respect and consideration for all other faiths ... everywhere an appeal was made to the mind and the heart; there was no force or compulsion" (Nehru [1946] 1985a: 134). As many scholars have noted, a kind of "cult of Ashoka" emerged in the first decade after Independence (Olivelle, Leoshko and Ray 2012). He not only represented the Indian nation to the global Buddhist community, but his ancient edicts outlawing the death penalty, providing free healthcare, and spreading a quasi-Buddhist civil religion (Lahiri 2015), were seen as increasingly relevant for the modern world. Nehru capitalized on this popular sentiment but also saw himself in Ashoka.

Relic Tours and Border Area Buddhists

One of the main avenues through which Nehru capitalized on the cultural capital of India's Buddhist past was the use of relics, or bodily remains (*sharira*) of ancient Buddhist masters. Reverence for relics has long been a noteworthy feature of Buddhist societies, and their use in political settings was by no means novel. Beginning in the late nineteenth century, the use of relics gained new traction when British colonial authorities redistributed a wide variety of India's Buddhist antiquities and corporeal remains across Asia in order to generate cultural goodwill and strengthen diplomatic connections with neighboring Buddhist nations. As noted earlier, Nehru had personally witnessed the re-enshrinement of Buddha relics at Sarnath's Mulagandhakuti vihara in 1931. This ceremony was just the tip of the iceberg. According to the historian Himanshu Prabha Ray (2014: 98–133), there were seven major discoveries of Buddha relics in India between 1851 and 1910. The first happened in Sanchi (1851) in Madhya Pradesh, followed by Sopara (1882) in Maharasthra, Girnar (1889) in Gujarat, Bhattiprolu (1891) in Andhra Pradesh, Piprahawa (1897) in Uttar Pradesh, Shahji-ki-Dheri near Peshawar (1908–09), and Mirpur Khas in Sindh (1910), the last two in present-day Pakistan. The handling of these relics were often inconsistent. Some were redistributed to museums and private collectors while others were re-enshrined at foreign and Indian viharas. But after the unearthing of the Sopara relics in 1882, there was a clear policy shift in the way these discoveries were managed (Ray 2014: 101–05).

In contrast to the discovery of earlier relics, which were routinely distributed to museums and collectors, the cultural and communicational landscape made news of the Sopara relics well known across the elite Buddhist world. From that point onwards, relic discoveries were regularly followed by memoranda from Buddhist organizations and governments requesting colonial officials to transfer the relics to Buddhist shrines where they could be worshipped according to designated Buddhist customs. When the colonial authorities recognized that the discoveries held not just an aesthetic value as museum artifacts, but a sacred presence that could be exploited for political purposes, they began using them to further geopolitical agendas. While Indian complaints regarding the dispersal of their national heritage to "foreign" entities after 1910 further complicated these diplomatic initiatives, the common practice was to distribute the relics either to Buddhist nations such as Burma or Ceylon or to re-enshrine them in the new Buddhist temples being constructed across India.

Not long after its establishment in 1891, the Maha Bodhi Society had taken an active role in negotiating with the government over the rightful ownership of relics. Although the Maha Bodhi Society had at times been an irritant to the viceroy, it possessed an international network of dignitaries and scholars that no other Buddhist organization in India could match. By the early 1900s, the colonial government increasingly relied on Maha Bodhi Society officials and Orientalist scholars to help arrange the "repatriation" and "re-enshrinement" of these relics. By Independence, the Society was not only itself the recipient of great many relics, but was seen by the new Indian leadership as the most reliable functionary for managing relic exhibitions and transfers. There were exceptions to this—independent relations and diplomatic offices provided other connections—but the Maha Bodhi Society's proximity to Nehru, Prasad, Mookerjee, and other government elites made it the obvious choice.

By coupling with the Maha Bodhi Society, the government of India was able to orchestrate several successful relic tours and exhibitions within and outside India's borders. It was the return to India of two Buddhist relics, in particular, that set the stage for some of the government's most vibrant celebrations of Buddhism. The relics of Sariputta and Mogallana, renowned disciples of the Buddha, had been first discovered at Sanchi in 1851 before being shipped to London, where they sat in the British Museum for most of the next century. After a decade of negotiation, the return of the relics to India was agreed upon in 1941. However, the danger of a submarine attack during the World War II postponed their departure until 1947. From 1947 to 1952, these relics traveled by plane, ship, train, automobile, on horseback, and on foot to Buddhist sites across India in Bihar, Assam, Sikkim, Ladakh, and Orissa, as well as reaching royal households, museums, and public exhibitions in Cambodia, Nepal, Burma, Thailand, Tibet, and Ceylon.

Throughout Nehru's rule, Buddhists in India's border regions were regularly given official state invitations to celebrate their religious events at major urban centres that held no clear association with Buddhism as well as at the ancient groves where the historical Buddha is said to have dwelt.[17] When Nehru brought the relics to majority-Buddhist regions along the borders, the rhetoric and performance surrounding the display was transformed. In Assam, a seventeen-day exposition of the relics began on 18 April 1950 (*MBJ* Vol. 58/6–7, 1950: 243–47). Organized jointly by the Government of Assam, the All-Assam Buddhist Association, and the Maha Bodhi Society, the Assam exposition coincided and shared the *pandal* with Congress's provincial conference in the state. The governor of Assam, Sri Prakasa, presided over a crowd of ten thousand devotees in Disangpani. A small party, led by the Maha Bodhi Society general secretary, Devapriya Valisinha, and Tan Yun Shan of Santiniketan, delivered speeches, collected funds for the construction of a Buddhist temple, and presided over a series of conversion ceremonies for leaders of the All-Assam Ahom Association. The speeches emphasized the "long-standing" connections between Assam and Buddhism and "the necessity of the revival of the Buddhist ideas of *karuna* [compassion], *metta* [loving kindness] and *mudita* [empathetic joy] all over the world" (247).

Following the Assam tour, the relics were carried to Ladakh in a trip financed entirely by the Central government and state ministries. Four years earlier, Nehru had visited the region, carrying bones believed to be those of Gotama Buddha himself. During his several-day tour, he exhibited the relics to the highest local incarnate lamas (Tibetan, *sprul sku*) and promised the Ladakhi lama, Bakula Rinpoche, that he would send more for future worship (Shakspo 1988: 442–43). Since that time, the social and political situation in Ladakh had become extremely fragile due to two destabilizing forces: first, India and Pakistan's competing claims over the region, leading to the first Indo-Pakistan war of 1947; and second, China's invasion of Tibet in 1950, which began the slow severance of Ladakh's cross-border trade and cultural links to Tibet (Aggarwal 2004). In 1948, Bakula traveled to Delhi with a seven-man delegation to discuss Ladakh's precarious position, and the plans for a relic exhibition in Ladakh were conceived in this meeting. Two years later, a police honor guard, seven Maha Bodhi Society officials, and one journalist accompanied the Buddhist relics from Calcutta to New Delhi (where Nehru met them at a public ceremony held at Birla's Buddhist temple on Reading Road), before moving on to Srinagar and then to Leh via a military airlift. For ten days, the Sariputta and Mogallana relics were exhibited at a number of monasteries across Ladakh that had "suffered most during Pakistani raids" (MSKB File no. 10/17, 1950). Several thousand people turned out to view and worship the exhibits, as local monastic and military elites mingled with Buddhist delegates.

Officially, such displays were a symbol of India's dedication to "non-violence, cooperation, friendliness and forgiveness" (MSKB File no. 10/17, 1950). However, as Toni Huber (2008: 341) argues, the relics sent "unequivocal signals" to the Ladakhi population "that the Indian nation they had just joined was sympathetic to and would even ritually support their Buddhist cultural identity." Maha Bodhi Society officials who traveled with the relic delegation were careful to articulate the government's support in terms that would resonate with any Buddhist audience: it was *vastu-dana* (the gift of material goods), *shiksha-dana* (the gift of education), and *dharma-dana* (the gift of dharma).

Exactly one year later, this same message was reiterated among a cosmopolitan Buddhist elite when the relics were carried across Sikkim, Tibet, and five prominent centers of Buddhist activity in the Darjeeling–

Kalimpong hills (*MBJ* Vol. 59/7, 1951: 261–64).[18] As in Ladakh, tens of thousands of devotees turned out to see the relics and "drink deep in the ocean of the bliss of Tathagata [Buddha]" (264). During the three-month exhibition, which was organized in conjunction with the Dalai Lama's visit just over the border in Yatung, a host of political elites from the border regions gathered to venerate the relics. These included the king and queen of Bhutan, the maharani of Burdwan, the Sikkimese royal family, the (exiled) Burmese prince and princess, and a host of European scholars and former members of colonial India's Frontier Raj. Due in part to the Dalai Lama's precarious and uncertain situation across the border—only months earlier the People's Liberation Army had occupied Lhasa, triggering his "pilgrimage" to Yatung—the relic exposition gained a heightened political sense and popularity that was witnessed by its frequent coverage in Tibetan, Hindi, and English newspapers.

When local officials discovered a Chinese government book entitled *Buddhism in China* circulating in Sikkimese marketplaces in 1955, the Ministry of External Affairs, under the advice of the political officer in Gangtok, instructed the Ministry of Information and Broadcasting to produce ten thousand copies of a comparable India-focused *History of Buddhism*, in Tibetan, Hindi, and English.[19] After the report reached Nehru's desk, the ministry instructed the Gangtok political officer to produce "as attractive a book as possible," which was "properly priced" at no more than one rupee per copy with at least two thousand copies distributed free of charge to "the various schools and libraries in the border areas" (MEANEF, File no. 37/7, 1955). Nowhere in the packet of files transferred back and forth across ministry desks does it state explicitly why Nehru and other officers felt it so important to publish a tri-lingual history of Indian Buddhism in a remote Indian district. Yet, the fact that the idea came about after learning of a similarly themed Chinese publication must be clearly understood as part of what the historian of international relations, Bérénice Guyot-Réchard (2018: 4), calls "state shadowing,"—those acts of "mutual observation, replication and competition" by which postcolonial states confronted each other in border regions where their presence and legitimacy was weakest. In short, the authorities believed that propagating Buddhism would send a clear message to the border communities that India and not China is their real "homeland". Just one year later, in 1956, the same geopolitical agenda was witnessed during the Dalai Lama's tense visit to India, when Nehru expressed his support behind plans to build a "Mahayana Institute of Tibetology" in Gangtok. On his way back to Tibet, on 10 February 1957, the Dalai Lama laid the foundation stone for the noted Buddhological institute, with Nehru and his daughter, Indira Gandhi, presiding over its grand inauguration roughly twenty months later.

There is also considerable evidence that the same civilizational logic of Buddhism being a pacifying, Indo-centric force was influencing the decisions of foreign affairs officers in north-east India. During the winter of 1949–50, New Delhi granted the Burmese government permission to launch a "Goodwill Mission" consisting of nine "carefully selected Buddhist monks to Assam whose object will be to strengthen the cultural ties existing between Burma and Assam" (MEANEFS File no. 147, 19 July 1949).[20] In short, integrating "Border Area Buddhists" into the national fold was critical to Nehru's political aspirations, and Buddhist symbols, whether material or immaterial, were central to accomplishing that mission.

Modern Buddhism and the Poetics of Power

At the time Nehru's government was securing loyalty at the borders and instilling a moral code at the centre, it also drew on the country's Buddhist resources to institute an informal policy of strengthening India's role in postcolonial Asia. Srirupa Roy (2006: 512fn21) has rightly noted that the dhammachakra flag symbolized the "double-edged nature" of Nehru's "universalist promise ... of a peaceful international order and of a strong and expansionist state". In the years leading up to Independence, Nehru viewed India as the symbol of anti-colonial resistance and anti-imperialism. However, in the new postcolonial order, he struggled to cast the nation in a new light, one in which it retained its stature as an anti-colonial leader, but also projected an image of self-sufficiency and world leadership. As he saw it, his aspirations for India were not just for the benefit of Indians, but of all Asian peoples. "The future that took shape in my mind," he wrote from a prison cell between 1942 and 1944, "was one of intimate co-operation, politically, economically and culturally, between India and the other countries of the world. But before the future came there was the present, and behind the present lay the long and tangled past, out of which the present had grown. So to the past I looked for understanding" (Nehru [1946] 1985a: 49–50).

As a product of his age, Nehru understood Buddhism to be the primary link between India and the rest of Asia. This idea coalesced smoothly with his post-Independence plan to establish India as a central player in international political affairs. During the Inter-Asian Relations Conference, which was convened in New Delhi in March 1947, Nehru laid forth the contours of his foreign policy for the next decade: "In this atomic age, Asia will have to function effectively in the maintenance of peace. Indeed, there can be no peace unless Asia plays her part ... the whole spirit and outlook of Asia are peaceful, and the emergence of Asia in world affairs will be a powerful influence for world peace" (SWJN Vol. 2: 507). Projecting India as an international leader whose stature rested not on its armies, but on its moral superiority and devotion to world peace, Nehru enlisted the nation to the Non-Aligned Movement (NAM) in 1955. The NAM, which was often called the "Third Way," attempted to formulate an alternative to the Cold War division between communist and non-communist blocs. As the balance of global political power oscillated between the USA and the USSR, Nehru argued that a new pan-Asian identity was an urgent necessity for global stability.

The assembly of world leaders at the Inter-Asian Conference in New Delhi also met up at other conferences, including an All-Asia Buddhist Convention held at the New Delhi Buddha vihara on 31 March 1947. During the meeting, nearly two dozen government officials from Ceylon, Siam, Burma, and Tibet met with leading Indian Buddhists to discuss the important role Buddhists could have in forming an "Asian Federation," or what one of the Ceylonese delegates (and future prime minister), S.W.R.D. Bandaranaike described as "a Brave New World" (*MBJ* Vol. 55/5–6, 1947: 149).[21] A recurring topic that day was the tremendous "sensitivity" being shown to Buddhism by the new leadership in Delhi. When Nehru met the delegates later that week, the most pressing matter they raised was the management of the Maha Bodhi temple at Bodh Gaya. The issue had been set aside during the Quit India movement but in May of the previous year, Rajendra Prasad as the chairman of the committee, along with the Maha Bodhi Society and Hindu Maha Sabha, had met in Patna, passing a further resolution to strip the current Hindu mahant of his legal ownership of the temple. With the mahant's continued opposition, the negotiations continued to stall, leaving Prasad with an ever-growing pile of letters on his desk.[22] Nehru responded by promising the delegates "all support for the restoration of Buddhagaya to the Buddhists," and just weeks later, he wrote to his secretary that Bodh Gaya should have a "certain international character" (SWJN Vol. 9: 110). Including foreign Buddhists on the Maha Bodhi temple advisory committee, he added, would be "a graceful gesture to the Buddhist world" (ibid).[23] On 19 June 1949, the Bodh Gaya Temple Act was passed, resulting in an eight-member committee, split evenly between Buddhists and Hindus with a final ninth vote to be decided by the governor of Bihar. The result was unsatisfactory to both parties, but in 1953 when the transfer was officially completed, Buddhists around the globe celebrated while the mahant counted his losses. The return of Buddhists to Bodh Gaya, it seems, was just one part of Nehru's pan-Asian vision.

The Nehruvian era also marked the beginning of a period when long-time Buddhist activists in India became allies of the Central and state governments, emerging as critical interlocutors in government initiatives abroad. When Burma gained its independence in January 1948, Rajendra Prasad attended the celebrations as part of India's first official delegation to the country. The Pali scholar and monastic from Bihar, Bhikkhu Jagdish Kashyap (1908–76) accompanied Prasad as a "Special Envoy". In the fifteen years since Kashyap had taken the vows of a Buddhist monk in Ceylon, he had studied widely across South and South-east Asia, gaining a deep knowledge of Buddhist history and building an extensive network of like-minded monastics and intellectuals. Presumably, it was these connections and skills that persuaded the government to bring him on other delegations to China and Tibet in the following decade. During Kashyap's visit to Burma with Rajendra Prasad, he delivered saplings of the bo tree at Bodh Gaya to various Burmese officials, invoking a tradition of ritual veneration and gift-giving (dana) that goes back to at least Tang China, when the Chinese monk, Xuanzang, returned from India with leaves from the Bodhi tree as gifts for the emperor. Following the visit, Prasad wrote to Nehru:

"Planting bo tress not bombs": Rajendra Prasad (far right), photographed here with
saplings and representatives from the Bodh Gaya Temple Management Committee

There is a great deal of goodwill on account of cultural relationship
with that country which could be canalized … [Kashyap] had
conversations with leading Buddhists, about establishing some sort of
a [Buddhist] cultural institution … its importance or necessity cannot
be questioned … we require such institutions—or perhaps "missions"
should be a better expression—not only in Burma but in all Buddhist
countries towards the east, south-east and north-east of India (RPCSD
Vol. 9: 167).[24]

The idea was received favorably at New Delhi. By year's end, Nehru
pushed the Central government to grant the Cambodian lawyer and
politician-turned–itinerant monk, Dharmavira Mahathera (1889–1999),
a plot of land in south Delhi. When Dharmavira established the Ashoka
Mission later that year, the property was little more than a thatched hut
with a small Buddhist shrine, but its central location at the national capital
alongside Nehru's support ensured its growth.[25]

In Japan, Nehru and other Indian leaders networked with Nichidatsu Fuji (1885–1985), the Japanese monk who, with the Birla family's financial support, built Buddhist temples in Calcutta (1935), Rajgir (1936), and Bombay (1940). With the straining of the relationship between Britain and Japan, Fuji returned to Kumamoto, his hometown, in 1938 "to contemplate what course of action he and [his Japanese sect] Nipponzan Myohoji should take" (Kisala 1999: 52). After Japan's defeat in the World War II, Fuji began constructing Peace Pagodas (*Shanti Stupas*) across the globe, proclaiming that the mighty Buddhist reliquaries could help save the world from destruction. Today, more than forty of these grand monuments can be found around the world—from India, Japan, the United States, and South Africa, to Latvia, Italy and beyond. Significantly, when the first Peace Pagoda was inaugurated in Kumamoto in 1954, Nehru and Indian delegates from the Gandhian Seva Sangha were present to transfer ten reliquary urns to Fuji and other priests, in front of a massive crowd numbering in thousands.[26]

Relics as de-colonizing initiatives, gave national leaders across Asia vectors of moral order, political legitimacy, and social unity. For instance, the exhibition and eventually permanent loan of a portion of India's Sanchi–Satdhara relics to Burma during 1950–52 was as highly politicized as it was popular. As Jack Daulton's (1999) detailed study shows, there were a series of high-profile events surrounding the relic transfers that involved Burma's political elite joining hands with Indian government representatives like S.P. Mookerjee, Nehru's former cabinet minister, Hindutva ideologue, and president of the Maha Bodhi Society. For the Buddhist public in Burma, the culmination of these affairs was undoubtedly the week-long festivities that marked the consecration and enshrinement of the calcite remains from India in Rangoon's [Yangon] Kaba Aye Pagoda (literally, "World Peace Pagoda"), a structure built to house the relics and widely touted at the time as the world's largest pagoda. The lavish ceremonies involved U Nu hoisting a gem-encrusted *hti* to the top of the pagoda's spire as fireworks glazed the sky—a local festival with theatrical performances, boxing matches, and an open-air cinema, all of which amounted to what Daulton calls "perhaps the most extraordinary celebration in modern Burmese history" (120). Other Theravadin nations greeted India's holy vestiges with equal enthusiasm. Six months after the celebration in Burma, Mookerjee traveled to Cambodia as the guest of honor at an exhibition of Indian relics. Here, the festivities were equally opulent. During the week-long exhibition in October 1952 at the Preah Vihear, situated within the Royal Palace complex in Phnom Penh, "tens and hundreds of thousands of people," including King Sihanouk, several ministers, military officials, and prominent monks were in attendance (Marston 2007: 107). From New Delhi's perspective, these events were signs that India's Buddhist heritage could indeed forge a brave new world.

By the early 1950s, the act of distributing Buddhist antiquities had become so commonplace that some government officials were worried about running out of relics, a fear that probably stemmed from a warning issued by India's director general of archaeology a decade before, that the source of ancient relics would soon be exhausted (MEASEA File no. Z/8141/10, 1953; File no. 1051, 1951). Such anxieties were evident in several diplomatic exchanges. For instance, in 1940, a Thai Goodwill Mission to India returned home with a steatite relic casket three inches high containing a small cylinder of gold with fragments of the Buddha's ashes and bone. The leader of the party explained to the chief secretary of India's Ministry of External Affairs that "the success of the Mission would be judged in Bangkok according to the value of the relics which it brought back" (MEAEB File no. 723-Secret, 1940). Later that day, after having "drank a whole bottle of champagne without being visibly affected," the Thai mission head added, "in confidence that it did not matter much if the relics were not genuine" (MEAEB File no. 723-Secret, 1940). Later, the Thai government reiterated that "here in Thailand these relics are confidently assumed to be those of the Buddha himself ... [and that] the casket containing the relics has been exposed to the public view and has been venerated by many thousands of people, including the highest personages in the land" (Letter from the Thai government to the Ministry of External Affairs, 11 Feb 1940, MEAEB File no. 723-Secret, 1940). A decade later, another request for Buddha relics, this time from the Thai-Bharat Cultural Lodge in Bangkok, had to be declined delicately. After much discussion, the request resulted in the distribution not of corporeal remains, as had often been the custom, but of the physical earth removed from "four sacred Buddhist pilgrim centres" (MEAIANZ File no. 1051, 1951). During a three-day ceremony in February 1953, an urn containing the sacred soil—taken from Lumbini, Bodh Gaya, Sarnath, and Kushinagar—was carried

Vice President S. Radhakrishnan (left) with Buddhist relics at the New Delhi Buddha vihara, 1956

by Thai monastics and government officials to the temple at Prachin Puri, where "thousands of people" gathered to venerate its installation inside the *chedi* of the Wat Saeng Swang in Bangkok (Letter from Raghunath Sharma, Director of Thai-Bharat Cultural Lodge to Prime Minister Nehru, 8 March 1953, MEASEA File no. Z/81841/10, 1953).

In November 1952, when the Sariputta and Mogallana relics were installed at a new vihara financed by the government in Sanchi, attendees included the "who's who" of the Asian Buddhist world. In addition to Nehru, Radhakrishnan, Mookerjee, and the Indian delegates of the Maha Bodhi Society, also present were: Prime Minister U Nu of Burma; Maharaja Kumar and Kumari of Sikkim; U Win, minister for sasana affairs in Burma; A. Ratnakaye, home minister of Ceylon; Kushok Bakula, a senior Ladakhi lama (and later an Indian ambassador to Mongolia), in addition to a wide range of representatives and ambassadors from non-Buddhist countries like France,

Nepal, and Pakistan. Weeks later, amidst the "chanting of Buddhist hymns and recitations of suttas to the accompaniment of blowing of conch-shells and ringing of bells," a near-identical list of political dignitaries was present in Calcutta (*Maha Bodhi Centenary Volume* 1991: 189). Only this time, the former and present prime ministers of Cambodia, and the Japanese and Thai ambassadors joined the distinguished gathering. Clearly, Nehru's declaration to the Constituent Assembly just five years earlier (*CAD* Vol. 4, 22 July 1947) that the Buddhist dhammachakra was a reminder that India was once "an international centre ... [and not] a tight little narrow country," was bearing fruit.

Prasenjit Duara (2001: 99–130) has shown that "civilizational" categories served as the trans-territorial basis for many twentieth century nationalist leaders in China, Japan, and Sri Lanka. Following these figures, Nehru was projecting India as the sole heir to a progressive and glorious civilization that was simultaneously unique, and therefore "national," and equally "trans-national" and part of the wider heritage of Asia. This idea, which contains an arguably irreducible tension between the exclusion of nationalism and inclusion of universalism, drew its power from India's place in Buddhism's origins. Nehru, of course, was astute enough to capitalize on these historical connections. Embellishing a universalist message of Buddhist fraternity, tolerance, and peace with slogans about pan-Asian unity, he argued that India was a kind of *axis mundi* for the Buddhist world. Following a cultural convention in Calcutta in 1949, he remarked: "It was gratifying to see all these nations of the Buddhist world looking to India, not only with friendship but as the *mother country* where their great religion originated" (Nehru 1985b: 267, emphasis added).

A Teaching in Impermanence: Tibet and the India–China Debacle

By 1954, state rituals supporting and using the language of Buddhism were central to the pan-Asian performances of India's "theatre state" (Geertz 1980). Perhaps nowhere did this become more obvious than in their attempts to assess and resolve the tumultuous political relationship between China, India, and Tibet. Between 1951 and 1958, there were at least five unofficial "friendship missions" led by Indian Buddhist monks, scholars, and officials to China.[27] The Buddhist links between the two countries were the focus of these delegations, and special efforts were made to visit the historical sites associated with the Chinese pilgrim, Xuanzang, whose seventh-century pilgrimage to India occupied centre stage in the early years of 1950s Sino-Indian relations. According to the historian Holmes Welch (1972: 173), "so important was Hsuan-tsang [Xuanzang] considered a symbol of Sino-Indian friendship that the temples connected with him in Sian [Xian] were among the first in China to be repaired [after the founding of the People's Republic of China in 1949] and at once began to be shown to Indian visitors." During the Indian mission to China in 1955, the first to be led by a government official (A.K. Chanda, the deputy minister of external affairs), the Indian delegates gifted Buddha relics and bo tree saplings to Ho Chi Minh, Zhou Enlai, and Mao Zedong (Report of Indian Cultural Delegation to China, MEAFEA, File no. 1/55 (Secret), 1955). In addition to visiting industrial centers and Chinese theatres, the Chinese government arranged for Indian officials to visit the "principal centres of cultural contact" between India and China in the past centuries, including the pagodas of Xuanzang and Kumarajiva. The premise was clear: revive memories of old links and symbols of ancient relations.

The most conspicuous example of Buddhist theatrics between India and China began in 1954 with the signing of the Sino-Indian Panchshil Agreement, which marked the apogee of the Hindi-Chini Bhai Bhai (Indo-Chinese Brotherhood) policy. The preamble to the accord, entitled Panchshil, purportedly in reference to the five (*panch*) principles of Buddhist morality (*shila*) details the rules of conduct between the two Asian superpowers.[28] The framework is indeed remarkably Buddhist: 1) Mutual respect for each other's territorial integrity; 2) Mutual non-aggression; 3) Mutual non-interference in each other's internal affairs; 4) Equality and mutual benefit; 5) Peaceful coexistence. By 1956, however, Sino-Indian relations were under increasing strain, and as the famous expression goes, the Sino-Indian brotherhood (*bhai bhai*) soon went "bye-bye," culminating in the deadly Indo-Chinese War of 1962.

The Buddha Jayanti celebrations of 1956 provide a sobering example of how Nehru's Buddhist statecraft deteriorated before his very eyes. One of the most important events during the celebration was the much-anticipated arrival of the fourteenth Dalai Lama. His visit, which was his first trip to

Indian soil, came amidst declining relations between India and China and recent uprisings among Tibetans in Kham (eastern Tibet) against the Chinese occupation. Just four years earlier, the notorious "Seventeen Point Agreement for the Peaceful Liberation of Tibet"—which effectively ceded control of the central Tibetan state to the People's Republic of China—had been signed by a Tibetan delegation, and there were serious questions about whether the Dalai Lama would stay in India. Throughout the course of his visit, there were continued rumors and news of ongoing Tibetan rebellions against the Chinese, thus exacerbating the situation. Here was another stunning example of the poetics of power central to India's postcolonial foreign relations. Although the Dalai Lama's visit to India's various Buddhist shrines and sites was ostensibly religious, most, if not all, of the public events were overshadowed by political affairs.

The major actors in the play—Nehru, Zhou Enlai (the Chinese premier), and the Dalai Lama—all struggled to push their own agendas. Although there was already explicit recognition that Tibet was a part of China in the Panchshil Agreement, throughout his travels the Dalai Lama, much to the chagrin of Beijing, was treated by India "like a head of state" (Shakya 1999: 151). One of the most important moments of the visit came in Bihar when the Chinese engaged in their own Buddhist ritual (dana) by donating money for the construction of a Xuanzang Memorial Hall in Nalanda, Bihar. This seemingly simple gesture of cultural goodwill was rich in political overtones. Rather than having a Chinese official present the gift, which was also coupled with the bodily remains of the intrepid Chinese pilgrim himself, the Dalai Lama was placed in charge of the ritual offering. The Chinese delegation then arranged for the Dalai Lama to present the relics to Nehru and announced that the Chinese government would be donating 300,000 yuan for the construction of a memorial hall to house the relics. By trying to make the Dalai Lama appear as a Chinese rather than a Tibetan delegate, Beijing was sending explicit signals to New Delhi, the international community, as well as the politically savvy Tibetan émigré in India. They were proclaiming that Tibet was theirs. These kinds of overtly political performances and attitudes behind the state Buddhist ceremonies of 1956 leads one to cast a justifiably skeptical eye on the entire Nehruvian decade of state Buddhist diplomacy.

The Competing Wills of Universalism and Nationalism

How do we reconcile the performance of politics, the aspirations of a benevolent, universal Buddhism, and the rational calculations of a bureaucratic state? While it is tempting to reduce everything to politics or to blindly ignore the political gerrymandering behind the public accolades, the complexity of human life and the habits, responsibilities, and logics inherent in political statecraft demand a more nuanced account. Ananya Vajpeyi (2012) suggests that Nehru's life shows two trends: one towards the idealism of non-violence, tolerance, and unity, and the other towards the realism of warring nation-states and state diplomacy. "The tension within the self," she writes, "between aspiration and instrumentality, between norm and purpose mirrors or replicates a larger contradiction in the very nature of the modern state, which cannot but pull in these two opposite directions in order to present itself as ethically desirable and worthy of dying for" (207). This tension, which Vajpeyi frames through the Indic categories of pragmatism (*artha*) and ethical order (dharma) is also found in the distance between Ashoka and the Buddha (Tambiah 1976). Nehru, it appears, was torn between these two models, and drew on both for personal sustenance as well as political inspiration at different times.

Yet the tension between Ashokan statecraft and Buddhist benevolence (*metta*), like the tension between nationalism and universalism, is difficult (if not impossible) to reconcile. Nehru's uses of Buddhism in the postcolonial state demonstrate this very dilemma: one turned towards Buddhist morality and universalism, and the other towards the national self-interest and territorial sovereignty. By linking nation with state through the ethical principles embodied by the dhammachakra and the lion pillar, Nehru offered an Indian alternative to the Cold War models of communism and democracy, and to Gandhian nationalism, by projecting modern Buddhism as a kind of enlightened nationhood. It was a project of self-definition upon which he felt the Indian state's future could be fashioned.

In the turbulent years after Independence, Nehru and other leading cabinet members attempted to institute all kinds of land and social reform policies, some of which, despite his deep vested interests in them, collapsed under the weight of a fractured India. For Nehru, the promotion of Buddhist tolerance, non-violence, and the legacy of Indian Buddhist civilization through national cultural events, institutes, relic exhibitions, and the national flag and insignia represented a less politically contentious vision of national development and reform. To be sure, in terms of their basic mechanics and choreography, many of these events differed little from those conducted by the viceroy's "humble servants" when the Union Jack still flew high across Delhi. In the Nehruvian age, the Buddhist rituals and idioms were simply adapted to the politics of the era in the form of Indian secularism, non-violence, and the Non-Aligned Movement. They were an integral part of Nehru's attempt to promote the development and welfare of the nation, temper the antagonisms between Hindu and Muslim factions, instill a sense of secular–spiritual belonging to the Indian state, and maintain the loyalty of the national frontiers. Nehru's idealistic vision, with its connection to a purportedly united Buddhist world and simultaneous rooting in the land of its origin, reflected a new sense of hope as the age of European empires in Asia came to an end. However, the memory of the dropping of atom bombs in Japan and the general unease in world politics by the mid-1950s with the Suez crisis, the revolution in Hungary, and the growing ideological clash between the USSR and the USA, weighed on Nehru's conscience. "So we hover between war and peace, between the atom [bomb] and the Buddha," he wrote to the Indian ambassador to the UN in 1956 (quoted in Gopal 1984: 32). In those tempestuous years, Nehru was forced to succumb to the bitter reality that while the nation's well-being can also be the world's well-being, the two do not always go hand in hand.

The first major rupture in his Buddhist politic came when Nehru's former law minister, B.R. Ambedkar, and nearly half a million of his followers converted to Buddhism in Nagpur. It was a triumphant moment for Ambedkar and for an oppressed population of dalits that had been unjustly forced to bear the heavy burden of social ostracism and violence. Yet, Ambedkar's Buddhism was in fundamental contradiction to Nehru's own vision. The latter's approach was typical of someone who held the reins of power (a modern-day Ashoka perhaps). He viewed it largely as a constellation of symbols and ideas that could serve as a solvent in *moments* of necessity: while he sweltered in a prison cell (Nehru 1941: 198), during civic celebrations of the Buddha Jayanti, or in the gifting of bo trees and

Buddha bones to neighboring states. To be sure, Nehru pursued a Buddhist internationalism in ways that no other politician had. Like Ambedkar, he boldly built Buddhism's civilizational prowess and moral leadership into the Indian national character and accorded it a quasi-missionary role. But he was uneasy about imparting the kind of full-fledged moral and ethical revolution that Ambedkar saw latent in the Buddha's dhamma. Ambedkar's Buddhism was steeped in an existential and political conviction that was as much about identity as it was about transcending identity via the realization of shunnyata or emptiness (Ambedkar 2011: 129–31).[29] This required a sustained and serious *everyday* commitment, and the courage to directly confront the most menacing of India's social ills—caste—even at the risk of immense social reprisal and antagonism.

Like most Indian leftists and liberal caste Hindus, Nehru believed that caste would disappear after the "progress" of "modernity" and economic socialist reforms. The annihilation of caste, in other words, played no role in Nehru's vision of resuscitating Buddhism. Rather than giving further energy to Nehru's secularized Buddhism, Ambedkar's conversion cut to the very foundations of this oppression and, in doing so, re-emphasized the historical antagonism between brahminism and Buddhism, Hindus and Buddhists. It did not flinch at the possibility of confrontation. Having personally experienced the failures of the secular state to rectify the wrongs inflicted upon the untouchables, Ambedkar's vision for dalit liberation hinged on a separate but universal Buddhist identity as the foundation of political rights. Ambedkar's renewed Buddhism was based on the equality of all people, the freedom of all people (liberty), and the conviction that people matter and belong to each other (fraternity). Although there are clear indications that Ambedkar's Buddhism was moving towards an enlightened, national identity for all Indians and not just dalits, his untimely death, just two months after the grand conversion, effectively undercut that momentum, shifting the parameters of Indian Buddhism towards continued struggle, agitation, and revolutionary fervor (Zelliot 2013: 198–203).

The ideals of reason, tolerance, and non-violent imperial expansion which the government's Buddhism symbolized had come under deep scrutiny, both by Nehru and by his critics. Growing dalit conversions to Buddhism and the Dalai Lama's exile to India in 1959 undermined Nehru's attempt to synthesize universalism and nationalism. Trapped in his own web of a universalizing Indian Buddhism, Nehru failed to see the limitations of his version of diplomacy, or what Joseph Nye (1990) famously called "soft power".[30] It was simply soft. When Chinese boots hit the ground in India in 1962, leading to India's devastating defeat in the Sino-Indian war, Nehru's Buddhist vision took a catastrophic blow. All the auguries had been there. By 1960, the Indian public had clearly caught wind of this alternative face of Buddhist diplomacy, as is evident from the immense skepticism leveled at the Burmese prime minister, U Nu's, "pilgrimage" to India that year. When in between Buddhist sites, Nu met with Nehru and the Russian premier Nikita Khruschev in Calcutta "for a casual talk about old times," as Nehru put it, the *Guardian* called the bluff, reporting that, "the real purpose [of] the visit was political and not religious" ("Nu meeting K," *Guardian*, 29 February 1960, in MEABB File no. 4/3, 1960).

Thus Have I Heard ...

For decades, studies of Buddhism in modern India have been guided by quantitative measures (like census figures) and entrenched academic theories that miss the forest for the trees. It is claimed that until Ambedkar's conversion in 1956, there was no Buddhism in modern India, and that Indian Buddhism, as the oft-repeated expression goes, "all but disappeared" between the twelfth and fourteenth centuries. But history rarely works this way. What may seem buried deep in the recesses of time may never really die. Places and objects remember what people forget and, despite efforts to expunge all memory of the past, it can always be resurrected. What today seems lost and abandoned can, tomorrow, be reborn again and serve as a resource for the future.

To understand modern Indian Buddhism, one cannot simply look at labels and titles. One has to carefully consider the full list of ingredients. In the century prior to the momentous events of the 1950s, Buddhism was an indispensable part of the daily lives of Indians from many walks of life and their primary way of belonging in the world. They spent their days reading and reinterpreting Buddhist scriptures, attending and delivering dhamma talks, building and rebuilding Buddhist shrines, and networking with Buddhists from near and distant lands, despite numerous disjunctures and unexpected transformations. The lives of Ambedkar, Birla, Bodhananda, Kosambi, Mahavir, Sankrityayan, Thass, and so many other figures help us realize that there is no one single identity at the heart of modern Indian Buddhism.

Buddhism continues to have an important but often unacknowledged role in Indian society till today. Although it no longer stands at the forefront of India's soft power diplomacy, having been surpassed by Bollywood and yoga, it still retains an important presence. The former Indian president, Pranab Mukherjee, delivered saplings of the bo tree from Bodh Gaya to Thailand in 2013, and to Korea and Vietnam in 2014, re-enacting Nehru's efforts in the 1950s. When the Chinese president Xi Jinping traveled to India on his first visit as head of state in 2015, the first stop on his itinerary was a specially crafted exhibition of images and posters detailing the presence of Buddhism in Gujarat and a comemmoration of the seventh-century Chinese bhikkhu, Xuanzang's, pilgrimage to India. During Prime Minister Narendra Modi's visit to Japan in August 2014, he and the late Japanese prime minister, Shinzo Abe, prayed at Buddhist temples together and released a series of tweets on how "looking at statues of Buddha, we were reminded of the deep historical ties between Japan and India" (@AbeShinzo, 30 August 2014). The medium has changed, but the performance of the politics and message remain the same.

Nehruvian Buddhism is not the only enduring entity. Visitors to dalit *melas* and bookshops in northern India will discover that translations of Buddhist works and texts authored by Ambedkar, Bodhananda, and Sankrityayan take up substantial shelf space. What has become especially pronounced among the Hindi-speaking dalit publics in north India, however, is the simultaneous trend of synthesizing Buddhism with devotion to the sants. Just as Bodhananda's works in the 1930s conceived of Buddhism and *nirguna* bhakti as a unified stream of anti-caste assertion against brahmanism, there is now "an unproblematic amalgamation of the traditions of the Kabirpanthis, Ravidasis and Buddhists by Dalit activists" (Hunt 2014: 47). Similarly, among many radical activists in India today, there is a parallel effort to couple Buddhism and Marxism on a single platform (Ilaiah 2001; Biswas 2008).

While these represent some of the most pronounced expressions, the nineteenth-century affinity for critical scholarship and restoration of Buddhist sites remains central to all such efforts. Every year, hundreds of thousands of Buddhist pilgrims and tourists from across the globe congregate at India's ancient Buddhist spaces to conduct Buddhist rituals. They meet

Buddhists from other parts of the world whose ritual performances and identities are both distinct and similar to their own. Of equal importance are the millions of dollars this spiritual tourism pumps into the local and national economy each year. Meanwhile, scholars and researchers at universities across India continue to give Buddhism a privileged place in the historiography of ancient India, understanding it to be one of the most important components of India's cultural heritage. All the while, the debates around whether Buddhism was actually anti-caste remain as vibrant as ever.

Although all of these developments can be traced back to the world this book has uncovered, there have also been significant changes since the 1950s that have altered Buddhism's direction and thus provide a natural end point for this study. Three of these are especially pertinent. The first stems from the tremendous influence that Tibetan Buddhists hold at Buddhist sites across India today. The popularity of the Dalai Lama (b. 1935), the influence of Tibetan lamas on Buddhism worldwide, and presence of some one hundred thousand Tibetan refugees in the country have revitalized Himalayan Buddhist practices and given Vajrayana Buddhism a popular respectability among Indians that it simply did not possess in the period prior to the 1950s. Secondly, beginning in the 1970s, S.N. Goenka's (1924–2013) vipassana movement has fundamentally altered the way middle-class Indians view Buddhism. Goenka's Buddhism, like the Indian state's version, is conceived of as secular and it is not unusual to find Sikhs, Hindus, Muslims, Christians, and other groups attending intensive ten-day silent meditation retreats at any of the fifty-plus dhamma centers operating in the country under his name.

Third, and perhaps the most powerful development of all, has been the continued prominence of the dalit Buddhist revolution. In contrast to Goenka's secular Buddhism which is perceived as a scientific tool open to anyone, regardless of identity, the conversion of several million more dalits since the 1950s has made the secular–religious divide more acute and raised the spectre of caste's corrosive influence. Mayawati (b. 1956), the former chief minister of Uttar Pradesh, India's most populous state—second only to China, Russia, the United States, and Brazil in population—has promised that she and millions of her followers will publicly convert to Buddhism if she gains control of the Central government ("Mayawati to embrace Buddhism,"

The Hindu, 17 Oct 2006). Since she poured millions of dollars into building towering monuments honoring the Buddha, Ambedkar, and other bahujan role models in places like Lucknow, Buddhism has emerged as the fastest-growing religion in the state. While Ambedkarite Buddhism continues to be (mis)understood by many Indians (and global Buddhists more widely) as an abnormal, deviant sect—less an "authentic" Buddhism than the political manifestation of casteist and communal thinking—it is an extremely important expression of social belonging and cultural meaning for millions. All of these new insertions into the Buddhist marketplace require a vastly different scholarly lens and for a study that has already encompassed a lot, they provide a convenient end point.

When I first conceived of this study, I was worried that there would not be enough material to sustain any concrete discussion. Many scholars, colleagues, and friends told me that Indian Buddhism was dead, so I had better seek out a different subject. Writing roughly a decade later, I must admit that I have only uncovered a fragment of all the materials. This book cannot, in any sense, be a complete history of modern Indian Buddhism. Instead, it has tried to explore its most formative strands through an examination of the people, places, objects, and ideas that gave it life. While conducting research for this book, I opted to read widely in the archives rather than narrowing in on a single text or individual. My main reason for doing so is to demonstrate the breadth of Buddhism in modern India. Without this sort of grand narrative, examples of Indian Buddhism would continue to be seen as one-off, localized instances, rarities that do not merit inclusion in wider historiography. They would, in other words, remain un-archived, to return to Pandey's (2012, 2013) expression. Naturally, I hope that this survey will force scholars to reconsider the legacy of modern Indian Buddhism and the role that India played in the formation of global Buddhisms.

However, I recognize that the book comes with real limitations, many of which stem from the multi-sited and multilingual methodology that I employed in order to connect what are otherwise seen as disparate histories of Buddhist revival. While I have done my best to make use of original sources, there are several instances where I have been forced to rely on translations and have been unable to engage extant scholarship composed in other languages, such as Tamil. This is perhaps unavoidable when working in such a linguistically rich land as India but it is certainly possible that something significant was lost in translation, or that evidence from other archives and linguistic corpora would alter my conclusions. Further, by not dwelling at length on one text or one individual or even one region, I may have missed the nuances and textured layers of meaning that can only arise from deep reading or localized studies. Undoubtedly, such blemishes— and I hope they are only that!—have crept into the text. Another central weakness of this work is its inability to uncover female voices. Indian women were certainly active in the formation of colonial India's Buddhism, but the written accounts I discovered and explored do little more than discuss them as objects or mark them as being present. By failing to integrate women's voices, I have essentially written a(nother) history of men's Buddhism. I take full responsibility for these and other shortcomings. However, if this research triggers further studies, even by those deeply critical of my analysis, and if it gets scholars of modern Buddhism and of modern India to finally speak to one another, I will consider it a success.

The Search for Buddhism in Modern India: A Final Consideration

In 1886, the Scottish historian and statistician, Sir William Wilson Hunter (1840–1900), proclaimed that, "the revival of Buddhism is always a possibility in India". Since then, revival has dominated the thinking of Indian Buddhism's modern transformation (Hunter 1886: 158). It was said to be occurring across Asia at that time, but its usage in the Indian context had a much more precise meaning. Revival referred not to the strengthening of a decaying or dying tradition but to the very rebirth and return of something that had been lost. For thousands of years, Buddhists have spoken of the decline of the sasana, but unlike in nineteenth-century Japan, Burma, or Ceylon, where Buddhism was still alive but said to be declining, Indian Buddhism was dead. For revivalists, it had become a "forgotten" thing of the past whose material presence and noble voice had disappeared under the oppressive vicissitudes of time. Where intricate images carved by hand into the side of a mountain had once inspired the public to live a more compassionate, loving life, they were now either hidden under a thick coat of impenetrable weeds, stigmatized as the dwelling places of social misfits, or functioning as commercial houses and competing religious shrines. Some Buddhist ideals had been retained but they were so hidden behind a veil of theological complexities and priestly rituals that only the most determined (or inventive) of scholars could unravel them. As archaeologists and philologists attempted to reconstruct this ancient world known only through memories, crumbling ruins, and mythical stories contained in different scripts and languages, the skeletal history that was ancient Indian Buddhism, made it ripe for possibilities. Where critical scholarship could not penetrate, imagination could.

Even the most rational of human beings relies on imagination to make sense of the world. Over the course of a single day, humans move between various states of being, revisiting the past, imagining known and unknown worlds and shaping them in highly inventive ways. The varied states that humans dwell in, or what Basso (1996) called place-worlds, are shaped by a near-infinite number of factors. Place-worlds may be constitutive of historical events (wars, famines, great migrations, etc.) or the "congenial places of experiential terrain" (3), the trivial and not-so-trivial moments of one's individual youth, upbringing, and life experiences. All human beings are bound by their own webs of significance, and the past is always mediated by the present as much the present by the past. Thus, the significance and meaning of these pasts will forever be invented and reinvented as long as someone is there to imagine them.

Place-making is, as Basso explains, "a way of constructing social traditions and, in the process, personal and social identities. We *are*, in a sense, the place-worlds we imagine" (7). This book has been full of place-worlds that have had real, tangible impacts, connected to everyday life: whether that of Ambedkar, Nehru, Sankrityayan, Subaji Bapu, Thass, or others, their Buddhist place-making had a truly live presence. When Indian patrons—jewelers, bankers, royal households, zamindars, and so on— supported scholars and pandits to recommission Buddhist artistic and literary works, they understood the creations as being somehow faithful to a Buddhist world that had fallen dormant and disappeared. When these works were then read (often aloud) and circulated among friends, family, and strangers, they were imagined as being authentic reproductions of the

Buddha's teachings. The revival, in other words, rested upon the notion that one could revive the "original" Buddhist scene. Is such a thing even possible? The term "revival," Holmes Welch (1968: 262) explains, "should mean that what has declined or expired is restored to the form it originally had ... in this sense nothing has ever been revived; rebirth has always to some been a new birth."

Modern Indian Buddhism was indeed a new birth, a restoration involving many older components but something distinctively designed in the present. Perhaps nowhere was this made more succinct than in an incredibly retrospective article composed by Dharma Gambhir Sinha, a writer for the All-India Buddhist Society. In June 1928, he alluded to how modernity had not so much revived Buddhism as it had reinvented it:

> [The Buddha] seems to be all things to all people .... To the Brahmins, He is the preacher of Purified Brahmanism .... To the ascetic, He is the Greatest Ascetic having performed the most rigorous form of asceticism; To the saints, He is Sakyamuni, and Mahamuni, the Great Saint; to the Heretics, He is the Greatest Heretic, having defeated many a heretic by His Supreme Wisdom and superphysical powers .... To the philosopher He is the Greatest Philosopher, for having taught the most practical philosophy of life; to the scientists, He is the Greatest, having discovered many scientific truths two thousand years before the dawn of modern science; to the nations of the world He is the Supreme Nation-builder and unifier for having been the upbuilder of so many Buddhist nations and the unifier for having united the ninety six nations of the world, not by physical force but by a bond of spiritual unity. To the internationalists, He is the Great Internationalist, having taught the message of international unity .... To the socialist, He is the Great Socialist for his message of social equality and social welfare and social progress. To the democrat, He is the Great Democrat for His principles of government by the people, for his Sangha, the Holy Brotherhood ... to the Liberal, He is the Supreme Liberal for his attitude towards His enemies, and for His principle of religious tolerance .... Of the modernists, He is the chief, because his views and principles tallied with all modernist ideas that led to human peace and welfare .... To the revolutionary, He is the

Chief, because He is the first to organize a revolution against caste tyranny and religious bigotry of the Brahmins. To the people of the world, He is the Greatest Cosmopolitan and all-uplifting teachings. To the lover of World-peace, He is an idol, as He is the Supreme Advocate of World, as His spiritual message leads all towards world peace, unity and brotherhood (*BI* Vol. 2/2, 1928: 108–09).

The way this Buddha and his corresponding Buddhisms were imagined and enacted has no pre-modern precedent: it constituted its own Navayana or New Vehicle.[1] For generations, a vast constellation of writers and thinkers across the globe had been inventing their own Navayana, consciously and unconsciously. Inventions never take place in a vacuum: there are always some antecedents, and varying degrees of indebtedness to those before us and around us cannot be avoided. Invention, in other words, has many mothers and fathers (although the "great man" theory of invention will probably long remain a more popular story).

Modern Indian Buddhism involved less the invention of anything as it did the reinvention of everything. There were significant continuities, but it spoke to a new global age. Like the formation of global Buddhism more widely, it had been crafted in conversations and encounters not just between Indians and Europeans, but between and among Asians living in an uncertain age of colonial interference, unequal rule, and yet unprecedented communication and awareness of one another. As Indians in the subcontinent confronted the social and political conditions of colonial rule, they did not focus only on the present. They lived in the world by looking backwards and forwards. The catalyst to re-enter Buddhist place worlds may have first been triggered by colonial education systems and Orientalist enterprises, but it gained its impetus from local interests shaped by long-running historical debates regarding caste, inequality, morality, social order, and belonging. Colonial rule brought new ways of thinking about these problems and a new language to describe them, but the recourse to Buddhism stemmed from a profound sense of connection with the traces of the past.

Traveling to Buddhist place worlds, whether real or imagined, was a process of discovery. More often than not, these discoveries tracked back to a point of imagined Buddhist origin where people were more decent than they are today. As Indians relived the past to find a better present and future, a classless, casteless, egalitarian society, free as much from the influences of colonial oppression and Western materialism as brahmanical discrimination and intolerable poverty, they found the Buddha. He was the untainted hero, the flesh-and-blood Indian savior who was also the Light of Asia, let alone the Jagadguru, the Teacher of the World, a universally admired figure. The experience of reading Buddhist scriptures in familiar and unfamiliar languages, of visiting known and unknown Buddhist spaces, listening to Buddhist teachings, of imagining the Buddha and Buddhism, was nothing short of liberation, the realization that tomorrow does not have to be like today.

Notes

Introduction

1 The total number of Buddhists listed in the most recent census at the time was 232,003 (East India Census 1943: 6).

2 Some scholars lay the primary blame on the sangha's own social failures and corruptions. Others point fingers at a resurgent and often antagonistic brahmanism. Most see the destructive raids of Muslim armies from the Central Asian steppe as the final culprit, although this thesis is becoming increasingly untenable. See, R.C. Mitra (1954); Sarao (2012); Verardi (2011); Truschke (2018).

3 With the exception of studies on Ambedkar, which typically see him as the starting point for Buddhist revival rather than part of a much longer genealogy, most critical studies have failed to consider Buddhism's impact on colonial Indian publics. Some noteworthy book-length exceptions include: Aloysius (1998); Ayyathurai (2011); Surendran (2013). Prior to these works, the late Dinesh Chandra Ahir (1989; 1991; 2010) paved the way in collecting histories of Indian Buddhist revival. Although one of the goals of this work is to de-center the conventional stories around India's Buddhist revival, including that of Ambedkar, the impact that the latter has had on modern Indian Buddhism is nearly as great as the sum of other parts. Some readers may be disappointed to see less space dedicated to Ambedkar in this work. What I hope the book shows is that although the immediate motives for Ambedkar's journey to Buddhism was deeply personal, it also belonged to a broader historical movement in which South Asians of different persuasions were pushed to engage with the Buddha, whether they liked it or not. If we fail to appreciate this wider setting, our understanding of Ambedkar will continue to be impoverished.

4 Emphasis added. Readers familiar with Pandey's argument, developed further in his book, *A History of Prejudice* (Pandey 2013), will recognize how my use differs slightly from his. Pandey's primary interests are in those

aspects of life which are deemed so trivial, everyday, and ordinary by those who experience them, that they rarely warrant entry into historical archive.

5   For instance, one of the most popular introductory textbooks on Buddhism used in North American colleges and universities (Mitchell 2008: 153–58), uses the term "extinction" as its header for the final chapter on Indian Buddhism.

6   "All but disappeared" has taken on a meme-like quality in innumerable works, repeated by dozens of scholars like Gethin (1998: 8), Lopez (2009: 6; 2012: 34), B. Turner (2014: 193), Keown (2013: 78), and Keown and Prebish (2013: 418). In Sarao's more recent work (2012: 6), he takes a more nuanced position and acknowledges that calling it a disappearance or death is not exactly an accurate characterization.

7   The doyen of modern Buddhist studies, Donald Lopez (2012: 39), writes, "there were no Buddhists living in India during the colonial period." Similarly, in an otherwise excellent work that does much to illuminate Buddhism's place in colonial India, the anthropologist, Steven Kemper (2015: 274fn102), reduces colonial India's living Buddhist communities to a single footnote, calling them "infinitesimal" (and therefore not deserving of discussion). For a critique of modern scholarship's stance on the "death" of Indian Buddhism, see McKeown (2019).

8   The history of the complex has been discussed in detail by Huber (2008: 193–231).

9   According to Sen (2017: 73), it is less clear whether this journey constituted a "religious pilgrimage".

10   Of the several re-creations that Brown discusses, the two latest constructions are the Schwegugyi temple in Pegu, dated to roughly 1460–70, and the Wat Chet Yot in Chiang Mai, dated to approximately 1455–70 (Brown 1988).

11   The Sanskrit manuscripts copied included the *Kalacakratantra* (dated 1447 CE, from the village of Kerki, Gaya district) and Shantideva's *Bodhicaryavatara* (dated 1436 CE, from Nalanda district).

12   In the twentieth century, many Newar Buddhists have turned away from Sanskrit Mahayana practices in exchange for Theravada-inspired models of Buddhism (LeVine and Gellner 2005).

13   The basis of the argument stems from the fact that the Buddha's birthplace falls within Nepal's national territory rather than India's. We should remember, however, that Nepal was only recognized by the British colonial government as an independent kingdom in 1923. From the perspective of the Raj, it was effectively seen as little different from other Indian protectorates during the century prior (Mojumdar 1973: 191). This may help explain why some colonial scholars, like Sylvain Lévi, tended to see Newar Buddhism as part of a wider Indic Buddhism. For a concise overview of the debate, see Gellner (2018).

14   On the nation's role in shaping historical paradigms, see Duara (1995); Anderson (1991).

15   For an insightful study of issues around the terms "periphery" and "borderlands" in the Indian context, see Baruah (1999, 2020).

16   Here, I rely on the Taw Sein Ko translation (*The Kalyani Inscriptions* 1892).

17   Hikosaka (1989: 177–98) dates the images to the end of the sixteenth century and is more ambivalent than Dehejia regarding their actual ritual use and production. Seshadri's (2009: 130) thoughtful review of the literary and archaeological evidence at Nagapattinam led him to wonder "if there was any native Buddhist population at all in the city or whether all the vihara activities were mainly for inland and foreign transit merchants." In a personal communication (29 June 2019), Arthur McKeown suggests these images were likely being produced for Shaiva communities and would have been heavily adorned with ritual vestments and fabrics to conceal their Buddhist identity. Ray (2015) has also provided a thorough examination of Nagapattinam's maritime landscapes and Buddhist past. Her argument that the port's Buddhist past has been marginalized due to broader historiographical trends focused on the expansion of agrarian states is well taken and serves as another explanation for why Buddhist histories from this region and period have failed to make bigger imprints in the historiography.

18   Some forty miles west of Nagapattinam, an inscription found outside a Shaiva temple in Kumbakonam district (taluk), dated 1579 or 1580, records the grant of land to the people of Tirumalairajapuram for a Buddhist temple (Tamil, *buddar-koyil*) as compensation for having to build a canal through the existing vihara's property (Rao 1927–28: 215–17; Vriddhagirisan [1942] 1995: 31–32).

19   In some cases, the difference in interpretation stems from the examination of a different set of data, but for the most part the evidence for Buddhism's post-fifteenth-century survival was well known to scholars writing after the 1930s.

20   As McKeown (2019) argues, both colonial and postcolonial scholars are well aware of these late Indian Buddhist masters, but in order to fit the data to the theory, they have continually redefined their definitions of Buddhism to denote only a strict adherence to institutionalized, monastic forms, thereby allowing them to dismiss Vajrayana Buddhist practices as inauthentic. This academic desire to define "authentic" and "inauthentic" forms of religion also speaks well to the Western encounter with Tibetan Buddhism. For much of the nineteenth and twentieth centuries, Tibetan Buddhism was seen as little more than "Lamaism"—a derogatory term. Yet, judging by the presence of Tibetan Buddhist centers in North America today, it has become one of the most "authentic" forms of Buddhism in the western hemisphere.

21   I am indebted to C. Bayly (2004); Jaffe (2004; 2019); Blackburn (2010); Green (2011); Turner, Cox, and Bocking (2013; 2020), for my understanding on this subject.

22   This model of networks and flows is by no means a rigid break with the past. Buddhist ideas, practices, and peoples have crossed Asia since its very inception through similar means (Frasch 1998; Sen 2003; Neelis 2011).

Chapter 1

1   Wilkinson's obituary was published in the well-known Calcutta newspaper,

The Friend of India (9 December 1841), abstracts of which were republished in *A Brief Notice of the Late Mr. Lancelot Wilkinson* (1853). Details about Subaji (whose full name was Ramacandra Shastri) are contained in a letter written by Wilkinson (1837: 401–02).

2   Many scholars have questioned whether Ashvaghosha is truly the author of this text. While the scholarly jury is hung on the subject, its historical authorship is less important in this context since what matters is that these particular audiences recognized it as a Buddhist and not an Upanishadic scripture. See, Bisgaard (1994: 11–15) for an insightful discussion of its authorship.

3   The "True Brahmin" discourse that Ashvaghosha employs here is just one of several approaches that Buddhists undertook to attack caste. For a comprehensive study covering the biological, genealogical, ethical, and epistemological critiques that Buddhists drew upon, see Eltschinger (2012).

4   On Wilkinson's support for local languages, see Sarma (1995–96: 185–99).

5   The commentary's official title was "Little Chisel" (*Laghutanka* or "Tunku" for short).

6   Soon after acquiring the manuscript, Wilkinson learned that Brian Hodgson and the Newar Buddhist scholar, Amritananda, had previously published an English translation in the Royal Asiatic Society in 1831. That translation was reproduced wholesale in the Wilkinson–Subaji edition.

7   My own research on its colonial Indian public reveals translations into English (1837, 1841, 1865, 1874, 1877, 1927, 1931), Bengali (1843), Tamil (1850), Marathi (1865), Malayalam (1868), Hindi (1927, 1931), and Nepali (1928). These translations are not to be confused with the Tamil and Bengali translations of the Upanishadic (*Sama Veda*) *Vajrasuchi*.

8   This is one reason why the oldest extant Indian-language manuscripts are typically found in drier landscapes along the Tibetan Plateau, the Afghanistan–Pakistan border, and arid regions of Central Asia.

9   While Indian writing systems were in use as early as the fourth century BCE, the regular use of writing to transmit knowledge—as opposed to recording the mundane, such as business transactions and land grants—came much later to the subcontinent. Up until the early centuries of the Common Era, oral techniques and "memory cultures" paved the way for the explicit transmission of knowledge, from generation to generation.

10   Buddhists also had no qualms in using terms such as *tirthika* (heretics, non-believers) and other forms of derision to describe non-Buddhist communities.

11   Sometimes this number varies between the eighth, ninth, or even twentieth. Other Puranas do not list him at all. Archaeological evidence indicates only limited spaces where the Buddha avatar's image was embodied in active ritual worship. The bulk of the evidence comes from seventh- and eighth-century Pallava inscriptions in Tamil as well as full reliefs of the Buddha avatar at the Dashavatara temple in Deogarh, Uttar Pradesh.

12   All references to the *Vishnu Purana* hereafter are to the Horace Hayman Wilson edition (*The Vishnu Purana* [1840] 1961), with occasional cross-reference, when noted, to the McComas Taylor translation (*The Vishnu Purana* 2021), which is based on the Baroda critical edition (1997–99).

13 The following section is indebted to Mitra (1954: 79–137) and Doniger (1976: 187–211).

14 It is not unusual for brahmanical Sanskrit works to conflate Jains and Buddhists—seeing them largely as two peas in a pod—and this tendency is reflected not only in philosophical discussions but also in narrative ones.

15 Verardi (2011: 141–77) argues that "apostate Brahmins" or brahmins who became Buddhists were most despised, often the subject of separate verses in texts laying out individualized punishments.

16 See Chapter 2 of *The Sarvadarsanasamgraha* (1882 translation), which presents a long list of Buddhist philosophical doctrines in order to refute them.

17 On Kumarila Bhatta, see Sharma ([1898–99] 1980: 1–33).

18 For a third possible ending to this story, see the seventeenth-century Tibetan account from Taranatha (1970: 226–34).

19 The "hidden Buddhist" (pracchannabauddha) polemic against Advaita Vedantins was typical of the wider intellectual terrain, with figures like Venkatanatha or Vedanta Deshika (1269–1370), the most important systematizer of the Vishishtadvaita school of Vedanta, regularly making distinctions between pracchannabauddha and "explicit Buddhists" (*prakata saugata*), the latter referring to those who represented more normative Buddhist ideas.

20 In his *The Untouchables,* B.R. Ambedkar (see [1948] 2020: 118) also pointed to the "spirit of [anti-Buddhist] hatred and contempt" visible in Sanskrit dramas such as the *Mricchakatika*. However, in their annotations to their critical edition of *The Untouchables*, Alex George and S. Anand contest Ambedkar's depiction, concluding instead that "the treatment of Buddhist characters in Sanskrit dramas is not uniform ... [and quoting the historian of Indian Theatre, M.L Varadpande, that] one must also note that the ascetics and monks of other cults were not spared by the playwrights" (139fn29).

21 And most seem to have been lost to posterity. Take Kshemendra (d. 1070 CE), the prolific poet known for his satires and recasting of classical works. Although he came from a Shaiva family and was said to have been a Vaishnava, he had a deep appreciation for Buddhist literature, as evidenced by his collection of Buddhist narratives, the *Bodhisattvadanakalpalata* (Wish-fulfilling Vine of Wondrous Tales of the Bodhisattva), composed around the year 1052 CE (Lin 2011). However, this text seems not to have had a wider currency in the Indic world until Sarat Chandra Das acquired a copy in Tibet in the 1880s.

22 These sectarian polemics cut multiple ways with Buddhists and Jains being ridiculed in devotional Shaiva and Vaishnava literature, and Buddhist and Jain works castigating each other as well as other Vaishnava and Shaiva systems. No stone, it appears, was left unturned.

23 Many scholars have also argued that the Jagannath temple was originally a Buddhist temple. While not certain, that possibility has always provoked anxiety for many devout Hindus and nationalists and was the center of an "acrimonious public debate" in colonial Bengal (Ghosh 2022). The contention

continues to generate an intense and often vitriolic public discussion, especially in light of its implication vis-à-vis the Babri Masjid at Ayodhya.

24   On the dating and composition of the *Madalapanji*, see Kulke (1993: 159–91).

25   In another recension, the Buddhists are able to escape the king's attempt to "smash the heads of the Buddhists to death" by cursing him and fleeing to the forest (*Madalapanji* 2009: 35).

26   During a visit to the ISCKON temple in Delhi in 2008, I was told a similar version of this story by one of the temple priests.

27   In his discussion of Buddhism, al'Fazl writes that the Buddha lived at Benares, Rajgir, and other nearby sacred places, and even reached Kashmir in his journeys. He notes that although Buddhism had once spread all the way to Kashmir, Tibet, and Scythia, it is only found in Pegu (Myanmar), Tenasserim (Myanmar), and Tibet. Interestingly, al'Fazl states that Akbar met with Buddhist leaders in Kashmir "but saw none among the learned".

28   Although it is difficult to establish exact mortality rates among European personnel in the Company at this time, coming to the colonies was certainly far more hazardous than Allen suggests, marked by wars and frequent outbreaks of famine as well as diseases like malarial fever, plague, cholera, dysentery, and influenza.

29   Most early Orientalists in India were better equipped in Persian than they were in Sanskrit or the Prakrits. Only after William Jones's late-eighteenth-century discovery that Greek and Sanskrit were related did a more comprehensive foray into India's pre-Islamic past take form. On the importance of Sanskrit for Orientalist studies, see Marshall (1970) and Trautmann (1997).

30   Wilkins, lived in India from 1770 to 1786, and is best remembered for his English-language translation of the Bhagavad Gita, published in 1785.

31   Despite its Eurocentric bias, the best study of these developments is found in Charles Allen's riveting works on the British discovery of Ashoka and the Buddha (Allen 2002, 2010, 2012).

32   These included *Asiatick Researches* (founded in Calcutta, 1788), *Transactions of the Literary Society of Bombay* (founded 1819), and *Journal of the Asiatic Society of Bengal* (founded in Calcutta, 1832). Other influential journals were *Journal Asiatique* (Paris, founded 1822), *Transactions of the Royal Asiatic Society of Great Britain and Ireland* (London, 1827), and *Journal des Savans* (re-established in Paris in 1816).

33   Fluent in Sinhalese and proficient in Burmese and Pali, Ratna Paula prepared a number of catalogues for the Asiatic Society libraries in Burma, Ceylon, and India and translated Buddhist works for scholars for over a decade (see Paula, 1834, 1838).

34   This was originally composed in January 1788. The condemnation of the Buddha was absolutely puzzling to Jones since the same pandits who spoke of his degraded teaching and practice described him as an incarnation of Vishnu. Jones's accounts of the oral traditions regarding the Buddha appear to have come from two of his Sanskrit teachers: Pandit Ramlochan and the retired Vaidya physician, Pandit Radhacant, who had previously worked for Warren Hastings, the governor general (Cannon 1990).

35 This text (Martin 1838) is in fact an edited selection of Buchanan's papers. After Martin published the work, he came under immense criticism for bowdlerizing Buchanan's Bengal papers and notes, while not even acknowledging the latter on the work's title page. Whether Buchanan himself or Martin used the word "infidel" in this passage remains a mystery, but it may have been an approximation of the derisive "tirthika," the term Jain and Buddhist texts often used to describe one another.

36 I have chosen to translate the term "nastika" in this particular context as "heretical" rather than "atheist," as is more usual today. For an insightful summary of this term in various historical contexts, see Nicholson (2010: 192–94).

37 The original report was published in the *Proceedings of the Madras Government, Revenue Department*, 7 November 1870. Boswell translates *lanja dib-balu* as the "harlot's hill". Holt (2005: 10), writing more than a hundred and twenty-five years later, remarks that this expression continues to be in use among the local populace.

38 Ashvaghosha's argument here is typical of what Eltschinger (2012) calls the Buddhist biological critique of caste.

39 Young speculates that this insecurity may have resulted from concerns over ritual pollution.

40 Of course, personal issues may have been relevant as well. Subaji may have condemned the *Vajrasuchi* in the hope that those who had berated his earlier support of Copernican science would see that he was not the European parrot they believed.

Chapter 2

1 The diversity of these new elites belies any simple classification. A few features, however, were particularly dominant. Most were male, came from upper-class families, and were of high caste status. For a useful analysis of the "new elites" typology, see Oberoi (1994: 260–79). For other uses, including that of "middle class" and "native intelligentsia," see Dalmia (1997), and Bayly (1998).

2 According to Nita Kumar (2012: 283), by the 1850s, there were eleven English colleges and forty high schools run by the government in British India with approximately 9,000 students enrolled. By contrast, there were ninety-two English-language missionary schools with roughly 13,000 students.

3 Elliot, alongside John Dowson, was the author of the eight-volume history, based on Persian sources, published posthumously as *History of India, As Told by Its Own Historians* (1867–77).

4 The preface to the first volume quoted here is in English while the remainder of the text is in Hindi with scattered passages in Urdu and English.

5 That the text's title, which declared history (itihas) as the "dispeller of darkness" (timir nashak), made clear not only Sivaprasad's judgement of its value in society but was also suggestive of popular European claims about India's "lack of history".

6   All translations are mine unless otherwise noted.

7   The idea that the Buddha marks the beginning of datable Indian history became so deeply entrenched in Indology that, according to Adheesh Sathaye (2015: 16–17), it was not until the mid-1970s that Indian scholars began to challenge such a view.

8   Part I begins in the first millennium of the Common Era, focusing primarily on the "Hindu" and "Muhammadan" periods up to the coming of the British. Part II contains the history of British India up through the present. Part III covers the social, cultural, and political history of the subcontinent from its earliest-known origins up through the present. Although Buddhism is not completely absent in the first two parts, it forms a significant section of Part III and is hence the focus of discussion here.

9   Compare Turnour (1838: 813) with Sivaprasad's Devanagri transcription ([1874] 1880: 54fn1) of the Buddha's Pali hymn at the moment of achieving enlightenment.

10 He seemed especially concerned that Jains would be offended because they were being equated with "meat-eating" Buddhist tantriks.

11 I suspect this was likely due to the Orientalist reliance on brahmanical interpretations of the past, which frequently lumped together Jains and Buddhists along with other shramana groups. Other Indian thinkers, such as Iyothee Thass also made similar arguments. According to Arun Prakash Raj (unpublished paper), Thass published a series of essays in 1913 in which he argued that Jains were originally Buddhists who after compromising with the brahmanical system became a breakaway sect. Such arguments were, not surprisingly, contested by local Tamil Jains. I am thankful to Arun for sharing his unpublished paper with me.

12 Although Sivaprasad doesn't provide further detail, the reference to the bones of the Buddha's disciples clearly concerns Alexander Cunningham's archaeological work at Sanchi–Satdhara in 1854, and the discovery of the relics of Mogallana and Sariputta. Sivaprasad's relationship with Cunningham likely kept him well informed of the latest research on Buddhist remains.

13 While Sivaprasad's drawing of parallels between the emancipation from slavery and serfdom, and the rise of Buddhism was wholly original (as far as I am aware), his references to Lincoln and Alexander II as the signs of a modern, liberal order were consistent with many of the other progressive Indian leaders of his day, from Mahadev Ranade to Jotirao Phule. Phule, for instance, dedicated his pioneering 1873 work *Gulamgiri* (Slavery) to "The Good People of the United States as a Token of Admiration for Their Sublime Disinterested and Self-Sacrificing Devotion in the cause of Negro Slavery, and with an earnest desire, that my countrymen may take their noble example as their guide in the emancipation of their Shudra brethren from the trammels of Brahmin Thraldom" (Phule [1873] 2002).

14 It is also possible that this comment could have been subtly aimed at the Raj.

15 Earlier in the text (14), he is more explicit, stating that "most of the Hindus [*bahutere vaidik hindu*]" alive today were formerly Buddhist (or Jain).

16 I have followed Joshi's 1874 translation (see Sivaprasad 1874: 82) for assistance in translating this section since the Hindi original was damaged.

17   The English translation was published as *A History of Hindustan* and the Urdu edition as *Ainah-i Tarikh Numa*.

18   These statistics are calculated based on the ten thousand copies reported in both 1864 and again in 1866. Cf. *RPENWP* (1864–65); *RPENWP* (1865–66): 46. The eighteen thousand is calculated by reports of ten thousand copies in Hindi, five thousand in Urdu and three thousand in English for *RPENWP* (1869–70), Part I: 91. Calculations for 1883 are derived from adding the total number of publications printed, listed on the title pages of Sivaprasad (1864–83), Pts I–III.

19   On nineteenth-century north Indian print cultures, see Stark (2007). On the politics of Britain's "civilizing mission," see Mann (2004).

20   For sample curricula in which the *Itihas* was used, see *RPENWP* (1869–70), Part I: 58 and Section IX: 213. According to Kumar (2012: 291–95), there were more than twenty-six different types of indigenous schools in the North-western Provinces in the 1870s with three dominant models: the *tols,* for higher education in Sanskrit, *pathshala*s that taught the vernaculars, and *maktab*s, that taught a combination of vernaculars with an emphasis on Urdu and Persio–Arabic literature.

21   On the crafting of Buddhism as a world religion, see Masuzawa (2005: 121–46).

22   A political agglomeration of the oppressed masses in India, typically signifying dalits and lower-order shudras.

23   The regular censorship campaigns against its use in schools seemed ineffective in stunting its popularity. For different takes on the *Itihas,* particularly as it relates to nationalist conceptions of India and pre-colonial historiographies, see Goswami (2004: 165–208) and Powell (1999). Neither Goswami nor Powell makes any references to its Buddhist content.

24   A list of his English-language publications (most of which were translated from Gujarati by Bühler and Dr Bhau Daji) includes twelve articles in the *Journal of the Bombay Branch of the Royal Asiatic Society,* eleven articles in the *Indian Antiquary,* and another six articles in miscellaneous periodicals.

25   A committed theist and leader of the Prarthana Samaj or Prayer Society, Bhandarkar found the Buddha's atheism to be lacking, its ethics less formed than that found in the Shanti and Anushasanika books of the Mahabharata.

26   Most of the nineteenth-century Asiatic Society fellows (whether Indian or European), it must be remembered, were not professional scholars of Buddhism but government bureaucrats like Babu Pratapchandra Ghosha and Babu Rashbihari Bose.

27   After being discovered by Cunningham in 1873, the complete structure at Bharhut was dismantled, packed, and shipped to the Indian Museum. For details of the complex political negotiations this required, see Singh (2004: 243–46). The Madras Museum also had its share of materials, including the complete Amaravati remains, brought to the museum in 1883. Other structures, like the Burmese pagoda currently held at Eden Gardens near Fort William in Calcutta, were only partially open to the public. After the British conquest of Prome in Burma in 1854, Lord Dalhousie had the local pagoda broken into pieces, shipped to Calcutta (along with three Burmese

carpenters) and then reassembled. On museums in India, see Guha-Thakurta (2004: 43–84).

28   By 1883, the Asiatic Society library possessed more than thirty thousand volumes in total with roughly eight thousand more in manuscript form. By 1917, the number of manuscripts stood at 11,264 (Shastri 1917: iii).

29   Although this was the most significant public collection in India, it was dwarfed by some of the largest European collections at the time. Cecil Bendall ([1883] 1992) lists 1,097 Buddhist Sanskrit manuscripts in the University Library, Cambridge.

30   Such ideas were no doubt being sparked by Henry Olcott and other Theosophists.

31   See the frontispiece of JBTSI Vol. 1/1 (1893). Among its more well-known members were Sir Alfred Croft, Henry Olcott, Norendronath Sen, Haraprasad Shastri, Hari Mohan Vidyabhusan, Heneviratne [later, Anagarika] Dharmapala, Sri Asutosh Mukhopadhyay [Mookerjee], Justice Gurudas Vandyopadhyaya, and Mahesh Candra Nyayaratna.

32   Later the group expanded its literary scope to include religious and social literature of Indian Buddhists found in Pali, Burmese, Siamese, Chinese, Korean, and Japanese texts with the hope of better understanding the history and geography of ancient India and "Indo-Aryan thoughts on Buddhism".

33   Among Risley's most enduring and pitiful legacies was his promotion of race science and the use of pseudoscientific methodologies like anthropometry, or the measurement of physical bodies to determine racial characteristics which influenced his census work deeply.

34   See Dharmapala Sarnath Notebook (DpNb, no. 25); Diaries of Chogyal Sidkeong Tulku (1901–02); Cunningham (1871); and Kosambi ([1924] 2010: 53–219).

35   The magnitude of Cunningham's research is captured well by Guha-Thakurta (2004: 42), when she describes Cunningham's writings as being seen then, as they are now, as "an archive: a source of constant citation, corroboration, and cross-reference in a field that their very authority had founded."

36   Unfortunately, very little is known of Babu Jamna Shankar Bhatt. He worked with Cunningham for over ten years, traveling to archaeological sites, interpreting ruins, conversing with locals, and reading and copying inscriptions when Cunningham was unable to do so himself. Although it is difficult to speak about their relationship with any precision, it is obvious that Cunningham held him in high regard, describing him as having "a very correct eye" and being "conversant with the true shapes of these ancient characters" (Cunningham 1877: i).

37   The outstanding success in using the Chinese texts, particularly those of Xuanzang, to map the ancient landscape on to the modern led to a paradigm shift in the Orientalist inquiry, where almost everything in the Chinese accounts were taken to be historically accurate. On Xuanzang's writings as a source for South Asian studies, see Trautmann and Sinopoli (2002: 495–501) and Deeg (2012: 89–113).

38   Nor did all shrines and temples form a part of the ASI's purview. Many were privately owned and managed, and therefore continued to be demolished and/or reworked within the confines of their own communities. Private

enterprises in Burma were also active in repairing ruined "pagodas" and renovating old ones. Lahiri (2012: 384–85) argues that many private owners were resistant to allowing the government to work on their properties since British officials often saw this as giving them rights over the shrines. At Bodh Gaya, for instance, the mahant insisted on paying for the dismantling and reconstruction of railing pillars "as he was afraid to lose his right over the temple if government paid for their relocation" (385).

39 These were published in Griffin's (1886) richly illustrated *Famous Monuments of Central India*, which includes the twenty-seven plates of Sanchi photographed by Dayal.

40 Although the title of this Urdu biography is not listed, the author reports that there were at least four other Urdu-language essays and books published on Buddhism at this time, most by S. Warman. Warman also apparently intended to produce an Urdu translation of Paul Carus's *The Gospel of Buddha* (*MBJ* Vol. 8/11, 1899–1900: 110).

41 On Beg, see Lahiri (2012: 367–68). Mahavir is discussed in the next chapter.

42 The complete events surrounding this have been retold in Allen ([2008] 2010), with the particulars of Mukherji's involvement on pp. 178–225.

43 Dharmapala's diaries contain many similar stories.

44 The *Lalitavistara Sutra* tells the story of the Buddha Shakyamuni in Sanskrit, from the time of his descent from the Tushita heaven to his first sermon at the Sarnath Deer Park.

45 These included Sanskrit, Latin, Greek, French, German, English, Persian, Urdu, Hindi, Bengali, and Odia.

46 Proof of Mitra's concern for preserving the past is found in a descriptive catalogue of manuscripts at the Asiatic Society, where it states that of the library's 11,264 Sanskrit manuscripts, 3,156 were acquired by Mitra! See Shastri (1917: iii).

47 For his comments on Hindu silences regarding Bodh Gaya, see Mitra (1878: 12–17). Other scholars of Buddhism, both Indian and European, often shared Mitra's assessment. For Cunningham, see Singh (2004: 39–40). For Indraji and Bühler, see Dharamsey (2012: Chapter Four).

48 According to Derek Waller (1990), the school was not very successful in its mission as only a few of the boys took up surveying, with Ugyen Gyatso and his brother-in-law, Rinzin Namgyal, becoming its most successful associates. On Rinzin Namgyal, see Madan (2004: 71–73, 131–32).

49 The greatest demographic shift resulted from Nepali laborers being recruited to work on the lucrative tea plantations in and around Darjeeling. The town had a very large English population as well. According to the *District Gazetteer*, the population rose from 10,000 in 1857 to a seasonal population in 1901 between 17,000 (cold weather) and 24,000 (in September). See O'Malley (1907: 39).

50 The 1901 *District Gazetteer: Darjeeling* describes four classes of "Bhutia Buddhists" in the Darjeeling district—1,550 Sikkimese Bhutias at Darjeeling, 3,450 Sherpa bhutias in the western end of the district, 2,350 Drukpa [Bhutanese] bhutias in Kalimpong, and 1,700 Tibetan bhutias found throughout (O'Malley 1907: 45–46).

51　In addition to founding the gompa (*yid dga' chos gling*), Lama Sherab was a highly regarded scholar of the Tibetan language, who trained many famous students. These included the Japanese monk–explorer, Ekai Kawaguchi, the Dutch linguist, M.A.J. van Malen, the police inspector, Sonam Wangfel Ladenla, and Calcutta University professor, Karma Sumdhon Paul.

52　It was probably not until the early 1900s when Das would have learned of the severe punishments, including execution, that some of his Tibetan hosts had to pay for assisting him, an agent of the British state. For a valuable overview into the larger geopolitical concerns and repercussions of Das's visits to Tibet, see McKay (2002).

53　The general public had to wait until the early 1900s for Das's complete memoirs to be cleared by British authorities, for the contents revealed too much of their clandestine support (see Waller 1990: 293fn40).

54　This concept had (and continues to have) a huge influence in both the popular and academic study of Buddhism in North America (Lopez 1998: 156–80).

55　Vidyabhusan was one of the first students to complete an MA in Pali at Calcutta University, for which he published *Kaccayana's Pali Grammar*, editing the text in Devanagari and translating it into English in 1901. He was later appointed as professor of Sanskrit and gained notoriety for his critical essays on Indian logic based on Sanskrit, Tibetan, and Pali sources. His magnum opus, *A History of Indian Logic* (1922), remains a valuable resource today.

56　After earning back-to-back degrees in Sanskrit from Calcutta University—acquiring the title "Shastri" after completing his MA—in 1883, he was appointed teacher of *alankara* and *vyakarana* (Sanskrit rhetoric and grammar) at Sanskrit College. In 1895, he became professor of Sanskrit at Presidency College. In 1900, he moved back to Sanskrit College as principal, where he remained until 1908. The title "Mahamahopadhyaya" was conferred by the government in 1898.

57　These two documents (HDBPB September 1892, Part B. and FDE April 1906, 1–4) reveal the pivotal role Haraprasad played in several government programs. For instance, in 1902–03, he was sought out by Curzon to serve as a "legal authority" in the Maha Bodhi temple proceedings. Before the Commander of the Indian Empire (CIE) decoration in 1911, he was also supplied with free copies of any work on archaeology, history, and antiquities published under the authority of the Government of India.

58　More recently, Shastri's reading of the Dharmaraj cult has been criticized by scholars of folkore, such as Frank Korom (1997).

59　Only the saraks of Cuttack were classified as Buddhist while those who lived in Bengal and Chutia Nagpur were considered a "Hinduized" form of Jains.

60　His accomplishments have been well documented in the anonymously authored *Pandit Nagendranath Vasu* (1916).

61　Compare with Vasu (1911: cclx).

62　A fourth criterion, based on ethnographic evidence, could also be applied. However, the precise details differed in this case. Where Haraprasad saw iconographic and ritual similarities between Newar Buddhist imagery and the Dharmaraj shrine in Janbazaar in Calcutta, Vasu based his conclusions on the annual gathering of saraks at the Khandagiri caves during the Buddha Purnima (Vasu 1911: ccxxxviii–ccxxix).

63   This practice is still visible across the subcontinent. See, for instance, S. Anand's (2004) journalistic report on the use of Buddha images in contemporary Tamil Nadu.

64   Central to this discourse was the larger and still enduring theory about the Jagannath temple's possible Buddhist origins, which began with Cunningham in the 1850s. Cunningham's argument has been long accepted by the most eminent scholars of South Asia including, Rajendralal Mitra, James Ferguson, Ananda Coomaraswamy, Sarvepalli Radhakrishnan, and many, many more. Bhima Bhoi's journey to the temple, in Vasu's argument, hinges on his understanding that the Jagannath image is actually that of the Buddha. For a critical review of the "Buddhist theory," see Starza (1993: 53–62).

65   The image was a gift from from a Japanese visitor—possibly the Shingi Shingonshu scholar, Masuda Jiryo (Jaffe 2017: 231–32). Sayajirao's influence on Buddhist studies would be channeled through other indirect avenues as well, most notably through the scholarship he provided to B.R. Ambedkar to study abroad.

66   For instance, both Dharmanand Kosambi and Rahul Sankrityayan, the two most influential north Indian scholars of Buddhism, studied with the Russian Orientalist, Fyodor Stcherbatski in Leningrad. Prior to this, Sankrityayan had studied Pali at Vidyalankara Pirivena in Ceylon. Two of Sankrityayan's most influential students, Jagdish Kashyap and Anand Kausalyayan, also studied at the Vidyalankara Pirivena at Sankrityayan's urging. Kosambi, who studied Pali at Vidyalankara Pirivena's sister institution, Vidyodara Pirivena, later spent long periods working on the *Visuddhimagga* in Cambridge at Harvard University. Kosambi's most distinguished student, P.V. Bapat, drew on Kosambi's connections to also study at Harvard. Bapat would eventually earn a PhD from Harvard for his critical comparison of the *Visuddhimagga* with the *Vimuttimagga*. These kinds of elite connections and networks are just the tip of the academic iceberg and in many ways parallel the monastic lineages and networks that criss-crossed Buddhist Asia at this time.

67   Sankrityayan's voluminous writings on Buddhism in Hindi were soon matched by his two students, Bhikkhu Jagdish Kashyap, who later oversaw a forty-one-volume edition of the Pali canon in Devanagari script, and Bhikkhu Anand Kausalyayan, who as early as 1942 had translated the Jatakas (#1–250) into Hindi (Bapat 1944: 11).

68   My usage of the term public is drawn primarily from the works of Novetzke (2008), Burchett (2019), and Warner (2002) and refers to those communities that "embrace otherwise unrelated people who all participate in the same discourse at different times and places" (Burchett 2019: 48).

69   Set in the Ashokan era, around the Buddhist sites of north-western India and Patna, the *Kanchanmala*, or Garland of Gold, marked the start of Haraprasad's side career as a historical novelist attempting "to allow proven facts to blend freely with imaginative reconstructions" (Guha-Thakurta 2004: 133). The text (Shastri 1882) was first serialized in 1882–83 & republished as a novel in 1916.

70 The group was first founded as the Calcutta Unitarian Committee in 1823. Later, they distanced themselves from the church, establishing the Brahmo Sabha in 1829 and finally the Brahmo Samaj in 1843. An appreciation for the Buddha's dhamma appears to have played no major role in the early development of the Brahmos, although many of its luminaries were exposed to living Buddhist cultures on the borders of Bengal as well as in Ceylon. Some of Rammohan Roy's later biographers, for instance, claimed that he spent his "early missing years" studying with Buddhist pandits in Benares or, alternatively, that he went to Tibet to study Buddhism. But these claims seem spurious since Roy's own writings never mention them. It seems that the references to Tibet actually indicate his journeys to Bhutan, since the most common north Indian word for this region "Bhot" simply designates the Buddhist Himalayan region at large. The record of his visit to Bhutan makes clear he was unimpressed by the "impure habits" of the Buddhist populace. See Bose (1825).

71 According to Kopf (1979: 283), this is the first full-length study of Buddhism in any modern Indian language. Aghore Nath Gupta's life is discussed in Damen (1983: 132) and Kopf (1979: 236–38).

72 Kopf (1979: 284) argues that, "the end product was a convincing case, at least from the Keshubite point of view."

Chapter 3

1 On Ambagahawatte IndaSabha and the Ramanna Nikaya's founding, see Malagoda (1972: 162–72).

2 On the Ramnna Nikaya, see Malagoda (1972: 162–72). Although numerically small in comparison to the other major Buddhist orders (nikaya) in the island, the Ramanna Nikaya's profile heightened greatly in the nineteenth century and was one of Henry Olcott's major allies in his quest to build a universal and liberal Buddhist order. The Ramanna Nikaya's influence in colonial India remains unstudied but it is clear that it had a pivotal impact in that many of the most influential Buddhist monastics in twentieth-century India were closely tied to the order, including the anti-caste Buddhist activist, Bhikkhu Bodhananda; Ambedkar's preceptor, U Chandramani; and Venerable Kripasaran, the founder of the Bengal Buddhist Association.

3 It is worth noting that for some modern Indian wrestlers, the Buddha is an exemplar who fits the mold of the ideal *brahmachari*, and therefore the model for north Indian wrestling ideology and identity (Alter 1992: 129). It is unclear whether this was part of Buddhism's appeal to Mahavir, but as John Powers (2012) has shown, discourses of masculinity, sex, and the body have long permeated Indian Buddhist texts.

4 Zarhee was clearly involved in a variety of affairs, as indicated by his frequent appearance in government documents and Maha Bodhi Society and Archaeological Survey of India reports. In English records, his name is variously spelled as Kee Zarhee, Zharhee, Moung Zarhee, Khee Jha Rhee, Khee Za Rhea.

5   Dharmapala's diaries provide good reason why Mahavir wanted to pursue this project independently. In the Sarnath Notebook (DpNb, No. 20), he writes: "In 1895 I set fire to the linga at Kusinara and the Saivaite Brahman was then the caretaker .... Then Mahavir Baba asked me to give over the place to him." If "setting fire" is to be taken literally, the problems Dharmapala caused for Mahavir would have been obvious, and yet even if we read that passage less literally, it is suggestive of the kind of aggressive, militant-like presence that Dharmapala often embodied and which Mahavir likely wished to avoid.

6   These included the most well-known national scholars like Dharmanand Kosambi (who lived with Mahavir in 1904) and Rahul Sankrityayan (who attended Mahavir's funeral in 1919), as well as Bhikkhu Bodhananda of Lucknow, a colleague of Mahavir's; Jagdish Kashyap, the great Pali scholar; Anand Kausalyayan, the Punjabi bhikkhu and Hindi writer who later took up the Ambedkarite Buddhist cause. A summary overview of the many eminent Indians in modern times who wore the saffron robe is provided in Ahir (1989) and Lal (2004).

7   For an insightful critique and alternative viewpoint into the world of working-class colonials and "plebeian cosmpolitans," see Turner, Cox, and Bocking (2020).

8   The British monk, Sangharakshita, who founded the Trailokya Bauddha Mahasangha Sahayaka Gana (TBMSG) in 1979, now one of the largest Buddhist organizations in India, also received his ordination from U Chandramani.

9   When U Chandramani, then still a novice, met Mahavir in Calcutta in the late 1890s, Mahavir sent him to Wasipur (Bihar) to study Sanskrit and Hindi from local pandits. Three years later, U Chandramani joined Mahavir at Kushinagar, and the two jointly managed the new vihara until Mahavir's death in 1919. See Tha Doe Hla (2002: 19–29).

10   Although the Weberian trope of an "other-worldly" sangha has been largely laid to rest, it is difficult to overestimate the degrees to which monastic communities successfully integrated themselves within the social, political, and economic fabric of the societies in which they arose. Had it not been for the sangha's wide range of activities in agrarian, medical, and banking affairs, Buddhism would not likely have emerged as the major pan-Indian and subsequently pan-Asian tradition that it became; nor would it have generated the exquisite artworks, monumental architecture, and literary masterpieces that materialized from such an economic basis and surplus.

11   It is important to recognize that not all Buddhists in India chose to join or establish such groups. In Kushinagar, Mahavir and U Chandramani made no such efforts until the early 1920s, when the Kushinagar Bhikkhu Sangha Association was formed for legal reasons. The lack of such an organization did not prevent them from engaging modern print technologies—they produced a thousand copies of the first Hindi translation of the Pali *Dhammapada* in 1909—but it is suggestive of the different social world they inhabited.

12   Although many of these organizations were shaped deeply by cosmopolitan urban cultures, they also marked the growing visibility of a hard-edged ethno-nationalist religious politics across South Asia, a wider symptom of

the nationalist fever sweeping the early twentieth-century world. On these wider colonial developments, see Ober (2019a).

13   As Washington (1993: 34) describes them: "[The Masters are] beings whose rigorous esoteric training and absolute purity have invested them with supernatural powers. Immortal and immaterial, the masters can inhabit material or semi-material bodies at will (this point is not quite clear) .... Communicating with one another by means of a sort of cosmic radio, they form a link between human beings and the chiefs of the divine hierarchy which rules the cosmos."

14   According to Johnson ([1994] 1997: 5), after the Olcott and Blavatsky settled permanently in India in 1880, the identity of the Masters became more Tibetan and Buddhist. Johnson (204) speculates that this may have been triggered by their growing contact with the Tibetologist, Sarat Chandra Das.

15   Olcott lived at Adyar for approximately twenty years in total, between 1880 and 1907, and Blavatsky for close to five between 1880 and 1885. On the remarkable gardens established at the TS headquarters in Adyar, see Srinivas (2015: 50–86).

16   The anti-Christian element in theosophy was much stronger in Blavatsky than it was in Olcott. The latter's criticism of Christianity was directed primarily towards its evangelical missionary efforts rather than the early teaching. Christian organizations were severe critics of Olcott and the theosophists more widely.

17   On the Anglicist divide in nineteenth-century Orientalism, see Trautmann (1997).

18   Olcott's division of a "spiritual East" and a "material West" was symptomatic of a wider world view, on which see Chatterjee (1993).

19   The Buddhist Theosopical Society had a formative impact on the Buddhist Sinhala society, establishing English-language schools parallel to Christian mission schools and drawing on the support of both clerical and lay figures across the island nation.

20   According to Prothero ([1996] 2011: 131), by the time Blavatsky died in 1891, the TS claimed 258 branches across six continents.

21   Prominent Indian contributors included, Camul Mukherjee, Damodar Mavalankar, Norendronath Sen, Babaji Dhabagirinath, Ramaswami Iyer, and T. Subba Row. The major sources for their discussion of Buddhism appear to have been Olcott's *Buddhist Catechism,* Sinnett's *Esoteric Buddhism*, and Blavatasky's *Isis Unveiled.*

22   For instance, the writings of the Pali scholar and influential Sinhalese monastic, Hikkaduve Sumangala, appeared in the journal.

23   On Hikkaduve, see Blackburn (2010).

24   Two important exceptions are Johnson (1995) and Srinivas (2015: 50–86).

25   Damodar's writings were published posthumously in three collections (Mavalankar 1940, 1978, 1982).

26   Damodar's body was never found and he remained an important rallying point for Theosophists, such as in 1909 when Annie Besant began reporting that he was going to return the next year "to lead the Theosophical Society". See, *MBJ* Vol. 17/1, 1909: 7–8.

27   I have been unable to find any further information on Babu Manohar Lall, other than brief references. In the preface to the thirty-third edition of the English text, Olcott (1897) reported the text to have been translated into "twenty languages, mainly by Buddhists, for Buddhists" (no page number).

28   Tukaram was also a close colleague of Jotirao Phule, and the duo published the first Marathi translation of the *Vajrasuchi*.

29   This document, dated 2 February 1884, is reprinted towards the end of Agarwal (2001).

30   Critical studies of Buddhism in Chittagong are scarce with Chaudhuri ([1982] 1987) and R.B. Barua (1978) being the most comprehensive (although problematic). See also, S.B. Barua (1990) and D.M. Barua (n. d.). Several works on the neighboring Arakan also shed light, such as Charney (1999, 2002), Leider (2010), D'Hubert and Leider (2011).

31   These included the *Padimukh* (codes of monastic conduct) and the *Maghakhamuja*, a short handbook of *Apadana* literature. The most well-known work he produced was an original account of the life of the Buddha (*Bauddharanjika*), based on a rare edition of the *Dhatuvamsa* composed in Arakanese script. Although completed in 1873 with the assistance of Nil Kamal, the *Bauddhranjika*'s publication was stalled after Kalindi's death and only published in an abridged version seventeen years later.

32   The study of Ceylon's Buddhist revival has been extensive. Some of the most helpful studies include Malagoda (1972); Bond (1988); Gombrich and Obeyesekere (1988); Blackburn (2010).

33   The analogy originated with Arnold (1885: 233).

34   These lectures were widely republished. See, for instance, "Col. Olcott on the kinship between Hinduism and Buddhism," *IM* 27 October 1892.

35   Olcott's own frictions with Besant on the question of improving the lives of the depressed classes bear mentioning. Olcott's schools for Tamil dalits, known as "Panchama Schools" (Basu 2011: 182–84), were clearly an anathema to Besant, who laid out her views on "The Uplift of the Depressed Classes" just two years after Olcott's death: "In every nation, we find as the basis of the social Pyramid, a large class of people, ignorant, degraded, unclean in language and habits ... it is ever on the verge of starvation ... suffers chronically from under-nutrition, and is a prey to the diseases which spring therefrom ... its children die off rapidly, ill-nourished, rickety, often malformed ... [this class] ought to be under continued control, and forced to labour sufficiently to earn its bread. In India, this class forms one-sixth of the total population, and goes by the generic name of the 'Depressed Classes'" (Besant 1909, quoted in BAWS Vol 9: 3–4). My thanks to S. Anand for alerting me to Besant's views on these matters.

36   Although Dharmapala abandoned the TS, he never abandoned theosophy, continuing to believe in the universal message of the Mahatmas, whose names still appeared in the *Maha Bodhi* journal he edited into the 1920s. Nor did Dharmapala's distance from the TS cut off the support he received from other theosophists, although this was due as much to his own social status as for his cause. See, Kemper (2015: 52–115).

37   The society's Bengali name, Bauddha Dharmankur Sabha, means the

"Society for the Germination of the Bauddhadharma". It often goes by the name, Bengal Buddhist Association, in English, and I follow that usage.

38   Other goals included: "(a) expunging the social evils, prejudices and superstitions by means of instruction, publications and lectures; (b) establishing Schools and 'Tolls' [Pali language institutes] in different villages for the development and culture of intellect and morality, (c) printing and circulating works on Buddhism, Pali Texts and translation of Buddhist scripture, etc."

39   Unless otherwise noted, my main source for the life of Kripasaran is Ram (2006).

40   By 1800, severe violence and new taxation schemes had led to what Company officials in 1800 described as a "very extraordinary and unexpected migration" of "no less than 35,000 [Arakanese] persons" to seek "protection in Chittagong". See "Chronicle for March 1800," 61, quoted in Charney (1999: 265fn622).

41   In historical literature, "Magh" is often written as "Mugg". The term has been dropped in recent decades because of its pejorative connotation and connection to the formerly robust slave trade and piracy in the region.

42   This is rather standard fare in the presentation of his life. See, for instance, Chowdury (2015) and the *Kripasaran Mahathera 125th Birth Anniversary Volume* (1990).

43   The Arakanese house was at 20/1 Gangadhar Babu's Lane, Bowbazar Street. See *MBJ* Vol. 1 (1892–93: 5). It later moved to 6 and then 10 Eden Street, all of which were short distances from one another. My estimate of the Barua population derives from the Census Comission's report of 2,903 Buddhists in Calcutta in 1891, most of whom were said to be Chinese (*Census of India* Vol. 6, Part I: Bengal, 1901: 157).

44   A BBA appeal for funds to build a Calcutta vihara was published in *MBJ* Vol. 12/1–2, 1903: 21. This document is signed by "Mahaweer [Mahavir] Bhikshu, Kripasaran Bhikshu, U Nanda Bhikshu, Ram Chandra Barua".

45   It is difficult to equate this in rupees, especially since these donations came over time, but the amount far exceeded that given to any other Buddhist organization in India. Foster's (1844–1930) philanthropic activities were well known to South Asians—she had many "gurus". She first met Dharmapala in Hawai'i in 1893 when he was returning from the World Parliament in Chicago. Despite only meeting two more times in person, during their four-decade long relationship, Foster was the Buddhist patron par excellence. Her donations came in incremental sums—Rs 3,000 in 1906; Rs 15,000 in 1908; Rs 50,000 in 1913, and a 50,000 USD bond in 1919, to name just a few. She was not the Maha Bodhi Society's only donor. Other means of support were substantial but compared to Foster (and the family trust Dharmapala inherited), they were negligible. Dharmapala's Sarnath diary (DpD) for 24 August 1920, reports that he had collected Rs 40,000 from Burma and Lanka since the organization's inception. Not an insignificant amount, but this was twenty-eight years of fund-raising: a single donation from Foster in 1913 exceeded that amount.

46   Some of the BBA's most generous benefactors included the princely states. Apart from preaching and relying on the subcontinent's ingrained tradition of ethical giving, all members were required to pay five rupees annually. A clause (#14) in the prospectus states: "*All the Buddhists of Calcutta* besides the members of the Association shall have to contribute a donation to this Association per annum according to their ability" (emphasis mine). How well this *zakat*-like demand played out is unclear.

47   Spurred on by allegations of financial mismanagement and fraud, Dharmapala printed a detailed record of Foster's donations in *MBJ* Vol. 37/1, 1929: 92–94.

48   The issue of "first" here should be contextualized, as the small Chinese community in Calcutta (Zhang 2014) may have already established a Buddhist temple by this period. If so, this would constitute the "first". However, what is striking is that the Chinese community in Calcutta is almost entirely absent in the colonial archives and does not appear to have engaged much in Buddhist affairs outside their own communities.

49   In addition to those discussed below, these included Sir R.W. Carlyle, member of the Governor General's council in charge of revenue and agriculture; the Calcutta High Court justices, H. Holmwood and Jogendra Chandra Ghosh. It also received the support of the rulers of several minor princely states, including Maharaja Sir Bijoy Chand Mahatab of Burdwan, Manindra Chandra Nandi, maharaja of Cox's Bazaar, and Raja Bhuban Mohan Roy, the Chakma chief of the Chittagong Hill Tracts in Rangamati. See *BBA* for longlists of their patrons, members, honorary members, etc.

50   For instance, several BBA monks, like Sammana Punnanada and Dharmavansa Thero, were employed by Calcutta University to teach in its Pali-language programs.

51   Kemper (2015: 29fn62) calls it "unclear" why there was not more "solidarity," suggesting class difference as the primary culprit. Contemporary writers associated with the Bengal Buddhist Association and Maha Bodhi Society frequently acknowledge the distant relationship but are silent on why they never formed a closer bond. I suspect that one of the reasons it has not been investigated further is that due to the close relationship between the two societies today, both are fearful that any digging up of the past may revive negative memories. Surendran (2013) appears to have missed these tensions, describing it as "a fruitful and cordial relationship" (68fn92).

52   Prominent among the society's members were the Panchen Lama (president), Sikyong Tulku, the Crown prince of Sikkim (vice president), and the notable scholar–translators, Kazi Dawa Samdup and Satish Chandra Vidyabhusan (resident secretaries).

53   O'Connor was one of three European-born "honorary advisors" on the board of the BSRS. Huber (2008: 277–79), one of the few scholars to recognize the society's importance, characterized the BSRS as a primarily secular institution interested in the management of archaeological sites, but the organization's aim was much more precise. Huber's misguided conclusions about the BSRS are likely due to the limited sources he had, which, as he notes (423fn83), are based on a single prospectus of the organization published in

the back of Satish Chandra Vidyabhusan's report on *The Tashi Lama's Visit to India (8th November 1905 – 17th February 1906)* (1907).

54   See, for instance, the notes from the meeting on 24 November 1907, where members expressed distrust of Dharmapala's understanding of the legal dynamics at Bodh Gaya (Darbar, 1906, File no. Nil, Part B, Paper reg: Buddhist Shrine Restoration Society).

55   Other notable Indian members included, Dharmanand Kosambi, Norendronath Sen, Babu Rashbihari Mukherji, and Surendranath Tagore, all individuals whom Dharmapala had once considered his friends. His sense of betrayal was sharp.

56   The judgment was given on 19 January 1909, and Dharmapala's appeal in the Calcutta High Court was dismissed without discussion just over a year later.

57   Dharmapala may have been turned off by the so-called decadence of the contemporaneous Bengali sangha, but the organization's rigorous missionary instinct appears to have appealed to other Buddhists in India. Around 1912 or 1913, the crown prince of Sikkim and incarnate lama (Tibetan, sprul sku), Sikyong Namgyal, invited the BBA's newest secretary and polyglot bhikkhu, Kali Kumar (d. 1914) to preach "orthodox Buddhism" among the Mahayana populace. The radical project, aimed as much at economic reforms as at religious ones, was short-lived and collapsed within just days of the Sikyong's premature death in 1914, when all Theravada Buddhists were expelled from the Mahayana Budddhist kingdom.

58   Of notable mention is the towering scholar of Tamil literature, U.V. Swaminatha Iyer (1855–1942). Aiyer is often credited wth restoring a large number of ancient and medieval Tamil works, especially Sangam works, which he turned from palm leaf manuscripts to print. This included the restoration of Tamil Buddhist literature, much of which was then unknown. For Iyer's first hand account of the scholarly Tamil scene in Buddhism in the 1890s, see Iyer (1980: 367–77).

59   On the debates and movements concerning the upliftment of "untouchable" castes in colonial Madras Presidency, see Basu (2011). Olcott's Panchama Free Schools, which targeted the children of untouchable labourers employed in tanneries and brick kilns, were highly regarded by colonial officials, and many students of these schools were able to secure lucrative employment in European and Eurasian households. See Basu (2011: 182–84) and Prothero ([1996] 2011: 137–38).

60   Olcott's and Thass's accounts were also published in several *MBJ* issues, such as Vol. 7/3 (1898–99: 23–24) and Vol. 7/4, (1898–99: 36–37). See also, Aloysius (1998, chapter three).

61   The letter was also published in *The Hindu*.

62   Olcott's position as president of the Theosophical Society restricted him from holding any proselytizing role, but he justified his involvement by accepting Thass's argument that the paraiyars were not "converting" to Buddhism but "reverting" to their "original" identity. For Olcott's perspective on these affairs, see Prothero ([1996] 2011: 136–42).

63   For a sociological analysis of these events, see Aloysius 1998: 50–57.

64   Following the ceremony, the men met with other monastics with whom

Olcott was particularly close, including Dharmapala and the heads of the Ramanna Nikaya.

65 At times, the organization also went by the title the South Indian Buddhist Society (SIBS). Recent archival work also suggests that Thass may have founded another Buddhist organization (Buddha Sangam) in Ootacamund in the years prior to his encounter with Olcott, as well as a Dravida Buddha Sangam in Madras shortly after his first meeting with Olcott but before his visit to Ceylon (Venkatachalapathy 2014).

66 Although colonial institutions benefited many dalits through educational schemes, colonialism had contradictory impacts, the most obvious of which was in its dual strengthening of brahmanical ideologies and violent exploitation and peasantization of India's bottom half. For three excellent studies, see Washbrook (1993); Jangam (2017); Teltumbde (2017b).

67 For a succinct overview, see S. Perumal (1998).

68 The names of thirteen other monks from Siam, Ceylon, and Burma are included in the South Indian Buddhists Petition, Home Department: Public Branch, Deposit # 141 (May 1917–18). See also, "Resolutions passed by the South Indian Buddhist Conference held at Bangalore on 21st November 1920," in Reforms Department, Franchise Branch, Part B, 172–73. Both documents are available in the National Archives, New Delhi.

69 In the 1911 report published by the Shakya Buddhist Society, Thass writes that "some 250 Buddhist visitors, Bikshshus [sic] and laymen and women from Holland, China, Japan, Burma, Ceylon, Siam, Singapore, Chittagong, Benares, Calcutta, Bodh Gaya and other places have called and stayed here on different occasions." See Appendix 4 in Aloysius (1998: 210).

70 The foundations for this movement stemmed from the Hindu Free Thought Union, later known as the Madras Secular Society. Founded by a small group of men and disseminated via the print journals, *Tattuva Vivesini* (in Tamil) and *The Thinker* and *Philosophical Inquirer* (both in English), the Madras Secular Society launched vitriolic attacks against the caste system and child marriage, questioned the existence of god, the divinity of Vedic scriptures, all the while endorsing the right of widows to remarry and women's rights to education. The group was known as far afield as Europe and the United States. It was the particular scourge of the Theosophical Society. The organization's influence is evident in the array of later Tamil rationalists who were discovered to have been voracious readers of their works and in some cases, even contributors. I am thankful to an anonymous reviewer for bringing V. Geetha's (2013) review essay on the Madras Secular Society to my attention.

71 My understanding of Thass's intellectual project and ideas is indebted greatly to the work of Aloysius (1998), Ayyathurai (2011), Geetha (1993), Geetha and Rajadurai (1993), Leonard (2017, 2019), and Rajangam (2018).

72 In Thass's report printed in 1911 by the Shakya Buddhist Society, he argues on the basis of Tamil sources that the actual birth of the Buddha occurred 3,397 years before (1,486 BCE). See, Appendix 4 in Aloysius (1998: 213).

73 The contents of the *Tamilian* from 1907 to 1914 have been studied in detail by Ayyathurai (2011). The magazine came to a halt in 1922, but was revived by G. Appadurai, who ran it from 1926 to 1935. Many of these articles were

later gathered and published in book form by the Kolar Gold Fields Buddhist associations—where they continue to be published even today.

74   He had serious misgivings about colonial rule as well, but his experiences with Congress leaders and at the Madras Mahajana Sabha, had led him to deeply distrust any rhetoric of swaraj. See Aloysius (1998: 1–49), for the wider context.

75   A noteworthy introduction to Narasu's life is Aloysius's in Narasu 2002.

76   Narasu also authored a major work on caste (Narasu 1922), approaching it as he did all things, with the same rationalist and scientific perspective that is visible in Ambedkar's writings.

77   Ambedkar's description of him in the preface to the 1948 edition of Narasu's, *The Essence of Buddhism,* is dramatic but perhaps apt: "Professor Narasu ... fought European arrogance with patriotic fervor, orthodox Hinduism with iconoclastic zeal, heterodox Brahmins with a nationalist vision and aggressive Christianity with a rationalistic outlook, all under the inspiring banner of ... the teaching of the great Buddha" (Narasu [1907] 1948: viii).

78   This kind of hyper-rationalized interpretation of the *Kalama Sutta* has been well critiqued by Bodhi (2010).

79   Nor were his interpretations of Buddhism highly regarded by more critically-minded academics. See, for instance, the devastating critique of Narasu's *The Essence of Buddhism* leveled by the noted Orientalist Louis de la Vallée Poussin (1913: 579–80).

80   Compare the transcript printed by the *MBJ* Vol. 36/7 (1928) as "The third South Indian Buddhist Congress" (329–32), with the same transcript printed as the "South Indian Buddhist Conference," in *ISR,* Vol. 38 (1927–28), 584–86. Numerous omissions in the *MBJ* reprint were clearly intentional edits that had nothing to do with space.

81   These kinds of tensions would appear again when Ambedkar (2011) made similar claims in his *The Buddha and His Dhamma.*

82   I am thankful to Gajendran Ayyathurai for translating Thass's essay.

83   The full details of this case (#OS 2736 of 1981 and # CS 274 of 1980) are beyond the scope of this book, but the gist of the problem (from the Maha Bodhi Society's perspective) is outlined in articles published in *MBJ* Volumes 40–43 (1932–34).

84   Bose, who is now often hailed as the "father of Indian modernism," trained under Tagore and had already spent several months painting Buddhist murals and images at Bagh and Ajanta in 1909 and again in 1921. The murals at the Nandan museum in Santiniketan were inspired by both these Buddhist sites. Many of Tagore's other students, like Asit Kumar Haldar and Kalipada Ghoshal, continued to represent the Buddhist past in art, architecture, and iconography, although, like the Tagores themselves, it was never numerically dominant. See Ray (2014: 228–33).

85   There is a certain irony in that some later scholars, like Rahul Sankrityayan, were deeply critical of Buddhist tantra and Mahayana devotionalism, and yet held Mahayana scholasticism in the highest regard, seeing it as the pinnacle of Indian thought.

86   Several of the speeches from this event were published in *MBJ* Vol. 33/1 and

2 (1925). According to these records, nearly two hundred senior monks from across the Bay of Bengal, along with two thousand lay devotees, attended the six-day conference from 6 to 12 December 1924. The purpose was to unify the various nikayas, and on 8 December 1924, a resolution was passed that all the monastics could perform Vinayaic activities together, and that they establish a new *sima* (sacred boundary for monastic ordination). However, the appeal for unity collapsed shortly after the convention's close. The wider significance of this event merits further study.

87   The prominent social reformer, V.R. Shinde (1873–1944), was similarly ambivalent about the Three Refuges, having declared himself a Buddhist in the 1920s. He was unwilling to take refuge in the dhamma or sangha, and only did so in the Buddha (Zelliot 1979: 397–98). Ambedkar had similar doubts about the sangha in the build-up to his public conversion in 1956 (Sangharakshita ([1986] 2006: 136).

88   Wadia was also close colleagues with Singaravelu and served as another link between the left-leaning union organizers, theosophists, and the Buddhist intelligentsia.

89   For earlier references to women's conferences in the Bengal Buddhist Association, see "Bauddha Sammilani," *MBJ* Vol. 11/7 (1902–03), 127–28.

90   He took the idea from Caroline Rhys Davids. The *Therigatha* is regarded by many scholars as the first body of literature ever composed by women. The poems are remarkable, highlighting women's perspectives on the ancient world and arguing unabashedly for the spiritual equality of men and women. The most widely consulted translation in India was undoubtedly Caroline Rhys Davids's English edition, *Psalms of the Early Buddhists* (1909).

91   Not that all of Narasu's contemporaries believed in the possibilities immanent in Burmese Buddhism. An important skeptic was Thass's brother-in-law, Rettamalai Srinivasan (1860–1945), the famed dalit activist who later worked closely with Gandhi. Srinivasan also accompanied Ambedkar to the Round Table Conferences but did not endorse the latter's decision to convert. According to an anonymous reviewer of this book, Srinivasan was equally critical of Tamil Buddhists, "arguing that the Burmese Buddhists with their vast and rich monasteries were hardly different from the Brahmins with their temples."

Chapter 4

1   Dharmapala also reportedly donated a thousand rupees to the Maha Sabha.

2   Although tailoring one's message is by no means the exclusive domain of Buddhists, it is important to recognize that this also has clear roots in the Buddhist concept of skillful means (*upaya*).

3   If one were to accept the terms of this debate, it would have to be said that Hinduism was a product of its encounter with Buddhism. Several Indian scholars from P.S. Jaini and Nalinaksa Dutt to B.M. Barua and Kashinath Upadhyaya made this argument many decades before. The driving force behind this argument today is Bronkhorst (2011).

4   And, of course, a substantial portion of what is now known as Hinduism is

the contribution of non-Vedic traditions like Buddhism and Jainism, Yoga and Samkhya, just as those traditions have been deeply shaped by Vedic brahmanical traditions. Nathan McGovern (2018) has suggested that these terms, brahmanical and non-brahmanical, are of little use in the ancient context, reflecting discourses that later Indic traditions and contemporary scholars imposed upon the past. McGovern's argument, compelling as it is, does not change the wider fact that over the course of time these traditions came to see each other as being in opposition, and as is so often the case in history, it is what one believes happened, rather than what actually happened, that comes to matter most.

5   For an excellent overview of the Buddhist–brahmanical interface, see the Special Issue of *Religions of South Asia* on "Representations of Brahmins and Brahmanism in Early Buddhist Literature," edited by Black (2009). Specialized studies make evident that although Buddhists shared a common vocabulary and set of practices with Hindus, they were distinct in innumerable ways. In addition to the Hindu politics discussed in this chapter, this distinctiveness has also been lost under the less than convincing trope of Hindu inclusivity, made famous by Paul Hacker. For two trenchant critiques, see Verardi (2011, Chapter 1), and Sanderson (2015).

6   It should be remembered that terms of identity for Buddhists were not colonial neologisms but were widely used in pre-colonial India as well. These included bauddha, saugata, prakata saugata ("explicit Buddhists," as opposed to pracchannna bauddha/saugata or "hidden Buddhists"), an expression used in polemics to denigrate Advaita Vedantins whose arguments sounded too Buddhist, or more literally had the "smell of Buddhists".

7   The exact phrasing of this passage actually changes in various editions of this work and becomes less emphatic over time. For instance, in the 1912 edition (p. 83), the passage reads: "Gautama was born, and brought up, and lived, and died a typical Indian. Hinduism had not yet, in his time, arisen."

8   But Vivekananda was astute, and like his Buddhist contemporary, Dharmapala, he offered a different vision for every audience. When in Europe and the USA, he often lavished praise on the Buddha, but when lecturing among Hindu audiences at home in India, he was deeply critical of not only Buddhists but also of the Buddha. His problems with Buddhism were many but most were doctrinally charged. According to Jyotirmaya Sharma (2013), three major issues stuck out: 1) the Buddha's disavowal of caste—for Vivekananda was firm in his belief that all individuals should adhere to their *svadharma* (Sharma 2013: 219); 2) the Buddha's "sectarianism" (for rejecting the Vedas and creating a new Hindu "sect"); and 3) the Theravadin Buddhist "denial of a noumenal world and their avowal of a phenomenal world" (Sharma 2013: 231–32).

9   The establishment of influential Muslim organizations and the Islamic ferment during the Khilafat movement had an equal bearing, galvanizing Hindu communal organizations into an aggressive, defensive action against the Muslim "other" (Jaffrelot 1996: 11–36).

10   Only decades prior, the Maha Sabha had claimed to represent "the whole of the orthodox classes of the Hindus in India," but now it claimed to represent "the united voice of the Hindu nation" (Zavos 2001: 120).

11 Being an atheist himself, Savarkar felt that religion was only one aspect of Hindutva and "not even the most important one". See Bapu (2013: 62).

12 Savarkar used the term "jati" for "race", a people "determined by a common origin and possessing common blood." This meant that although Indian Christians and Muslims had abandoned India, since they had Aryan blood, they could return to "their long lost kith and kin" by "re-converting" to an Aryan religion (quoted in Bapu 2013: 70).

13 The temple was the brainchild of B. Shiva Prasad Gupta, the owner of the Gyan Mandal, one of the most important Hindi presses in north India, and the Hindu Sanskritist Babu Raghava Das. See *ISR* Vol. 47/9, 1936: 130–31.

14 See, for instance, the *Naradiya Purana* I. 15. 50–52: "A *brahmana* who enters a Buddhist temple even in a time of great calamity cannot get rid of the sin by means of hundreds of expiations since the Buddhists are heretical critics of the sacred *Vedas*" (quoted in Holt 2005: 10).

15 These passages come from HDPB, File no. 198, Part B.

16 *ISR*, 25 August 1923, in "Newspaper Extracts related to Hindu Maha Sabha," Government of India, Home Department: Political Branch, File no. 198, Part B, National Archives of India.

17 The expression *arkabandhu* or "friend of the Sun" could also refer to Shakyamuni's Solar lineage.

18 A significant portion of their argument rests on the notion that the Bhagavad Gita predated the Buddha's teachings. Such a chronology is largely unaccepted today, and some scholars even argue that significant sections of the Bhagavad Gita were composed in response to the ascendancy of Buddhism. For the seminal study in this vein, see Upadhyaya (1968).

19 This, they contend, is based on the extensive number of ritual mantras where the Buddha's name is recited. These include the *Buddha Pratahsmaranam* or early-morning salutation to the Buddha in the *Garuda Purana* (2.31.35), the *Buddha Dhyanam* or meditation on him in the *Agni Purana* (49.8), the *Buddha Bratapuja* in the *Varaha Purana* (49), the *Buddha Gayatri* or Vedic formula of address to the Buddha in the *Linga Purana* (2.48.28–33), and *Buddha Namaskarah* or salutation to the Buddha in the *Meru Tantra* (Maitreya and Yogiraja 1924: 27–30).

20 A near-identical argument was propounded by Pandit Shyama Shankar, the private secretary to the maharaja of Jhalawar, in his *Buddha and His Sayings, with Comments on Re-incarnation, Karma, Nirvana, etc.* (1914). Shankar argued that early Buddhism had been completely transformed by its foreign practitioners and that early Buddhists worshipped Brahma as the supreme god and believed in a soul (atman).

21 It is possible that Gandhi's more offensive tone during the 1925 Vesak was meant to appease the uproar among Sanatan Dharmists during the latest round of discussion on the Maha Bodhi temple at the All-India Hindu Maha Sabha just months before.

22 See also, Gandhi's "Reply to Buddhists" Address, Colombo, 15 November 1927, in *CWMG* Vol. 40: 367–72.

23 Even by the end of 1926, more than 200 of its 362 branches were in the northern provinces (Bapu 2013: 23–24).

24   Its wider membership included numerous caste associations made of rajputs and jats, talukdars (landed classes), banking magnates, and the nobility of several Hindu princely states. While many of these figures were early supporters of the Congress, the differences were apparent. The Maha Sabha felt that the Congress had not only failed to protect upper-caste Hindu interests in the legislature but was too "soft" on Islam, which it saw as the primary threat to its imagined Hindu nation. Under the growing influence of V.D. Savarkar, the Maha Sabha's once cozy relationship with the Congress began to unravel in the late 1920s, before coming to a tumultuous end in 1938 when the Congress declared the Maha Sabha a "communal organization" and banned its members from holding dual membership in the group.

25   A copy of this report is available in *MBJ* Vol. 34/1, 1926: 2–50. It is notable that three of the committee's four members would later have a profound impact on modern Buddhism. There was the Bihari Congressman, Rajendra Prasad, who later became independent India's first president and was a major force behind the Nehruvian state's uses of Buddhism. Then there was K.P. Jayaswal, one of the foremost historians of ancient India and head of the Bihar and Orissa Research Society. Lastly, and most importantly, was Rahul Sankrityayan, the pioneering historian, travel writer, and manuscript-hunter. During the committee meeting, Sankrityayan was still known by his Hindu name, Sadhu Ramodar Das. Three years later his Sinhalese Buddhist preceptor gave him robes (*cīvara*) as a bhikkhu and a new identity as Rahul Sankrityayan.

26   Mookerjee's father, Asutosh, was president of the Maha Bodhi Society from 1916 to 1924 and also one of the driving forces behind the institutionalization of Buddhist studies at Calcutta University in the early 1900s during his tenure as vice chancellor.

27   For instance, when Dharmapala attended the World Parliament in Chicago, he opened his first speech, which had been drafted by Hikkaduve Sumangala, by explaining that Buddhists are followers of a single "arya dharma, miscalled Buddhism by Western scholars." Quoted in Snodgrass (2003: 84).

28   According to a study conducted by *Forbes Magazine* in 2007, the scion of the Birla family, Kumar Birla, is the eighth wealthiest individual in India and the eighty-sixth wealthiest in the world with a net worth of eight billion US dollars (Karmali 2007). In 1919, the branches of the old business, "Baldeodas Jugalkishore," were amalgamated into the Birla Brothers Limited, with the effective management turning to Ghanshyam Das (1893–1984), JK's younger and more well-known brother. See, Kudaisya (2003: 48).

29   The Devanagari or Hindi–Nagari movement was an organized political effort beginning in mid-nineteenth century colonial India aimed at enshrining Hindi and the Devanagari script as India's official state language and script. Best exemplified by the popular political slogan "Hindu, Hindi, Hindustan," the movement helped solidify the notion that Hindi language was intimately connected to the Hindu religion and Hindu nation (King 1994). Cow protection movements coalesced in colonial India during the same time. Led by a spectrum of religious leaders, but most notably Mahatma Gandhi and the Arya Samaj founder, Dayanand Sarasvati, it aimed to ban the slaughter of cows—whose killing was largely opposed by Hindu, Jain, and Sikh

communities—at the expense of many Muslim and so-called untouchable communities whose livelihoods were often tied to cattle rearing and slaughter. The issue of cow protection was a source of immense religio-political antagonism and violence, especially between Hindus and Muslims, and it remains so into the twenty-first century. Although the movement is primarily associated with India, cow protection was and still is a significant issue in the neighbouring Buddhist countries of Myanmar (Burma) and Sri Lanka (Ceylon). Buddhists in colonial India were largely supportive of the cow protection measures.

30   It is noteworthy that they were also behind the publication of the journalist Baburao Vishnu Paradikar's *Tikawali Gita* in 1914. This Hindi-language translation of the Bhagavad Gita was one of the most popular Hindi books of the decade, gaining much of its notoriety and controversy due to its cover picture of Mother India (Bharat Mata) with the Gita in one hand and a sword in the other. The book was eventually banned by the British government on the basis that it incited violence.

31   According to Kudaisya (2003: 105), in the late 1920s, GD began to move away from Malaviya and the Hindutva ideologues, feeling that their politics were too sectarian and injurious to constitutional progress. After the 1932 Round Table Conference, when Malaviya's position on the minorities question differed from Gandhi's, GD severed all political links with Malaviya, although they maintained a close family bond. JK, on the other hand, continued to support Malaviya's projects, including providing him with a monthly allowance of Rs 3,000. After Gandhi was assassinated by a member of the Maha Sabha, which led Nehru to arrest more than 25,000 of its members (Kudaisya 2003: 269), JK's support for right-wing Hinduism came under increasing scrutiny. When JK tried to persuade his younger brother to release some of his friends who had been jailed by Nehru, his brother responded, "I don't know why you believe that they have been propagating Sanatana Dharma. They have been propagating some sort of *Shaitan* [Satan] Dharma" (270).

32   There remain some questions regarding this donation. Ray (2014: 114–15) reports that he donated the money for the construction, but Birla's name is nowhere to be found on the temple inscription of major donors—and his Rs 5,000 donation would have certainly been entered there since it would have made him the third largest donor after Mary Foster and Dharmapala. Only in the 1933 volume of the *MBJ* (Vol. 41/12 (1933), 527–28), is Birla ever listed as a donor for the Dharmarajika vihara, and while the language is vague, it seems to indicate he gave the money during the event (or shortly thereafter) in order to fund the vihara's *expansion*. It is unclear when JK first took an interest in Buddhism, although his presence in Calcutta and the family connections with Japanese Buddhist merchants may have sparked such ties. On Japanese corporate involvement in 1920s India, see Jaffe (2019: 114–50).

33   Much of his support for publishing Buddhist scriptures was conducted via the Maha Bodhi Society's Hindi Translation Fund, which in turn supported the researches of the three most prolific Indian Buddhist bhikkhu scholars— Rahul Sankrityayan, Anand Kausalyayan, and Jagdish Kashyap. He also regularly covered the "entertainment expenses" at the Mulagandhakuti

vihara celebrations and was a major financer of Professor Tan Yun Shan's Sino-Indian Cultural Society at Tagore's Visva-Bharati University, whose primary researches concerned Chinese and Indian Buddhism.

34   This list is not exhaustive and only includes the most well-known and/or relevant Buddhist projects that JK and the Birlas financed. For instance, not included in the list are the many Buddha images that the Birlas donated to temples across the country. I have also excluded the Birlas' involvement in the Darjeeling and local Chinese Buddhist scene since much of this activity has been difficult to trace in any precise detail.

35   In *Untouchable Freedom,* Vijay Prashad (2000: 104–06, 129–217) describes a similar strategy in the Birla family's construction of Hindu temples among valmikis, an untouchable caste in northern India. According to Joel Lee (2021: 170), in the fifty years since G.D. Birla provided funds for the first valmiki temple in Lucknow in 1956, "another ten Valmiki temples and statues would be erected in the city, all funded and inaugurated by privileged caste Hindu politicians of the Congress, and later, the Bharatiya Janata Party (BJP): mayors, cabinet ministers, governors, and even a prime minister."

36   This is discussed in further detail in the next chapter.

37   Such resolutions had been in vogue at Maha Sabha committee meetings since the early- to mid-1920s.

38   I am indebted to Padma Dorje Maitland for his careful reading of these images, the further details of which are outlined in our forthcoming essay (Ober and Maitland) in *Comparative Studies in South Asia, Africa, and the Middle East.*

39   In 1947, Moonje paid tribute to J.K. Birla, singling him out in the family for being "unique" in that his "charities are almost entirely concerned with the cause of Hindus" (quoted in Kudaisya 2003: 255fn93)

40   Although Jainism is also linked to ahimsa, it seems that Buddhism monopolized discussions in the historical imagination of the national elite.

41   Moonje regularly castigated Buddhism for ruining India and entered into several long debates with Buddhists and scholars of Buddhism on this issue (see: *MBJ* Vol. 43/9, 1935: 457; Vol. 43/10, 1935: 487–89; Vol. 45/10, 1937: 471; Vol. 46/6, 1938: 266–71). For Savarkar, the "first degeneration of the Hindu nation" occurred when Ashoka "strangled India" through his propagation of "non-violence, righteousness and toleration". This allowed the Huns and Scythians who were superior in "fire and sword" to destroy the formerly "magnificent empire of Chandragupta" and strip away India's "manhood for centuries" (quoted in Bapu 2013: 64).

42   One way this played out was in his and his father's long history of charitable support for cow sanctuaries and bird refuges. See Kudaisya 2003: 41.

43   This included Kalidas Nag, the Greater India Society's first president and later editor of the *Maha Bodhi*, the linguists P.C. Bagchi and Suniti Kumar Chatterji, both members of the Maha Bodhi Society, and Sameer Chandra Mookerjee, who regularly contributed to the *Maha Bodhi*.

44   In early-twentieth-century India, scholars like Satish Chandra Vidyabhusan and Sarat Chandra Das often argued that Buddhism was a missionary force

that spread Indo-Aryan culture. For a critical review of this idea, see Walters (1992) and Learman (2004).

45   Kausalyayan was a former Arya Samaji who under Sankrityayan's influence traveled to Lanka in 1928 to study Pali and ordain under Venerable Lunupokne Dhammananda of the Vidyalankara Pirivena. Through Dharmapala's London Buddhist Mission, Kausalyayan taught Buddhism in Europe for two years before returning to India where he became an outspoken Buddhist activist–monk, noted as much for his ultra-nationalilst Nagari stance (which brought him into close contact with many right-wing Hindus) as his polemical criticisms of Vedic and brahmanical culture (which simultaneously put him at odds with right-wing Hindus). From 1941 to 1951, he was the general secretary of the Rashtrabhasha Prachar Samiti, which propagated a Sanskritized Hindi in contrast to Gandhi's Hindustani. After Ambedkar's conversion in 1956, Kausalyayan became one of the dalit movement's most energetic Buddhist activists. On Kausalyayan, see Medhankar (2002).

46   Bombay was in fact the first site of action for Fuji with a "seminary"—essentially a thatched hut—established there in 1932. Sometime between 1935 and 1940, a foundation was eventually laid for what came to be a small but impressive temple built in the same architectural style as the other Birla temples. The temple quarters in the rear of the current structure was complete by 1940 but when Fuji and several of his colleagues were imprisoned or deported at the beginning of the World War II, the remainder of the temple's construction ceased. It was officially inaugurated only in 1956.

47   On Ottama, see Mendelson (1975: 202–04).

48   For summary accounts of the Buddhist motifs and symbols, like the "Gautama Gate" at the Maha Sabha's Nagpur convention in 1938, see *BP* Vol. 7/1, 1939: 1059–61. As far as I am aware, Ottama was the only Buddhist bhikkhu to ever be elected president of the All-India Hindu Maha Sabha. But other monastics, like Bhikkhu Nyanasir of the New Delhi vihara, served as the president of the New Delhi branch of the Hindu Maha Sabha (see, *MBJ* Vol. 47/11, 1939: 521).

49   According to the *MBJ* (Vol. 44/12, 1936: 548–57), the plot of land was acquired by a group of Barua Buddhists living in New Delhi, with Sarbananda Barua the driving force. On Sarbananda Barua, see *MBJ* (Vol. 43/12, 1935: 605). While traveling through India in 2014–15, I was also told by different individuals from across India that Ambedkar was responsible for inspiring Birla to build the temple. An allusion to this is found in Kausalyayan (1968: 117–18), who reports that Ambedkar criticized Birla for failing to build a more appropriate shrine for a figure of the Buddha's stature.

50   Gandhi entered both temples and was then "virtually held prisoner for nearly an hour" as garlands were tossed into the temple from the sidewalk.

51   During the laying of the foundation stone on 31 October 1936, approximately thirty leaders, including Bhai Parmanand (of the Maha Sabha), J.K. Birla, Devapriya Valisinha (general secretary, Maha Bodhi Society), Bhikkhu Maruyama (Japan), Bhikkhu Anand Kausalyayan (India), Lt Col Ramsher Jung (Nepal), and the consul general of Japan, Konezawa, held a "tea party" at the Maha Sabha headquarters, located on the other side of the Birla temple.

52 The history of the All-India Buddhist Society (AIBS) illustrates the influence of the Maha Sabha quite well. The AIBS regularly petitioned the colonial state for Buddhist representation in provincial affairs, but as was the norm throughout its short lifespan, these petitions were mostly rejected by government officials. In response, the AIBS turned to the Maha Sabha for assistance, since the organization had a larger political footprint and clout, and by 1933, AIBS memoranda and requests were being sent via the Hindu Maha Sabha's office in New Delhi. See, letter no. 5450, dated 13 November 1933, in HDPB no. 332 (1933).

53 Sanchi too provided a model for Mayawati's memorials to anti-caste leaders at the massive Ambedkar Memorial Park in Lucknow, opened in 2008 (Belli 2014). Like the Birla-funded projects discussed above, these projects also sought to re-territorialize the nation. But, rather than construct a vision of India as a Hindu nation, they imagined it as a site for a new Buddhist republic.

54 This is an English translation of his Hindi article that originally appeared in *Vishvamitra*, a popular Hindi weekly from Calcutta.

55 Gandhi's reaction and further context is discussed in Ober (2013: 139–40).

56 See, "Tape 176: My Eight Main Teachers," by Sangharakshita, available at https://www.freebuddhistaudio.com/texts/lecturetexts/176_My_Eight_Main_Teachers.pdf. Sanghrakshita studied under Kashyap at BHU in 1949–50.

57 See, for instance, Kausalyayan (1937), where he describes Sanatan Dharma as a cheap religion (*sasta dharma*) and the source of our slavery (*hamari gulami*).

58 Bhikshu Morita, head of the Bombay (Worli) Nipponzon Myohoji Mandir, personal communication, 27 February 2015.

59 A leading advocate in the Lahore High Court, Sheo Narain was also the President of the Punjab Historical Society for many years. Best remembered today for his scholarship on Persian and Urdu literature, he was also a prolific essayist, which were frequently authored under his pen-name "Shamin." His turn to Buddhism began in the late 1880s when he launched a study of comparative religion and "came to the conclusion that Buddhism will suit my requirements as the best of all religions" (Narain 1933: 259). Over the course of the next several decades, Narain published some two dozen essays on Buddhism in English in addition to numerous essays and books in Urdu. This included a 200-page Urdu work on *Buddha and His Teachings* (the Urdu title is unknown), that he self-published in 1900 (for reviews published in the *Tribune, Punjab Observer,* and *Indian Mirror,* see MBJ Vol. 9/7, 1900–01: 119). He and Dharmapala were also close colleagues. After Sheo Narain retired, he built a small cottage in Sarnath, and eventually donated much of his private library to the Maha Bodhi Society. Much of that collection is now found in Sarnath's Mulagandhakuti vihara library.

Chapter 5

1 Although Ambedkar had known of Chandramani for over a decade, it was only a month before that he approached the revered Arakanese bhikkhu

from Kushinagar to serve as his dhamma preceptor. See, "Letter 177," in Ambedkar (1993: 192).

2   This is not to say that all of the ritual practices and settings were identical, only that these kinds of conversion events were far from novel. Of course, the sheer size and scope of Ambedkar's conversion was unprecedented in Buddhist history. For a summary of the 1956 conversion ceremony, see Beltz (2005: 55–58),

3   Most of the new Buddhists were mahars, although the movement also briefly gained momentum among urban jatavs (chamars) in western UP, particularly in Agra (Lynch 1969: 129–65).

4   The total number of Buddhists listed in the 1961 census was 3,250,227 with 2,789,501 of those in Maharashtra. The number of dalits who actually took diksha is undoubtedly much larger, but due to the loss of scheduled caste "privileges" that occurred in becoming Buddhist, significant numbers did not report their conversion. See Zelliot (2013: 172–73, 207–09).

5   That teacher (and the author of the text) was K.A. Keluskar, a prominent social reformer in Maharashtra who remained close friends with Ambedkar until the end of his life.

6   On the Nashik statement, see Keer ([1971] 2009: 261–65).

7   The Bahujan Samaj Party was founded in 1984 by the dalit politician Kanshi Ram. The party's use of the term bahujan generally refers to scheduled castes, scheduled tribes, other backward castes (OBC), and other minority groups.

8   The passage comes from the *Mahavagga* of the *Vinaya Pitaka*.

9   My use of the term to denote both categories does not mean there was necessarily any sense of shared identity and unity between or among these various bahujan populaces, although attempts to mobilize and organize these communities were frequently made, including by the Buddhist activists examined in this chapter. Rather, the bahujan populace was composed of various groups, marked by numerous differences, including but not limited to caste, language, ethnicity, and religion.

10 The term scheduled caste encompasses various untouchable groups and was first used in the early 1900s. Another common administrative category is "depressed classes". The term scheduled castes became more popular in the 1940s through the rise of Ambedkar's Scheduled Caste Federation and after the Scheduled Caste Order of 1950, which was meant to reserve government jobs and benefits for this group.

11 Gandhi dubbed untouchables as harijans, or children of god, a term that many find patronizing. Dalit, a term popularized by Ambedkar's followers and which literally means "oppressed or ground down," is the name currently used by most former untouchables with Ambedkarite leanings. Achoot, literally "untouched". is generally conceived today as a deeply offensive and pejorative term, although it should be recognized that many north Indian dalits attempted to reinvent the term as a symbol of pride and purity in the mid-twentieth century (Rawat 2015).

12 There is a vast body of literature on caste (see Rao 2009 for a comprehensive review), but perhaps its most poignant and systematic critique occurs in Ambedkar ([1936] 2014).

13   The text was included as a part of Tukaram's *Jatibhed Viveksar* [A Critique of Caste Divisions] (1865). For a summary of this text, see O'Hanlon (1985: 42–45). Tukaram later became an important leader of the Bombay Theosophical Society in the 1880s and 1890s.

14   In another demonstration of the *MBJ*'s censorship of touchy subjects, Bodhananda's speech was not mentioned in their report on the event.

15   The journal ceased publication in July 1940 and restarted in 1941. In the late 1950s, the journal also included a Marathi-language section, clearly aimed at its new mahar audience with roughly four to five articles each month. It is still published today but only on an annual basis and in a bilingual Hindi–English format. Its early editors were mostly monastics, including Sangharatana (1912–84, b. Ceylon), Dharmarakshita (1923–77, b. India), Dharmajyoti (dates unknown), Anand Kausalyayan (1905–88, b. India), Sasanasiri (1899–1966, b. Ceylon), and Dhammaratana (1917–85, b. Ceylon). Brief biographical entries on several of these monastics are found in Lal (2004).

16   Other contributors also included prominent Hindi litterateurs like Sohanlal Dwivedi and Hazari Prasad Dwivedi.

17   These letters were republished in book form as Kausalyayan (1940).

18   One of the most well-known "Hindu–Buddhist" reformers—and a colleague of Ambedkar's—was the barefoot upasaka and brahmin, A.R. Kulkarni. After founding the Buddha Society in Nagpur in 1944, Kulkarni gave up his legal practice, and combined his mastery of the pen with an itinerant lifestyle, to preach Buddhism at Hindu pilgrimage sites across north and central India. Significantly, Kulkarni's Buddha Society was an important base for dalit activists and intellectuals growing up in Nagpur in the 1940s. In Kulkarni's vision, to become a Buddhist, "it was only necessary to accept the teaching of Lord Buddha in the heart, to abide by the Five Precepts and to honour the Buddha, the Dhamma and the Sangha." Although some of the Buddha Society's clientele found Kulkarni's "Hindu–Buddhist" identity paradoxical, his lucid explanations of Buddhist doctrine in Hindi, Marathi, and English alongside arguments of why "Buddhism is the only hope for the Depressed Classes of India" undoubtedly did a tremendous amount to popularize Buddhism among a wider audience (*MBJ* Vol. 56/12, 1949: 414–15).

19   For instance, during Periyar's celebration of the Buddha Jayanti on 27 May 1953, he led his followers in the smashing of Ganesha statues before the Town Hall in Tiruchirappalli. A court case was filed against Periyar and two of his companions, although in the final judgement, the act was not considered an offence to religious sensibilities (Section 295 of the Indian Penal Code) because they only broke images that they themselves made or bought and not those worshipped in a temple. See Aloysius (2006).

20   There were, however, distinct differences between those izhavas who lived in British Malabar and those who lived in the princely states of Travancore and Cochin, where caste oppression was often said to be some of the most severe in the subcontinent.

21   Krishnan's home was also located on Paran Square, which was a major hub in early twentieth-century Kerala for progressive intellectuals, artists, and political activists. The various organizations housed there, including

a women's club, the Empire Printing Press, and a public library, are representative of his diverse public engagements.

22 Jinarajadasa was president of the Theosophical Society from 1946 to 1953 and had long been involved in South Asian Buddhist affairs. He was also a builder of Buddhist temples, including the Buddhist structure at Adyar in 1925. In many ways, he represented the emerging new-age characteristics of theosophy but also the end of a theosophical era in which Buddhism occupied the pivotal role. (On his life, see Srinivas 2015: 50–86.)

23 In his words, "Hinduism is a religion which is not founded on morality. Whatever morality Hinduism has it is not an integral part of it" (Ambedkar 1950: 118).

24 He continues: "The bulk of the converts to Buddhism are from the Nair caste, but after the final disappearance of Buddhism they are grouped along with the Ilavas [izhavas] and thus the number of the Ilava [izhava] community swelled up. This accounts for the close resemblance between the Nair and the Ilava [izhava] communities in social customs, religious practices, etc." (Alexander 1949: 134–35).

25 See, for instance, the pamphlets distributed by the district judge, Ayyakutti, who was also vice president of the Kerala Buddhist Association, in "Not Hindus but Buddhists: Appeal from Cochin," *MBJ* Vol. 34/12, 1926: 606–07. The izhava claim to a Buddhist past may have also been motivated by caste tensions with nayars (nairs), who although classified as shudras, were seen by some izhavas as a group that had collaborated with brahmins and were therefore rewarded with a higher status, although still clearly lower than the ruling elites. See also Kumar (2014).

26 On Ananda Maitreya, see Gombrich and Obeysekere (1988: 299–313). They describe him as "undoubtedly one of the leading figures of contemporary Buddhism," and as a "model of Buddhist character and learning". Maitreya had earlier studied and taught at Ananda College in Colombo, Ceylon (originally founded in 1891 by Olcott's Buddhist Theosophical Society).

27 According to the *MBJ* Vol. 45/8, 1937: 383, the mission is "chiefly financed by Birlaji".

28 On the relationship between Ambedkar and Gandhi, particularly as it related to the Round Table Conferences and Poona Pact, see Lelyveld (2011: 208–40), and Guha (2018: 421–47).

29 He also used these opportunities to dispute the idea that the Buddha was an atheist and to criticize meat-eating and the killing of animals for human consumption in Sri Lanka.

30 This was despite his own admission that "probably, a fifth-form boy from Nalanda Vidyalaya would plough me in a Buddhist catechism" (Speech presented at the Vidyodaya College, 15 November 1927, in *CWMG* Vol. 40: 370).

31 By the mid-1930s, however, when the Hindu Maha Sabha's transformation from a reformist Hindu organization to a radical political party was near complete, its new leadership, led by figures like Savarkar and Bhai Parmanand, saw Buddhism as an acceptable "national" alternative to the "de-nationalizing" religions of Christianity and Islam (Jaffrelot 2005: 136–37).

32 My primary source for the life of Bodhananda is Jigyasu (1965). After

Bodhananda's death in 1952, several short obituaries also appeared in the *MBJ*, the most useful of which is *MBJ* Vol. 60/8, 1952: 286–89.

33   Some later accounts and researchers have reported that Dharmapala was also present during this ceremony. However, it is very curious that it is not reported in Dharmapala's diaries nor in the *MBJ*, since the journal regularly advertised its newest "converts" and would have certainly publicized such an event.

34   When the prominent British Buddhist, B.L. Broughton, visited Bodhananda at his vihara in 1931, he described him as "an Indian bhikkhu of strikingly noble appearance...[who] is moved to tears when, in his addresses he contrasts the glorious days of Buddhism with its present state." See *MBJ* Vol. 39/8, 1931: 358.

35   The society's early activities are difficult to determine but by the 1920s it was regularly holding lectures in Hindustani, distributing free Buddhist literature in Urdu and Hindi, and organizing community service projects among orphaned children and the urban poor. For instance, during the Buddha Jayanti of May 1928, free copies of the *Dhammapada* in Hindi and Urdu were distributed and there were three "well attended" Hindustani lectures on "Buddha and Buddhism," "Buddhism in Daily Life," "Three Refuges and five Moral Precepts," along with two English lectures on "Lord Buddha" and the "Four Aryan Truths". The first three lectures were delivered by Shiva Charan Lal and his son Ganga Charan Lal, the former of whom was also the first president of the All-India Buddhist Society. See, letter from Ganga Charan Lal, secretary to the "Bharatiya Buddha Sangha," published in *MBJ* Vol. 36/12, 1928: 464–65.

36   For an insightful study of the social and political world these communities inhabited, see Gooptu (2001), and on Lucknow in particular, see Duncan (2020).

37   Jigyasu was arguably the most important anti-caste publisher and pamphleteer in north India during the mid-twentieth century. On Hindi dalit publishing, with much discussion on Jigyasu's importance, see Hunt (2014: 4–131).

38   In 1947, Bodhananda also produced a popular manual on Buddhist rituals (*Bauddh-carya-padhdhati,* Lucknow: Buddh Vihar, 1947), which after Ambedkar's conversion was republished in multiple editions (including a Marathi translation).

39   It is important to recognize that although Bodhananda pursued the same emancipatory ideology as Swami Achutanand and the other Adi-Hindu/Adi-Dravida activists, his inclusion of both shudras and dalits in this category was more unique. While this may appear to be a trivial matter, in the politics of the moment, such an argument was rare. Relationships between and among so-called low-caste and untouchable communities were then, as they still often are, characterized by large degrees of tension and mistrust. Bodhananda's writing of the history of *both* groups together can be seen as an effort to reach a broader base and mobilize a larger bahujan consciousness.

40   Bodhananda clearly locates this original path in the sramanic traditions and while he often describes it as Buddhism and Jainism (*buddh aur jain*

dharm), detailed references to Jainism are extremely rare. This could have been a consequence of his own preference for Buddhism or simply a lack of knowledge about Jain traditions. In any case, the implicit meaning of the text is clear: the religion of the ancient Indians is Buddhism.

41 The reference to "The Light of Asia" is clearly an ode to Edwin Arnold. Bodhananda remarks that foreign scholars (*videshi vidyanom*) accept the Buddha as the Light of Asia (*Asia ke jnanalok ka surya*) or literally the "Sun of Asia's Wisdom" (57).

42 Several became the north Indian torch-bearers of dalit–bahujan movements of later years. These included Chandrika Prasad Jigyasu, the founder of the popular Bahujan Kalyan Prakashan or Common People's Welfare Press; Raisaheb Ramcharan, the prominent dalit politician and advocate; and Lal Chedi Sathi, the founder of the UP branch of the Republican Party of India. See also Duncan (2020).

43 According to Singh (in Bodhananda 2009: 183), during one of Ambedkar's visits to the Lucknow vihara in the 1940s, the latter expressed his frustration at not being able to acquire a copy of Lakshmi Narasu's *The Essence of Buddhism*, the text that he republished with his own introduction in 1948. The book was apparently out of print, and Bodhananda supplied him with his own copy.

44 This was contained in a letter from Ambedkar to Subhedar Savadkar in spring 1933.

45 Although not a Buddhist, Gour, who was the former mayor of Nagpur, and Delhi University's first vice chancellor (1922–29), had in 1929 also published a 650-page study of Buddhism entitled *The Spirit of Buddhism*. He was also a regular contributor to the *Maha Bodhi* in the 1930s. In the 1920s and 1930s, the Nationalist Party—not to be confused with the Indian National Congress—was the main opposition in the Central Legislative Assembly.

46 Some conclusions have certainly been based more on speculation than on fact. For instance, Deslippe's (2013) argument that the Brooklyn-born bhikkhu, Lokanatha, was "a catalyst to perhaps the largest mass religious conversion in modern history" (176) is spurious and seems like little more than a desperate attempt to bolster Lokanatha's legacy.

47 Although the precise details of their conversation are not known, it shows that Ambedkar was aware that the Bombay Buddha Society already managed a Buddhist space, Ananda vihara, located in the grounds of Nair's hospital. So Ambedkar's suggestion can only have meant that the vihara was either too inaccessible to the general public or, more likely, too elite and Hindu in its orientation, being frequented primarily by upper-caste Hindu reformers.

48 Eventually Kosambi resigned from the temple after a disagreement with J.K. Birla over the role of violence in Hindu scriptures and culture. See, Ober (2013: 139–40).

49 Many of these speeches have been compiled in Ambedkar 2013: 263–330.

50 The English translation cited above is from Mangesh Dahiwale in https://velivada.com/2015/05/03/buddha-jayanti-and-its-political-significance-dr-babasaheb-ambedkar. The English text has been edited slightly.

51 When Ambedkar attended a meeting at the Bombay branch of the Royal

Asiatic Society in July 1950, he was accused of "opportunitism". See "Advocacy of Buddhism," *TOI*, 26 July 1950.

52   The Bharatiya Ved Vidyalaya (school) was founded in 1914 by Medharthi's father, Dr. Fakiray Ram. The school's curriculum was largely modeled after the gurukuls of the Arya Samaj but also included a Pali curriculum and housed several Buddhist statues. For instance, Bhikkhu Lokanatha and Bhikkhu Gyan Keto both visited there in 1937, donating two Buddha images crafted from brass and marble to the school. Later, both Ambedkar and J.K. Birla donated statues to the school.

53   Dharmarakshita would also participate in Ambedkar's conversion ceremony at Nagpur in 1956. In addition to Chandramani and Dharmarakshita, there were five other monks that shared the stage with Ambedkar, all of whom hailed from Ceylon but had spent much of their life in India: Ven. Pragyananda, the Sinhalese disciple of Bodhananda who oversaw the Lucknow Risaldar vihara until his death in 2017; Ven. Hammalawa Saddhatissa (1914–1990), the prominent author who later held a number of academic appointments at universities in the UK and Canada; Ven. H. Dhammananda (dates unknown), who oversaw Bombay's Bahujan vihara after Kosambi's departure; and Ven. Sangharatana (d. 1984), the Sinhalese bhikkhu in charge of the Sarnath branch of the Maha Bodhi Society.

54   Kausalyayan's descriptions of these early meetings, although colored by his own Buddhist activism, provide important clues about the depth of Ambedkar's devotion to Buddhism at this time and also why he waited so long before holding a public conversion ceremony. See, Kausalyayan (1968: 117–26).

55   See the insightful introductory essays provided by Kancha Ilaiah Shepherd, and Alex George and S. Anand, in Ambedkar ([1948] 2020).

56   On Dewey's influence on Ambedkar, see Zelliot (1920: 79–85).

57   For an important assessment of Ambedkar's arguments on these doctrines and their place within a wider framework of Buddhist hermeneutical traditions, see Queen (1996).

58   The jurist in Ambedkar recognized the importance of law, but Martin Fuchs (2001: 261) is right when he argues that Ambedkar saw law not as the basis of society but as the necessary mechanism to force and punish those unwilling or unable to accept "the sense of a fundamental, reasonable principle of 'sociality'".

59   In particular, numbers 1–8 and 19. For a list and discussion of these vows, see Beltz (2005: 57–58).

60   While the "snake and mongoose" expression is widely attributed to Patanjali, McGovern (2018) has shown that there is no textual evidence to actually support such claims. Nonetheless, as often in history, it is the perception of reality that matters more than reality.

61   See, "Letter to Shri V.S. Kardak," 4 December 1956, in Ambedkar (1993: 199). Ambedkar writes: "The Buddhist Marriage ceremony is simple. There is no home [sic, *homa* or Vedic fire] and there is no sapta-padi [seven steps around the Vedic fire]. The essence of the ceremony lies in placing an earthen pot newly made between the bridegroom on a stool and to fill it brimful with

water. The bride and the bridegroom [are] to stand on two sides of the pot. They should place a cotton thread in the water pot and each hold one end of the thread in their hands. Some one should sing the *Mangal Sutta*. Both bride and bridegroom should wear white clothes".

62   The use of the term "Harijan" here remains a mystery. It is well known that Ambedkar abhorred the appellation, so it seems odd that he would have used it, and it is possible that the editors at the *MBJ* edited his speech or just reported it that way.

63   The reviewer (*MBJ* Vol. 67/12, 1959: 352–53) was Lobzang Jivaka (1915–62), or Michael Dillon, an English Buddhist monk who studied under Sangharakshita and later at Rizong gompa in Ladakh, where he was ordained. Jivaka called Ambedkar's interpretation "dangerous". Jivaka's late-in-life conversion to Buddhism has often been minimized in favor of a discussion of the fact that he was born as a woman and was one of the first—if not the first— individuals in history to successfully undergo a sex-change operation.

64   The TBMSG is undoubtedly the most well organized Buddhist organization among Ambedkarite Buddhists but some critics accuse it of appropriating Ambedkar (see, Beltz 2005: 199, 218–21, for a concise discussion).

65   For instance, in 1959, three years after Ambedkar's death, the Buddha Sasana Council of Burma issued a hostile review of Ambedkar's *The Buddha and His Dhamma,* something which was no doubt ignited by Ambedkar's criticisms of the sangha in Burma (see, Beltz 2005: 203). In the years building up to the 1956 conversion in Nagpur, Ambedkar had been in touch multiple times with the Buddha Sasana Council requesting support for his movement, concluding that "if I fail the blame must lie at the door of the Buddhist countries for failure to rise to the occasion" (Ambedkar 1956: no page numbers).

66   Marxist critique is latent in much of Ambedkar's writings, but Ambedkar's problem with the socialist solution was its argument that material factors alone were responsible for the growth and development of differences. Although he was not entirely consistent in his views, sometimes stressing brahmin political and economic power over religious ideologies, in his mind the caste-based social structure that developed in Indian society was primarily rooted in the ideologies of religion, not economic conditions. In Anupama Rao's (2009: 124) estimation, it was Marx, not Gandhi, that was Ambedkar's primary "intellectual adversary".

Chapter 6

1   Thass, for instance, was deeply critical of the Congress as well as Dharmapala. Singaravelu's later commitments to communism were also in opposition to the Shakya Buddhists, who felt that its theoretical analysis of economic class overlooked the underlining social structures of caste and untouchability. According to Anand Teltumbde (2017a: 28–29), Singaravelu's analysis of social inequalities and the problem of untouchability adhered to traditional Marxist thought. For an insightful first hand account of the tensions within the Shakya Buddhist Society between 1902 and 1904, see Kosambi (2010: 124–48).

2   Singaravelu goes on to argue that Jesus as an Essene was also a communist and that Plato, More, Morris, and others taught vague notions of communism, but that it was Karl Marx who gave it a "scientific and definite form so as to be applicable in practice."

3   One of the reviewers of this work informs me that Singaravelu's relationship to Buddhism "has since been criticized and framed differently within Tamil debates" (Anonymous Reviewer, 28 March 2022) and that his embrace of both Buddhism and Marxism was more superficial than his biographers have claimed. Even if this is the case—and my own linguistic shortcomings make me a poor judge of the contemporary Tamil-language scholarly corpus—Singaravelu's engagements with Buddhism and the imaginative genealogy he drew between it and Marxism is further evidence of the critical space that these discourses held at this particular historical juncture.

4   My understanding of Kosambi's life is drawn from Meera Kosambi's introduction in Kosambi (2010). Also see Ober (2013, 2020).

5   On *The Light of Asia,* and its modern global impact (including in India), see Ramesh's (2021) meticulously researched and eye-opening study. For a narrow discussion focused on its influence in India, see Ober (2020).

6   On socio-religious reform movements in British India, see Jones (2006) and on Vidyodaya as a hub for new Buddhist praxis, see Seneviratne (1999).

7   Woods traveled to India on multiple occasions, and remained a long-time friend of Kosambi, even financially supporting his family in the 1930s when Kosambi was jailed for his involvement in the Non-Cooperation movement. In total, Kosambi spent nearly eight years at Harvard on four separate trips (1910–12, 1919–22, 1926–29, 1933–34). According to Eleanor Zelliot (1979: 392), Kosambi earned a doctorate from Harvard in 1929. In previous publications I've also followed Zelliot's assessment but according to Kosambi's great-grandson, Dilip Prasad, Kosambi was never awarded the degree (personal communication, 1 July 2022).

8   While the Communist Party of India (CPI) was founded in 1924, it should be noted that, in 1920, M.N. Roy and six of his colleagues had founded a party by the same name in Tashkent. The Tashkent faction struggled for acceptance among India's domestic communists, and only after the split within the CPI in 1964 did a new branch entitled the CPI-Marxist (CPI-M) claim the earlier date as its official founding. See Overstreet and Windmiller (1959: 34–38) on the origins of the Tashkent CPI, the rise of "radical" communist politics in early 1920s India, particularly vis-à-vis the trade union movement. Much historical scholarship now describes the colonial-era CPI as the "undivided CPI".

9   On Dorjiev, see Snelling (1993). Many Kalymk and Buryatian "Buddhist agents" like Dorjiev were indispensable to the geopolitical goals of the Bolsheviks (Andreyev 2001: 349–62).

10 A thorough discussion of the Buddhist Marxist context in Russia is discussed in Tolz (2011: 142–47); Schimmlepennick van der Oye (2010: 171–98).

11 Chowdhuri (2007: 155). Although the latter part of this argument had been expressed for a decade by the CPI, many Indians—whether on the "right" or the "left"—were deeply sceptical of the CPI, believing it to be too closely linked to the Comintern and the Soviet machinery.

12   My reading of *Indian Civilization and Non-violence* stems from Pandit Vishvanath Damodar Sholapurkar's Hindi translation of the entire text (Kosambi [1935] 2010). An English translation of the last chapter is also found in Kosambi ([1909–49] 2010: 327–57). When quoting sections from the last chapter, I use Meera Kosambi's English translation (Kosambi [1909–49] 2010) for ease and reference. All other translations refer to the Hindi edition.

13   The English translation of the play is available in Kosambi ([1909–49] 2010: 358–408).

14   Kosambi's son, D.D. Kosambi, is typically seen as the "father" of India's Marxist historiography.

15   For a list of his publications, see Bhattacarya (2005: 205–15). In the Buddhist studies world, Sankrityayan is best known for his recovery of a great many "lost" Sanskrit manuscripts in Tibet.

16   Technically, Kosambi's upasampada occurred in Burma and not in Ceylon, where his vows remained that of a novice (*samanera*).

17   According to Seneviratne (1999:160fn41), the anti-imperialist Marxist rhetoric of the Vidyalankara monks was primarily in opposition to imperialism as related to colonialism but not to the Marxist definition of imperialism as an extension of capitalism.

18   I do not mean to imply here that the reading of Marx is necessarily evidence of support for his theories. On the contrary, many Vidyalankara monks were at the forefront of anti-Marxist campaigns. In the cases where Sinhalese intellectuals actually worked to demonstrate the compatibility between Buddhism and Marxism, this often arose as an effort "to counter the established elite's attempt to get some monks and others to portray Marxism as the enemy of Buddhism" (Seneviratne 1999:144fn22). My reason for pointing this out is to invite attention to both the availability of this literature and the frequency with which these ideas were being discussed. This would have no doubt inspired intellectuals like Sankrityayan to think about these issues more deeply and lead him to form his own judgements.

19   There is neither the space nor the time here to explore the details of these incredible journeys and the impact that they had on the wider world of modern Buddhology and Indology. In addition to his famed expeditions in Tibet (1929–30, 1934, 1936, 1938), these years also involved extensive travel to other parts of Asia and Europe, including a long journey to western Europe (1932–33), Ladakh and Lahaul (1933, 1936), Japan, Korea, Manchuria, and Russia (1935), Nepal (1936), Iran, Afghanistan, and Russia (1937–1938) in addition to several cross-country journeys through India and Ceylon.

20   Narendra Dev's studies in Indology at Queen's College had led him to Buddhism. During the peak of his political career, from the 1940s until his death in 1956, Dev published a number of influential works on Buddhist history and philosophy. These included a four-volume Hindi translation of Vasubandhu's *Abhidharmakosha* (based on Poussin's French translation from the Chinese) and a seven-hundred-page tome on Buddhist philosophy (*Bauddhadharma-darshan*) that won India's most distinguished literary award from the Sahitya Akademi in 1956. During Dev's incarceration at Ahmednagar Fort in 1942, he helped the future Indian prime minister,

Jawaharlal Nehru, write the sections on Buddhist history and logic that appeared in *The Discovery of India.*

21 As the kisan sabha saw it, the "agrarian problem" referred primarily to issues of bonded labor, population pressures, overtaxation, rural debt, farming techniques, and landownership.

22 This essay was first published in 1956 in *New Age*, the organ of the Communist Party of India. It has also been republished in multiple other venues often under different titles such as "Buddhism and Marxism."

23 According to Sankrityayan, there were other features equally responsible for Buddhism's downfall, but the sangha's material wealth was at the center of his thesis.

24 Buddhist themes framed many works of the Progressive Writers' Movement. Yashpal, for instance, arguably the most important Hindi writer of the twentieth century after Premchand, regularly invoked Buddhism's historical failures to inspire political activism in the present day. In his third novel, *Divya* (1945), set in the second century BCE in north-west India, Buddhism's caste radicalism is portrayed as a threat to the brahmanical order. Yashpal derived much of his knowledge of Buddhism from Bodhananda, whom he knew personally while living in Lucknow, but unlike Bodhananda, Yashpal was more critical of Buddhism, and it remained an object of critique in *Divya* for its assertion of a "fatalistic" doctrine of karma, "cowardly" asceticism, and institutional misogyny. See Cohen (2020).

25 Ambedkar too had a vested interest in the topic, understanding the sense of competition between the two systems and hoping to prevent communism from making any further inroads into Buddhist Asia (the recent Chinese invasion of Tibet being of especial focus). Although deeply influenced by Marxism himself, he had an uneasy relationship with the Indian left, especially the CPI. The reasons for this were complex, including personal distrust, caste tensions (the CPI was dominated by brahmins), and political competition over their "natural" constituencies (since dalits formed a major bloc in the working classes of Maharashtra). For an insightful analysis, see Teltumbde (2017a).

Chapter 7

1 The Flag Committee, headed by Rajendra Prasad, included Abul Kalam Azad, B.R. Ambedkar, C. Rajagopalachari, K.M. Munshi, and Sarojini Naidu.

2 According to the speech Mehta delivered that day, the delegation was supposed to have been led by another of India's elite feminist leaders and writers, Sarojini Naidu (1879–1949).

3 This second century CE Buddha statue had been brought to Government House (present-day Rashtrapati Bhavan or "President's House") shortly after Independence as part of the "Masterpieces of Indian Art" exhibition. It remains in the house to this day. For a discussion of its exhibition, see Guha-Thakurta (2004: 175–204).

4 Work at these sites was conducted by a number of different organizations, such as the Archaeological Survey of India and the public works department. Most projects were undertaken in preparation for the annual Buddha Jayanti celebrations and included everything from adding medical and

travel facilities, the construction and repair of rest houses, the building and maintenance of roads, as well as minor repairs to existing monuments. For instance, to prepare for the 1956 Buddha Jayanti at Bodh Gaya, a number of "improvements" were made to the Maha Bodhi temple complex, "including the excavation of a large lotus tank just south of the Temple, the construction of a new *pradakshina* (circumambulation) path, the repair of several small shrines within the compound, the establishment of an Ashokan pillar near the Lotus Tank, the electrification of the entire compound, and a major face-lift given to the Temple itself" (Doyle 1997: 201).

5   This massive project was headed by Bhikkhu Jagdish Kashyap, who edited the majority of the series. The first volume was published in 1956 to coincide with the 2,500th anniversary of Buddha Jayanti and the final volume was completed in 1961. The same government initiative also sponsored the publication of a twenty-five-volume Buddhist Sanskrit series (*Bauddhagranthavali*), seventeen volumes of which were edited by P.L. Vaidya, the director of the Mithila Institute in Darbhanga. The remainder of the series was edited by S. Bagchi and completed in the 1970s.

6   The stark contrast between the unfettered purity of the Buddha and his teaching as opposed to the layered orthodoxy and dogma of Buddhism as religion is a defining trait in Nehru's understanding. Shortly after this passage, he writes: "When I visited countries where Buddhism is still a living and dominant faith … there was much I did not like. *The rational, ethical doctrine had become overlaid with so much verbiage, so much ceremonial, canon law*" (Nehru [1946] 1985a: 130–31) [emphasis mine].

7   These kinds of nationalist claims have in recent decades become a source of friction with Nepalese officials, who argue that on account of the Buddha's birthplace being located in Lumbini, the Buddha was in fact Nepalese and not Indian (Gellner 2018).

8   A letter from Rajendra Prasad to R.R. Diwakar, the governor of Bihar, in which he tells the latter to get on All India Radio and celebrate the Buddha Jayanti in order to spread Gandhi's message of non-violence, is suggestive of the new milieu. See, Letter from Prasad to Diwakar, 20 February 1949, in *RPCSD* 1984: 38–39.

9   See Ambedkar's penetrating work, *What Congress and Gandhi Have Done to the Untouchables* (1945) (in *BAWS* Vol. 9) which details his opposition to the Congress.

10   Although Ambedkar's formal public conversion to Buddhism did not occur until October 1956, he had been publicly declaring himself to be a Buddhist since at least the early 1950s.

11   Recently, in an email received on 16 June 2020, Jairam Ramesh shared a typescript of documents from the National Archives of India which indicates that the decision to decline Ambedkar's request for funds also stemmed from formal policies put in place during the Buddha Jayanti that distinguished between "literary, philosophical, ethical and scientific works" which could be supported with state funds and "religious works" which were to be avoided. While this documentation does in fact complicate the reasons for refusing Ambedkar's request, the personal angle remains critical, especially when

one considers that the lack of collaboration between Ambedkar and Nehru at Buddhist events pre-dating the collapse of the Hindu Code Bill. I have not found any evidence of a *single* Buddhist event where both men shared the dais.

12   On his experiences with the theosophists and his later reservations about the group, see, Nehru (1941: 26–28). Notably, it was through the Theosophical Society, still at that time under the heavy influence of the American Buddhist, Henry Olcott, that he read the *Dhammapada* (in English translation).

13   A list of individuals, countries, and organizations represented at the inauguration is available in Appendix 1 of *History of the Mulagandha Kuty Vihara* (2010).

14   "Pandit Nehru's Letter and Gift to the Maha Bodhi Society," *The MBJ* Vol. 40/1 (1932), no page number. Italics mine. The flag and letter are at the Dharmapala Museum in Sarnath.

15   He and his daughter, Indira (who later became prime minister) regularly attended the Mulagandhakuti vihara celebrations in Sarnath throughout the 1930s and 40s. In 1937, he inaugurated the centre for Buddhist and Sino-Indian studies ("Cheena Bhavan") at Santiniketan (*ISR* Vol. 49/32, 1937: 507).

16   Nehru was in fact so impressed by Ashoka that according to the Hindi poet, Harivansh Rai Bachchan, his daughter, Indira Gandhi (her full name was Priyadarshini Indira) was actually named after Ashoka—Priyadassi being the name that Ashoka took up after his renunciation. See Bachchan (1998: 466).

17   For instance, in Calcutta in 1949, Sanchi in 1952, Bodh Gaya throughout the 1950s, and in New Delhi in 1956.

18   Namely, Kalimpong, Darjeeling, Kurseong, Ghoom, and Tindharia.

19   Later, the number was increased to twelve thousand. See Letter from T.N. Kaul, joint secretary, Ministry of External Affairs to P.M. Lad, secretary, Ministry of Information and Broadcasting, 3 September 1955, in MEANEF, File no. 37/7, 1955.

20   These monks were from the "Hill Tract Buddhist Mission", under the direct support of Prime Minister U Nu.

21   Bandaranaike, then a minister of local administration, was elected prime minister in a landslide election in 1956. His term met a tragic end three years later when a Buddhist monk assassinated him. Other foreign leaders in attendance included the education minister in Ceylon, Dr C.W.W. Kannanagara; Justice U Kyaw of the Mint of Burma; Vira Dhammawara of Siam; Daynananda Priyardasi, president of the United Lanka Congress; and Khenchen Losang Wangyal, the Dalai Lama's representative in Delhi.

22   A segment of these papers is housed at the National Archives of India in New Delhi under the Rajendra Prasad Private Papers collection, File No. 1-R/38, Collection No. 2, Sub: Buddha Gaya Temple.

23   While Nehru recognized the goodwill that could be acquired by transferring control to the Buddhists, the transfer of the temple out of the Shaiva mahant's hands also served as part of his Land Reforms Act to demolish zamindari. The mahant was the largest landowner (zamindar) in all of Bihar, a region

with one of the highest rates of inequality in property ownership (Geary 2014).

24   See also RPCSD Vol. 10: 332–34.

25   In 1975, Dharmavira moved to the USA, and the Ashoka Mission was reorganized under its new president, Ven. Lama Lobzang from Ladakh. Since the early 2000s, the Ashoka Mission has emerged as a major organizer of international Buddhist events in India, including holding one of the largest Buddhist conferences in modern history in New Delhi in 2011.

26   It is notable that this event occurred in conjunction with the second session of the World Conference of Pacifists, the first session having been held the year prior at Gandhi's former ashram in Wardha.

27   There was an "Indian friendship mission" in October 1951, an Indian "goodwill delegation" in 1954, an Indian "cultural delegation" in 1955 led by Raghu Vira, another "friendship mission" in 1956 led by P.V. Bapat and Jagdish Kashyap, and a "cultural delegation" led by Rahul Sankrityayan in 1958.

28   According to Arpi (2004: 114), the use of the term was actually introduced by President Sukarno of Indonesia when he gave the name *Pantaja Sila* to Indonesia's "Five Principles" of national policy in 1945.

29   Here I am drawing on several valuable suggestions and insights into Ambedkar's Buddhism offered by S. Anand in a preliminary review.

30   According to Nye (1990), soft power refers to the ability of governments to coerce other governments into doing what they want without force or violence. Put simply, soft power means "getting others to want what you want".

Thus Have I Heard ...

1   Contrary to popular thought, Ambedkar did not coin the word Navayana. There remains a great deal of uncertainty as to whether Ambedkar even used the appellation at all. According to Ashok Gopal (personal communication, 25 October 2022), all of the evidence points to Ambedkar's discussion with press reporters in Nagpur on 13 October 1956—one day after the public conversion—in which it was reported that he used the term. According to Gopal, "Ambedkar's reported answer makes it clear that he was not coining or trying to promote a new term ... the offhandedness of the remark is crystal clear." I am thankful to Ashok Gopal and S. Anand for their assistance in clarifying this issue. Although I am unsure of the term's precise origin, Har Dayal spoke of a Navayana as early as 1927, and it was widely used by Japanese Buddhists in Hawai'i in the 1930s. It also features in the title of a popular English work by the British Buddhist, Capt. J.E. Ellam, *Navayana: Buddhism and Modern Thought* (1930).

Bibliography

A Brief Notice of the Late Mr. Lancelot Wilkinson of the Bombay Civil Service with his Opinions on the Education of Natives of India, and on the State of Native Society. 1853. Cornhill: Smith, Elder & Co.

Agarwal, C.V. 2001. *The Buddhist and Theosophical Movements, 1873–2001.* Calcutta: Maha Bodhi Society.

Aggarwal, Ravina. 2004. *Beyond Lines of Control: Performance and Politics on the Disputed Borders of Ladakh, India.* Durham: Duke University Press.

Ahir, D.C. 1989. *The Pioneers of Buddhist Revival in India.* New Delhi: Sri Satguru Publications.

———. 1991. *Buddhism in Modern India.* New Delhi: Sri Satguru Publications.

———. 1994. *Buddha Gaya through the Ages.* New Delhi: Sri Satguru Publications.

———. 2010. *Buddhism in India: Rediscovery, Revival and Development.* New Delhi: Buddhist World Press.

Alexander, P.C. 1949. *Buddhism in Kerala.* Annamalainagar: Annamalai University.

Allen, Charles. 2002. *The Buddha and the Sahibs: The Men Who Discovered India's Lost Religion.* London: John Murray.

———. [2008] 2010. *The Buddha and Dr. Führer: An Archaeological Scandal.* New York: Penguin.

———. 2012. *Ashoka: The Search for India's Lost Emperor.* London: Abaacus.

———. 2015. *The Prisoner of Kathmandu: Brian Hodgson in Nepal 1820–43.* Chicago: Haus Press.

Almond, Philip C. 1988. *The British Discovery of Buddhism.* Cambridge: Cambridge University Press.

Aloysius, G. 1998. *Religion as Emancipatory Identity: A Buddhist Movement among the Tamils under Colonialism.* New Delhi: New Age International Publishers.

———. (ed.). 1999. *Iyotheethasar Sinthanaigal II.* Palaymkottai: St. Xavier's College Folklore Resources and Research Centre.

———. 2006. *Periyar aur Bauddh Dharma.* Translated from Tamil into Hindi by Moses Michael. New Delhi: Samyak Prakashan.

Alter, Joseph S. 1992. *The Wrestler's Body: Identity and Ideology in North India.* Berkeley: University of California Press.

Ambedkar, B.R. [1929–1956] 1979–2020. *Babasaheb Ambedkar Writings and Speeches [BAWS].* Edited by Vasant Moon. Bombay: Education Department, Government of Maharashtra.

———. 1950. "The Buddha and the Future of His Religion." *Maha Bodhi*, Vol. 58/4: 117–118, 199–206.

———. 1956. "Dr. Ambedkar's Letter to Buddha Sasana Council, Rangoon (Burma)." Accessed on 21 December 2021 at: https://velivada.com/2015/07/19/dr-ambedkars-letter-to-buddha-sasana-council-rangoon-burma/

———. 1993. *Letters of Ambedkar*. Edited by Surendra Ajnat. Jalandhar: Bheem Patrika Publications.

———. 2011. *The Buddha and His Dhamma: A Critical Edition*. Edited and with an introduction by Aakash Singh Rathore and Ajay Verma. New Delhi: Oxford University Press.

———. 2013. *Ambedkar Speaks* Vol. II. Edited by Narendra Jadhav. New Delhi and Seattle: Konark Publishers.

———. [1936] 2014. *Annihilation of Caste: The Annotated Critical Edition*. Edited by S. Anand with an introduction by Arundhati Roy. New Delhi: Navayana.

———. [1948] 2020. *Beef, Brahmins, and Broken Men: An Annotated Critical Selection from The Untouchables*. Edited and annotated by Alex George and S. Anand. With an introduction by Kancha Ilaiah Shepherd. New Delhi: Navayana.

Anand, S. 2004. "Bodhi's Tamil Afterglow." *Outlook India*. 19 July. Accessed at: https://www.outlookindia.com/magazine/story/bodhis-tamil-afterglow/224559.

Anderson, Benedict. 1991. *Imagined Communities: Reflections on the Origin and Spread of Nationalism*. Rev. ed. London: Verso.

Andreyev, Alexander. 2001. "Russian Buddhists in Tibet, from the end of the nineteenth century – 1930." *Journal of the Royal Asiatic Society*. Vol. 11/3: 349–62.

Annual Report for the Bengal Buddhist Association. 1912–1918. Calcutta: Bauddha Dharmankur Sabha.

App, Urs. 2012. *The Cult of Emptiness: The Western Discovery of Buddhist Thought and the Invention of Oriental Philosophy*. Kyoto: University Media.

Appadurai, Arjun. 1990. "Disjuncture and difference in the global cultural economy." *Public Culture*. Vol. 2/2: 1–24.

Archaeological Survey of India Annual Reports (1871–1924). Calcutta and New Delhi: Government of India

Arnold, Edwin. 1879. *The Light of Asia or the Great Renunciation (Mahabhinishkramana) Being the Life and Teaching of Gautama, Prince of India and Founder of Buddhism, as told in Verse by an Indian Buddhist*. London: Trübner & Co..

———. 1885. *India Revisited*. London: Kegan, Paul, Trench, Trübner & Co.

Arpi, Claude. 2004. *Born in Sin: The Panchsheel Agreement, the Sacrifice of Tibet*. New Delhi: Mittal Publications.

Aydin, Cemil. 2007. *The Politics of Anti-Westernism in Asia: Visions of World Order in Pan-Islamic and Pan-Asian Thought*. New York: Columbia University Press.

Ayyathurai, Gajendran. 2011. "Foundations of Anti-caste Consciousness: Pandit Iyothee Thass, Tamil Buddhism and the Marginalized in South India." PhD diss., Columbia University.

Bachchan, Harivansh Rai. 1998. *In the Afternoon of Time: An Autobiography*. Abridged and translated from the Hindi by Rupert Snell. New Delhi: Penguin.

Bader, Jonathan. 1991. "Conquest of the Four Quarters: Traditional Accounts of the Life of Sankara." PhD diss., Australian National University.

Bakker, Freek. 2009. *The Challenge of the Silver Screen: An Analysis of the Cinematic Portraits of Jesus, Rama, Buddha and Muhammad.* Leiden: Brill.

Banerjee-Dube, Ishita. 2009. *Religion, Law and Power: Tales of Time in Eastern India, 1860–2000.* London: Anthem Press.

Banerji, Babu Chandrasekhara. 1870. "Antiquities of the Cuttack Hills." *Journal of the Asiatic Society of Bengal.* Vol. 39/3: 158–71.

Bapat, P.V. 1944. "Buddhist Studies: 1918-1943." *Annals of the Bhandarkar Oriental Research Institute.* Vol. 25/1–3: 1–35.

Bapat, P.V. (ed). 1956. *2500 Years of Buddhism.* New Delhi: Government of India.

Bapu, Prabhu. 2013. *Hindu Maha Sabha in Colonial North India, 1915–1930: Constructing Nation and History.* London: Routledge.

Barua, Deb Mitra. n.d. "Modern Buddhist Reformation in Chittagong and Extended Bengal: A Blind Spot of Modern Buddhist Studies." Unpublished paper.

Barua, Dipak Kumar. 2007. "Historical perspective of contemporary Buddhism and its followers in India." *Journal of the Department of Pali,* Vol. 14: 8–37.

———. 2014. "Theravada Buddhism in Bengal under British Colonialism." In *The Wisdom: 150th Birth Anniversary Volume of Karmayogi Kripasaran Mahasthavir,* edited by Bhikkhu Kachayan, 29–43. New Delhi: Dialogue of Wisdom.

Barua, Rabindra Bijoy. 1978. *The Theravada Sangha.* Dhaka: Asiatic Society of Bangladesh.

Barua, Sitangshu Bikash. 1990. *Buddhism in Bangladesh.* Chittagong: Prajna Printers.

Baruah, Sanjib. 1999. *India Against Itself: Assam and the Politics of Nationality.* Philadelphia: University of Pennsylvania Press.

———. 2020. *In the Name of the Nation: India and Its Northeast.* New Delhi: Navayana.

Basso, Keith. 1996. *Wisdom Sits in Places: Landscape and Language among the Western Apache.* Albuquerque: University of New Mexico Press.

Basu, Raj Sekhar. 2011. *Nandanar's Children: The Paraiyans' Tryst with Destiny, Tamil Nadu 1850–1956.* New Delhi: Sage Publications.

Bauddh, Jugal Kishor Acarya. 2008. *Jahan Bhagavan Buddh Mahaparinirvan ko Prapta Hue: Kusinara.* New Delhi: Samyak Prakashan.

Bayly, Christopher. 1998. *Indian Society and the Making of the British Empire.* Cambridge: Cambridge University Press.

———. 2004. *The Birth of the Modern World, 1780–1914: Global Connections and Comparisons.* Oxford: Blackwell.

Bayly, Susan. 2000. "French Anthropology and the Durkheimians in Colonial Indochina". *Modern Asian Studies.* Vol. 34/3: 581–622.

———. 2004. "Imagining 'Greater India': French and Indian Visions of Colonialism in the Indic Mode." *Modern Asian Studies.* Vol. 38/3: 703–44.

Belli, Melia. 2014. "Monumental Pride: Mayawati's Memorials in Lucknow." *Ars Orientalis.* Vol. 44: 85–111.

Bellwinkel-Schempp, Maren. 2004. "Roots of Ambedkar Buddhism in Kanpur." In *Reconstructing the World: B.R. Ambedkar and Buddhism in India,* edited by Surendra Jondhale and Johannes Beltz, 221–44. New Delhi: Oxford University Press.

———. 2011. "Bhakti and Buddhism: Text, Content and Public Representation of Dalit Religiosity in Uttar Pradesh." *Neuer Buddhismus als gesellschaftlicher*

Entwurf: zur Identitätskonstruktion der Dalits in Kanpur, Indien, edited by Peter Schalk, Gabriele Reifenrath and Heinz Werner Wessler, 187–233. Uppsala: Uppsala Universitet.

Beltz, Johannes. 2005. *Mahar, Buddhist and Dalit: Religious Conversion and Socio-Political Emancipation*. New Delhi: Manohar.

Bendall, Cecil. [1883] 1992. *Catalogue of the Buddhist Sanskrit Manuscripts in the University Library, Cambridge*. Publications of the Nepal German Manuscript Preservation Project. Stuttgart: Steiner.

Berkwitz, Stephen. 2010. *South Asian Buddhism: A Survey*. London and New York: Routledge.

Bevir, Mark. 2003. "Theosophy and the Origins of the Indian National Congress." *International Journal of Hindu Studies*. Vol. 7/3: 99–115.

Bharati, Agehananda. 1976. "Monastic and Lay Buddhism in the 1971 Sri Lanka Insurgency." In *Religion and Social Conflict in South Asia*, edited by Bardwell L. Smith, 101–12. Leiden: Brill.

Bharucha, Rustom. 2006. *Another Asia: Rabindranath Tagore and Okakura Tenshin*. Oxford: Oxford University Press.

Bhatta Jayanta. 2005. *Agamadambara* [Much ado about religion]. Translated from the Sanskrit by Csaba Dezsó. New York: Clay Sanskrit Library.

Bhattacarya, Abhijit. 2005. *Mahapandit Rahul Sankrityayan ke Vyaktitvantaran*. Kolkata: Anand Prakashan.

Bhattacharya, Ramkrishna. 1994. "From Buddha to Marx." In *Essays on Indology: Birth Centenary Tribute to Mahapandita Rahula Sankrityayana*, 118–21, edited by A. Chattopadhyaya. Calcutta: Manisha Granthalaya.

Bird, James. 1847. *Historical Researches on the Origin and Principles of the Bauddha and Jaina Religions; Embracing the Leading Tenets of their System, with Accounts of the Scriptures in the Caves of Western India, with Translations of the Inscriptions of Those of Kanari, Karli, etc*. Bombay: American Mission Press.

Bisgaard, Daniel James. 1994. *Social Conscience in Sanskrit Literature*. New Delhi: Motilal Banarsidass.

Biswas, Swapan K. 2008. *Nine Decades of Marxism in the Land of Brahminism*. Calicut: Other Books.

Black, Brian (ed.). 2009. Special Issue on "Representations of Brahmins and Brahmanism in Early Buddhist Literature." *Religions of South Asia*. Vol. 3/1.

Blackburn, Anne. 2010. *Locations of Buddhism: Colonialism and Modernity in Sri Lanka*. Chicago: University of Chicago Press.

Blavatsky, Helena Petrovna. 1877. *Isis Unveiled: A Master-Key to the Mysteries of Ancient and Modern Science and Theology*. New York: J.W. Bouton.

Bloch, Ester, Marianne Keppens, and Rajaram Hegde. 2009. *Rethinking Religion in India: The Colonial Construction of Hinduism*. London: Routledge.

Bodhananda, Bhadant Mahasthavir. 1947. *Bauddh-carya-padhdati*. Lucknow: Buddh Vihara.

———. [1933] 2012. [=Bodhananda, Bhadant Mahathera]. *Bhagavan Gautama Buddha*. New Delhi: Samyak Prakashan.

———. [1930] 2009. [=Bodhananda, Bhikkhu]. *Mool Bharatvasi aur Arya*. New Delhi: Samyak Prakashan.

Bodhi (Bhikkhu). 2010. "A Look at the Kalama Sutta." *Access to Insight* (Legacy Edition), 5 June 2010. Accessed on 6 July 2016, at http://www.accesstoinsight. org/lib/authors/bodhi/bps-essay_09.html

Boer, Roland. 2014. "Revolutionary Christianity: Friedrich Engels and the Aufhebung of Religion." *Political Theology Today.* Accessed June 2017 at: http:// www.politicaltheology.com/blog/revolutionary-christianity-friedrich-engels-and-the-aufhebung-of-religion/

Bond, George. 1988. *The Buddhist Revival in Sri Lanka: Religious Tradition, Reinterpretation and Response.* Columbia: University of South Carolina Press.

Borges, Jorge Luis. 1948. "On Exactitude in Science." In *Jorge Luis Borges: Collected Fictions,* translated by H. Hurley. New York: Penguin.

Bose, Kishen Kant. 1825. "Account of Bootan, translated [from the Bengali] by D. Scott." *Asiatick Researches, Or, Transactions of the Society Instituted in Bengal, for Inquiring Into the History and Antiquities, the Arts, Sciences, and Literature of Asia.* Vol. 15: 128–56.

Bose, Ram Chundra. 1886. "Art. III—Buddha as a Man." *The Calcutta Review.* Vol. 82/163: 65–84.

Boswell, J.A.C. 1872. "On the Ancient Remains in the Krishna District." *Indian Antiquary.* Vol. 1: 152–53.

Bronkhorst, Johannes. 2011. *Buddhism in the Shadow of Brahmanism.* Leiden: Brill.

Brown, Rebecca. 2009. "Reviving the Past: Post-Independence Architecture and Politics in India's Long 1950s." *Interventions.* Vol. 11/3: 293–315.

Brown, Robert. 1988. "Bodhgaya and Southeast Asia." In *Bodhgaya, the Site of Enlightenment,* edited by Janice Leoshko, 101–24. Bombay: Marg Publications.

Buchanan, Francis. [1798] 1992. *Francis Buchanan in Southeast Bengal, 1798: His Journey to Chittagong, the Chittagong Hill Tracts, Noakhali, and Comilla.* Edited by Willem van Schendel. New Delhi: Manohar.

———. 1801. "On the Religion and Literature of the Burmas." *Asiatick Researches; or, Transactions of the Society Instituted in Bengal, for Enquiring into the History and Antiquities, the Arts, Sciences, and Literature, of Asia.* Vol. 6: 163–308.

[Buchanan =] Hamilton, Francis. 1819. *An Account of the Kingdom of Nepal and of the Territories Annexed to This Dominion by the House of Gorkha.* Edinburgh: Archibald Constable and Company.

———. [1811–12] 1925. *The Journal of Dr. Francis Buchanan (afterwards Hamilton), kept during the survey of the districts of Patna and Gaya in 1811–1812.* Gaya: Superintendent of Government Printing, Bihar and Orissa.

Buddhamitra, Bhikshu. 1999. *Svatantra Senani Mahasthavir Bhikshu Mahavir.* Kushinagar: International Buddhist Trust Committee.

Burchett, Patton. 2019. *A Genealogy of Devotion: Bhakti, Tantra, Yoga, and Sufism in North India.* New York: Columbia University Press.

Burgess, James. 1902. "Extracts from the Journal of Colonel Mackenzie's Pandit of His Route from Calcutta to Gaya in 1820." *Indian Antiquary.* Vol. 31: 65–75.

Bysack, G.D. 1890. "Notes on a Buddhist Monastery at Bhot Bágán (Howrah)." *Journal of the Asiatic Society of Bengal.* Vol. 59/1: 50–99.

Caitanya Caritamrta of Krsnadasa Kaviraja: A Translation and Commentary. 1999. Translated from the Bengali by Edward Dimock with an introduction by

Edward Dimock and Tony Stewart. Edited by Tony Stewart. Cambridge, Mass.: Harvard University Press.

Cannon, Garland. 1990. *The Life and Mind of Oriental Jones: Sir William Jones, the Father of Modern Linguistics*. Cambridge: Cambridge University Press.

Chandavarkar, Rajnarayan. 1997. "From Communism to 'Social Democracy': The Rise and Resilience of Communist Parties in India, 1920–1995." *Science and Society*. Vol. 61/1: 99–106.

———. 1998. *Imperial Power and Popular Politics: Class, Resistance and the State in India, c. 1850–1950*. Cambridge: Cambridge University Press.

Chandramani, Mahasthavir Bhikkhu. 1968. "Tathagata ke liye." In *Ek Bindu, Ek Sindhu: Svargiya Jugalakishor Birla*, edited by Dev Datta Shastri, 278–79. Mathura: Shrikrishna Janmasthan Sevasamgha.

Chandramohan, P. 1987. "Popular Culture and Socio-Religious Reform: Narayana Guru and the Ezhavas of Travancore." *Studies in History*. Vol. 3/1: 57–74.

Charney, Michael W. 1999. "Where Jambudipa and Islamdom converged: Religious change and the emergence of Buddhist communalism in early modern Arakan (fifteenth to nineteenth centuries)." PhD diss., University of Michigan.

———. 2002. "Beyond state-centered histories in western Burma, Missionizing monks and intra regional migrants in the Arakan littoral, c. 1784–1860." In *Maritime Frontier of Burma: Exploring Political, Cultural and Commercial Interaction in the Indian Ocean World, 1200–1800*, edited by Jos Gommans and Jacque Leider, 213–24. Leiden: KITLV Press.

Chatterjee, Partha. 1993. *The Nation and its Fragments: Colonial and Postcolonial Histories*. Princeton: Princeton University Press.

———. 2010. *Empire and Nation: Selected Essays*. New York: Columbia University Press.

Chaudhari, K.K. (ed.). 1990. *Source material for a history of the freedom movement in India, Vol. XI, Civil Disobedience Movement, April-September 1930*. Bombay: Gazetteers Department, Government of Maharashtra.

Chaudhuri, Sukomal. [1982] 1987. *Contemporary Buddhism in Bangladesh*. Calcutta: Atisha Memorial Publishing Society.

Chia, Jack Meng-Tat. 2020. *Monks in Motion: Buddhism and Modernity across the South China Sea*. New York: Oxford University Press.

Chopel, Gendun. 2014. *Grains of Gold: Tales of a Cosmopolitan Traveler*. Translated from the Tibetan by Thupten Jinpa and Donald S. Lopez, Jr. Chicago: University of Chicago Press.

Chowdhuri, Satyabrata Rai. 2007. *Leftism in India, 1917–1947*. New York: Palgrave Macmillan.

Chowdhury, Hemendu Bikash. 1990. "Kripasaran Mahathera." In *Jaggajyoti: Kripasaran Mahathera 125th Birth Anniversary Volume*, 1–10. Calcutta: Bauddha Dharmankur Sabha.

———. 2015. "Karmayogi Kripasaran." *Mohajivan*. 22 February. 34–38.

Chudal, Alaka Atreya. 2016. *A Freethinking Cultural Nationalist: A Life History of Rahul Sankrityayan*. New Delhi: Oxford University Press.

Chung, Tang. 1999. *In the Footsteps of Xuan Zang: Tan Yun-shan and India*. New Delhi: Indira Gandhi National Centre for the Arts.

Cohen, Ashley. 2020. "New Materialism and Charvaka Marxism in Yashpal's *Divya* (1945)." Unpublished paper.

Collingwood, R.G. [1933] 2013. *An Autobiography and Other Writings*. Edited by David Boucher and Teresa Smith. Oxford: Oxford University Press.

Constituent Assembly Debates: Official Reports. 1947. Government of India. Vol. 4: 14–31 July.

Cort, John. 2012. "Indology as authoritative knowledge: Jain debates about icons and history in colonial India," in *Trans-colonial Modernities in South Asia,* edited by Michael S. Dodson and Brian A. Hatcher, 137–61. London: Routledge.

Cox, Laurence. 2013a. "Rethinking early Western Buddhists: beachcombers, 'going native' and dissident Orientalism." *Contemporary Buddhism*. Vol. 14/1: 116–33.

———. 2013b. *Buddhism and Ireland: From the Celts to the Counter-Culture and Beyond*. Sheffield: Equinox.

Cumberland, R.G. (ed.). 1865. *Stray Leaves from the Diary of an Indian Officer, containing an account of the famous temple of Jaggurnath* [sic]*, its daily ceremonies and annual festivals and a residence in Australia.* London: Whitefield, Green & Son.

Cunningham, Alexander. 1843. "An Account of the Discovery of the Ruins of the Buddhist City of Samkassa." *The Journal of the Royal Asiatic Society of Great Britain and Ireland*. Vol. 7/2: 241–49.

———. 1871. *Four Reports made during the years 1862 – 1863 – 1864 – 1865*. 2 vols. Simla: Government Central Press.

———. 1877. *Corpus Inscriptionum Indicarum, Vol. I, Inscriptions of Asoka*. Calcutta: Office of the Superintendent of Government Printing.

D'Hubert, Thibaut. 2019. "India Beyond the Ganges: Defining Arakanese Buddhism in Persianate Colonial Bengal." *The Indian Economic and Social History Review*. 56/1: 1–31.

D'Hubert, Thibaut and Jacques P. Leider. 2011. "Traders and Poets at the Mrauk U Court: Commerce and Cultural Links in Seventeenth-Century Arakan." In *Pelagic Passageways: The Northern Bay of Bengal before Colonialism,* edited by Rila Mukherjee, 77–111. New Delhi: Primus Books.

Dalmia, Vasudha. 1997. *The Nationalization of Hindu Traditions: Bharatendu Harischandra and Nineteenth-century Banaras*. New Delhi: Oxford University Press.

Damen, Frans L. 1983. *Crisis and Religious Renewal in the Brahmo Samaj (1860–1884): A documentary study of the emergence of the "New Dispensation" under Keshab Chandra Sen*. Leuven, Belgium: Department Oriëntalistiek.

Das, Sarat Chandra. 1893. *Indian Pandits in the Land of Snow*. Edited by Nobin Chandra Das. Calcutta: Baptist Mission Press.

———. 1894. "Report on the proceedings of the second quarterly meeting." *JBTSI*. Vol. 2/2: i–vi.

———. 1902. *Journey to Lhasa and Central Tibet*. Edited by William Woodville Rockhill. Second edition, revised. New York: E.P. Dutton & Company.

Das, Sisir Kumar. [1995] 2006. *History of Indian Literature: 1911–1956. Struggle for Freedom: Triumph and Tragedy*. New Delhi: Sahitya Akademi.

Dash, Narendra Kumar. 2007. *Buddhism in Indian Literature*. Shimla: Indian Institute of Advanced Study.

Dash, Sarita. 2002. *The Bauddhatantis of Orissa: Culture, Identity and the Resurgence of an Ancient Guild of Buddhist Weavers*. Batagaon, Puri: Society for Environmental Action and Restoration of Cultural Heritage, Orissa.

Datta, Hirendra Nath. 1904. "Theosophy: In creeds and nations." *Theosophy in India*. Vol. 1/1.

Daulton, Jack. 1999. "Sariputta and Mogallana in the Golden Land: The Relics of the Buddha's Chief Disciples at Kaba Aye Pagoda." *Journal of Burma Studies*. Vol. 4: 101–28.

Davidson, Ronald. 2002. *Indian Esoteric Buddhism: A Social History of the Tantric Movement*. New York: Columbia University Press.

Davis, Ronald L., and Yi Zhong. 2017. "The Biology of Forgetting—A Perspective." *Neuron*. Vol. 95/3: 490–503.

Deeg, Max. 2012. "'Show me the land where the Buddha dwelled...' Xuanzang's 'Record of the Western Regions' (*Xiu ji*): A Misunderstood Text?" *China Report*. Vol. 48/1 & 2: 89–113.

Dehejia, Vidya. 1988. "The Persistence of Buddhism in Tamil Nadu." *Marg*. Vol. 39/4: 53–74.

Deslippe, Philip. 2013. "Brooklyn Bhikkhu: How Salvatore Cioffi Became the Venerable Lokanatha." *Contemporary Buddhism*. Vol. 14/1: 169–86.

Dev, Narendra. [1956] 2011. *Buddha-dharma-darshan*. New Delhi: Motilal Banarsidass.

Dewey, John. [1934] 2013. *A Common Faith*, 2nd edition, with an introduction by Thomas Alexander. New Haven: Yale University Press.

Dharamsey, Virchand. 2012. *Bhagwanlal Indraji: The first Indian archaeologist: Multidisciplinary approaches to the study of the past*. Vadodara: Darshak Itihas Nidhi.

Dharmapala, Anagarika. 1898–1899. "Was Sankaracharya a Buddhist?" *MBJ*. Vol. 7/6.

———. 1899–1900a. "Buddhism and Brahmanism." *MBJ*. Vol. 8/5.

———. 1899–1900b. "Was Shankara a Buddhist?" *MBJ*. Vol. 8/4.

———. 1908. "The Place of Women in the Buddhist Church." *MBJ*. Vol. 16/2.

Dharmarakshit, Bhikshu. 1949–50 [V.S. 2006]. *Kushinagar ka Itihas*. Devariya: Kushinagar Prakashan, Bauddha Vihar.

Dhere, Ramchandra Chintaman. 2011. *The Rise of a Folk God: Vitthal of Pandharpur*. Translated from the Marathi into English by Anne Feldhaus. New York: Oxford University Press.

Doniger, Wendy. 1976. *The Origins of Evil in Hindu Mythology*. Berkeley: University of California Press.

———. 2009. *The Hindus: An Alternative History*. New York: Penguin Press.

Doyle, Tara N. 1997. "Bodh Gaya: Journeys to the Diamond Throne and the Feet of Gayasur." PhD diss., Harvard University.

Droit, Roger-Pol. [1997] 2003. *The Cult of Nothingness: The Philosophers and the Buddha* [originally published as *Le culte du néant: Les philosophes et le Bouddha*], translated from the French into English by David Streight and Pamela Vohnson. Chapel Hill: University of North Carolina Press.

Duara, Prasenjit. 1995. *Rescuing History from the Nation: Questioning Narratives of Modern China*. Chicago: University of Chicago Press.

————. 2001. "The Discourse of Civilization and Pan-Asianism." *Journal of World History*. Vol. 12/1: 99–130.

Duncan, Ian. 2020. "The Mallah and Ram Charana in the United Provinces." *Contributions to Indian Sociology*, Vol. 54/3: 440–65.

Dutt, R.C. 1893. "Proceedings of the Society." Edited by Sarat Chandra Das. *JBTSI*. Vol. 1/2.

East India Census 1941, Vol. 1: Abstract of Tables. 1943. London: His Majesty's Stationery Office.

Ellam, J.E. 1930. *Navayana: Buddhism and Modern Thought*. London: Rider.

Eltschinger, Vincent. 2012. *Caste and Buddhist Philosophy: Continuity of Some Buddhist Arguments against the Realist Interpretation of Social Denominations*. Translated from French to English by Raynald Prévèreau, in collaboration with the author. New Delhi: Motilal Banarsidass.

Ferguson, James. 1884. *Archaeology in India, with Especial Reference to Babu Rajendralal Mitra*. London: Trübner and Co.

Finney, Patrick. 2014. "The ubiquitous presence of the past? Collective memory and international history." *International History Review*, Vol. 36/3: 443–72.

Fischer-Tiné, Harald. 2009. *Low and Licentious Europeans: Race, Class and White Subalternity in Colonial India*. New Delhi: Orient Longman.

Fitzgerald, Timothy. 1999. "Politics and Ambedkar Buddhism in Maharashtra." In *Buddhism and Politics in Twentieth-century Asia*, edited by Ian Harris, 79–104. London: Continuum.

Franco, Fernando, Jyotsna Macwan and Suguna Ramanathan. 2004. *Journeys to Freedom: Dalit Narratives*. Kolkata: Samya.

Frasch, Tilman. 1998. "A Buddhist network in the Bay of Bengal: Relations between Bodhgaya, Burma and Sri Lanka c. 300–1300." In *From the Mediterranean to the China Sea: Miscellaneous Notes*, edited by C. Guillot, D. Lombard and R. Ptak, 69–92. Wiesbaden: Harrassowitz.

Freschi, Elisa. 2016. "Venkatanatha's Engagement with Buddhist Opponents in the Buddhist Texts He Reused." *Buddhist Studies Review*. Vol. 33/1–2: 65–99.

Fuchs, Martin. 2001. "A Religion for Civil Society? Ambedkar's Buddhism, the Dalit Issue and the Imagination of Emergent Possibilities." In *Charisma and Canon: Essays on the Religious History of the Indian Subcontinent*, edited by Vasudha Dalmia, Angelika Malinar and Martin Christof, 250–73. Oxford: Oxford University Press.

Gandhi, Mohandas K. [1896–1948] 1999. *Collected Works of Mahatma Gandhi, Volumes 1–98*. New Delhi: Publications Division Government of India.

Geary, David. 2014. "The Decline of the Bodh Gaya Math and Afterlife of Zamindari." *South Asian History and Culture*. Vol. 4/3: 366–83.

————. 2017. *The Rebirth of Bodh Gaya: Buddhism and the Making of a World Heritage Site*. Seattle: University of Washington Press.

Geertz, Clifford. 1980. *Negara, the Theatre State in Nineteenth Century Bali*. Princeton: Princeton University Press.

Geetha, V. 1993. "Rewriting History in the Brahmin's Shadow." *Journal of Arts & Ideas*. Vol. 25 & 26: 127–38.

————. 2013. "'Atheist Intrigues' in the Old Madras Province." *Frontline*. 1 November.

Geetha, V., and S.V. Rajadurai. 1993. "Dalits and Non-Brahmin Consciousness in Colonial Tamil Nadu." *Economic and Political Weekly*. 25 September: 2091–98.

Gellner, David. 1992. *Monk, Householder, and Tantric Priest: Newar Buddhism and Its Hierarchy of Ritual*. Cambridge: Cambridge University Press.

———. 2018. "Politics of Buddhism in Nepal." *Economic and Political Weekly*. Vol. 50/3 (20 January): 17–20.

Gethin, Rupert. 1998. *The Foundations of Buddhism*. Oxford and New York: Oxford University Press.

Ghosh, Ujaan. 2022. "The God of Controversy: Hindu History Writing of Jagannatha's Buddhist Past." Unpublished paper presented at the Association for Asian Studies, March.

Gombrich, Richard and Gananath Obeyesekere. 1988. *Buddhism Transformed: Religious Change in Sri Lanka*. Princeton: Princeton University Press.

Gooptu, Nandini. 2001. *The Politics of the Urban Poor in Early Twentieth-century India*. Cambridge: Cambridge University Press.

Gopal, S. 1975. *Jawaharlal Nehru: A Biography, 1889–1947*. Vol. I. London: Jonathan Cape.

———. 1984. *Jawaharlal Nehru: A Biography: 1956–1964*. Vol. III. London: Jonathan Cape.

Goswami, Manu. 2004. *Producing India: From Colonial Economy to National Space*. Chicago: University of Chicago Press.

Gour, Hari Singh. 1936. "The Future of the Harijans." *MBJ*. Vol. 44/1: 8–13.

Green, Nile. 2011. *Bombay Islam: The Religious Economy of the West Indian Ocean, 1840–1915*. Cambridge: Cambridge University Press.

Guha, Ramachandra. 2018. *Gandhi: The Years That Changed the World, 1914–1948*. New York: Alfred A. Knopf.

Guha, Sumit. 2019. *History and Collective Memory in South Asia, 1200–2000*. Seattle: University of Washington Press.

Guha-Thakurta, Tapati. 2004. *Monuments, Objects, Histories: Institutions of Art in Colonial and Post-Colonial India*. New York: Columba University Press.

Guneratne, Arjun. 2002. *Many Tongues, One People: The Making of Tharu Identity in Nepal*. Ithaca and London: Cornell University Press.

Gupta, Aghore Nath. [1882] 1957. *Sakyamuni Charitra o Nirbana-tattva*. 4th ed. Calcutta: Naba-bidhan Publications.

Gupta, Charu. 2017. *The Gender of Caste: Representing Dalits in Print*. Seattle and London: University of Washington Press.

Guyot-Réchard, Bérénice. 2018. *Shadow States: India, China and the Himalayas, 1910–1962*. Cambridge: Cambridge University Press.

Habib, Irfan. 1998. "The Left and the National Movement." *Social Scientist*. Vol. 26/5–6: 3–33.

Halbfass, Wilhelm. 1991. *Tradition and Reflection: Explorations in Indian Thought*. Albany: State University of New York.

Hallisey, Charles. 1995. "Roads taken and not taken in the study of Theravada Buddhism." In *Curators of the Buddha,* edited by Donald S. Lopez Jr, 31–62. Chicago: University of Chicago Press.

Hammerstrom, Erik. 2015. *The Science of Chinese Buddhism: Early Twentieth-Century Engagements*. New York: Columbia University Press.

Hansen, Thomas Blom. 1999. *The Saffron Wave: Democracy and Hindu Nationalism in Modern India*. Princeton: Princeton University Press.

Harding, John, Victor Sogen Horn, and Alexander Soucy (eds). 2020. *Buddhism in the Global Eye: Beyond East and West*. London: Bloomsbury Academic.

Harris, Ian (ed.). 1999. *Buddhism and Politics in Twentieth-century Asia*. London: Continuum.

Hawley, John Stratton and Mark Juergensmeyer. 1988. *Songs of the Saints of India*. New York: Oxford University Press.

Hikosaka, Shu. 1989. *Buddhism in Tamil Nadu: A New Perspective*. Madras: Institute of Asian Studies.

Hirsch, Francine. 2005. *Empire of Nations: Ethnography and the Making of the Soviet Union*. Ithaca: Cornell University Press.

Hodgson, Brian. 1827. "On the extreme resemblance that prevails between many of the symbols of Buddhism and Saivism." *The Quarterly Oriental Magazine, Review, and Register*. Vol. 7/14: 218–22.

———. 1831. "A Disputation respecting caste by a Buddhist, in the form of a series of propositions supposed to be put by a Saiva and refuted by the Disputant." *Transactions of the Royal Asiatic Society of Great Britain and Ireland*. Vol. 3/3: 160–69.

———. [1827–28] 1874. *Essays on the Languages, Literature and Religion of Nepal and Tibet together with further papers on the Geography, Ethnology and Commerce of those Countries*. London: Trübner.

Holdich, Thomas Hungerford. 1906. *Tibet, the Mysterious*. New York: Frederick A. Stokes Company.

Holt, John. 2005. *The Buddhist Visnu: Religious Transformation, Politics and Culture*. New York: Columbia University Press.

Hortsmann, Monica. 2015. "The Example in Dadupanthi Homiletics." In *Texts and Telling: Music, Literature and Performance in North India,* edited by Francesca Orsini and Katherine Butler Schofield, 31–60. Cambridge: Open Book Publishers.

Houben, Jan E.M. and Saraju Rath. 2012. "Introduction: Manuscript Culture and Its Impact in "India": Contours and Parameters." In *Aspects of Manuscript Culture in South India,* edited by Saraju Rath, 1–54. Leiden: Brill.

Huber, Toni. 2008. *The Holy Land Reborn: Pilgrimage and the Tibetan Reinvention of Buddhist India*. Chicago: University of Chicago Press.

Hunt, Sarah Beth. 2014. *Hindi Dalit Literature and the Politics of Representation*. New Delhi: Routledge.

Hunter, William Wilson. 1881. *The Imperial Gazetteer of India*: *Volume II, Bengal to Cutwa*. London: Trübner.

———. 1886. *The Indian Empire: Its People, History, and Products*. London: Trübner.

Ilaiah, Kancha. 2001. *God as Political Philosopher: Buddha's Challenge to Brahminism*. Calcutta: Samya.

Imam, Abu. 1966. *Sir Alexander Cunningham and the Beginnings of Indian Archaeology*. Dacca: Asiatic Society of Pakistan.

Indraji, Bhagavanlal. 1882. *Antiquarian Remains at Sopara and Padana. Being an account of the Buddhist Stupa and Asoka Edict recently discovered at Sopara, and of other antiquities in the neighbourhood*. Bombay: Education Society Press.

Ives, Christopher. 2009. *Imperial-Way Zen: Ichikawa Hakugen's Critique and Lingering Questions for Buddhist Ethics*. Honolulu: University of Hawai'i Press.

Iyer, Swaminatha. 1980. *The Story of My Life*. Translated from the Tamil by Sri S.K. Guruswamy and edited by A. Rama Iyer. Tiruvanmiyur: Dr. U.V. Swaminatha Iyer Library.

Jaffe, Richard. 2004. "Seeking Shakyamuni: Travel and the Reconstruction of Japanese Buddhism." *Journal of Japanese Studies*. Vol. 30: 65–96.

———. 2019. *Seeking Sakyamuni: South Asia in the Formation of Japanese Buddhism*. Chicago: University of Chicago Press.

Jaffrelot, Christophe. 1996. *The Hindu Nationalist Movement in India*. New York: Columbia University Press.

———. 2003. *India's Silent Revolution: The Rise of the Lower Castes in North India*. New York: Columbia University Press.

———. 2005. *Dr. Ambedkar and Untouchability: Fighting the Indian Caste System*. New York: Columbia University Press.

———. 2010. *Religion, Caste and Politics in India*. New Delhi: Primus Books.

Jagadiswarananda, Swami. 1941. "Bhagavan Buddha." *MBJ*. Vol. 49/7: 298–99.

Jangam, Chinnaiah. 2017. *Dalits and the Making of Modern India*. Oxford: Oxford University Press.

Jeffrey, Robin. 1976. "Temple Entry Movement in Travancore, 1860–1940." *Social Scientist*. Vol. 4/8: 3–27.

Jha, Ashutosh. 1999. "Compile all my poems [and] it would be my autobiography: Nagarjun." *Indian Literature*, Vol. 43/6: 196–206.

Jigyasu, Chandrika Prasad. 1965. *Bhadant Bodhanand Mahasthavir*. Lucknow: Bahujan Kalyan Prakashan.

Johnson, Paul. 1995. *Initiates of Theosophical Masters*. Albany: State University of New York Press.

———. [1994] 1997. *The Masters Revealed: Madame Blavatsky and the Myth of the Great White Lodge*. New Delhi: Sri Satguru Publications.

Jones, Kenneth. 1976. *Arya Dharm: Hindu Consciousness in 19th Century Punjab*. Berkeley: University of California Press.

———. 2006. *Socio-religious Reform Movements in British India*. Cambridge: Cambridge University Press.

Jones, William. 1790. "On the Chronology of the Hindus." *Asiatick Researches*, Vol. 2: 111–147.

Joseph, Stella. 2008. "Print and Public Sphere in Malabar: a study of early newspapers (1847–1930)." PhD diss., University of Calicut.

Joshi, L.M. 1983. *Discerning the Buddha: A Study of Buddhism and of the Brahmanical Hindu Attitude toward It*. New Delhi: Motilal Banarsidass.

Juergensmeyer, Mark. [1982] 2009. *Religious Rebels in the Punjab: The Ad Dharma Challenge to Caste*. New Delhi: Navayana.

Kalama Sutta. 2013. Translated from the Pali by Soma Thera. *Access to Insight* (Legacy Edition), 30 November 2013. Accessed on 5 July 2016 at http://www.accesstoinsight.org/lib/authors/soma/wheel008.html.

Kalekar, Kakasahab. 1968. "Jugalkishorji aur Bauddh-dharm." In *Ek Bindu, Ek Sindhu: Svargiya Jugalakishor Birla*, edited by Dev Datta Shastri, 47–48. Mathura: Shrikrishna Janmasthan Sevasamgha.

Kaplonski, Christopher. 2014. *The Lama Question: Violence, Sovereignty, and Exception in Early Socialist Mongolia*. Honolulu: University of Hawai'i Press.

Karmali, Naazneen. 2007. "India's Richest." *Forbes*, 12 August. Accessed at: http://www.forbes.com/2007/08/05/india-billies-richest-oped-cx_nka_0813billies.html.

Karpiel, Frank J. 1996. "Theosophy, Culture, and Politics in Honolulu, 1890–1920." *Hawaiian Journal of History*. Vol. 30: 177–89.

Kashyap, Jagdish. 1961. "Rahulji: Mere Gurubhai." *Journal of the Bihar Research Society*. Vol. 47: 7–10.

Kausalyayan, Anand. 1941. *Buddh aur Unke Anucar*. Prayag: Chatrahitakari Pustakamala.

——. 1940. *Bhikshu ke Patra*. Prayag: Nagari Press.

——. 1937. "Buddh-dharm aur Brahman-dharm." *DD*. Vol. 3/4: 35–36.

——. [1941] 1991. *Bhagavadgita aur Dhammapad*. Nagpur: Diksha Bhoomi.

——. 1968. *Yadi Baba Na Hote*. Nagpur: Diksha Bhoomi.

Keer, Dhananjay. [1964] 2002. *Mahatma Jotirao Phooley: Father of the Indian Social Revolution*. Bombay: Popular Prakashan.

——. [1971] 2009. *Dr. Ambedkar: Life and Mission*. 3rd edition. Bombay: Popular Prakashan.

Kemper, Steven. 2015. *Rescued from the Nation: Anagarika Dharmapala and the Buddhist World*. Chicago: University of Chicago Press.

Keown, Damien and Charles Prebish (eds). 2013. *Encyclopedia of Buddhism*. London and New York: Routledge.

Keown, Damien. 2013. *Buddhism: A Very Short Introduction*. Oxford: Oxford University Press.

Kerala District Gazetteers: Kozhikode Supplement. 1981. Edited by Adoor K.K. Ramachandran Nair. Trivandrum: Government of Kerala Press.

Khare, R.P. 1984. *The Untouchable as Himself: Ideology, Identity and Pragmatism among Lucknow Chamars*. Cambridge: Cambridge University Press.

King, Christopher. 1994. *One Language, Two Scripts: The Hindi Movement in Nineteenth Century North India*. Bombay: Oxford University Press.

Kipnis, Ira. [1952] 2004. *The American Socialist Movement, 1897–1912*. Chicago: Haymarket Books.

Kisala, Robert. 1999. *Prophets of Peace: Cultural Identity in Japan's New Religions*. Honolulu: University of Hawai'i Press.

Klostermaier, Klaus. 1979. "Hindu Views of Buddhism." In *Developments in Buddhist Thought: Canadian Contributions to Buddhist Studies*, edited by Roy C. Amore, 60–82. Waterloo: Wilfrid Laurier University Press.

Kopf, David. 1969. *British Orientalism and the Bengal Renaissance: The Dynamics of Indian Modernization, 1773–1835*. Berkeley: University of California Press.

——. 1979. *The Brahmo Samaj and the Shaping of the Modern Indian Mind*. Princeton: Princeton University Press.

Korom, Frank. 1997. "'Editing' Dharmaraj: Academic Genealogies of a Bengali Folk Deity." *Western Folklore*. Vol. 56/1: 51–77.

Kosambi, Dharmanand. [1909–49] 2010. *Dharmanand Kosambi: The Essential Writings*. Edited and translated from the Marathi into English by Meera

Kosambi, and with an introduction by Meera Kosambi. Ranikhet: Permanent Black.

———. [1935] 2010. *Bharatiya Sanskriti aur Ahimsa.* Translated from the Marathi into Hindi by Pandit Vishvanath Damodar Sholapurkar. New Delhi: Samyak Prakashan.

Krishna Mishra. 2009. *Prabodhacandrodaya* [The rise of wisdom moon]. Translated from the Sanskrit by Matthew Kapstein, New York: Clay Sanskrit Library.

Kudaisya, Medha M. 2003. *The Life and Times of G.D. Birla.* New Delhi: Oxford University Press.

Kulke, Herman. 1993. "Reflections on the Sources of the Temple Chronicles of the Madala Pañji of Puri." In *Kings and Cults: State Formation and Legitimation in India and Southeast Asia,* edited by Herman Kulke, 159–91. New Delhi: Manohar.

Kumar, Basant. 1994. *A Rare Legacy: Memoirs of B.K. Birla.* Bombay: Image Incorporated.

Kumar, Nita. 2012. "India's trials with citizenship, modernization and nationhood." In *Mass Education and the Limits of State Building, c. 1870–1930,* edited by Laurence Brockliss and Nicola Sheldon, 283–304. New York: Palgrave.

Kumar, Udaya. 2014. "Dr. Palpu's Petition Writings and Kerala's Pasts." *Nehru Memorial Museum and Library Occasional Paper* 59.

Lach, Donald F. 1965–93. *Asia in the Making of Europe.* 9 vols. Chicago: University of Chicago Press.

Lahiri, Nayanjot. 2012. *Marshalling the Past: Ancient India and Its Modern Histories.* New Delhi: Permanent Black.

———. 2015. *Ashoka in Ancient India.* Cambridge, Mass.: Harvard University Press.

Lal, Angne. 2004. *Buddha Sasana ke Ratna: 32 bauddh bhikshuon ke vyaktitva evam krititva par abhutapoorva granth.* Lucknow: Prabuddh Prakashan.

Lang, Jon. 2002. *A Concise History of Modern Architecture in India.* New Delhi: Permanent Black.

La Vallée Poussin, Louis de. 1913. "Bibliographie: *The Essence of Buddhism* by P. Lakshmi Narasu" *Anthropos.* Vol. 8/2–3: 579–80.

Learman, Linda (ed). 2004. *Buddhist Missionaries in the Era of Globalization.* Honolulu: University of Hawai'i Press.

Lee, Joel. 2021. *Deceptive Majority: Dalits, Hinduism, and Underground Religion.* Cambridge: Cambridge University Press.

Leider, Jacques. 2008. "Forging Buddhist credentials as a tool of legitimacy and ethnic identity: A study of Arakan's subjection in nineteenth-century Burma." *Journal of the Economic and Social History of the Orient.* Vol. 51: 409–59.

———. 2010. "Southeast Asian Buddhist Monks in the Peregrinação: Tracing the 'Rolins' of Fernao Mendes Pinto in the Eastern Bay of Bengal." In *Fernao Mendes Pinto and the Peregrinação: Studies, Restored Text, Notes and Indexes,* edited by Jorge M. dos Santos Alves, 145–62. Lisbon: Fundacao Oriente et Imprensa Nacional-Casa da Moeda.

Lelyveld, Joseph. 2011. *Great Soul: Mahatma Gandhi and His Struggle with India.* New York: Alfred A. Knopf.

Leonard, Dickens. 2017. "One Step Inside Tamilian: On the Anti-Caste Writing of Language." *Social Scientist.* 45/1–2: 19–32.

————. 2019. "From Discourse to Critique? Iyothee Thass and the Dalit Intellectual Legacy." In *Multilingualism and the Literary Cultures of India: Proceedings of the seminar on Multilingualism and the Literary Culture Organized by the Sahitya Akademi on 27-29 March 2014 at Hyderabad.* Edited by M.T. Ansari, 200–34. New Delhi: Sahitya Akademi.

Leoshko, Janice. 2003. *Sacred Traces: British Explorations of Buddhism in South Asia.* Hants, England: Ashgate.

LeVine, Sarah and David Gellner. 2005. *Rebuilding Buddhism: The Theravada Movement in Twentieth-Century Nepal.* Cambridge: Harvard University Press.

Lewis, Todd. 2000. *Popular Buddhist Texts from Nepal: Narratives and Rituals of Newar Buddhism.* Translations in collaboration with Subarna Man Tuladhar and Labh Ratna Tuladhar. Albany: State University of New York.

Liang, Chi Chao. 1924. "China's Debt to India." *Visva-Bharati Quarterly.* Vol. 2/3: 251–61.

Lin, Nancy. 2011. "Adapting the Buddha's Biographies: A Cultural History of the Wish-Fulfilling Vine in Tibet, Seventeenth to Eighteenth Centuries." PhD diss., University of California Berkeley.

Ling, Trevor. 1979. *Buddha, Marx and God: Some Aspects of Religion in the Modern World.* Ann Arbor: University of Michigan Press.

Lopez Jr., Donald S. (ed). 1995. *Curators of the Buddha: The Study of Buddhism under Colonialism.* Chicago: University of Chicago Press.

Lopez Jr., Donald S. 1998. *Prisoners of Shangri-La: Tibetan Buddhism and the West.* Chicago: University of Chicago Press.

————. 2009. *Buddhism and Science: A Guide for the Perplexed.* Chicago: University of Chicago Press.

————. 2012. *The Scientific Buddha: His Short and Happy Life.* New Haven: Yale University Press.

————. 2013. *From Stone to Flesh: A Short History of the Buddha.* Chicago: University of Chicago Press.

Lorenzen, David N. 2006. *Who Invented Hinduism: Essays on Religion in History.* New Delhi: Yoda Press.

Lynch, Owen M. 1969. *The Politics of Untouchability: Social Mobility and Social Change in a City of India.* New York: Columbia University Press.

Madalapanji: The Chronicle of Jagannath Temple (Rajabhoga Itihasa). 2009. Translated from the Odia by K.S. Behera and A.N. Parida. Bhubaneswar: Amadeus Press.

Madan, P.L. 2004. *Tibet: Saga of Indian Explorers (1864–1894).* New Delhi: Manohar.

Maha Bodhi Centenary Volume, 1891–1991. 1991. Calcutta: Maha Bodhi Society of India.

Maitreya and Vishvanatha Prasad Mishra. 1924. *Buddha-mimaṃsa.* Benares: Tripathi.

Maitreya and Yogiraja. 1924. *The Buddha Mimansa: The Buddha and His Relation to the Religion of the Vedas.* Calcutta: Thacker, Spinck & Co.

Malagoda, Kitsiri. 1972. *Buddhism in Sinhalese Society, 1750–1900: A Study of Religious Revival and Change.* Berkeley: University of California Press.

Malaviya, Pandit Padhamkant. 1968. "Mahamana Malaviya aur Jugalkishor Birla."

In *Ek Bindu, Ek Sindhu: Svargiya Jugalakishor Birla*, edited by Dev Datta Shastri, 68–70. Mathura: Shrikrishna Janmasthan Sevasaṃgha.

Mallinson, James. 2019. *"Kalavañcana* in the Konkan: How a Vajrayana *Hathayoga* Tradition Cheated Buddhism's Death in India." *Religions.* Vol. 10/4: 1–33.

Manjapra, Kris. 2012. "Knowledgeable Internationalism and the Swadeshi Movement, 1903–1921." *Economic and Political Weekly.* Vol. 47/42: 53–62.

Mann, Michael. 2004. "Torchbearers upon the Path of Progress: Britain's Ideology of a 'Moral and Material Progress' in India." In *Colonialism as Civilizing Mission: Cultural Ideology in British India,* edited by Harald Fischer-Tiné and Michael Mann, 1–28. London: Anthem Press.

Manu's Code of Law: A Critical Edition and Translation of the Manava-Dharmasastra. 2005. Translated from the Sanskrit by Patrick Olivelle with the editorial assistance of Suman Olivelle. Oxford and New York: Oxford University Press.

Marshall, P.J (ed). 1970. *The British Discovery of Hinduism in the Eighteenth Century.* Cambridge: Cambridge University Press.

Marston, John. 2007. "The Cambodian Hospital for Monks." In *Buddhism, Power and Political Order,* edited by Ian Harris, 104–20. London: Routledge.

Martin, R. Montgomery. 1838. *The History, Antiquities, Topography and Statistics of Eastern India.* 3 vols. London: Allen and Lane.

Masuzawa, Tomoko. 2005. *The Invention of World Religions, or How European Universalism Was Preserved in the Language of Pluralism.* Chicago: University of Chicago Press.

Mavalankar, Damodar. 1940. *Damodar: The Writings of a Hindu Chela.* Edited by Sven Eek. Adyar: Theosophical Publishing House.

———. 1978. *Damodar and the Pioneers of the Theosophical Movement.* Adyar: Theosophical Publishing House.

———. 1982. *The Service of Humanity.* Santa Barbara: Concord Grove Press.

McGovern, Nathan. 2018. *The Snake and the Mongoose: The Emergence of Identity in Early Indian Religion.* New York: Oxford University Press.

McKay, Alex. 2002. "The Drowning of Lama Sengchen Kyabying: a preliminary enquiry from British sources." In *Tibet Past and Present: Tibetan Studies I: the proceedings of the 9th international seminar for Tibetan Studies, Leiden 2000,* edited by Henk Blezer, 263–80. Leiden: Brill.

McKeown, Arthur. 2019. *Guarding of a Dying Flame: Shariputra (c. 1335–1426) and the End of Late Indian Buddhism.* Cambridge: Harvard University Press.

McMahan, David. 2008. *The Making of Buddhist Modernism.* Oxford: Oxford University Press.

Meadowcroft, Keith. 2006. "The All-India Hindu Maha Sabha, untouchable politics, and 'denationalising' conversions: the Moonje-Ambedkar Pact." *South Asia: Journal of South Asian Studies.* Vol. 29/1: 9–41.

Medhankar, Bhadant Savangi. 2002. *Dr. Bhadant Anand Kausalyayan: Jivan-darshan.* Nagpur: Buddh Bhoomi Prakashan.

Mendelson, E. Michael. 1975. *Sangha and State in Burma: A Study of Monastic Sectarianism and Leadership.* Ithaca: Cornell University Press.

Missionary Expedition. 1881. Calcutta: Brahmo Tract Society.

Mitchell, Stephen. 2008. *Buddhism: Introducing the Buddhist Experience.* Oxford: Oxford University Press.

Mitra, Rajendralal. 1882. *The Sanskrit Buddhist Literature of Nepal*. Calcutta: Asiatic Society of Bengal.

Mitra, R.C. 1954. *The Decline of Buddhism in India*. Santiniketan: Visva-Bharati Press.

Mitra, Rajendralal, August Friedrich Rudolf Hoernle, and Pramatha Nath Bose. 1885. *Centenary Review of the Asiatic Society of Bengal from 1784 to 1883*. Calcutta: Asiatic Society of Bengal.

Mitra, Rajendralal. 1875–1880. *The Antiquities of Orissa*, Vol. 1 (1875) and 2 (1880). Calcutta: Government of India.

———. 1877. *The Lalita Vistara, or Memoirs of the Early Life of Sakya Sinha*. Edited from the Sanskrit with an introduction by Rajendralal Mitra. Calcutta: Asiatic Society of Bengal.

———. 1878. *Buddha Gaya: The Hermitage of Sakya Muni*. Calcutta: Bengal Secretariat Press.

Mojumdar, Kanchanmoy. 1973. *Political Relations Between India and Nepal, 1877-1923*. New Delhi: Munshiram Manoharlal.

Monier-Williams, Monier. 1889 [1883]. *Buddhism in its Connexion with Brahmanism and Hinduism, and in its contrast with Christianity*. New York: MacMillan and Co.

Monius, Anne. 2001. *Imagining a Place for Buddhism: Literary Culture and Religious Community in Tamil-speaking South India*. Oxford: Oxford University Press.

Mookerjee, Sameer Chandra. 1921. "Essential Steps to India's Regeneraton: An address to the Indian public assembled at the Baisak Festival at the Chaitya Vihara, Calcutta." Two-part essay in *MBJ*. Vol. 29/7: 242–47, and Vol. 29/8: 284–89.

———. 1923. "The need for coalition between Hindus and Buddhists," *MBJ*. Vol. 31/6: 210–14;

———. 1924. "Why India Needs Buddhism," *MBJ*. Vol. 32/4: 162–71.

Moon, Vasant. 2001. *Growing up Untouchable in India: A Dalit Autobiography*. Translated from the Marathi by Gail Omvedt with an introduction by Eleanor Zelliot. New York: Rowman and Littlefield.

Mukherjee, Prabhat. 1940. *History of Medieval Vaishnavism in Orissa*. Calcutta: R. Chatterji.

Mukherji, Babu Purna Chandra. 1899. *Archaeological Survey of India: A Report on a Tour of Exploration of the Antiquities, in the Tarai, Nepal the Region of Kapilavastu during February and March, 1899*. No. 26. Government of United Provinces: Public Works Department.

Murugesan, K, and C.S. Subramanyam. 1975. *Singaravelu: First Communist in South India*. New Delhi: People's Publishing House.

Nakamura, Hajime. [1980] 1999. *Indian Buddhism: A Survey with Bibliographic Notes*. New Delhi: Motilal Banarsidass.

Narain, Sheo. 1923. "Revival of Buddhism." *MBJ*. Vol. 31/7: 254–62.

———. 1933. "In memoriam." *MBJ*. Vol. 41/7–8: 259–61.

Narasu, P. Lakshmi. 1922. *A Study of Caste*. Madras: K.V. Raghavulu.

———. [1907] 1976. *The Essence of Buddhism*. 1912 edition with a foreword by Anagarika Dharmapala. 1948 edition with a preface by Dr Bhimrao Ambedkar. New Delhi: Bharatiya Publishing House.

———. 2002. *Religion of the Modern Buddhist*. Edited and introduced by G. Aloysius. New Delhi: Samyak Prakashan.

———. [1916] 2009. *What is Buddhism?* With an introduction by Devapriya Valisinha in the 1946 edition. New Delhi: Samyak Prakashan.

Nariman, G.K. 1920. *Literary History of Sanskrit Buddhism: From Winternitz, Sylvain Levi, Huber.* Bombay: D.B. Taraporevala Sons & Co.

Neelis, Jason. 2011. *Early Buddhist Transmission and Trade Networks: Mobility and Exchange within and beyond the Northwestern Borderlands of South Asia.* Leiden: Brill.

Nehru, Jawaharlal. [1934–35] 1982. *Glimpses of World History.* New Delhi: Jawaharlal Nehru Memorial Fund.

———. [1936] 1941. *Toward Freedom: The Autobiography of Jawaharlal Nehru.* New York: John Day.

———. [1946] 1985a. *The Discovery of India.* New Delhi: Oxford University Press.

———. 1982–87. *Selected Works of Jawaharlal Nehru.* Vol. 1–9. Edited by S. Gopal. New Delhi: Jawaharlal Nehru Memorial Fund.

———. 1985b. *Jawaharlal Nehru, Letters to Chief Ministers: 1947–1964.* Vol. 1. Edited by G. Parthasarathi. New Delhi: Oxford University Press.

Neminath Maharaj, Acharya Swami. 1956. *Is the Republic of India Secular?* Calcuta: D.L. Bardiya.

Nichidatsu, Fuji. [1972] 1975. *My Non-violence: An Autobiography of a Japanese Buddhist.* Translated from the Japanese by T. Yamaori. Tokyo: Japan Buddha Sangha Press.

Nicholson, Andrew. 2010. *Unifying Hinduism: Philosophy and Identity in Indian Intellectual History.* New York: Columbia University Press.

Novetzke, Christian. 2008. *Religion and Public Memory: A Cultural History of Saint Namdev in India.* New York: Columbia University Press.

Nye, Joseph. 1990. "Soft Power." *Foreign Policy.* No. 80: 153–71.

O'Hanlon, Rosalind. 1985. *Caste, Conflict and Ideology: Mahatma Jotirao Phule and Low Caste Protest in Nineteenth-Century Western India.* Cambridge: Cambridge University Press.

O'Malley, L.S.S. 1907. *Bengal District Gazetteers: Darjeeling.* Calcutta: The Bengal Secretariat Book Depot.

Ober, Douglas. 2013. "'Like embers hidden in ashes, or jewels encrusted in stone': Rahul Sankrityayan, Dharmanand Kosambi and Buddhist activity in late British India." *Contemporary Buddhism.* Vol. 14/1: 134–48.

———. 2019a. "Buddhism in Colonial Contexts." *Oxford Research Encyclopedia of Religion.* 30 October. Accessed 10 January 2023. https://oxfordre.com/religion/view/10.1093/acrefore/9780199340378.001.0001/acrefore-9780199340378-e-565.

———. 2019b. "From Buddha Bones to Bo Trees: Nehruvian India, Buddhism, and the Poetics of Power." *Modern Asian Studies.* Vol. 53/4: 1312–50.

———. 2020. "Socialism, Russia, and India's Revolutionary Dharma." In *Buddhism in the Global Eye: Beyond East and West,* edited by John Harding, Victor Sogen Hori and Alexander Soucy, 71–86. London: Bloomsbury Academic.

———. 2021. "Translating the Buddha: Edwin Arnold's *Light of Asia* and Its Indian Publics." *Humanities.* Vol. 10/3: 1–18.

Ober, Douglas and Padma Dorje Maitland. Forthcoming. "Temple Architecture and Modern Hindu Appropriations of Buddhism." *Comparative Studies in South Asia, Africa, and the Middle East.*

Oberoi, Harjot. 1994. *The Construction of Religious Boundaries: Culture, Identity, and Diversity in the Sikh Tradition.* Chicago: University of Chicago Press.

Ojha, P.N. 1986. *Homage to Bhikkhu Jagadish Kashyap: A Commemorative Volume.* Nalanda: NavaNalanda Mahavihara.

Olcott, Henry. 1883. "The Theosophical Society and Its Aims." *A Collection of Lectures on Theosophy and Archaic Religions,* 1–17. Madras: A. Theyaga Rajier.

———. 1890. "Net Results of Our Indian Work." *The Theosophist.* Vol. 12/1.

———. [1881] 1897. *Buddhist Catechism.* Adyar: Theosophical Society.

———. 1900. *Old Diary Leaves: The Only Authentic History of the Theosophical Society, Second Series, 1878–83.* London: Theosophical Publishing Society.

———. 1902. *The Poor Pariah.* Madras: published by the author.

Olivelle, Patrick, Janice Leoshko and Himanshu Prabha Ray (eds). 2012. *Reimagining Asoka: Memory and History.* New Delhi: Oxford University Press.

Omvedt, Gail. 2003. *Buddhism in India: Challenging Brahmanism and Caste.* New Delhi: Sage Publications.

Ottama, U, Bhadant Bodhananda, and Chandrika Prasad Jigyasu. 1933. *Bhagavan Gautama Buddha: Jivani aur Updesh.* Calcutta: Kishkamitra Press.

Overstreet, Gene and Marshall Windmiller. 1959. *Communism in India.* Berkeley: University of California Press.

Pandey, Gyanendra. 2012. "Un-archived Histories: The 'Mad' and the 'Trifling'." *Economic and Political Weekly.* Vol. 47/1, 7 January: 37–41.

———. 2013. *A History of Prejudice: Race, Caste and Difference in India and the United States.* Cambridge: Cambridge University Press.

Pandit Nagendranath Vasu: A Sketch of His Life and Works. 1916. Calcutta: Kumudini Kanta Ganguli.

Paula, Ratna. 1834. "Translation of an inscription in the Pali and Burma languages on a stone slab from Ramavati, (Ramree Island), in Arracan, presented to the Asiatic Society by H. Walters, Esq. CS, as explained by Ratna Paula." *Journal of the Asiatic Society of Bengal.* Vol. 3/29: 209–14.

———. 1838. "Restoration and translation of the inscription on the large Arracan bell now at Nadrohighat, Zillah Alligarh, described by Captain Wroughton in the *Journal of the Asiatic Society,* December 1837." *Journal of the Asiatic Society of Bengal.* Vol. 7/76: 287–96.

Perreira, Todd LeRoy. 2012. "Whence Theravada? The Modern Geneaology of an Ancient Term." In *How Theravada Is Theravada? Exploring Buddhist Identities,* edited by Peter Skilling, Jason A. Carbine, Claudio Cicuzza, Santi Pakdeekham, 443–571. Chiang Mai: Silkworm Books.

Perumal, S. 1998. "Revival of Tamil Buddhism: A Historical Survey." In *Buddhism in Tamil Nadu: Collected Papers,* edited by G. John Samuel, R.S. Murthy and M.S. Nagarajan, 529–42. Chennai: Institute of Asian Studies.

Peterson, Indira Viswanathan. 1989. *Poems to Siva: The Hymns of the Tamil Saints.* Princeton: Princeton University Press.

Phule, Jotirao. 2002. *Selected Writings of Jotirao Phule.* Edited by G.P. Desphande. New Delhi: Leftword.

Pittman, Donald. 2001. *Towards a Modern Chinese Buddhism: Taixu's Reforms.* Honolulu: University of Hawai'i Press.

Pollock, Sheldon. 1989. "Mimamsa and the Problem of History in Traditional India," *Journal of the American Oriental Society.* Vol. 109/4: 603–10.

———. 2006. *The Language of the Gods in the World of Men: Sanskrit, Culture, and Power in Premodern India.* Berkeley: University of California Press.

———. 2011. "Introduction." *Forms of Knowledge in Early Modern Asia: Explorations in the Intellectual History of India and Tibet, 1500–1800,* 1–16. Durham and London: Duke University Press.

Powell, Avril A. 1999. "History textbooks and the transmission of the pre-colonial past in northwestern India in the 1860s and 1870s." In *Invoking the Past: The Uses of History in South Asia,* edited by Daud Ali, 90–133. New Delhi: Oxford University.

Powers, John. 2012. *A Bull of a Man: Images of Masculinity, Sex, and the Body in Indian Buddhism.* Cambridge, Mass.: Harvard University Press.

Prasad, Rajendra. 1984. *Dr. Rajendra Prasad: Correspondence and Select Documents.* Vols 3–10. Edited by Valmiki Choudhary. New Delhi: Allied Publishers.

Prashad, Vijay. 2000. *Untouchable Freedom: A Social History of a Dalit Community.* New Delhi: Oxford University Press.

Prothero, Stephen. [1996] 2011. *The White Buddhist: The Asian Odyssey of Henry Steel Olcott.* 2nd edition. Bloomington: Indiana University Press.

Pryor, Richard. 2012. "Bodh Gaya in the 1950s: Jawaharlal Nehru, Mahant Giri and Anagarika Munindra." In *Cross-disciplinary Perspectives on a Contested Buddhist Site: Bodh Gaya Jataka,* edited by David Geary, Matthew R. Sayers, and Abhishek Singh Amar, 110–18. London: Routledge.

Pullapilly, Cyriac. 1976. "The Izhavas of Kerala and their historic struggle for acceptance in the Hindu society." *Journal of Asian and African Studies.* Vol. 11/1: 24–46.

Queen, Christopher. 1996. "Dr. Ambedkar and the Hermeneutics of Buddhist Liberation." In *Engaged Buddhism: Buddhist Liberation Movements in Asia,* edited by Christopher S. Queen and Sallie B. King, 45–72. Albany: State University of New York Press.

Radhakrishnan, Sarvepalli. 1946. "Presidential Address at the 12th All-India Oriental Conference at Benares Hindu University." In *Proceedings and Transactions of All India Oriental Conference 1943–44.* Benares: Banaras Hindu University.

———. 1950. *Dhammpada: With Introductory Essays, Pali Text, English Translation and Notes.* Oxford: Oxford University Press.

———. 1956. "Foreword." In *2,500 Years of Buddhism,* edited by P.V. Bapat, v–xvi. New Delhi: Ministry of Information and Broadcasting.

Rahman, Smita A. 2010. "The presence of the past: negotiating the politics of collective memory." *Contemporary Political Theory,* Vol. 9/1: 59–76.

Raj, Arun Prakash. "Constructed Buddhism and Living Jainism: Encounters and Dialogues in the Early Twentieth-Century Madras Presidency." Unpublished paper.

Rajangam, Stalin. 2018. "Living Buddhism." Unpublished lecture delivered at "The Genealogies of Dalit Learning and Humanist Buddhism in 19th and 20th Century India." University of Toronto. 25 October.

Ralhan, O.P. 1998. *Communist Party of India.* New Delhi: Anmol Publications Pvt. Ltd.

Ram, Rajendra. 2006. *Karmayogi Kripasharan Mahasthavir Bauddhdharm ka Dhruvatara*. Kolkata: Bauddha Dharmankur Sabha.

Ram, Ronki. 2012. "Beyond Conversion and Sanskritisation: Articulating an Alternative Dalit Agenda in East Punjab." *Modern Asian Studies*. Vol. 46/3: 639–702.

Ramesh, Jairam. 2021. *The Light of Asia: The Poem that Defined the Buddha*. New Delhi: Penguin Viking.

Rao, Anupama. 2009. *The Caste Question: Dalits and the Politics of Modern India*. Berkeley: University of California Press.

Rao, G. Venkoba. 1927–28. "Kumbakonam Inscription of Sevvapa-Nayaka." *Epigraphica Indica*, Vol. XIX. Calcutta: Government of India Central Publication Branch.

Rao, V. Narayan. 2008. "Buddhism in Modern Andhra: Literary Representations from Telugu." *The Journal of Hindu Studies*. Vol. 1/1–2: 93–119.

Rawat, Ramnarayan S. 2011. *Reconsidering Untouchability: Chamars and Dalit History in North India*. Bloomington: Indiana University Press.

———. 2015. "Genealogies of the Dalit political: the transformation of *achhut* from 'Untouched' to "Untouchable' in early twentieth-century north India." *The Indian Economic and Social History Review*. Vol. 52/3: 335–55.

Ray, Haraprasad. 1993. *Trade and Diplomacy in India-China Relations*. New Delhi: Radiant Publishers.

Ray, Himanshu Prabha. 2007. "Narratives of Faith: Buddhism and Colonial Archaeology in Monsoon Asia." *Asia Research Institute, Working Papers Series*. No.99: 1–42.

———. 2014. *The Return of the Buddha: Ancient Symbols for a New Nation*. New Delhi: Routledge.

———. 2015. "A 'Chinese' Pagoda at Nagapattinam on the Tamil Coast: Revisiting India's Early Maritime Networks." *Occasional Publication* 66. New Delhi: India International Centre.

Report on the progress of education in the northwestern provinces. 1864–1870. Allahabad: Government Press.

Rhys Davids, Caroline (tr.). 1909. *Psalms of the Early Buddhists*. London: Pali Text Society.

Rhys Davids, T.W. 1877. *Buddhism: A Sketch of the Life and Teachings of Gautama, the Buddha*. London: Society for Promoting Christian Knowledge.

Risley, Herbert Hope. 1915. *The People of India*. 2nd Edition. Edited by William Crooke. Calcutta and Simla: Thacker, Spink & Co.

Robinson, Catherine. 2006. *Interpretations of the Bhagavad-Gita and Images of the Hindu Tradition*. London and New York: Routledge.

Rodrigues, Valerian. 1993. "Making a Tradition Critical: Ambedkar's Reading of Buddhism." In *Dalit Movements and the Meanings of Labour in India*, edited by Peter Robb, 299–338. New Delhi: Oxford University Press.

Roy, Shukla. 1988. *Indian Political Thought: Impact of Russian Revolution*. Calcutta: Minerva Publications.

Roy, Srirupa. 2006. "A Symbol of Freedom: The Indian Flag and the Transformations of Nationalism, 1906-2002." *Journal of Asian Studies*. Vol. 65/3: 495–527.

Sabukuttan, K. 2002. *C. Krishnan and Social Change in Kerala.* Kottayam: Lalu Books.

Sahajanand, Swami. 1995. *Swami Sahajanand and the Peasants of Jharkhand: A View from 1941 [Jharkhand ke Kisan].* Edited and translated from the Hindi by Walter Hauser. New Delhi: Manohar.

Sanderson, Alexis. 2015. "Tolerance, Exclusivity, Inclusivity and Persecution in Indian Religion during the Early Medieval Period." In *Honoris Causa: Essays in Honour of Aveek Sarkar,* edited by John Makinson, 155–224. New York: Allen Lane.

Sangari, Kumkum, and Sudesh Vaid (eds). [1990] 1999. *Recasting Women: Essays in Indian Colonial History.* New Brunswick: Rutgers University Press.

Sangharakshita, Bhikkhu. 1952. "A Buddhist Bible?" *MBJ.* Vol. 60/5–6: 221–23.

———. 1991. *Facing Mount Kanchenjunga: An English Buddhist in the Eastern Himalayas.* Birmingham: Windhorse Publications.

———. 1996. *In the Sign of the Golden Wheel: Indian Memoirs of an English Buddhist.* Birmingham: Windhorse Publications.

———. [1986] 2006. *Ambedkar and Buddhism.* New Delhi: Motilal Banarsidass.

Sankrityayan, Rahul. 1942. *Volga se Ganga.* Allahabad: Kitab Mahal.

———. 1957. *Jinka Main Kritagya.* Allahabad: Kitab Mahal.

———. [1957] 1975. *Navdikshit Bauddh.* Edited by Pragyananda Mahasthavir. Lucknow: Buddh Vihara.

———. 1984. *Selected Essays of Rahul Sankrityayan.* New Delhi: People's Publishing House.

———. [1956] 1994. "Buddhist Dialectics." In *Essays on Indology: Mahapandita Rahula Sankrityayana Birth Centenary Volume,* edited by Alaka Chattopadhyaya, 1–9. Calcutta: Manisa.

———. [1930] 2011. *Buddhacharya.* New Delhi: Samyak Prakashan.

———. [1956] 2011. *Mahamanav Buddh.* New Delhi: Samyak Prakashan.

———. [1944–63] 2014. *Meri Jivan Yatra.* Vols. I–IV. New Delhi: Radhakrishna Prakashan.

Sarao, K.T.S. 2002. "Double Tragedy: A Reappraisal of the Decline of Buddhism in India." *International Journal of Buddhist Thought and Culture.* Vol. 1: 97–107.

———. 2012. *The Decline of Buddhism in India: A Fresh Perspective.* New Delhi: Manoharlal.

Sarasvati, Dayanand. 1987. *Autobiography,* 3rd revised edition. Edited and translated from the Hindi by K.C. Yadav. New Delhi: Manohar.

Sarkar, Benoy Kumar. 1916. "Sino-Japanese Buddhism and Neo-Hinduism." *Modern Review.* Vol. 20: 39–47.

———. 1922. *The Futurism of Young Asia and Other Essays on the Relations between the East and the West.* Berlin: Springer.

Sarma, Sreeramula Rajeswara. 1995–96. "Sanskrit as Vehicle for Modern Science: Lancelot Wilkinson's Efforts in the 1830s." *Studies in History of Medicine and Science.* Vol. 14: 189–99.

Sathaye, Adheesh. 2015. *Crossing the Lines of Caste: Visvamitra and the Construction of Brahmin Power in Hindu Mythology.* Oxford: Oxford University Press.

Satyadevji, Shri Svami. 1923. *Shribuddha Gita.* Agra: Lavaniyan Publishing House.

Savarkar, V.D. [1923] 1938. *Hindutva: Who is a Hindu?* New Delhi: Central Hindu Yuvak Sabha.

Schimmelpennick van der Oye, David. 2010. *Russian Orientalism: Asia in the Russian Mind from Peter the Great to the Emigration.* New Haven: Yale University Press.

Schopen, Gregory. 1991. "Archaeology and Protestant Presuppositions in the Study of Indian Buddhism." *History of Religions.* Vol. 31/1: 1–23.

Scott, David. 2004. *Conscripts of Modernity: The Tragedy of Colonial Enlightenment.* Durham: Duke University Press.

Sen, Keshab Chunder. [1881–1882] 1956. *Sadhusamagam: Discourses on Pilgrimage to the Prophets.* Edited and translated from the Bengali by Jamini Kanta Koar. Calcutta: Navavidhan Publication Committee.

Sen, Tansen. 2003. *Buddhism, Diplomacy and Trade: The Realignment of India-China Relations, 600–1400.* Honolulu: University of Hawai'i Press.

———. 2016. "Taixu's Goodwill Mission to India: Reviving the Buddhist Links between China and India." In *Buddhism in Asia: Revival and Reinvention,* edited by Nayanjot Lahiri and Upinder Singh, 293–322. New Delhi: Manohar.

———. 2017. *India, China, and the World: A Connected History.* Lanham: Rowman & Littlefield.

Seneviratne, H.L. 1999. *The Work of Kings: The New Buddhism in Sri Lanka.* Chicago: University of Chicago Press.

Seshadri, Gokul. 2009. "New Perspectives on Nagapattinam: The Medieval Port City in the Context of Political, Religious, and Commercial Exchanges between South India, Southeast Asia and China." In *Reflections on the Chola Naval Expeditions to Southeast Asia,* edited by Hermann Kulke, K. Kesavapany, and Vijay Sakhuja, 102–34. Singapore: Institute of South-east Asian Studies.

Shakspo, N.T. 1988. "The Revival of Buddhism in Modern Ladakh." In *Tibetan Studies: Proceedings of the 4th Seminar of the International Association for Tibetan Studies,* edited by Helga Uebach and Jampa L. Panglung, 439–48. Munich: Schloss Hokenkammer.

Shakya, Tsering. 1999. *Dragon in the Land of Snows: A History of Modern Tibet since 1947.* London: Pimilico.

Shankar, Pandit Shyama. 1914. *Buddha and His Sayings, with Comments on Re-incarnation, Karma, Nirvana, etc.* London: Francis Griffiths.

Sharma, Arvind. 2003. "Did the Hindus Lack a Sense of History?" *Numen.* Vol. 50: 190–227

Sharma, Jyotirmaya. 2013. *A Restatement of Religion: Swami Vivekananda and the Making of Hindu Nationalism.* New Haven and London: Yale University Press.

Sharma, P.S. [1898–99] 1980. *Anthology of Kumarila Bhatta's Works.* New Delhi: Motilal Banarsidass.

Shastri, Dev Datta (ed.). 1968. *Ek Bindu, Ek Sindhu: Svargiya Jugalakishor Birla.* Mathura: Shrikrsna Janmasthan Sevasamgha.

Shastri, Haraprasad. 1882. "Kanchanmala." *Bangadarshan.* Vol. 9: 141–50, 157–71, 208–13, 272–86, 323–26, 387–93, 418–29, 476–94.

———. 1894. "Discovery of Living Buddhism in Bengal." *Proceedings of the Asiatic Society of Bengal.* Vol. 1/2: 135–38.

———. 1895a. "Buddhism in Bengal since the Muhammadan Conquest." *Journal of the Asiatic Society of Bengal.* Vol. 64: 65–68.

————. 1895b. "Sri Dharmamangala: A Distant Echo of the *Lalita Vistara*." *Journal of the Asiatic Society of Bengal*. Vol. 64: 55–64.

————. 1897. *Discovery of Living Buddhism in Bengal*. Calcutta: Hare Press.

————. 1917. *A Descriptive Catalogue of Sanscrit Manuscripts in the Government Collection, under the Care of the Asiatic Society of Bengal. Vol 1: Buddhist Manuscripts*. Calcutta: Baptist Mission Press.

Shastri, Tephun Tenzin. 2005. *Freedom Fighter: The Untold Story of the Tibetan Freedom Movement in Exile: The Life of Gan Thupten Jungney (Gan Gose La) Foremost Exiled Freedom Activist*. Edited by Katrina Swenson. Sarnath: Tibetan Monastery.

Shields, James Mark. 2012. "Blueprint for Buddhist Revolution: The Radical Buddhism of Seno' Girō (1889–1961) and the Youth League for Revitalizing Buddhism." *Japanese Journal of Religious Studies*. Vol. 39/2: 333–51.

Shin'ichirō, Hori. 2015. "Evidence of Buddhism in 15th Century India: Clues from the Colophon of a *Kalacakratantra* Manuscript in Old Bengali Script." *Journal of Indian and Buddhist Studies*. Vol. 63/3: 228–34.

————. 2017. "Buddhism in 15th Century Eastern India: Sanskrit Manuscript Evidence and Tibetan Sources." Paper delivered to the International Association of Buddhist Studies, Toronto, 23 August 2017.

Silk, Jonathan. 2020. "Indian Buddhist Attitudes toward Outcastes: Rhetoric around Candalas." *Indo-Iranian Journal*. Vol. 63: 128–87.

Singh, Upinder. 2004. *The Discovery of Ancient India: Early Archaeologists and the Beginnings of Archaeology*. New Delhi: Permanent Black.

Singh, Upinder and Nayanjot Lahiri. 2010. *Ancient India: New Research*. New Delhi: Oxford University Press.

Sinnett, Alfred. 1883. *Esoteric Buddhism*. Boston and New York: Houghton, Mifflin and Company.

Sivaprasad, Raja. [1864] 1883. *Itihas Timir Nashak*. Part I. Allahabad: Government Publishing House.

————. 1874. *Itihas Timir Nashak*. Part II. Benares: Government of India Medical Hall Press.

————. [1874] 1880. *Itihas Timir Nashak*. Part III. Allahabad: Government Publishing House.

Slusser, Mary Shepherd. 1988. "Bodhgaya and Nepal." In *Bodhgaya, the site of enlightenment*, edited by Janice Leoshko, 125–42. Bombay: Marg Publications.

Snelling, John. 1993. *Buddhism in Russia: The Story of Agvan Dorzhiev, Lhasa's e\ Emissary to the Tsar*. With a foreword by Stephen Batchelor. Longmead: Element Books.

Snodgrass, Judith. 2003. *Presenting Japanese Buddhism to the West: Orientalism, Occidentalism, and the Columbian Exposition*. Chapel Hill: University of North Carolina Press.

Srinivas, Smriti. 2015. *A Place for Utopia: Urban Designs from South Asia*. Seattle and London: University of Washington Press.

St. Sekkizhaar's Periya Puranam. 1995. Translated from the Tamil by T.N. Ramachandran. Vol. 2. Thanjavur: Tamil University.

Stark, Ulrike. 2007. *An Empire of Books: The Naval Kishore Press and the Dissemination of the Printed Word in Colonial India*. New Delhi: Orient Blackswan.

———— . 2012. "Knowledge in context: Raja Shivaprasad as hybrid intellectual and people's educator." In *Trans-colonial Modernities in South Asia,* edited by Michael S. Dodson and Brian A. Hatcher, 66–91. London: Routledge.

Starza, O.M. 1993. *The Jagannatha Temple at Puri: Its Architecture, Art, and Cult.* Leiden: Brill.

Stcherbatski, Fyodor [=Stcherbatsky, Theodore]. 1970. *Further Papers of Th. Stcherbatsky.* Translated from the Russian into English by H.C. Gupta and edited by D. Chattopadhyaya. Calcutta: R.D. Press.

Stoddard, Heather. 1986. *Le Mendiant de l'Amdo.* Paris: Société d'Ethnographie.

Stolte, Carolien. 2016. "Compass Points: Four Indian Cartographies of Asia, ca. 1930-1955," In *Asianisms: Regionalist Interactions and Asian Integration,* edited by M. Frey and N. Spakowski, 49–74. Singapore: NUS Press.

Stone, Jacqueline. 2003. "Nichiren's Activist Heirs: Sōka Gakkai, Risshō Kōseikai, Nipponzon Myōhōji." In *Action Dharma: New Studies in Engaged Buddhism,* edited by Christopher Queen, Charles Prebish and Damien Keown, 63–94. London: Routledge.

Strahan, Lt Col G. 1889. *Report of the Explorations of Lama Serap Gyatso, 1856-68 in Sikkim, Bhutan and Tibet.* Published under the direction of Col. H.R. Thuillier, Surveyor General of India. Dehra Dun: Survey of India.

Strong, John. 2015. *Buddhisms: An Introduction.* London: OneWorld.

Stuart, Daniel M. 2020. *S.N. Goenka: Emissary of Insight.* Boulder: Shambhala.

Sumedha Thero, K. Siri (ed.). 2010. *History of the Mulagandha Kuty Vihara Sacred Relics and Wall Paintings at Isipatana—The First Preaching Place of the Buddha.* Sarnath: Mulagandha Kuty Vihara.

Surendran, Gitanjali. 2013. "The Indian Discovery of Buddhism: Buddhist Revival in India, c. 1890–1956." PhD diss., Harvard University.

Tambiah, Stanley. 1976. *World Conqueror and World Renouncer.* Cambridge: Cambridge University Press.

Taranatha. 1970. *History of Buddhism in India (dpal dus kyi 'khor lo'I chos bskor gyi byung khungs nyer mkho).* Translated from the Tibetan by Lama Chimpa and Alaka Chattopadhyaya. Simla: Indian Institute of Advanced Study.

Teltumbde, Anand. 2017a. "Bridging the unholy rift." In *B.R. Ambedkar: India and Communism,* edited by A. Teltumbde. New Delhi: LeftWord Books.

———— . 2017b. *Dalits: Past, Present and Future.* New York: Routledge.

Templeman, David. 1997. "Buddhaguptanatha: A Late Indian *Siddha* in Tibet." In *Tibetan Studies: Proceedings of the 7th Seminar of the International Association of Tibetan Studies, Graz, 1995,* Vol. II, edited by H. Krasser, M.T. Much, E. Steinkellner, and H. Tauscher, 955–66. Wien: Verlag der Österreichischen Akademie der Wissenchaften.

Tha Doe Hla. 2002. *The Life Story of Sri Bhaddanta Chandramani Mahathera.* Translated from the Burmese by Sein Tun Aung. Varanasi: U Chandramani Foundation.

The Ain-I-Akbari by Abul Fazl Allami. 1873–1907. Translated from Persian by H. Blochmann and H.S. Jarrett. Vols I–III. Calcutta: Asiatic Society of Bengal.

The Kalyani Inscriptions Erected by King Dhammaceti at Pegu in 1476: Text and translation. 1892. Translated from the Mon and Pali by Taw Sein Ko. Rangoon: Government Printing.

The Sarva-darsana-samgraha or Review of the Different Systems of Hindu Philosophy by Madhava Acharya. 1882. Translated from the Sanskrit by E.B. Cowell and A.E. Gough. London: Trübner & Co.

The Vishnu Purana: A System of Hindu Mythology and Tradition, translated from the original Sanskrit and illustrated by notes chiefly from other Puranas. [1840] 1961. Translated from the Sanskrit by Horace Hayman Wilson with an introduction by R.C. Hazara. Calcutta: Punthi Pustak.

The Visnu Purana: Ancient Annals of the God with Lotus Eyes. 2021. Translated from the Sanskrit by McComas Taylor. Acton: Australian National University Press.

Therigatha: Poems of the First Buddhist Women. 2015. Translated from the Pali by Charles Hallisey. Cambridge, Mass.: Harvard University Press.

Tolz, Vera. 2011. *Russian's Own Orient: The Politics of Identity and Oriental Studies in the Late Imperial and Early Soviet Periods*. New York: Oxford University Press.

Trautmann, Thomas. 1997. *Aryans and British India*. Berkeley: University of California Press.

———. 2012. "Does India Have History? Does History Have India?" *Comparative Studies in Society and History*. Vol. 54/1: 174–205.

Trautmann, Thomas and Carla Sinopoli. 2002. "In the Beginning was the Word: Excavating the Relations between History and Archaeology in South Asia." *Journal of the Economic and Social History of the Orient*. Vol. 45/4: 492–523.

Trevithick, Alan. 1999. "British Archaeologists, Hindu Abbots and Burmese Buddhists: The Maha Bodhi Temple at Bodh Gaya, 1811-1877." *Modern Asian Studies*. Vol. 33/3: 635–56.

———. 2007. *The Revival of Buddhist Pilgrimage at Bodh Gaya (1811-1949): Anagarika Dharmapala and the Maha Bodhi Temple*. New Delhi: Motilal Banarsidass.

Tripathy, Shyam Sunder. 1988. *Buddhism and Other Religious Cults of South-east India*. New Delhi: Sundeep Prakashan.

Truschke, Audrey. 2015. "Dangerous Debates: Jain responses to theological challenges at the Mughal court." *Modern Asian Studies*. Vol. 49/5: 1–34.

———. 2018. "The Power of the Islamic Sword in Narrating the Death of Indian Buddhism." *History of Religions*. Vol. 57/4 (May 2018): 406–35.

Tsui, Brian. 2010. "The Plea for Asia: Tan Yunshan, Pan-Asianiams and Sino-Indian Relations." *China Report*. Vol. 46/4: 353–70.

Tucci, Giuseppe. 1931. "The Sea and Land Travels of a Buddhist Sadhu in Sixteenth Century." *Indian Historical Quarterly*. Vol. 7/4: 683–702.

Turner, Alicia. 2014. *Saving Buddhism: The Impermanence of Religion in Colonial Burma*. Honolulu: University of Hawai'i Press.

Turner, Alicia, Laurence Cox, and Brian Bocking. 2013. "A Buddhist Crossroads: Pioneer European Buddhists and Globalizing Asian Networks, 1860–1960." *Contemporary Buddhism*. Vol. 14/1: 1–16.

———. 2020. *The Irish Buddhist: The Forgotten Monk Who Faced Down the British Empire*. New York and Oxford: Oxford University Press.

Turner, Bryan. 2014. *War and Peace: Essays on Religion and Violence*. London: Anthem.

Turnour, George. 1837. *The Mahawanso in Roman Characters with the Translation Subjoined and an Introductory Essay on Pali Buddhistical Literature* Vol. 1. Ceylon: Cotta Church Mission Press.

———. 1838. "Pali Buddhistical Annals," *Journal of the Asiatic Society*. Vol. 7/2: 686–701.

Upadhyaya, K.N. 1968. "The Impact of Early Buddhism on Hindu Thought (with Special Reference to the Bhagavadgita)." *Philosophy East and West*, Vol. 18/3: 163–73.

Vajpeyi, Ananya. 2012. *Righteous Republic: The Political Foundations of Modern India*. Cambridge, Mass.: Harvard University Press.

van der Veer, Peter. 2001. *Imperial Encounters: Religion and Modernity in India and Britain*. Princeton: Princeton University Press.

Vasanthakumaran, P. 2003. *The Godfather of Indian Labour: M. Singaravelar*. Chennai: Poornima Publishers.

Vasu, Nagendranath. 1911. *The Modern Buddhism and Its Followers in Orissa*. Calcutta: U.N. Bhattacharyya Press.

———. 1912. *The Archaeological Survey of Mayurabhanja*, Vol. I. Calcutta: Hare Press.

Venkatachalapathy, A. R. 2014. "From a footnote to the forefront." *The Hindu*. 24 December. Accessed on https://www.thehindu.com/opinion/op-ed/From-a-footnote-to-the-forefront/article10955928.ece.

Verardi, Giovanni. 2011. *Hardships and Downfall of Buddhism in India*. New Delhi: Manohar.

Victoria, Brian. [1997] 2006. *Zen at War*. 2nd edition. Lanham: Rowman and Littlefield Publishers.

Viswanathan, Gauri. 1998. *Outside the Fold: Conversion, Modernity and Belief*. Princeton: Princeton University Press.

———. [1989] 2014. *Masks of Conquest: Literary Study and British Rule in India, with a New Preface by the Author*. New York: Columbia University Press.

Vivekananda, Swami. 2016. *The Complete Works of Swami Vivekananda*, Vol. 6. Kolkata: Advaita Ashrama Publication Department.

Vriddhagirisan, V. [1942] 1995. *Nayaks of Tanjore*. New Delhi: Asian Educational Services.

Waddell, L.A. 1893. "A 16th Century Account of Indian Buddhist shrines by an Indian Buddhist Yogi, translated from the Tibetan." *Proceedings of the Asiatic Society of Bengal*. January–December. 55–61.

Waller, Derek. 1990. *The Pundits: British Exploration of Tibet and Central Asia*. Lexington: University of Kentucky Press.

Walters, Jonathan. 1992. "Rethinking Buddhist Missions." PhD diss., University of Chicago.

Warner, Michael. 2002. "Publics and Counterpublics." *Public Culture*. Vol. 14: 49–90.

Washbrook, David. 1993. "Land and Labour in Late Eighteenth-Century South India: The Golden Age of Pariah?" In *Dalit Movement and the Meanings of Labour in India,* edited by Peter Robb, 49–90. Oxford: Oxford University Press.

Washington, Peter. 1993. *Madame Blavatsky's Baboon: Theosophy and the Emergence of the Western Guru*. London: Secker & Warburg.

Waterhouse, David (ed.). 2004. *The Origins of Himalayan Studies: Brian Houghton Hodgson in Nepal and Darjeeling*. London: Routledge.

Wayman, Alex. 1966. "Review of *Indian Pandits in the Land of Snow.*" *Journal of Asian Studies*. Vol. 25/4: 778.

Weber, Max. 1978. *Economy and Society: An Outline of Interpretive Sociology.* Vols I and II. Edited by Guenther Roth and Claus Wittich. Berkeley: University of California Press.

Welch, Holmes. 1968. *The Buddhist Revival in China.* Cambridge, Mass.: Harvard University Press.

———. 1972. *Buddhism Under Mao.* Cambridge, Mass.: Harvard University Press.

Wilkins, Charles. 1788. "Translation of a Sanskrit Inscription, Copied from a Stone at Booddha [sic] Gaya." *Asiatick Researches.* Vol. 1: 284–87.

Wilkinson, Lancelot. 1834. "On the Use of the Siddhantas in Native Education." *Journal of the Asiatic Society of Bengal.* Vol. 7: 504–19.

———. 1837. "Proceedings of the Asiatic Society." *Journal of the Asiatic Society of Bengal* Vol. 6/65: 401–02.

Yajnik, Javerilal Umashankar. 1889. "Memoir of the late Pandit Bhagvanlal Indraji, LL.D, Ph.D." *The Journal of the Bombay Branch of the Royal Asiatic Society.* Vol. 47/2: 18–46.

Yengde, Suraj. 2019. *Caste Matters.* New Delhi: Viking Penguin.

Young, Richard Fox. 2003. "Receding from Antiquity: Hindu Responses to Science and Christiainity on the Margins of Empire, 1800–1850." In *Christians and Missionaries in India: Cross-Cultural Communication since 1500,* edited by Robert Eric Frykenberg, 183–222. Oxford: Routledge.

Yu, Xue. 2016. "Buddhist Efforts for the Reconciliation of Buddhism and Marxism in the Early Years of the People's Republic of China." In *Recovering Buddhism in Modern China,* edited by Jan Kiely and J. Brooks Jessup, 177–215. New York: Columbia University Press.

Zavos, John. 2001. "Defending Hindu Tradition: Sanatana Dharma as a Symbol of Orthodoxy in Colonial India." *Religion.* Volume 31/2: 109–23.

Zelliot, Eleanor. 1979. "The Indian Rediscovery of Buddhism, 1855-1956." In *Studies in Pali and Buddhism: A Memorial Volume in Honor of Bhikkhu Jagdish Kashyap,* edited by A.K. Narain, 389–406. New Delhi: B.R. Publishing Company.

———. 1992. *From Untouchable to Dalit: Essays on the Ambedkar Movement.* New Delhi: Manohar.

———. 2013. *Ambedkar's World: The Making of Babasaheb and the Dalit Movement.* New Delhi: Navayana.

Zhang, Xing. 2014. "Buddhist Practices and Institutions of the Chinese Community in Kolkata, India." In *Buddhism across Asia,* Vol. 1, edited by Tansen Sen, 429–58. Singapore: Institute of South-east Asia Studies.

Ziegenbalg, Bartholomäus. [1713] 2005. *Genealogy of the South Indian Deities: An English Translation of Bartholomäus Ziegenbalg's Original German Manuscript with a Textual Analysis and Glossary.* Translated by Daniel Jeyaraj. London and New York: Routledge.

Acknowledgements

Some twenty years ago, I stepped off an airplane in Delhi as a young college student. I had been captivated by Indo-Tibetan Buddhism—I suppose I was a kind of "prisoner of Shangri-La," to use Donald Lopez's (1998) expression—but back then I had no idea that the next two decades of my life would lead me to write a book on Buddhism in India. In the years that followed, I traveled regularly to many places inextricably tied to the history of Buddhism (Leh, Bamiyan, Sarnath, Kardze, Paro, Bangkok, Mrauk U, Kathmandu, Nagpur, Adyar, Bagan, Dharamsala). And over time, these sites and others like them, began to form a pattern—a network, perhaps—and the basis of my understanding of a global Buddhism that was so deeply shaped by the idea of India. Only later did I fully realize that much of that idea was of recent historical provenance.

But in between visits to temple towns and villages, archives and libraries, thriving pilgrimage sites and desolate ruins, I also camped, climbed mountains, fell in love, had a son, lost loved ones, and lived a life far removed from South Asian Buddhism. For a long time, I thought this book would never be published. Then, in the very months surrounding the outbreak of the Covid-19 pandemic, my professional academic career (if there ever was one) was rescued by three strangers from afar: S. Anand at Navayana in Delhi, and Anand Venkatkrishnan and Andrew Ollett, both at the University of Chicago. S. Anand expressed confidence in this book, and importantly, an offer to publish it. This was then unexpectedly followed by invitations from Anand and Andrew to join the University of Chicago as a visiting fellow in their research project on Entanglements of the Indian Past, funded by the Neubauer Collegium. That fellowship not only provided the time to rewrite large sections of this work, but it also led me to reconsider professional academia. In retrospect, a book like this should probably not have taken so long to publish but it did, and the fact that it has finally appeared at all is thanks to Anand, Anand, and Andrew.

This was not the first time that I benefited from the support of others. This book was made possible due to the assistance of innumerable researchers, scholars, librarians, archivists, family members, and friends around the world. Most of the research was conducted during my trips to India, Sri Lanka, Myanmar, and Nepal between 2012 to 2017, including a longer stint in 2014–15 as a Fulbright–Nehru fellow in India, thanks to the support of the United States–India Education Foundation (USIEF). Other field research was supported by the University of British Columbia's (UBC) Institute of Asian Research, Department of Asian Studies, Universal Buddhist Temple Scholarship, and Tina Morris and Wagner Foundation Fellowship. But the foundation for my work was laid a decade earlier, first as a student in India, Nepal, and Tibet, followed by a taste of Buddhist monastic life in Bhutan, and then several years leading tours in India, Pakistan, Afghanistan, and Tibet. In the end, the book is as much a product of the seemingly endless hours I spent in South Asian and North American libraries, temples, and archives, as it is of the time I spent exploring the archaeological sites, urban streets and village walkways that criss-cross the subcontinent.

All works of history depend on archives and special thanks are due to the staff at several institutions: Sarnath's Mulagandhakuti Library; New Delhi's National Archives of India, and Nehru Memorial Museum and Library; Calcutta's Maha Bodhi Society, and National Library; Adyar's Theosophical Society; Lucknow's Uttar Pradesh State Archives; Gangtok's Sikkim State Archives, and Institute of Tibetology; Yangon's Myanmar National Archives; Colombo's National Library; Thimphu's National Library and Archives; the University of Chicago's Special Collections at the Regenstein Library; and the University of British Columbia Library. I would also like to acknowledge the Association for Asian Studies (AAS)–National Endowment for the

Humanities (NEH) Publication Support Fund whose generous grant helped offset publishing costs and procure images. Parts of this book have been published in earlier versions in *Modern Asian Studies,* and in *Buddhism in the Global Eye.* I am thankful to Cambridge University Press and Bloomsbury Academic, respectively, for granting permission to republish these articles.

At the University of British Columbia in Vancouver, where much of this work was first written, Harjot Oberoi has been constant in his encouragement and guidance for more than ten years. Tsering Shakya has also been an endless bastion of positivity since the very beginning, offering advice, endless conversation, and connections. Three anonymous reviewers read the entirety of the manuscript and their comments strengthened the book in numerous ways. Special thanks are to one reviewer in particular (you know who you are!), whose detailed comments, recommendations, and suggestions read like something of a critical essay itself, and pushed me to rewrite significant sections of the book.

Although most of the work was written between Chicago, Delhi, Dharmasala, Durango, Sarnath, and Vancouver, it has taken inspiration from many colleagues around the globe. I am especially grateful to David Geary for all his support, collaboration and leadership on our Buddhist Homelands project. Numerous other scholars and researchers helped me track down rare sources, shared recommendations, lent their ear and challenged me in my thinking, either via emails, phone calls, or at conferences. In particular, I owe a wealth of additions and suggestions for improvement from the following: Acharya Tashi Wangchuk, Alex George, Alicia Turner, Anne Blackburn, Arthur McKeown, Arun Prakash Raj, Ashley Cohen, Ashok Gopal, Bendi Tso, (late) Bhikkhu Bodhipala, Bhikkhu Morita, Bhikkhu Upananda, Catherine Becker, David Ellingson, Deb Mitra Barua, Dhondup Tashi Rebkong, Dilip Prasad, Elizabeth Williams-Oerberg, Gajendran Ayyathurai, (late) Geshe Ngawang Nornang, (late) Hemendu Bikash Chowdhury, Gitanjali Surendran, Jairam Ramesh, Jessica Main, John Marston, Joy Dixon, Laurence Cox, Mallory Hennigar, Mark Turin, Max Deeg, Myintz Zaw, Padma Dorje Maitland, Pema Bhante, Richard Jaffe, (late) Shanti Swarup Bauddh, S. Anand, Sraman Mukherjee, Steven Kemper, Swargajyoti Gohain, Tarang Bauddha, Tsering Shakya, Upinder Singh, Venerable Buddhamitra, Venerable Pragyadeep, and Whitney Cox.

Thank you for your good sense, your research, criticisms, collaborations, and support. To anyone I've forgotten, I'm sorry!

As all of this makes clear, I did not produce this book on my own. Although I take credit for all of its faults and errors, its presentation here is also due to the exceptional work of the editorial team at Navayana—S. Anand, Alex George, S.K. Ray Chaudhuri, and Shyama Haldar. Alex George deserves the credit for bestowing upon this book its brilliant title, a last-minute change, and for patiently reading through my (only sometimes?) painful prose. S. Anand has been meticulous, driven, supportive, energetic, and never failed to impress me. I have never had another editor but I suspect he has set the bar high. I thank Anurag Jadhav for the map. I also owe a special thanks to Dylan Kyung-Lim Bentley White at Stanford for his support of this project and willingness to see it through. I am honored to have it appear in the South Asia in Motion Series.

Lastly and most importantly, this book would never have been completed were it not for the support of my family. Tommy, Jamie, Tanya, and Becs never cease to remind me of the importance of healthy living, as veritable demonstrations of energetic strength (*virya*). I'm more than fortunate to have a mother who is the very model of the four immeasurables (*apramana*). Thank you for everything. My deepest gratitude is to EJ and Rowan, to whom this book is dedicated. EJ: I know this book has impacted you nearly as much as it has me. Thank you for your sacrifice and generosity (dana), your patience (*kshanti*), honesty (*sacca parami*), and loving kindness (metta). And finally, to Rowan, for bringing so much joy (*mudita*) into my world.

Douglas Ober
Durango, Colorado, 2022

Picture credits

Chapter 2

Sir Alexander Cunningham (p.79): Public Domain. Sandes, E.W.C. 1935. The Military Engineer in India, Vol. II. Chatham: Institution of Royal Engineers.

Workers conducting repairs in Sanchi (p.85): Printed with permission from Bridgeman Images, British Library, Photo 1001/1 (1342), photographed by Lala Deen Dayal, 1881.

Sarat Chandra Das (p.92): Public Domain. Das 1902.

Chapter 3

Mahavir Singh (p.107): Public Domain. From Kausalyayan 1941.

Anagarika Dharmapala (p.123): Wikimedia Commons.

Theosophical Society (p. 125): Printed with permission from the Theosophical Society of America.

Venerable Kripasaran (p. 130): Public Domain. *MBJ*, 1926.

P. Lakshmi Narasu (p. 141): Wikimedia Commons.

Chapter 4

Jugal Kishore Birla in New Delhi (p. 163): Public Domain. *MBJ*, 1951.

Chapter 5

Ambedkar and Savita, conversion ceremony in Nagpur (p. 186): From the collection of Vijay Surwade.

Leaders of the Malabar Buddhist Movement (p. 200): Public Domain. *MBJ*, 1925–26.

Risaldar Park vihara, c. 1940 (p. 208): Public Domain. *MBJ*.

Inside the Risaldar Park vihara, 2015 (p. 208): Photograph by Douglas Ober.

Bhikkhu Bodhananda (p. 209): From Ottama, Bodhananda, and Jigyasu 1933.

Ambedkar at the World Buddhist Conference (p.219): From the collection of Vijay Surwade.

Chapter 6

Dharmanand Kosambi (p.233): Courtesy of Dilip and Anil Prasad.

Chapter 7

Buddhist delegates with Jawaharlal Nehru (p.253): Published with permission from the Tibet Museum, Dharamsala, India

The first cabinet of independent India (p.259): Public Domain

Rajendra Prasad with saplings (p.273): Public Domain

S. Radhakrishnan with Buddhist relics (p.276): [Alamy]

Index

From Raj to Republic: Sovereignty, Violence, and Democracy in India
Sunil Purushotham (2021)

The Greater India Experiment: Hindutva Becoming and the Northeast
Arkotong Longkumer (2020)

Nobody's People: Hierarchy as Hope in a Society of Thieves
Anastasia Piliavsky (2020)

*Brand New Nation: Capitalist Dreams and Nationalist
Designs in Twenty-First-Century India*
Ravinder Kaur (2020)

Partisan Aesthetics: Modern Art and India's Long Decolonization
Sanjukta Sunderason (2020)

Dying to Serve: the Pakistan Army
Maria Rashid (2020)

In the Name of the Nation: India and Its Northeast
Sanjib Baruah (2020)

Faithful Fighters: Identity and Power in the British Indian Army
Kate Imy (2019)

Paradoxes of the Popular: Crowd Politics in Bangladesh
Nusrat Sabina Chowdhury (2019)

*The Ethics of Staying: Social Movements and
Land Rights Politics in Pakistan*
Mubbashir A. Rizvi (2019)

Mafia Raj: The Rule of Bosses in South Asia
Lucia Michelutti, Ashraf Hoque, Nicolas Martin, David Picherit, Paul
Rollier, Arild Ruud and Clarinda Still (2018)

For a complete listing of titles in this series, visit the
Stanford University Press website, www.sup.org.

CPSIA information can be obtained
at www.ICGtesting.com
Printed in the USA
JSHW020025080223
37448JS00001B/1